DESIGNING AND CONSTRUCTING INSTRUMENTS FOR SOCIAL RESEARCH AND EVALUATION

JB JOSSEY-BASS

DESIGNING AND CONSTRUCTING INSTRUMENTS FOR SOCIAL RESEARCH AND EVALUATION

David Colton and
Robert W. Covert

1807
WILEY
2007

John Wiley & Sons, Inc.

Published by Jossey-Bass
A Wiley Imprint
989 Market Street, San Francisco, CA 94103–1741—www.josseybass.com

Jossey-Bass books and products are available through most bookstores. To contact Jossey-Bass
directly call our Customer Care Department within the U.S. at 800–956–7739, outside the U.S. at
317–572–3986, or fax 317–572–4002.

Jossey-Bass also publishes its books in a variety of electronic formats. Some content that appears in print
may not be available in electronic books.

Library of Congress Cataloging-in-Publication Data
Colton, David, 1948-
   Designing and constructing instruments for social research and evaluation/David Colton
and Robert W. Covert.
      p. cm.
   Includes bibliographical references and index.
   ISBN-13: 978-0-7879-8784-8 (cloth)
   1.   Social sciences—Research—Methodology. 2.   Evaluation—Methodology. I. Covert, Robert W.,
1943- II. Title.
   H62.C583 2007
   300.72—dc22

                                                                                    2007026748

Printed in the United States of America
FIRST EDITION

HB Printing   10 9 8 7 6 5 4 3 2 1

CONTENTS

PART THREE: ORGANIZATION AND ADMINISTRATION   279

FIGURES, EXHIBITS, TABLES, AND INSTRUMENTS

Figures

Exhibits

Tables

Instruments

PREFACE: ASKING AND ANSWERING

When word of the people's discontent reached the grand vizier, he had trouble sleeping, for, you see, he was a conscientious ruler who had the welfare of his people at heart. He called upon the captain of guards and directed him to question members of the populace.

Dutifully, the captain of the guards rounded up one hundred people, men and women, and asked them a series of questions to discover the cause of their discontent. Now the captain was an imposing fellow, some six feet four inches tall and muscular. He wore a scimitar in a scabbard, and the medals he had won for his bravery in battle adorned his waistcoat. When he addressed the citizens, his voice had a hard and commanding tone, and he looked at them with the steely glare of a man ready for combat, which of course was how he approached all tasks.

"The grand vizier has commanded that you provide information about the quality of life in our kingdom. First, I want to know if you believe that taxes are too high?"

In unison all one hundred citizens responded, "No," although records of this session suggest that some citizens responded less enthusiastically than others.

"Ah yes, good." replied the captain of the guards. "Now tell me, do you think that the laws of the land are administered fairly?"

In unison all one hundred citizens responded, "Yes," although it was noted that one citizen had recently lost property in a dispute with the vizier's second cousin's nephew.

"Splendid," said the captain of the guards, and he exhaled a sigh of relief, for he did not relish bringing bad news to the grand vizier. "And do you citizens agree with the new law prohibiting mules in the marketplace?"

In unison all one hundred citizens responded, "Yes," although several were merchants whose businesses were hurt by the new law.

And so the questioning went, and the captain of the guard was pleased that each time the citizens replied in unison and each time there was complete agreement to his question. Armed with this information (for the captain of the guards never went anywhere without being fully armed), he returned to the grand vizier. "Good news, my ruler," he declared. "Although there is some grumbling among the populace, the people I spoke to, who were a diverse lot, all had good things to say about you and your administration. Sleep soundly now, for truly the kingdom is in good hands."

The grand vizier did indeed sleep soundly, at least for a day or two, until word again reached him of the people's discontent. Now this sorely vexed the vizier, for he had the best interests of his people at heart. But he was also confused, because what the people had told the captain of the guards was clearly at odds with what he continued to hear. For that reason he sent for Halcolm, a teacher and counselor, and asked him to go forth among the people to determine the source of their displeasure. Halcolm agreed to this task with the understanding that he would speak to the people in confidence, so that they could speak freely without fear of reprisal.

Now Halcolm was a man of simple and plain means, very undiscerning in appearance. His voice was calm and reassuring, and people tended to feel comfortable in his presence. While buying some fruit in the marketplace, he asked the vendor, "I've been thinking of opening a stand in the marketplace to sell candlesticks and other brass goods. Do you think I could make a profit at that?" The vendor smiled and replied, "Yes and no. Surely you should have a good market for your wares. But as to making a profit, it will be hard given the current tax rate. When the vizier decided to build an addition to the palace, he upped our taxes by 20 percent! I'll be happy when that project is over, and the taxes are reduced."

Further down the marketplace, Halcolm spoke with a rug vendor and asked the same question. "Yes," the rug vendor replied, "you will certainly have a market for brass goods. However, the laws of the land are often applied unevenly, and they create a lot of headaches for us. For example, you might be fined if your cart is too close to the street. Also, since the vizier passed the rule outlawing mules in the marketplace, it is becoming increasingly difficult to carry our wares into town to sell. If changes aren't soon made, many of us will go out of business. In the end, we, the vizier, and ultimately the entire kingdom will suffer under these rules. Now don't get me wrong. I have great respect for the grand vizier. He has been a good and just ruler in the past. It is just that recently I think he has lost touch with the people."

Halcolm continued his project and met with a number of people in the marketplace, at religious shrines, and at the theater. After several days of asking his questions he returned to the grand vizier and shared his findings. "Perhaps I have been out of touch," sighed the vizier. "I will immediately revise my plans for constructing and financing the palace addition. Also, I will establish a committee to examine our laws and rewrite them so that they are fair and just. Thank you, Halcolm, for finding out what really troubled our citizens. I am pleased that the people were so honest in their responses. If I had depended on what people told the captain of the guards, my kingdom might have gone down in ruin," and as he spoke those words, he glared at the captain of the guards, who was also present at this meeting.

"Thank you for your kind words," responded Halcolm, "but I would like to add that as a teacher and counselor, it is my job to know how to ask the right questions and how to ask questions right. You would not, however, want me to lead your army into battle. For that, you would want your captain of the guards, who is an excellent tactician and great warrior." With that, the grand vizier smiled, the captain of the guards smiled, and Halcolm smiled, for in addition to knowing how to ask a good question, Halcolm knew how to phrase a good answer.

(With special thanks to Michael Quinn Patton, for providing the evaluation profession a role model in the guise of Halcolm.)

Increasingly, individuals and organizations are being asked to collect, manage, and use information for decision making, particularly to improve the quality of services and products. Rather than being based on intuition or hunches, decision making is viewed as being a *data-driven* process, one that is systematic and produces trustworthy information.

The purpose of this book is to provide the reader with a systematic, nontechnical and commonsense approach to developing instruments for data collection and analysis. We have written the book as a guide for both those who are using or developing instruments for the first time and those with experience who want to hone their skills, people ranging from students to agency personnel to program managers to researchers. The book does not require any technical expertise and is written for all levels of readers.

Throughout the text we use the term *instrument* generically to describe any format for collecting data, such as attitudinal questionnaires, checklists, and political polls. And as we note in the text, the process for developing an instrument is the same whether that instrument will be used for self-rating (by a respondent) or whether another person (an observer) will fill it out.

There are literally thousands of instruments that have been developed and marketed to fulfill distinct needs for information. However, we have found that informational needs are often unique to a particular person, organization, situation, time, or event. Consequently, these needs can be met only by designing and developing a questionnaire for that specific purpose and situation. Additionally, finding a previously developed instrument may be time consuming, and the cost of purchasing the instrument may prove to be greater than the cost of developing a new instrument that uniquely fits your needs.

The approach presented here is based on the underlying assumption that the process of constructing an instrument is both a creative and a technical venture. It involves not only being very familiar with the content or substance of the topic of interest but also developing good questions or items and presenting them in a format accessible to the people who will have to complete the instrument. Consequently, this book is designed to help you create an instrument that will obtain the information you seek.

Throughout we emphasize the need to ensure that an instrument will produce trustworthy and accurate data. To that end, we provide guidelines for reviewing and revising to enhance data validity and reliability. Additionally, we stress the importance of involving, throughout the process of instrument construction, the different groups of people who will be affected by the data generated. These groups, referred to as *stakeholders,* include the instrument designer(s), decision makers (such as administrators, policymakers, and funding agencies), agency personnel, clients, and raters or respondents.

The ideas in this book are based on the authors' experience in several hundred evaluation projects over the past twenty-five years. In addition, they have been presented in a variety of settings, from the university classroom to workshops on questionnaire construction. Moreover, in writing this text, we have addressed *you,* the reader, directly, as if we were present to advise you through this process. We hope this familiarity will make you more comfortable and less intimidated as you undertake the challenge of designing an instrument.

This book is organized around the process of instrument construction and takes the reader through each of the steps. The chapters in Part One present the conceptual basis for designing and constructing instruments for data collection and analysis. We describe how instruments fit into the process of social inquiry and how different types support specific informational needs. Before you decide on the type of instrument to construct, it is important to understand the variety of approaches available for gathering information about a particular research or evaluation question. These chapters describe the various types of instruments as well as the components of an effective instrument. We also introduce such concepts as validity and reliability.

The chapters in Part Two offer guidance in constructing questionnaires and other forms of instrumentation, helping you to define the purpose of your study, to understand and choose among the different ways to format items, and to pre-test and construct items that will meet your informational needs.

Part Three provides guidelines for organizing the instrument, administering it, and reporting the results to stakeholders and decision makers. This is to ensure that the effort you put into obtaining reliable data, through a well-designed instrument, is not compromised when you actually carry out the measurement process.

To give you opportunities for applying the information presented in this text, the chapters conclude with examples of instruments. These instruments have been developed to meet different informational needs, and many come from the public domain. Each one is discussed and critiqued, and reviewing these samples can help you hone your skills both as a user of instruments and as a developer and designer of your own questionnaires.

Feedback

A central theme of this book is that instrument construction is a process of continual development and refinement. We welcome feedback and the sharing of information that can improve both the substance and presentation of our material. Please contact us through the publisher.

Acknowledgments

Our view that instrument construction involves constant revision has certainly held true during the development of this book. We want to express our appreciation to Daniel M. Stuhlsatz, of Mary Baldwin College, Staunton, Virginia, who reviewed an early version of the manuscript, and to Gary Skolits, of the University of Tennessee, Knoxville, Tennessee, who reviewed a revised version. Their feedback at both stages of development was incorporated into successive drafts.

We also want to acknowledge the students who have taken the instrument construction class we teach at the Curry School of Education, University of Virginia, as this book was in part written to address the topics and questions that typically arise there. Student projects have also provided useful resources, and one group in particular, the class of 2003, also reviewed and provided feedback for an early version of the manuscript. We offer special thanks to Tracey Armstrong, Ronda Bryant, Dan Bublitz, Holly Conti, Antoinette Ewell,

Alan Fortescure, Jeanne Hineline, Sa Rah Ho, Amelia Hunt, Catherine Johnson, Jae Hyun Jun, Jennifer Mabry, Ana Paula Loucao Martins, Shizuka Modica, Yi Ni, Ana Palla, Margaret Peak. Nikkia Sheppard, Doug Toti, Dave Wolcott, Trimika Yates, Hyunsil Yoo, and Yubo Zhang. The multicultural makeup of this class led to very interesting discussions on translating instruments into different languages.

We also offer a special thank-you to our families for their support and encouragement during this drawn-out but fulfilling writing project. Finally, we thank the editorial staff at Jossey-Bass, in particular Elspeth MacHattie and Rachel Anderson, for their assistance in helping us through the publication process.

June 2007   David Colton
                                                                        Waynesboro, Virginia
                                                                         Robert W. Covert
                                                                              Faber, Virginia

THE AUTHORS

David Colton comes to the area of instrument construction as both a practitioner in the field and an educator and evaluator. He received his BA degree in secondary education and MEd degree in reading education from Salisbury University, in Salisbury, Maryland, an MPA degree from James Madison University, in Harrisonburg, Virginia, and an PhD degree, with a major in evaluation, from the University of Virginia at Charlottesville. Over the past thirty years he has worked in a variety of management and program development positions with the Maryland and Virginia public mental health systems. His current position involves evaluation, performance measurement, and quality improvement for an inpatient treatment facility serving children and adolescents. He has published a number of articles on quality improvement and cultural change in human service agencies, and his Checklist for Assessing Organizational Readiness for Reducing Seclusion and Restraint is used by mental health organizations throughout the United States, Canada, and Europe. For the past seventeen years, Colton has served as an adjunct instructor with the health care administration program at Mary Baldwin College, in Staunton, Virginia, and for the past five years he has taught the course on instrument construction at the Curry School of Education, University of Virginia.

Robert W. Covert is associate professor in the program area of research, statistics and evaluation at the Curry School of Education, University of Virginia.

He received his BS degree in math from Grove City College, in Grove City, Pennsylvania, his MEd degree in math education, and his PhD degree in educational psychology, with a specialization in research and statistics, from Temple University, in Philadelphia, Pennsylvania. An active member of the evaluation community, he served as the second president of the American Evaluation Association and was responsible for that group's membership services for over ten years. He is a recipient of the Robert Ingle Service Award, presented by the American Evaluation Association for continuous contribution to its leadership and mission. He has conducted over 500 evaluations, primarily in the education and social services sectors. As a faculty member at the University of Virginia he has designed and taught a variety of methodological courses, including instrument construction, computer statistics lab, and introduction to qualitative research methods. In addition he has designed and currently teaches a popular course in multicultural education, and he has conducted AEA presessions in instrument construction and multicultural issues for evaluators.

DESIGNING AND CONSTRUCTING INSTRUMENTS FOR SOCIAL RESEARCH AND EVALUATION

PART ONE

CONCEPTS

CHAPTER ONE

INTRODUCTION

In this chapter we will

- Explain the purpose and function of a social science instrument.
- Describe nomenclature used to describe instruments.
- List and describe the components of an instrument.
- Outline the steps in the instrument construction process.

We are living in a time characterized as the information age, and we encounter data-gathering instruments in all facets of our lives. For example, we are familiar with polls that gather information about political preferences and voting behaviors. Surveys of potential voters try to predict who will be elected or what proposition will pass. Media commentators remind us of the margin of error associated with a survey or note that an election is still too close to call.

The proliferation of instruments to provide data and information for decision making is not unique to political polls. Survey questionnaires can be used to obtain factual information and to assess attitudes and beliefs across a variety of topics and groups. For example, surveys can assess consumer behaviors, client satisfaction with services, employee attitudes, and the general public's values and beliefs. The federal government is perhaps the greatest consumer and user of survey questionnaires, as these instruments are used to collect data about such topics as criminal activity, educational needs, services to the mentally ill, and health care utilization, not to mention the data for the U.S. Census.

You may be familiar with other forms of measurement instruments as well. For example, many organizations conduct annual evaluations of employee work performance. Often these evaluation instruments use scales to rate job performance on a number of attributes, such as attendance, ability to work with others, or the ability to complete work tasks in a timely manner. Although the intended purpose of a checklist or rating instrument such as an employee evaluation is different from the purpose of a survey questionnaire, the same principles are used in constructing these instruments.

As you read this introduction, you are likely thinking of instruments that you have personally used or have been asked to complete, including instruments related to your work or study. And as a reader of this text, you are also interested in creating an instrument, perhaps in conjunction with a research project or job-related activity.

Social science instruments are tools for the collection and measurement of data, and the purpose of this book is to describe how good instruments are constructed. We use the adjective *good* because there are indeed standards and guidelines that can produce an efficient and effective instrument rather than a mediocre one. Our goal is to help you identify the components that make for a "good" instrument, one that provides trustworthy information. As you will see, no instrument is perfect, as there are many ways to pose a question. However, by being aware of the conditions that affect your results, you can create an instrument that effectively meets your need for information.

We believe that instrument construction is as much an art as it is a science. Research has demonstrated that some approaches to instrument development can increase the accuracy and dependability of responses. And statistical tests can be used to measure the consistency of people's responses. Nevertheless, much of what you will do involves common sense, interpersonal skills, and to a degree even creativity. You should not shy away from developing your own instrument because you believe the process is too technical.

We compare instrument construction to the activities of a painter creating a work of art. The first stage involves conceptualizing the project, a purely mental process in which the artist begins to visualize the subject and what it should look like when completed. The designer of a questionnaire goes through a similar process as he or she defines the purpose of the study, obtains information about the subject to be studied, and contemplates the items that might be included. The next step is preparatory. The artist may develop a number of sketches to define the subject, conceptualize the composition of the painting, and experiment with the use of color. Similarly, through an iterative and interactive process, the creator of a questionnaire will draft the instrument, test the items, and revise and modify both individual items and the instrument format.

An artist may set the canvas aside from time to time to evaluate its progress. During such periods, the artist may experiment with subtle changes in composition, colors, or techniques for applying the paint. The questionnaire designer will also fine-tune the instrument, often in response to feedback from content experts or potential users. Items may be reworded, different item types may be tried, and the layout of items within the instrument may be reorganized. In the end both painter and questionnaire designer must reach a point where they are comfortable that their goals have been attained and the product is ready to be unveiled.

Instrumentation

An *instrument* is a mechanism for measuring phenomena, which is used to gather and record information for assessment, decision making, and ultimately understanding. An instrument such as a questionnaire is typically used to obtain factual information, support observations, or assess attitudes and opinions. For example, a survey may ask respondents to list the type of soap they purchase (factual information), recall how often they purchased the item in the past year (an observation), and consider the factors that influenced their purchase, such as smell, touch, or appearance (attitudes toward the product). The term *subjective* describes information that originates within an individual and is reflected by items that measure attitudes, feelings, opinions, values, and beliefs. Information that is *objective* attempts to be free of personal interpretation and is typified by data that are observable.[1]

Some instruments consist of all objective items, like the medical history questionnaire at the end of this chapter. Respondents are asked to provide demographic information such as their weight, height, and age as well as information about their physical health, such as allergies and previous illnesses. Conversely, some instruments are designed to obtain primarily subjective responses, such as information about political preferences. Although political polls include objective demographic questions, the body of the instrument consists of items that require the respondent to express an opinion or attitude.

In the social sciences most instruments are of the paper-and-pencil variety, meaning that the individual completing the instrument is expected to record information on a form. Even when other media are to be used, a paper-and-pencil instrument will probably need to be developed initially. For example, a marriage counselor might use videotape to record the interactions between a husband and wife. However, a written instrument might then be applied to count the number of times a particular word or phrase or body gesture is used or to rate a type of interaction. A marketing survey organization might collect information over the telephone but record responses with a paper-and-pencil instrument. More and more, instruments are being constructed that can be completed on a computer. This medium has the advantage of reaching many people quickly and the software often allows the user to tabulate results easily. However, even when the process of collecting or entering information varies—pen, pencil, keyboard, mouse, or verbal encoding—the basic construction of the instrument remains the same, regardless of the medium.

We can categorize instruments in several ways. One approach is based on a *mode of administration:* who is responsible for completing the instrument? Some instruments, such as polls or medical history questionnaires, rely on *self-report,* where the respondent supplies the information directly. For example, many interviews, telephone surveys, and some psychometric assessments are initiated by a second party; nonetheless, because the information is provided directly by the respondent, we classify these instruments as self-report.

Another mode of administration is *observation,* where information about an individual is obtained by someone external. Examples of observation instruments are employee performance appraisals, student assessments of faculty, and behavior checklists. These instruments collect data about characteristics intrinsic to an individual even though the respondent is not queried directly. For example, as part of conducting a screening process for attention deficit disorder, a teacher might use a behavior checklist to record the number of times a student is off task.

An external rater or observer is also used when information is needed about things rather than people. For example, a medical records director might develop a checklist to assess whether all the required documentation has been filed in a clinical chart. Similarly, when researchers need information from existing sources, such as medical, personnel, or student records, they may need an instrument designed specifically for data extraction. External raters usually require training to ensure that they obtain the data in the manner required by the instrument developer and are consistent with other observers or raters.

Some instruments use a combination of approaches and formats. The Achenbach questionnaires (Achenbach, 1991) consist of three instruments that provide information about a child's behaviors and emotional state. The Youth Self-Report (YSR), which has various item formats, such as checklists, fill in the blanks, and rating scales, is completed directly by the youngster who is the focus of evaluation. As its title implies, the mode of administration is self-report. The Child Behavior Checklist (CBCL) is completed by the child's parent or guardian and consists essentially of the same items as the YSR, although worded slightly differently. The Teacher Report Form (TRF) attempts to measure the same attributes, but the questions are formulated to address the child's behaviors in an academic setting. Thus both the CBCL and the TRF are based on parent, guardian, or teacher observation and assessment. The results from each of these three instruments can be used, either individually or collectively, for assessment and diagnostic purposes by a mental health professional.

Both approaches provide the instrument designer with challenges. For example, one of the advantages of constructing an instrument for completion by external raters is the opportunity to interact with and train the observers. This can produce very high levels of consistency between raters. However, this is also time consuming and costly. Conversely, self-report instruments are subject to each respondent's personal interpretation of an item, which may or may not be what you, as instrument designer, had intended. In either case it is important to test and revise the instrument to minimize these potential problems.

We can also try to classify instruments by *use* or *purpose*. Although this approach provides a nomenclature for describing instruments, as we shall see, it is not easy to make distinctions based solely on intended use.

The array of instruments used in the social sciences, ranges from academic tests to survey questionnaires. It is perhaps better to think of them as a continuum (as in Figure 1.1), rather than as distinct categories, as these instruments may be put to use for more than one purpose and often share common elements. For example, results on an achievement test can be used as a measure of cognition in the same manner as an intelligence test, although the latter would more likely be categorized as a psychometric instrument than a test. Additionally, some instruments, such as tax forms, may not fit easily into a single grouping. The overlapping circles in Figure 1.1 illustrate that these are not distinct or exclusive categories.

One major group of instruments listed in Figure 1.1 is tests. "A *test* is a collection of items developed to measure some human educational or psychological attribute" (Worthen & Sanders, 1987, p. 302). One aspect of a test is that a *correct* answer or level of performance is anticipated. Although tests and other instruments share commonalities, the theories and properties underlying test development are sufficiently different from those underlying instruments as to exclude tests from further discussion in this text.

Rating scale is a generic term describing instruments that are evaluative and that make use of an item format where response choices are ordered on a continuum. The system of judging athletic performances in such events as ice skating and diving is an example of a rating scale. A rating scale differs from a ranking in that the instrument designer predetermines the scale and the respondent selects *one value*, such as *strongly agree* on a scale that ranges from *strongly disagree* to *strongly agree*. During the process of ranking, the respondent creates a hierarchy, placing *all* the values in order, for example from *strong* to *weak*, or from *most important* to *least important*.

FIGURE 1.1: CATEGORIES OF SOCIAL SCIENCE INSTRUMENTS.

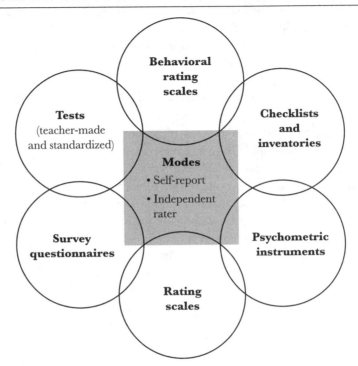

Aiken (1975, p. 12) notes that "rating scales are a primary tool in contemporary assessment methodology, second only to teacher-made achievement tests in frequency of use for rating people, objects, and events."

Rating scales are used to measure attitudes and opinions and also to record direct observation and assessment. Rating instruments are often used to assess the performance of individuals, organizations, programs, and services. For example, professional review organizations often use rating scales to determine if schools or hospitals meet criteria for accreditation or licensure. The following example is adapted from hospital accreditation standards.

EXAMPLE

Treatment plans provide evidence of input from patients and their families (check one):

——Always   ——With a few minor   ——Not consistently   ——Rarely   ——Never
                    exceptions

Performance and behavior rating instruments use rating scales specifically designed to measure an individual's ability to complete a task or perform an activity. Examples of performance instruments are employee job evaluations and the assessment instruments used in rehabilitation and education. These instruments are typically completed by an external observer or rater. Behavior measures may be designed to be descriptive and not evaluative, that is, not judging the value of what is observed but establishing whether it occurred. Such an instrument might use items with a response choice of *present* or *not present*. Behavior measures may also be primarily evaluative, as in a job performance appraisal where the task is to make a qualitative assessment of performance. In that case the response choices might rate an aspect of job performance from *satisfactory* to *unsatisfactory*, or from occurring *none of the time* to *all of the time*.

Checklists are used to determine the presence or absence of an attribute and to count the prevalence of an item or event.[2] These instruments may use a variety of item formats, including scales, rank order, dichotomous choices (*yes* or *no*, *present* or *not present*), and open-ended questions. One example of a checklist is an instrument used to count the number of computers and computer accessories in a school building. The checklist might be used to indicate if the computer equipment is located where it was originally assigned and to record the property number. The checklist might also include criteria for making qualitative assessments; for example, it might contain a rating scale for evaluating aspects of equipment quality, such as working condition and need for hardware upgrades.

Another example of a checklist is a list of tasks that should be completed to ensure that a process or product is complete. The instructions for building a model airplane might be written as a checklist for instance. Checklists may be organized sequentially for such things as projects where one action must be performed before another can occur—part F of the model airplane may not fit into part G unless it has first been glued to part E.

Checklists may be designed to be self-report instruments or to be completed by an independent observer or rater. Moreover, they may be completed for just one entity (such as one individual) or for multiple entities, possibly chosen by sampling methods. For example, if you are developing a checklist for auditing records (such as medical charts or personnel files) and there are hundreds or thousands of them, you could use random sampling to obtain a representative sample of the records, rather than auditing all of them.

In the broadest terms, an inventory is simply a list of objects, goods, or attributes. The word is also used as a verb to describe the process of compiling the list; one might *inventory* one's supplies, for example. In the social sciences the term *inventory* describes an instrument used to assess a person's interests, characteristics, or skills. One example is the Vineland Adaptive Behavior Scales (Sparrow, Balla, &

Cicchetti, 1984), a developmental inventory that measures adaptive living skills, such as ability to dress oneself and manage a personal budget. An important aspect of developmental inventories is that the items are usually listed sequentially where acquisition of basic skills is a precursor to demonstrating more complex skills; a child typically acquires the ability to hold a spoon, knife, or fork before the ability to cut up food without assistance.

As with other instruments, the mode of administration can be either self-report or observer based. A patient recovering from a stroke might be asked to complete (self-report) an inventory of skills developed as a result of participating in physical therapy. An external rater completing a developmental inventory might observe the same person completing activities of daily living (toileting, personal hygiene, and so forth) and check off whether the individual can or cannot complete the task. An inventory may set a threshold at which observations stop, such as when the individual cannot complete five items in a row. The information obtained can be weighed against normative data to provide a comparative level of functioning. For example, an adaptive living inventory might indicate that, as the result of a stroke, an elderly individual's physical functioning (gross motor skills to carry out the activities of daily living) is significantly diminished in comparison to the functioning of similarly aged adults.

Survey, poll, attitude scale, and *questionnaire* are terms used interchangeably to describe instruments designed to obtain factual information and to assess beliefs, opinions, and attitudes. Questionnaires typically make use of rating scales and open-ended questions. Specific sampling methodologies may be used to obtain responses that are representative of the population of interest (see the following discussion). Questionnaires are typically designed as self-report instruments.

Considerations in the Use of Survey Questionnaires

Surveys are frequently used when information is needed from large numbers of individuals. However, because there are a number of ways of obtaining information, the pros and cons of using a survey as your method of data collection should be considered in each case.

Surveys can be used to explore relationships. You may believe that certain respondents are predisposed to certain decisions—for example, that women, more so than men, rely on appearance and scent when purchasing a particular product. You can obtain data to support this supposition by comparing the demographic data supplied by respondents to their responses on specific items.

Surveys can be used to examine attitudes and beliefs. When assessing attitudes and beliefs there are no right or wrong answers; instead you are interested in the nature of respondents' values, perceptions, and feelings. Surveys are adept in garnering this information because a number of item formats, including multi-item scales, can be used for both data collection and verification.

Surveys can be used to obtain sensitive information. Respondents are often not comfortable with sharing information about their financial status, legal involvement, or lifestyles in person—through an interview or focus group, for example. Similarly, workers may be reluctant to share information about their employer (such as working conditions) for fear of retaliation if they can be associated with their responses. Surveys that are properly designed and administered and that ensure confidentiality or anonymity can address these obstacles.

Surveys can be combined with other data-gathering approaches. Your survey may provide meaningful results but also suggest that you need to gather additional information not readily assessed by preselected items. For example, you may wish to follow-up your survey that has provided information that can be generalized to the population of interest with a number of interviews that can provide details and explanations the survey was unable to capture.

Despite the many benefits that surveys afford, they also have limitations:

Surveys are mistakenly perceived to be more time and cost effective than other approaches to information gathering. When interventions are evaluated using randomized experimental designs, it may take months or even years to produce results. Qualitative approaches present a similar problem; it may take many months to conduct interviews or videotape situations. In some cases, such as anthropological research, a study may be carried out over a number of years. In comparison to these approaches, surveys are often assumed to be fairly efficient to produce, administer, and analyze. In fact, development of an effective survey may take months by the time one ensures that the instrument produces reliable and trustworthy information. The U.S. General Accounting Office (1986) estimates that it takes about nine months to develop a questionnaire, administer the survey, analyze and interpret the data, and report the results. In some complex situations, the GAO notes, the survey process can take up to eighteen months to complete. For example, if the survey is to be administered by telephone or in person, additional time needs to be allotted for training of the surveyors to guarantee consistent application of questionnaire items. Consequently, surveys should not be chosen solely for perceived efficiency.

By design, surveys limit data acquisition. Qualitative researchers are not limited to set questions or item responses, and qualitative methods are said to produce "rich and thick" information. For example, respondents may provide information the interviewer did not request. "In comparison, surveys are limited in their ability to capture unsolicited but meaningful information, because the items limit the response choices. Although there are ways to extend the amount and type of information you can acquire (for example, by using open-ended items and allotting space for comments), establishing the questions in advance does limit the information you will obtain. Careful and thoughtful design of the questionnaire can increase the likelihood of capturing the information you are interested in, although it can never completely overcome the limitation posed by defining your questions in advance.

Surveys are subject to misinterpretation. One goal of instrument development is to reduce ambiguity. Ambiguity occurs when respondents misunderstand the meaning of an item and respond to it from their interpretation rather than its intended meaning. Additionally, if the questionnaire is administered as a telephone survey, the surveyor's inflection and tone in reading items may influence the respondent's choice. Misinterpretation can be reduced by pretesting the instrument. Additionally, training can increase consistent presentation of survey questions by telephone surveyors and reduce the impact of tonal quality on the respondent's understanding of the question.

In summary, survey research methods provide a unique process for gathering data. Considering the benefits and limitations of surveys can help you decide whether a survey will provide you with the information needed to support your theory or answer your questions. Careful and thoughtful design can also help you overcome some of the inherent limitations associated with surveys.

Psychometric instrument is a broad term used to describe an array of instruments designed to assess cognitive, affective, and physical functioning and personality traits. Consequently, some psychometric instruments can be just as easily categorized as behavior rating instruments or inventories, such as the Vineland Adaptive Behavior Scales. Examples include instruments designed to assess depression or psychosis, intelligence, self-esteem, and hyperactivity. Psychometric instruments developed to assess vocational abilities and aptitudes are used to predict an individual's suitability for an occupation or a specific job. Some psychometric instruments are very specialized and make use of pictorial response sets. For example, the Children's Apperception Test (Bellak & Bellak, 1993) and the Rorschach inkblot test (Exner & Weiner, 1994) use drawings and abstract designs to solicit responses. Psychometric instruments can be completed through self-report or by an independent observer.

A unique subcategory of psychometric instruments consists of those designed for behavior analysis. Behaviors are measured before, during, and after treatment to determine if an intervention is producing the desired effect as evidenced by changes in the frequency or duration, or both, of a targeted behavior. The number of times the behavior occurs may be counted, or a behaviors may be classified into discrete categories such as *occurred* or *did not occur,* or *correct* or *incorrect* (Kazdin, 1982). Frequency counts are typically tallied for predetermined blocks of time (such as fifteen-minute intervals) or by providing a list of frequency ranges for each observation (such as "Number of Occurrences: 0 to 1, 2 to 4, 5 to 7, 8 or more"), or the observer may just count the occurrences.

Considerations in the Use of Observation Instruments

Many instruments are designed to support the observation and recording of human activity. One example is the ubiquitous job appraisal, used to support personnel decisions such as granting pay raises and promoting, demoting, or retaining employees. Observation instruments are also often used to provide feedback to individuals; such as checklists to observe a teacher's instructional and classroom management skills. In this situation the information can be used by a master teacher to assist with mentoring and coaching. In many human service fields, including mental health, rehabilitation, and education, checklists and inventories employing observational rating are used to identify deficits that may then be the target of treatment efforts.

Observational instruments present many of the same challenges to the developer as do questionnaires. For example, like questionnaire respondents, observers may misunderstand the meaning of an item and rate it based on their personal interpretation rather than the meaning that you had intended.

Perhaps the greatest challenge in the development of observational instruments is ensuring that different raters provide similar ratings when observing the same event at the same time. The extent to which different raters agree on their ratings is referred to as *interrater reliability,* which we'll examine in more depth in Chapter Four. Here it suffices to say that enhancing rater consistency will require additional time in the development and training stages.

As you read these descriptions you probably realized that although researchers would like to be able to make clear distinctions between these various instruments, one of the difficulties in categorizing instruments by purpose is that the terminology often has multiple, overlapping meanings. For example, *rating scale* may describe an entire instrument or any item within an instrument that is developed along a measurable continuum. So a checklist, inventory, or poll can be composed of rating scale items. And as we shall examine later in this book, the word *scale* can have a definition that is distinct from the term *rating scale* even though these terms are often used synonymously. Similarly, the term *survey* is used to describe a type of instrument as well as the method of administration (as in "conducting a survey"). Finally, an instrument might fit the definition of more than one instrument type; for example, an inventory might be constructed as a checklist; a behavior rating scale might fit the definition of a psychometric instrument. The sample instrument at the end of this chapter was designed to evaluate instruction. On the one hand it functions as a survey by soliciting opinions about the course, instructor, and learning environment. On the other hand it functions as a performance measure to judge the merit or value of different aspects of training. We use these terms to help us communicate our intentions to others, an in, "I am developing a questionnaire, which will be administered as a telephone survey." However, as instrument designer, your primary task is to develop an instrument (which may be a questionnaire, checklist, inventory, and so on) that measures what you intend to measure.

Components of an Instrument

Typically, there are six parts to an instrument, and all or most will be included regardless of the intended purpose or the process used to collect the data. Although we explain the purpose of each component individually, in reality the components function together to create an integrated document. The ability of a respondent or a rater to complete an instrument is based on the quality of each component as well as the instrument as a whole. You may find it helpful to refer to Instrument 1.A at the end of this chapter (the University of Virginia Continuing Education Workshop Evaluation) as we present each section.

Title. The title helps to convey the purpose of the instrument. It is placed at the top center (usually) of the instrument and is the first thing that someone will see when handling the document. The title should be consistent with the instrument's intended purpose.

Introduction. The purpose of an introduction is to explain why you constructed the instrument, how you will use it, and the type of information you want to obtain. It may also contain information about how the instrument and its contents will be managed—for example, how you will ensure the respondent's confidentiality as a participant. The introduction may be conveyed on a separate page or as a separate section at the beginning of the instrument. A 1998 survey (Instrument 7.A) administered to more than ninety thousand public employees in Virginia, included a cover letter from the state governor saying: "I am keenly interested in your concerns about our State government in general and your personal experience as an employee." The purpose of this survey was also described in the instructions for completing the instrument: "This survey will be used to better understand the views of the State's work force" (Office of the Governor, Commonwealth of Virginia, 1998). Notice how these statements convey that the instrument will be used to obtain data reflecting opinions and beliefs.

Directions or instructions. Directions should be given at the beginning of the instrument and within the instrument where respondents need guidance to complete items—for example, when there is a change in item format. External raters or observers will also need comprehensive directions, to ensure interrater consistency.

The purpose of directions is to guide the respondent through the instrument and to assist in obtaining the type of information sought. They should be brief and clear; the directions on the workshop evaluation are concisely stated in one sentence.

Items. At the heart of the instrument are the items, and as we explain in this book, a multitude of item formats can be used to solicit information. *Selection items* provide the respondent with potential choices (that is, choices given in advance) from which the respondent makes a selection. A rating item consists of a *stem,* which is a phrase, sentence, or question that elicits information, and the *response set,* from which the respondent makes the selection. The response choices may form a graded continuum, or scale, or they may be alternatives. An example of a selection item with a scaled response set is being asked to *rate* your experience with a product as *satisfactory, somewhat satisfactory, somewhat unsatisfactory,* or *unsatisfactory.* An example of an item with alternative choices is being asked to *select* your age from a list of age ranges. Another example of a selection item is being asked to *rank* your choices. In this case you must consider, compare, and order all the response alternatives, rather than selecting just one of them.

Supply items, such as open-ended questions, require respondents to provide the answer themselves. Such responses tend to be more descriptive and provide opportunities for more elaboration. However, they may also measure more than the respondent's knowledge; for example, they may also reflect writing skills and language development. Consider the following question, written first as a selection item and then as a supply item:

Examples

1. I would recommend this organization as a place of employment (circle one):

Strongly Disagree   Disagree   Agree   Strongly Agree

2. What would you recommend about this organization as a place of employment?

In the first example, the selection item, the responses may be easier to score and categorize. This might be a factor if the question is to appear in an instrument administered to hundreds of people. However, the second example, the supply item, may elicit a better sample of the respondent's range of knowledge or attitudes, producing more information than the first example would provide. However, analysis of hundreds of lengthy narratives would be more labor intensive.

Demographics. The demographic section gathers such information about the respondent as age, gender, occupation, and marital status. It should solicit only information that is vital to the project. An instrument used to obtain information about an object will solicit descriptive information about that object. For example, the demographic section of a checklist to audit medical records might include space to record the record number, the date the audit was completed, and the name of the auditor. The demographic section can be placed at either the beginning or end; Chapter Twelve examines the advantages and disadvantages of each placement.

Closing section. Depending on the purpose of the instrument, it may include a closing section. A survey, for example, might use this section to thank the individual for responding and also to repeat certain information, such as the return address.

Selecting an Appropriate Instrument

As the creator of an instrument, you have some latitude as to the type of instrument to develop, such as a questionnaire, checklist, or inventory; the mode of administration to use; and ultimately the item format(s) to use, such as open-ended questions, rating scales, or ranking items. The decision about the type of instrument and item format(s) will typically be based on the following considerations.

The purpose of the study. The type of instrument to use is usually determined by identifying the type of information you need. In turn, the type of information you require should emerge from defining the purpose of your study. For example, a marketing questionnaire would be suggested if the purpose of your study is to identify consumer characteristics. We'll examine this process in more detail in Chapter Five.

The research design. Identifying the purpose of the study will also suggest some research designs and information-gathering strategies, such as an experiment using random assignment, survey research, or naturalistic inquiry (Chapter Two). The design may therefore suggest instrumentation. For example, a research design based on naturalistic inquiry and fieldwork would imply the use of an observational recording form.

Object of measurement. Closely related to the purpose of the study is the question of who or what will be the focus of inquiry. If the answer to this question is a what, then you will need to develop an instrument that will be completed by an independent or external rater. If the answer to the question is a who, then the options will include self-report as well as an independent rater.

Data collection methodology. In the design phase of instrument construction, it is important to consider the type of data that might be produced and how those data will be collected. This information can help in determining the item format to use. For example, if data are to be collected by multiple independent observers, that might suggest using items with predetermined response choices.

Resources. The design of the instrument and consequently the choice of instrument can also be influenced by the resources available during all phases of your study. For example, will you be the sole instrument designer, or will it be a group effort? What are the time constraints: how much time do you have to design, test, and administer the instrument? Who will do the data collection and the data analysis? These questions should help as you consider the instrument and item format(s) to use.

Taken together these considerations should help you decide on the type of instrument to develop. For example, in order to respond to a school board request, an elementary school principal needs to know for how many hours during the school day children are engaged in reading. The principal could ask her teachers to guesstimate the amount of time, or she could use a more systematic approach, such as having teachers keep a written record. To make data collection more efficient, the principal decides to develop a checklist, so that the teachers need only circle the times that students are engaged in reading activities. In developing this instrument the principal takes into account a number of factors, such as the type of information needed, how data will be collected, and available resources (that is, she is sensitive to the limited amount of time that teachers have to collect the data).

The Process of Instrument Construction

As we discussed earlier, artists typically go through a number of steps in the creation of a painting. First, they may draft a number of preliminary sketches of their subject, drawing the subject from different angles, varying the lighting, and if painting the human figure, trying different poses. Some artists like to make color sketches in pastel chalks or watercolors before committing to a final product in oil or acrylic paint. And even after they have begun applying paint to canvas, they may make changes during the process of actually completing the painting.

This process of constantly revising a composition is an *iterative* process, and instrument construction, like painting a picture, should be viewed as a systematic yet creative activity that requires continual refinement and revision (Figure 1.2). Although there are clearly steps that must be completed in this process, instrument construction may not always progress sequentially. For example, after you receive feedback from a friend, colleague, or potential user of the instrument, you may find you need to rewrite specific items or reorganize the instrument itself. Consequently, the following activities should be viewed as part of a creative cycle.

Articulate the purpose and focus of the study. This is perhaps the most important activity, and yet it is often overlooked or minimized. Specifying the purpose helps you identify the themes or concepts you want to understand, the methodology you might use, the type of instrument to develop, and the questions or items that

FIGURE 1.2: STEPS IN THE INSTRUMENT CONSTRUCTION PROCESS.

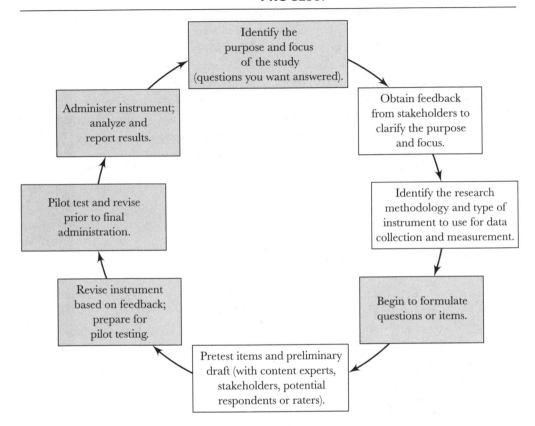

you might include in the instrument to obtain the information you seek. Part of this process involves reviewing literature (books, journal articles, and so on) relevant to the topic. Discussing your project with others who are familiar with its topic can help you identify aspects to focus on or exclude from the study. This is important if the study has been commissioned, as you may need to negotiate the purpose and content of the study. Additionally, you may want to speak with potential respondents, as they too can provide information and their personal perspective about the topic. In considering the approach to use to collect and analyze the data (that is, the methodology), ask whether the topic lends itself to qualitative approaches such as interviews or focus groups, to examination of archival data, to a survey, or to an experimental design.

Failure to complete this activity could result in obtaining information that does not answer your question or that does not provide useful and accurate information for decision making. Drafting a purpose statement can also assist in specifying how the data will be collected and who will complete the instrument.

Activity review and check. It is important to share your purpose statement with others and to obtain feedback that can clarify and focus the project.

Formulate items. This is both a technical and creative process. It is based on your knowledge of the topic, the information you have described in your purpose statement, and your review of supportive information to help in the creation of specific items. For example, if you are going to conduct an assessment of employee satisfaction, you will probably want to know, prior to designing the questionnaire, what the organization does and how it is organized. Additionally, you will want to understand some of the management theories and concepts that apply to the understanding of employee satisfaction. This information will assist you in brainstorming and writing out questions or items. This process may also involve examining similar instruments to see how others have carried out this measurement. (You may even decide that rather than create a new instrument you will use or adapt an existing instrument, being sure to cite the original source[s], respect copyright, and pay a fee if the instrument is proprietary.)

This creative process may be a solitary or a group endeavor. At this stage, items may be written as questions or statements, and no attempt is made to format them into, for example, open-ended questions or selected response items. Additionally, during this activity decisions can be made about the specific information to obtain. For example, if you have decided to create a survey that will be administered only to women, there is no need to include a demographic question asking for the respondent's gender.

Activity review and check. Obtain feedback from others on item validity: do the items appear to ask for information that will answer your question or obtain the information you need for decision making? Modify your items based on this feedback.

Structure and format the items. The next activity is to decide on the item format or formats that will provide the information you need efficiently and effectively. This decision will depend in part on the purpose of your study. For example, an instrument designed to support observations of another's behaviors might suggest the use of a behavior rating scale, whereas an instrument with items that ask for opinions will likely suggest the use of a scale measuring the respondent's level of agreement with a statement. And depending on what you want to measure, you might incorporate a variety of item formats in the instrument.

Activity review and check. Obtain feedback from content experts (individuals knowledgeable in the subject you are studying) as well as from potential respondents. This feedback is used to determine whether the items make sense and are unambiguous and whether the information you obtain from the items will provide you with the information you want. This feedback can also assist in identifying problems with instrument administration. Do individuals who will use an observational instrument agree on the meaning of the items and what they are supposed to observe and report?

Organize and format the instrument. At this stage you are ready to organize items so that they flow in a logical order, and depending on the purpose of the instrument, you may need to consider the content of the instructions and the demographic section.

Activity review and check. Typically, you will want to pretest the instrument as a complete document rather than item by item. This pretest determines how long it takes to complete the instrument and identifies places where respondents or raters had difficulty completing the instrument due to bottlenecks or confusing items or instructions. This is an important activity, as an incomprehensible or awkwardly formatted instrument may result in a low response rate (for a survey questionnaire) or unreliable data (for a checklist or behavior rating instrument).

Administer and revise the instrument. Even though you have taken steps to correct problems during instrument design and construction, the responses from the first administration may suggest improvements, and you may find that the instrument requires further revision if you intend to use it again. Such revision is a common activity with instruments used to measure performance, as repeated administrations will certainly highlight shortcomings or portions of the instrument that need to be corrected. You may find problems in the administration of the instrument that can be improved as well.

Summary

In this chapter we provided a definition of an instrument, described the parts of an instrument, and listed the steps in the instrument construction process. We also described some ways that instruments might be categorized and pointed out that the terminology researchers and evaluators use to describe these categories can be somewhat indefinite. A major theme is that instrument construction is an iterative process— as you will find yourself repeatedly revising and refining the instrument in response to feedback—and therefore it is an activity that is both technical and creative.

Instrument 1.A: Illustrating the Parts of a Questionnaire

Throughout this book we present sample instruments or items to illustrate our themes and main points. These samples can provide guidance as you design your own instrument and when you need to evaluate instruments designed by others. We use our first example to illustrate the components of an instrument.

The Continuing Education Workshop Evaluation Form (Instrument 1.A) was developed a number of years ago to evaluate a continuing education workshop and its instructors. The results are provided to the instructors so they can use this information to revise and improve the curriculum and classroom instruction. The title of the form is printed in bold type at the top of the page. The title—Continuing Education Workshop Evaluation Form—clearly connotes the instrument's purpose. The demographic section consists of three items: course title, course number, and schedule number. The questionnaire is typically completed at the conclusion of the training, and participants are given the demographic information to fill in these blanks at that time. Further down the page is a line for the instructor's name. The form provides for the rater's anonymity, as the individual completing the form does not provide identifying information. The instructions are concisely stated in one sentence and are printed near the top of the page.

Through experience, the department using this form has identified those few questions that produce meaningful information, resulting in a very concise instrument. For example, the instrument makes use of both selection items and open-ended statements. Each item is preceded by a number. Items 1 through 7 are to be rated on a *Likert* response scale, from *strongly agree* to *strongly disagree*. *Not applicable* (NA) and *no opinion* or *neutral* (N) options have been provided in the response set. The items address instructor skills, the physical environment, and course content. Items 8, 9, and 10 provide space for written comments. In order to be concise, this instrument does not include an introductory or a closing section.

The instrument is organized coherently and logically. Large black boxes are printed in the response matrix corresponding to item 8 to indicate that this is an open-ended item; for clarity and continuity, black boxes should also have been printed after items 9 and 10. The instrument is designed for automated data collection, using an optical mark recognition device (Scantron). For each of the first seven items, the respondent darkens an oval corresponding with the appropriate description on the scale printed near the top of the page. This facilitates data collection. Alternatively, respondents might have checked a box or circled a number.

The Workshop Evaluation Form also highlights the difficulty of categorizing instruments and the need to clearly define an instrument's intended purpose. The instrument's primary function appears to be to work as a survey questionnaire, by soliciting opinions about the course, instructor, and learning environment. When it is used for this purpose, an instructor can use the findings to improve the content and process of a workshop. However, items 1 through 5 of this form could also be used by a supervisor to assess student opinions about the instructor's skills and abilities. When used for this purpose, the instrument functions as a performance appraisal.

INSTRUMENT 1.A: WORKSHOP EVALUATION.

Continuing Education Workshop Evaluation Form

Course Title: _____

Course Number: _____

Schedule Number: _____

Name of Instructor: _____

Please assess each of the following statements based on the key by filling in the bubble in the column that best represents your opinion.

	Instructor #					Schedule #				
	⓪	⓪	⓪	⓪		⓪	⓪	⓪	⓪	⓪
	①	①	①	①		①	①	①	①	①
	②	②	②	②		②	②	②	②	②
	③	③	③	③		③	③	③	③	③
	④	④	④	④		④	④	④	④	④
	⑤	⑤	⑤	⑤		⑤	⑤	⑤	⑤	⑤
	⑥	⑥	⑥	⑥		⑥	⑥	⑥	⑥	⑥
	⑦	⑦	⑦	⑦		⑦	⑦	⑦	⑦	⑦
	⑧	⑧	⑧	⑧		⑧	⑧	⑧	⑧	⑧
	⑨	⑨	⑨	⑨		⑨	⑨	⑨	⑨	⑨
	⑩	⑩	⑩	⑩		⑩	⑩	⑩	⑩	⑩

SA - Strongly Agree	A - Agree	N - No Opinion or Neutral	D - Disagree	SD - Strongly Disagree	NA - Not Applicable

	SA	A	N	D	SD	NA
1. The objectives for the course were clearly stated.	☐	☐	☐	☐	☐	☐
2. The instructor effectively taught the stated objectives.	☐	☐	☐	☐	☐	☐
3. The intructor used a variety of teaching strategies (two or more of the following: lecture, discussion, small group activity, visual/audio aids, individual assistance).	☐	☐	☐	☐	☐	☐
4. The workshop demonstrated how to apply the strategy or process presented.	☐	☐	☐	☐	☐	☐
5. The instructor demonstrated openness and receptivity to student needs and opinions.	☐	☐	☐	☐	☐	☐
6. Facilities and equipment (e.g., audiovisual equipment) were adequate. If not, comment below.	☐	☐	☐	☐	☐	☐
7. The subject matter was relevant to my professional needs.	☐	☐	☐	☐	☐	☐
8. What I liked best about this course was:	■	■	■	■	■	■
_____	☐	☐	☐	☐	☐	☐
_____	☐	☐	☐	☐	☐	☐
_____	☐	☐	☐	☐	☐	☐
_____	☐	☐	☐	☐	☐	☐
9. To strengthen the course I would suggest:	☐	☐	☐	☐	☐	☐
_____	☐	☐	☐	☐	☐	☐
_____	☐	☐	☐	☐	☐	☐
_____	☐	☐	☐	☐	☐	☐
_____	☐	☐	☐	☐	☐	☐
10. Additional workshops, courses, or programs I would like the University Continuing Education to offer:	☐	☐	☐	☐	☐	☐
_____	☐	☐	☐	☐	☐	☐
_____	☐	☐	☐	☐	☐	☐
_____	☐	☐	☐	☐	☐	☐
_____	☐	☐	☐	☐	☐	☐

Source: University of Virginia Department of Continuing Education. Reprinted with permission.

Instrument 1.B: Medical History Questionnaire

Instrument 1.B, a medical history questionnaire, was created by extracting items from several different medical history questionnaires that were readably available from sites on the Internet and is provided as an example of an instrument based solely on items that solicit objective information. The instrument illustrates various item formats as it uses both open (supply) and closed (selection) items such as checklists and dichotomous (*yes* or *no*) response sets.

INSTRUMENT 1.B: SAMPLE MEDICAL HISTORY.

Name: _____ _____ Date of Birth: _____ Current Age: _____

Gender: ☐ Male ☐ Female Health Care Insurance: ☐ Yes ☐ No

If Yes, name of insurer: _____ Policy No.: _____

Do you have a present or past history of: (*check all that apply*)

☐ ADHD	☐ Diabetes	☐ Pneumonia
☐ Alcohol Abuse	☐ Eating Disorder	☐ Skin Problems
☐ Anemia	☐ Heart Disease	☐ Single Cell Anemia
☐ Arthritis	☐ Hepatitis	☐ Sleep Problems
☐ Asthma	☐ Hernia	☐ Smoking
☐ Back Problems	☐ High Blood Pressure	☐ Thyroid Disorder
☐ Cancer	☐ High Cholesterol	☐ Tuberculosis
☐ Chronic Cough	☐ HIV/AIDS	☐ Urinary Tract Infection
☐ Dental Problems	☐ Measles	☐ Whooping Cough
☐ Depression/anxiety	☐ Mumps	☐ Other (please specify):

Are you currently on any medications: ☐ Yes ☐ No
If Yes, please list the medications here:

Do you have any allergies: ☐ Yes ☐ No
If Yes, please list your allergies here:

Exercise History:

In what kind of exercises or sports do you currently participate?
How often do you participate?
How many years have you participated in these activities?

To be completed by nurse:

Height: _____ Weight: _____ Blood Pressure: _____ Pulse: _____
Vision: Without Glasses: Right ____ / Left ____ With Glasses: Right ____ / Left _____

Thank you for completing this form.

This medical history questionnaire also requires two modes of administration. Although it is primarily designed to be a self-report instrument, with the client providing the information, data to complete the last section are obtained by a nurse. Note that there are no instructions at the beginning of the instrument; instead, directions are provided as necessary in the body of the questionnaire. Additionally, a purpose statement is probably not needed as the instrument is designed to be used in a specific setting, such as a doctor's office, or during the hospital admissions process.

Instrument 1.C: Example of a Checklist

The Research Evaluation Checklist (Lutz, 2006) was developed to assist stakeholders evaluate research projects and reports. For example, this checklist might be used by an agency institutional review board (IRB) to assess a research proposal. Consequently, it is also a useful instrument for someone (perhaps you) who is planning a research project or is documenting the results of a project.

This is a simple *yes* or *no* checklist, with the reviewer literally checking a box when the document being examined contains the required information or leaving the box blank when the information is not present. Items are clustered by themes and concepts. This example illustrates the kind of checklist described in this chapter. Although the checklist itself offers no instructions, it appears in a manual that describes how it might be used, as follows:

> The second checklist is longer and will be useful when completing a thorough evaluation of a research report. The questions are organized according to the components of a research report. (Part III [of the manual], Getting the Most Out of a Research Report, provides a definition of a research report and describes its typical contents.) People who have little or no experience in evaluating research may wish to select questions from the second checklist rather than using all of them. Some questions include terms that may be unfamiliar to you. Be sure to check for their definitions in the Glossary in Part IV, Understanding the Language of Research. In Part II and Part III, certain terms will appear in underlined *italics* the first time they are used. Their definitions can be found in the Glossary [Lutz, 2006, p. 11].

INSTRUMENT 1.C: RESEARCH EVALUATION CHECKLIST.

Significance of the Study
❑ What makes the study useful, important or of interest to you?
❑ What do you want to know from the *research*?
❑ Did the researchers clearly explain why they did the study?
❑ Have the researchers convinced you of the importance of the study?
❑ Does the study address a *gap in knowledge* or provide new information about the topic or issue?
❑ Were *constructs, variables* and terms clearly defined?
❑ Was a clear *rationale* presented for the constructs or variables examined in the study?
❑ Were consumers or family members involved in helping to *design* the study?
❑ Were board members, administrators or agency staff involved in helping to design the study?

Research Questions and Hypotheses
❑ Were the research questions and hypotheses clearly stated?
❑ Did the research questions and hypotheses accurately forecast what would take place in the study?

Methodology
❑ Were the procedures clearly described?
❑ Could someone repeat the study after reading the *methods* section?
❑ Were appropriate criteria used to select the *sample*?
❑ Were methods used to prevent *bias* in the study?
❑ Were the procedures and instruments *reliable* and *valid*?
❑ Were the procedures and instruments free of potential bias (for example, age, gender, racial or ethnic)?
❑ Was a *control group* needed to address the main question of the study?
❑ Was an appropriate control or *comparison group* used in the study?
❑ What steps did the researchers take to prevent harm or distress to the research participants?
❑ Was the study approved by an institutional review board (IRB) or a similar committee on ethics?

Sample, Representativeness, and Generalizability
❑ Did the researcher justify the size of the sample?
❑ Did the researcher describe the methods used to determine sample size?
❑ Was the sample size sufficient to find significant results?
❑ Do the characteristics of the sample match those of the *population* of interest?
❑ Did the *study setting* match the location where the results will be applied?

Statistical Methods and Results

❑ Did the researchers use appropriate statistical tests to evaluate hypotheses or answer the research questions?

❑ Did the researchers use the appropriate statistical tests for *small sample sizes*?

❑ Did the researchers clearly identify the *major findings* of the study?

Discussion, Limitations, and Implications

❑ Did the researchers identify the limitations and biases of the study?

❑ Did the researchers discuss how the limitations and biases influence the results?

❑ Did the researchers discuss recommendations from or practical implications of the findings?

❑ Did the researchers discuss what future studies could be done on this topic or issue?

❑ Did the researchers state how they will use the findings?

❑ Did the researchers recommend how others can use the findings? For example, did they indicate that the findings might be used to:

    ❑ improve a current practice or service?

    ❑ develop or revise a policy?

    ❑ change a mental health law?

    ❑ support a request for funding?

    ❑ support implementation of a new program or service?

Source: Adapted from Heacock, Koehoorn, & Tan, 1997; Kazdin, 1998; Krathwolh, 1988; Centers for Disease Control and Prevention, 2006; National Alliance on Mental Illness, 2006; Lutz, 2006. Reprinted with permission.

Endnotes

1. Despite our best efforts, we humans "filter" what we observe, based on prior experience. Consequently, two people may see the same event, but interpret it differently, and if asked to measure the event using some form of observational instrument, they may come up with decidedly different ratings; consider, for example, the scores different judges give to an ice-skating performance.

2. Scriven (2000, p. 1) defines checklist as, "a list of factors, properties, aspects, components, criteria, tasks, or dimensions, the presence or amount of which is to be separately considered, in order to perform a task."

Key Concepts and Terms

attitude scale

behavior rating

checklist

instrument

inventory

item

Likert response scale

mode of administration

objective

observation

poll

performance rating

psychometric instrument

questionnaire

rating scale

response set

selection item

self-report

stem

subjective

supply item

survey

test

CHAPTER TWO

INSTRUMENTS AND SOCIAL INQUIRY

In this chapter we will

- Describe approaches to social inquiry.
- Examine how methodology influences the selection and construction of instruments.

As with any human endeavor, there is a history helping to explain how and why we do what we do when we engage in social inquiry. The purpose of this chapter is to provide a conceptual basis for the use of social science instruments in social inquiry. We explain what makes the social sciences a science, describe approaches to systematic inquiry, and explain the role of instruments in measurement and information gathering.

Instruments and Questionnaires in the Context of Social Science Research

Social science refers to the application of a systematic approach to understanding human actions and interactions. Social scientists refer to this process as *sense making*, an attempt to give meaning to our existence by asking questions that lead us to try to explain such very basic concepts as, What is truth? What is reality? How do we make sense of the world? The approaches used in social science inquiry are the same across the social science disciplines: political science, sociology, anthropology, education, psychology, and management and business administration. Ultimately, the purpose of social science and of the methodologies used to conduct social inquiry is to better understand, explain, and influence human behavior.

From an historical perspective, the social sciences were not always scientific. Early attempts to explain human behavior were often based solely on observation, description, and conjecture, and for much of human history, events were explained as being the result of divine intervention, luck, or chance. Such basic attempts to comprehend situations are referred to as *ordinary knowing,* and for thousands of years this was the primary approach to sense making (Judd, Smith, & Kidder, 1991). Ordinary knowing is characterized by intuition, hunches, observation, inference, and past experience. Historically, understandings of beliefs, social relationships, and human behavior were most often formulated on political and religious philosophy (for example, the concept that kings obtained their authority to rule through divine right), rather than on systematic inquiry to define underlying causal relationships. This began to change in the mid- to late nineteenth century, when it was demonstrated that the methodologies employed in the natural and physical sciences, including measurement, experimentation, systematic observation, and the use of statistical analysis, could be adapted to questions of social relevance.

In the late nineteenth century, research in biology and medicine increased understanding of human physiology, and the work of Darwin helped to build a conceptual basis for understanding human development. If human physiological mechanisms could be explained, perhaps the cognitive and behavioral attributes of humans, individually (psychology) and collectively (sociology), could be as well. And if human biology could be examined by application of scientific methods, why couldn't these same methods be used to understand human thought and behavior? Consequently, in the late nineteenth and early twentieth centuries, the methods used in the physical sciences were applied to the study of human behavior and relationships, resulting in social science as a systematic discipline of inquiry.

One of the factors that helped to "legitimize" the social sciences as a science was the use of measurement and statistical analysis. Measurement provides a means for the systematic classification and coding of information. Measurement is a critical factor in the development of instruments because we want to construct items that will produce data that can be organized in a coherent, logical, and replicable fashion. In turn this supports a methodical approach for analysis, such as the use of statistics to examine trends, patterns, and associations or to test hypotheses.

The social sciences also gained legitimacy by employing probability theory and statistics in describing and explaining human behavior. Probability had long been used in biology and the other natural sciences for understanding and predicting variation among observations. By the early nineteenth century, probability theory was being applied as a way of understanding the effects of population growth. Statistics were originally referred to as *political arithmetic*. The term *statistic* is derived from the German word *statistik*, which meant information important to matters of the state. By the late 1800s and early 1900s, statistical analysis had become the primary means of analyzing data in the social sciences. For example, Frederick Taylor, referred to as the "father of scientific management," carried out his work at the turn of the twentieth century and was among the first to use statistics to measure and predict work output (Albanese, 1981). It was also during this period that British statistician Karl Pearson derived his formula for calculating correlations (the strength of a relationship between variables), which is now foundational for many forms of social research. With measures and statistics as analytical tools, social scientists could finally lay claim to methods as rigorous as those employed in the natural and biological sciences (Porter, 1986).

The adaptation of scientific methods, measurement, and statistical analysis to social inquiry created a systematic approach, overcoming many of the shortcomings present in methodologies based solely on observation and description. First, social science research is grounded in theory. In general use *theory* often refers to an unverified assumption, but a scientific theory is a logical explanation that has been tested repeatedly and is well supported by evidence. Researchers develop hypotheses (assumptions) about these theories and then conduct empirical research, or systematic observation and measurement, in an attempt to examine and produce evidence to support or refute these hypotheses. Scientific theories are never fully proven; however, they are confirmed as hypothesis testing develops a body of supportive evidence. The strength of this evidence is often increased when a study replicates and builds upon prior research.

Second, systematic inquiry requires that there be rules and standards to guide research. Such guidelines ensure that other researchers can replicate a study in an attempt to support or refute earlier findings. They also ensure that the sources of information used in a study are credible and appropriate for the research. A popular belief or explanation may sound and appear plausible, but to be proven it must withstand the scrutiny of systematic inquiry and replication. For example, a study published in a prestigious medical journal found that infertile women who were prayed for by prayer groups became pregnant twice as often as those who did not have people praying for them. However, upon investigation it was found that the research methods were unsystematic, the results could not be reproduced, and questions were raised about the integrity of the researchers (Flamm, 2004).

Third, social science research employs accepted methodologies for conducting research, as well as accepted methodologies for collecting, analyzing, and interpreting data. There are a number of these methodologies, and a research question may suggest a specific method for collecting and analyzing the data, or it may suggest a variety of methods and the researcher must choose the one that best fits his or her skills, situation, and resources. Indeed, in the real world, inquiry methods and data are never completely tidy:

> A scientist is characterized neither by a willingness to believe or a willingness to disbelieve, nor yet a desire to prove or disprove anything, but by the desire to discover what is, and to do so by observation, experiment, verification, and falsification. So doing, the scientist expects that others will take the trouble to check his findings, for it is only by such independent testing that his finding can be verified. Scientists do not believe in fundamental and absolute certainties. For the scientist, certainty is never an end, but a search; not the ordering of certainty, but its exploration. For the scientist, certainty represents the highest degree of probability which attaches to a particular judgment at a particular time level, a judgment or conclusion that has been arrived at by experiment, inference, or observation. ... Scientists lack a superstitious regard for the catchwords of science, and believe that all knowledge is infinitely perfectible [Montagu, 1984, pp. 7–8].

Until the mid-twentieth century, scientific research was positivist in outlook. The philosophy of positivism holds that only that which can be observed can be studied, for every effect there is a cause, and it is possible to understand the world well enough that phenomena can be predicted and controlled (Trochim, 2001). The natural and physical sciences set the stage for positivism because, for the most part, these sciences were working with constants, such as the speed of light or the number of electrons in an element. These constants hold true even though individuals may experience them differently. Additionally, physicists, astronomers, biologists, and chemists could directly observe many of the things they wanted to measure. For example, Galileo was the first to use a telescope to observe Jupiter's moons and calculate the motion of their orbits.

In contrast, social science phenomena behave in a very different manner. Unlike physical phenomena, the activities that social scientists study are situational: that is, they may differ within and between situations or settings, and they may change over time. For example, people's attitudes toward government and political leaders may change in response to these leaders' statements and actions, a change that may appear as a rise or fall in a presidential approval rating. Additionally, the social sciences acknowledge the existence of multiple realities: Social and cultural phenomena are experienced differently by individuals, and social science attempts to understand the world as experienced by individuals or groups of individuals through their *shared realities*. Finally, social and behavioral scientists are often interested in attributes that cannot be directly observed, such as psychological and social states, including depression, anxiety, self-esteem, locus of control, and the like. At best, social science instruments attempt to measure characteristics associated with these states (referred to as *constructs*). If a social scientist is interested in knowledge and cognitive abilities, the instrument might attempt to measure some observable aspect of knowledge, such as the ability to recall information or the breadth of an individual's vocabulary. Consequently, social science instruments may or may not obtain information that represents a direct measure of the subject of interest.

Today, most physical and social scientists have adopted a philosophical approach to inquiry referred to as *postpositivism*. This means that although the methods used to examine phenomena must be rigorous and systematic, it is understood that not all phenomena can be easily understood, explained, or predicted. Contemporary astronomers and physicists, for example, now find that the things they need to measure often cannot be directly observed, such as atomic particles. Unable to account for all of the matter and energy that their calculations demonstrate must exist in the universe, they have postulated the existence of dark matter and dark energy, which can be inferred from gravitational effects but are undetectable using current methods of measurement (Freedman & Turner, 2003).

Lincoln and Guba (1985) make this distinction between positivism and postpositivism (which they refer to as the *new paradigm*): "Where positivism is concerned with surface events or appearances, the new paradigm takes a deeper look. Where positivism is atomistic, the new paradigm is structural. Where positivism establishes meaning operationally, the new paradigm establishes meaning inferentially. Where positivism sees its central purpose to be prediction, the new paradigm is concerned with understanding. Finally, where positivism is deterministic and bent on certainty, the new paradigm is probabilistic and speculative" (p. 30).

In addition to trying to answer *why* questions, social scientists are often interested in *what, how,* and *if* questions. For example, they may be interested in how a particular program works, if clients are receiving the intended outcome of services, or if employees are carrying out their job duties as assigned. The results of such inquiry are often used to make value judgments about programs, processes, people, and products, such as whether a program should continue to be funded, whether services need to be added or reduced, or whether an employee will receive a raise in pay. For social scientists investigating such questions, the use of instruments allows them to measure program and individual efforts and effects consistently and systematically.

It is sometimes difficult to believe that many of the approaches we currently use to collect and analyze data were developed just a few generations ago, and that others have been developed in our lifetimes. For example, systematic measurement, even in the physical sciences, is relatively new. In eighteenth century France, there were multiple measures for a foot, which varied between 10.6 and 13.4 inches, and different measures for a pound, bushel, and liter. During that period, physical measures differed not only between countries, but between cities within a country and even between neighborhoods within a city (Strauss, 1995). One of the first psychometric instruments, the Stanford-Binet Test of Intelligence, was developed by Alfred Binet in 1905 and adopted for systematic use in the United States by Lewis Terman in 1916 (Kamin, 1995). Development of tests and measures of academic achievement flowered in the early twentieth century, as reflected in the publication of E. L. Thorndike's pioneering text on measurement in 1904 (Worthen, Borg, & White, 1993). In regard to survey questionnaires, Babbie notes that even though one of the first surveys of political attitudes was conducted in 1880, for the most part "contemporary survey research is a product of American researchers in this century" (1990, p. 37). For example, it was during the 1924 and 1928 presidential campaigns that the Hearst newspaper chain ran preelection polls in almost every state of the union. George Gallup started his polling organization in 1935, and in 1936, using a random sample of potential voters, successfully predicted that Franklin Roosevelt would be reelected president (Newport, 2004).

It was also during this period that the format for questionnaire items was being honed. In 1929, L. L. Thurstone explored the theory of attitude measurement and developed a schema for categorizing responses along a continuum that allowed measurement on both sides of the continuum; that is, responses to a series of items could be used to measure both agreement and lack of agreement. In 1932, Rensis Likert developed a format for item construction that asked respondents to indicate their level of agreement with an item (*strongly agree, agree, disagree,* and *strongly disagree*). This has probably become the most frequently used format for constructing items to measure opinions and beliefs (Judd et al., 1991). Additionally, the values associated with the items could be added together to create a score reflecting the strength of the relationship between the items and the underlying concept that the instrument attempts to measure.

Over time the methods developed for social science research have been adapted to virtually all activities requiring measurement and analysis. The following section describes the principal approaches to social inquiry. Although there are many ways to gather information, almost all require some form of instrument.

Methods of Inquiry

Instrument construction is just one facet of the larger process of discovery and decision making. To ensure that you are obtaining the information you want and need, it is important to clarify the purpose of your study, define the questions that need to be addressed, identify potential sources of information, construct data-gathering instruments, and apply a systematic approach for collecting and analyzing the data. In this section we will outline a process for focusing your study or project and describe the relationship between instruments and approaches to data collection and analysis (illustrated in Table 2.1).

Table 2.1 illustrates the process of defining a project and the relationship between instruments and other steps in the process. The first phase is to state the purpose of your project; this can be stated as a question, such as, "What is the relationship between standardized testing and curriculum development?" or a declarative statement (hypothesis), such as, "Standardized tests lead to more effective curriculum." Not all instruments are developed for the purpose of social inquiry; they may also be designed for such more mundane but pertinent activities as evaluating people, products, processes, and programs in conjunction with problem solving and decision making. For example, you may want to develop an observation instrument to provide teachers with information about student behaviors to improve the teachers' classroom management skills, or you may need a screening instrument to determine the level and type of services to provide to clients referred to a mental health clinic. Regardless of the underlying rationale—social science research or evaluation for decision making—it is important to start the project by focusing and clarifying the process.

The next step is to formulate the questions that need to be answered in order to understand and, possibly, resolve the problem. For example: What are "good" and "bad" classroom behaviors, and can I distinguish between them? Is it important to know how often these behaviors occur? Are there student characteristics that I need to be aware of? Are there teacher characteristics that affect student behavior? And so forth. These questions bring into focus what will be studied and what data will need to be generated in order to answer the questions.

Methodology refers to how we will go about understanding the phenomenon or question of interest and addresses the approaches used to collect, analyze, and interpret information. As we will see in the next section, methodology suggests informational needs and sources and thus the type of instrument needed, which in turn will suggest whether you can use an existing instrument (off the shelf or adapted to your situation) or will need to construct an instrument to meet your unique circumstances and informational needs.

There are two broad categories of methodologies: *qualitative* and *quantitative*. Qualitative methods involve "open-ended explorations of people's words, thoughts, actions, and intentions" as a means of obtaining information (Judd, et al., 1991, p. 299). An interview that results in a written transcript, field notes reflecting direct observation of participants, and video-recordings are examples

TABLE 2.1: STUDY PLANNING GRID.

Purpose Statement

State the major consideration, concern, or question to be addressed.

Methodology

State the conceptual and technical basis for collecting, analyzing, and interpreting the data (quantitative, qualitative, or mixed method).

Questions	Instrument	Information Collection Strategies	Information Analysis & Interpretation	Reporting
Formulate the questions that help to focus the study by pointing out and clarifying the areas of concern. Can also identify resources needed to implement the study.	Identify the mechanism(s) for obtaining information to support decision making and understanding. May be off the shelf or developed to meet the particular situation and informational needs.	Describe the specifics of the information collection procedures. For example, how, when, to whom, and under what conditions will the instrument(s) be administered?	Describe the process that will be carried out to facilitate answering the questions. To what extent do the data and how they were obtained influence how they should be analyzed?	Consider the reporting decisions: Who should receive the information? What type of information should each of the individuals receive? When should people receive it? In what format should it be presented?

Source: Adapted from Worthen and Sanders (1987, p. 244).

of qualitative approaches. Quantitative approaches typically focus on "how much, how often or how many" (Judd et al., 1991, p. 174) and therefore often make use of data that are numerical or can be converted to numerical data, such as a questionnaire that uses a response scale numbered 1 to 5. As the term suggests, mixed-method approaches make use of both qualitative and quantitative measures.

The approach selected influences data collection and instruments. Consider the number and type of activities associated with using a checklist to rate teacher interactions and classroom management skills; they include (1) identification and training of observers to use the checklist; (2) gaining access and approval to observe teachers in the classroom; (3) creating an observation schedule; (4) determining the duration of each observation; (5) assessing observer consistency before, during, and after the observations; (6) designing an observation process that is as unobtrusive as possible; and (7) identifying how data will be stored for tabulation and analysis. In part the ways these activities are carried out is dependent on the instrument, because the number, wording, and format of the items may have an effect on such factors as the frequency and duration of each observation as well as inter-observer reliability.

Choice of methodology also helps to frame how obtained information is analyzed and interpreted. Content analysis is a method for analyzing narrative data, such as the transcripts of individual and group interviews, whereas statistical analysis and the use of tables and charts are approaches to summarizing and analyzing numerical data. An important consideration at this stage is that the trustworthiness of your results is only as good as the trustworthiness of the data that your instrument produces.

The final step is reporting the data, and you should consider who will receive and use the results, when and in what manner they will be delivered, and the type of information you will present. On the one hand, information about teacher-student interactions might be shared with the teacher (or even the class) as part of a coaching and mentoring process. In this case, reporting is informal and used to enhance the quality of teaching. On the other hand, your examination of teacher and student behaviors may have been conducted as part of a systematic investigation and the results published in a peer-reviewed journal. In some cases you may need to present the instrument used to capture data and explain how you have demonstrated that it is providing the results it should and in a consistent manner.

Methodology and Instruments

The selection of a methodology will depend on many factors, such as the question to be addressed, available resources, the time you have available to conduct your study, and your skills and expertise when working with a particular approach; there are no hard, definite rules that determine which approach to take. Let's suppose that a school system has asked you to obtain information about teacher job satisfaction. Given the number of schools and teachers, you may find that the most expedient approach is to administer a questionnaire to a sample of teachers in the system. Conversely, if you are concerned that this method will limit teachers' responses, you might interview or hold group discussions with a selected number of teachers at each school. The questionnaire will provide a broad overview of how a sample of teachers in the school system perceive job satisfaction, whereas the interviews or focus groups will provide in-depth information from a selected few teachers. Time permitting, you could use both approaches, so that the responses from the interviews and focus groups enhance and expand on the results of your survey.

Qualitative approaches include descriptive information, such as long narratives obtained from interviews, anecdotal reports from observations, and responses to open-ended questions asked on surveys and tests. The qualitative approach is typified by an investigator's journal of observations and impressions. Qualitative approaches are often used in anthropology, sociology, organization development, and program evaluation. Descriptive information may be derived from interviews that use open-ended questions to initiate discourse and that result in open-ended responses. The researcher who observes behaviors in a natural setting, such as a schoolyard, is engaging in a field study. This approach allows the researcher to understand the children's behaviors in a particular context and at a particular time. Data from this type of research may be derived from observation notes, videotapes, audiotapes, interviews, or reflective papers. Information may also come from archival data, such as personnel records, program documents, or classroom syllabi.

Another qualitative approach is the use of *focus groups* to obtain information from a group of individuals on a particular topic. Focus groups are often used to conduct needs assessments or to engage in brainstorming and creative problem solving and, as we will see, to participate in the construction and pretesting of your instrument. Data from this type of research may include audiotapes, meeting minutes, or reflective papers.

Open-ended and essay questions on tests reflect a qualitative approach, as they require test takers to synthesize and communicate information in their own words. For example, the test takers may be asked to present and defend a position or write a theme comparing and contrasting a topic.

Qualitative data can be sorted and categorized and can even be given numerical values that lend themselves to quantitative analysis. For example, you can sort narratives according to recurring themes or compare-and-contrast responses, or you can compare information to preestablished criteria. You can also code the data—1 if a theme is present and 0 if not present—and then count the frequency of occurrence or determine a statistical correlation between the values (Trochim, 2001, pp. 155–156). When analyzing qualitative data, such as interview transcripts, it is important to consider the context in which the information is being shared as well as what is actually being said. This suggests that the researcher must be observant and aware of subtleties. Whereas quantitative approaches attempt to summarize information concisely, often through the use of tables, graphs, or statistical values, qualitative approaches are characterized by rich and thick description. For example, the final product of a study that applied qualitative approaches might be a case study that uses multiple perspectives to describe an individual, group, organization, or situation.

Instruments are often developed in conjunction with qualitative approaches to data gathering, the most frequent being a questionnaire to guide interviews. Such questionnaires typically consists of a series of open-ended questions to initiate interaction. As the interview proceeds, additional questions arise from the discussion. This differs from open-ended items in a questionnaire, where there is no opportunity for follow up based on a response.

Quantitative approaches create data that can be sorted, categorized, and counted, and the aggregate data can be summarized numerically through graphs, charts, statistical analysis, and the like. Several designs are associated with gathering quantitative date, particularly the randomized experiment, which is often considered the most rigorous, or "gold standard," approach. Its basic design involves the random assignment of subjects to either a control group or an experimental group. The experimental group receives a treatment or participates in a program different from that given to the control group. Measures are taken of both groups at the beginning and end of the experiment. The use of random assignment to rule out intervening factors means that if there is a difference found between the groups, social scientists can attribute the difference to the treatment or program with a high degree of confidence.

Because social scientists examine programs that involve people, providing a treatment or service to one group, the experimental group, and not the other, the control group, raises some concerns. For example, if a reading program has been designed to increase the reading capabilities of fourth graders, would it be equitable to exclude some students because their nonparticipation is required to prove the value of the reading program? Owing to such concerns, alternative approaches, referred to as *quasi-experimental* designs, have been developed that do not require random assignment and the use of control groups. For example, a researcher might introduce an intervention at scheduled intervals and take repeated measurements over time. Even though there is no control group, changes that might occur over time could be interpreted as being a response to the intervention.

One of the primary goals of quantitative research methods is that under certain circumstances, the results can be extrapolated to groups beyond the sample involved in the experiment or survey. For example, if research on a reading program is conducted with a random sample of fourth graders attending a public school system, then researchers may be able to generalize their results to all public school fourth-grade students. In the same way, the results of a survey of a thousand randomly selected, eligible voters can be extrapolated to the entire population of eligible voters, which could total in the tens of millions.

The use of surveys and polls is considered a quantitative approach because the closed-ended questions typically included in a survey questionnaire produce quantitative data and statistical analysis can be used to make sense of these data; for example, it is possible to calculate the frequency of responses for a particular survey item and to analyze those data by comparing the responses to another variable, such as gender or age. Nonetheless, surveys and polls might also be considered a mixed-method approach, because some questionnaire items, such as open-ended questions or requests for respondents to offer comments, do produce qualitative data. Another example of overlap occurs with *content analysis,* an approach to classifying descriptive information. The initial aspect of this process is qualitative; a system of categories is developed, often reflecting themes, phrases, or words embedded in the narrative. However, once categories are identified, the frequency with which they occur can be tabulated and reported as a numerical value. For example, you might count the number of times that a particular word, phrase, or theme appears in the text and possibly attribute some level of significance to the frequency of those occurrences, particularly if they share a situational context.

In contrast to approaches for obtaining measurements from many respondents, single-subject research is a quantitative approach used to understand individual cases, such as a one person or one situation. Typically in such cases, some form of observation instrument is constructed to measure change over time. For example, an observer might be assigned to collect data about a child who bites her nails. After a period in which a data baseline is established, an intervention is introduced, and data continue to be collected. If the intervention is successful, we would expect the nail biting to decrease or discontinue entirely. To ensure that the intervention and not some other variable is producing the desired results, the investigator may modify the intervention or discontinue it to see if any changes in the nail-biting behavior occur. In this case the methodology suggests the use of an observation instrument, such as a behavior checklist.

Observation instruments are not always developed to measure change. Often they are constructed to provide individuals with feedback about a behavior, as they do when used for personnel evaluation. They can also be used to expedite data extraction; for example, when a researcher needs to obtain data from a pre-existing source such as a personnel or medical record.

There are many ways to report quantitative data. Statistical output such as correlational values and probability levels can tell us about the strength of a relationship or indicate a how confident we can be that a result is due to a specific intervention and not another factor. Graphs, charts, and histograms are visual means of presenting data. Frequency tables are often used to summarize numerical results. Consequently, one advantage of reporting quantitative information, as compared to qualitative information, is that data can be easily summarized and reported concisely.

In summation, a variety of quantitative and qualitative approaches are available for carrying out research and decision making—collecting, analyzing, and interpreting data. Ultimately, the purpose for collecting data will have an influence on the type of information sought, the method (qualitative or quantitative) or research design most appropriate to that approach, and the choice or design of the instrument. It is important therefore to consider the purpose of your research to determine the most effective methodology to employ. Experimental and quasi-experimental designs, for example, are more likely to be implemented when a researcher is interested in understanding cause-and-effect relationships. Qualitative approaches, such as naturalistic inquiry are most suitable when trying to understand human behavior and social relationships in the environment where they occur. Surveys are typically used to gather factual information or to assess attitudes and beliefs. In addition, depending on the area of interest and the resources available, quantitative and qualitative methods may be used together, to broaden the range of information made available and to complement the data collected under each approach. For example, the information you obtain from a survey may whet your appetite for more detailed information that can be obtained only through individual or focus group interviews.

Finally, care must be taken as approaches to information gathering cannot always be easily categorized as either qualitative or quantitative. For example, nominal group technique helps group members to identify and analyze themes. Nurses may meet as a group, for example, and each nurse is asked to write down a problem he or she believes affects patient services. The nurses share their problems within the group, and a list is developed. Then the group facilitator initiates discussion about the problems. At this stage the process is entirely qualitative. However, during the next stage the group is asked to *rank* the problems, a quantitative process, so that problem solving can begin with the most intensive problems and end with the less serious areas of concern.

How We Know What We Know

In the first chapter we stated that strategies exist to help you develop a "good" instrument, one capable of providing trustworthy information. So you may be wondering how these strategies, or guidelines, are derived. The answer, in a nutshell, is through research. Instrument construction is a process that can be studied, analyzed, and improved. Research has focused on various aspects of the instrument construction process, including how to craft items that are clear and unambiguous, how to anticipate respondent choices, and how to administer the instrument so that it reflects the population of interest.

One research approach is to create two or more versions of the same instrument, using items that have slightly different wording. In this way the effect language and syntax have on respondent behavior can be studied. For example, one study used four versions of a questionnaire to examine the impact that language (using positively or negatively worded stems) and the order of response alternatives (listing *strongly disagree* or *strongly agree* first) have on respondents' choices. The researcher was also interested in detecting whether a primacy effect was operating. A primacy effect occurs when people tend to select the first response option (such as *strongly disagree* or *strongly agree*) regardless of the question. The author concluded that the results of the study revealed

> no evidence that the directionality of Likert response alternatives should be a concern in the design of at least some types of surveys. While this may or may not be an issue for many survey designers, it is a question frequently asked by those learning to design such surveys, and perhaps it is in the back of the minds of many seasoned survey designers. A primacy effect was not observed in this experiment. This indicates that at least sometimes it may not make any difference which direction is used as related to the technical adequacy and stability of the results obtained [Barnette, 2001, p. 81].

The Gallup Organization, one of the leading polling companies in North America, routinely conducts studies to improve instrument design. For example, it is often assumed that voters unilaterally support tax cuts; however, one Gallup study indicated that "it depends" on how you ask the question. Respondents to a survey were split into two groups and asked the same root question about budget surpluses. However, the response sets differed. In addition to tax cuts, one group was given the option of increasing spending on specific government programs such as education, Medicare, and defense. The other group was given the alternative of spending the surplus on other, nonspecified programs. As reflected in the following table, even this slight variation in wording produced a significantly different response pattern (Newport, 2004, pp. 231–232). The question, asked in March 1999, was this: "As you may know, the federal government is currently running a budget surplus, meaning it is taking in more money than it spends. President Clinton and the Republicans in Congress agree that most of the surplus money should be used for Social Security, but they disagree over what to do with the rest. How would you prefer to see the rest of the budget surplus used?"

Alternative 1 and Response Pattern		Alternative 2 and Response Pattern	
To tax cuts	36%	To tax cuts	74%
To fund new retirement savings accounts as well as increase spending on education, defense, Medicare, and other programs	59%	To increase spending on other government programs	21%
No opinion	5%	No opinion	1%

Another approach is to compare the results of one item to the results of other items in an instrument. This may produce evidence of questionnaire reliability and validity, which we will examine in more detail in Chapter Four. The following article abstract describes how statistical analysis was used in one study to provide support that the study instrument was measuring what it was designed to measure:

> Overall, the results indicate that the Suicide Screening Inventory (SSI) is a moderately good assessment instrument for evaluating the risk of suicide in adjudicated delinquents. Specifically, the results indicated moderate internal consistency for the SSI, which should be sufficient for a short screening tool like the SSI. The SSI was also found to have high content validity, meaning that experts at assessing suicide likelihood considered the questions on the SSI useful and important. Other findings indicated that the SSI had good convergent validity with the RADS assessment of depressive symptoms and that the SSI had good consequential validity, based on the qualitative data on four incarcerated youths who attempted suicide. Participants were 382 male offenders and 60 female offenders who had been consecutively admitted to 2 secure correctional facilities in Wisconsin. Participants completed the SSI and the RADS, a self-report measure designed to determine the severity of depressive symptoms in adolescents. The reliability of the SSI was assessed using split-half reliability coefficients in an odd-even item format. Cronbach's alpha was used as the reliability estimate and t tests were used to assess the content validity. Limitations of the study . . . include its use of a nonrandom sample of youths at two facilities, calling into question the generalizability of the findings. Future research should evaluate the reliability and validity of the SSI for assessing suicide risk outside of corrections populations [Kaczmarek, Hagan, & Kettler, 2006, p. 204].

Throughout this book we will present research-based recommendations for crafting items. However, it is important to recognize the limitations associated with social science research: it is understood that the results obtained from any studies are situational and context bound. In other words, a set of results may be unique to a particular study and may not generalize to your situation. As Barnette (2001) noted of the study involving positive and negative wording, results may be due to "differences in types of surveys, the focus of the survey, and the relationship of the topic to the respondent" (p. 77). That is why, as we explain later in the text, it is important to pretest your items and the entire instrument before implementing it. Additionally, it is important to keep in mind that results that appear erroneous may also be instructional. Newport (2004), for example, contends "that variations based on environmental and situational factors do not undermine the value of survey results as important scientific data, but actually enhance it. This type of variation instead serves as the basis for a more thorough and compelling understanding of humans' views on important matters. Our objective as pollsters becomes one of figuring out why responses sometimes vary according to question wording and other conditions" (pp. 222–223).

The Art of Instrument Construction

The purpose of this chapter has been to present an introduction to instrument construction by providing a conceptual and historical background to the process. Although instrument construction must be organized and systematic, it is also a very creative process. As such, it is as much about conceptualization, spontaneity, practice, and serendipity as it is about technical or scientific precision.

We have purposely chosen the metaphor of painting a picture as a way of conveying the art of instrument construction, but a comparison to virtually any artistic endeavor or art form will suffice, whether dancing, singing, woodworking, gardening, or building model trains. To be an effective designer of social science instruments, you should have an interest in the topic you want to study and some interest in the instrument construction process itself. Few people engage in hobbies and arts in which they have limited interest; the power of the creative process comes from personal enthusiasm and attention to subject. One way to develop that interest is to read about the subject you want to study. Individuals who paint for a living or as a hobby often build a library of books describing painting techniques and art history. If you are interested in studying gender roles in large corporations, it makes sense to obtain books and journal articles related to that topic. The same holds true for instrument construction and there is no reason why this book should be your sole source of information on the subject. Ideally, your personal library will come to include a variety of materials on instrument design, survey methods, and social science methodology.

Instrument construction is also a highly creative process. Although we will examine that element in more depth in Chapter Five, the same mental processes that go into conceptualizing a painting apply to the design and development of instruments as well. Creativity arises from personal experience, thinking and processing, and mental imagery. Determining items to include in your instrument may (and should) come from your research into the subject. How those items are worded will come from experience, trial (and error), thinking, and meditating.

An individual unfamiliar with New York City stopped a man on the street and asked, "How do I get to Carnegie Hall?" Replied the man, "Practice." This advice applies not only to the arts but is good guidance for instrument designers as well. Most artists who paint in the abstract style have first developed their drafting skills and can also paint objects realistically—in his early works, before becoming known for his cubist style, Picasso displayed precise draftsmanship. Similarly, you will find that your instrument construction skills and expertise increase the more that you engage in the process. Fortunately, instrument construction is an iterative process. By that, we mean that you put the instrument out to others for review and feedback and then use the information to revise and improve the instrument. It is not at all surprising to administer an instrument that has evolved and looks quite different from your initial effort.

Finally, instrument construction is a learning process. The more you engage in the activity, the more you will perceive the subtleties involved in the design and administration of your instrument. Through experience you will recognize when an item is worded unclearly and when it captures the ideas you have in mind. You will also gain appreciation for the process of instrument construction. For example, a student of ours was pleased that she had designed a simple and easy to administer questionnaire. It consisted of seventeen items with rating and ranking scales. It was only after she administered the instrument that she appreciated the enormity of her next task. Each questionnaire produced about 25 pieces of information. With 115 respondents, the "simple" instrument produced 2,875 pieces of data!

Throughout this book, we will continue to use the painting metaphor. Not every painter can be a Picasso, Monet, or O'Keeffe, and not every instrument designer will be a Likert, Thurstone, or Gallup. However, by learning the techniques of instrument construction and by expressing your creative instincts, you can and will develop effective instruments for social science inquiry.

Instrument 2.A: A Political Poll

Instrument 2.A is composed of standard items that appear on questionnaires developed by a variety of polling organizations. The items typify the way opinion questions are worded. To minimize bias the wording on some questions is usually rotated in polls; for example, a political poll might list *Democrat* as the first choice on half of the questionnaires and *Republican* as the first choice on the other half. Notice that the response choices vary in order to match the question; it would not be appropriate to use a single response scale, such as *strongly disagree* to *strongly agree*, as that does not fit all the items. Lastly, notice that the demographic questions are limited to essential information and that given an adequate sample size and appropriate mode of administration it would be difficult to identify the respondent.

INSTRUMENT 2.A: POLITICAL OPINION POLL.

We're interested in how you view current events. Please place a check in the box ☑ that best describes how you feel about the question. It should take no more than 10 minutes to complete the following fourteen items.

Do you approve or disapprove of the way the President is handling his job?	☐ Approve	☐ Disapprove	☐ Unsure
Do you approve or disapprove of the way Congress is handling its job?	☐ Approve	☐ Disapprove	☐ Unsure
Do you think the Congress is in touch with what is going on in the country?	☐ In touch	☐ Not in touch	☐ Unsure
Generally speaking, would you say things in this country are heading in the right direction, or are they off on the wrong track?	☐ Right direction	☐ Wrong track	☐ Unsure
Do you think America is ready to elect a woman president, or not?	☐ Ready	☐ Not ready	☐ Unsure
In general, do you believe that members of Congress are honest and trustworthy in their conduct?	☐ Honest	☐ Not honest	☐ Unsure
When it comes to who pays what in taxes, do you think the federal income tax system is basically fair or basically unfair?	☐ Fair	☐ Unfair	☐ Unsure

Do you think the federal government should guarantee health insurance for all Americans, or isn't this the responsibility of the federal government? ☐ Should guarantee ☐ Not their responsibility ☐ Unsure

Please tell me whether you favor or oppose a constitutional amendment to allow voluntary prayer in public schools. ☐ Favor ☐ Oppose ☐ Unsure

Do you consider the amount of federal income tax you have to pay as too high, about right, or too low? ☐ Too high ☐ About right ☐ Too low

Do you approve or disapprove of the way Congress is handling ethics in government? ☐ Approve ☐ Disapprove ☐ Unsure

Which party do you believe is doing a better job of handling the nation's business? ☐ Repub. ☐ Democratic ☐ Neither

Do you think the federal government should or should not require labels on food saying whether it has been genetically modified or bio-engineered? ☐ Should ☐ Should not ☐ Unsure

Right now, do you think the quality of the environment in the country as a whole is getting better or getting worse?" ☐ Getting better ☐ Getting worse ☐ Same

Which of the following do you think is the most important problem facing this country today? (check one)

☐ National defense
☐ Economy/jobs
☐ Highways and transportation infrastructure
☐ Environment
☐ Energy
☐ Social Security
☐ Drug abuse
☐ Health care
☐ Other: _____

Your Gender:

☐ Female   ☐ Male

Your Age:

☐ Under 21
☐ 21 to 30
☐ 31 to 40
☐ 41 to 50
☐ 51 to 60
☐ 61 to 70
☐ 71 and older

Instrument 2.B: Mental Health Screening Form

As explained in this chapter, one of the primary reasons for constructing a questionnaire is to produce information for decision making. The Mental Health Screening Form-III is presented to clients upon admission to a hospital unit or center for substance abuse treatment. These individuals may also have co-occurring mental health problems, such as depression, phobias, or thought disorders, which can influence treatment. The purpose of the questionnaire is to screen for mental health problems so that therapy can be provided holistically.

The first page of the instrument provides information to treatment providers and is not presented to the client filling out the form. This page describes the purpose of the questionnaire, how items should be scored, and how the results should be interpreted. For example, some items cluster together, and if a respondent answers in the affirmative it is an indicator that further evaluation and assessment should be considered.

The instrument that the client completes begins on a new page. The title is clearly indicated at the top of the page and the instructions section explains the purpose of the instrument. The instructions do not specifically state that the respondent is to circle the appropriate response, but the layout supports that mode of recording the response. The *yes* responses are totaled, and the higher the score the more likely the individual is to need more intensive evaluation and the more aware the treatment provider should be of the potential for a co-occurring disorder. The questionnaire does not include demographic items, such as age, gender, ethnic group, weight, and so forth, because that information is available from other sources in the client's medical record. Additionally, demographic information may not be essential because this questionnaire is used for screening and not diagnostic purposes. However, because medications are often prescribed and adjusted based on such factors as gender, weight, and age, an instrument used diagnostically probably would ask about these characteristics.

INSTRUMENT 2.B: MENTAL HEALTH SCREENING FORM-III.

Guidelines for Using the Mental Health Screening Form-III

The Mental Health Screening Form-III (MHSF-III) was initially designed as a rough screening device for clients seeking admission to substance abuse treatment programs. Each MHSF-III question is answered either "yes" or "no." All questions reflect the respondent's entire life history; therefore all questions begin with the phrase "Have you ever . ."

The preferred mode of administration is for staff members to read each item to the respondent and get their "yes" and "no" responses. Then, after completing all 18 questions (question 6 has two parts), the staff member should inquire about any "yes" response by asking "When did this problem first develop?"; "How long did it last?"; "Did the problem develop before, during, or after you started using substances?"; and,

"What was happening in your life at that time?" This information can be written below each item in the space provided. There is additional space for staff member comments at the bottom of the form.

The MHSF-III can also be given directly to clients for them to complete, providing they have sufficient reading skills. If there is any doubt about someone's reading ability, have the client read the MHSF-II instructions and question number one to the staff member monitoring this process. If the client can not read and/or comprehend the questions, the questions must be read and/or explained to him/her.

Whether the MHSF-III is read to a client or s/he reads the questions and responds on his/her own, the completed MHSF-III should be carefully reviewed by a staff member to determine how best to use the information. It is strongly recommended that a qualified mental health specialist be consulted about any "yes" response to questions 3 through 17. The mental health specialist will determine whether or not a follow-up, face-to-face interview is needed for a diagnosis and/or treatment recommendation.

The MHSF-III features a "Total Score" line to reflect the total number of "yes" responses. The maximum score on the MHSF-III is 18 (question 6 has two parts). This feature will permit programs to do research and program evaluation on the mental health-chemical dependence interface for their clients.

The first four questions on the MHSF-III are not unique to any particular diagnosis; however, questions 5 through 17 reflect symptoms associated with the following diagnoses/diagnostic categories: Q5, Schizophrenia; Q6, Depressive Disorders; Q7, Post-Traumatic Stress Disorder; Q8, Phobias; Q9, Intermittent Explosive Disorder; Q10, Delusional Disorder; Q11, Sexual and Gender Identity Disorders; Q12, Eating Disorders (Anorexia, Bulimia); Q13, Manic Episode; Q14, Panic Disorder; Q15, Obsessive-Compulsive Disorder; Q16, Pathological Gambling; Q17, Learning Disorder and Mental Retardation.

The relationship between the diagnoses/diagnostic categories and the above cited questions was investigated by having four mental health specialists independently "select the one MHSF-III question that best matched a list of diagnoses/diagnostic categories." All of the mental health specialists matched the questions and diagnoses/diagnostic categories in the same manner, that is, as we have noted in the preceding paragraph.

A "yes" response to any of questions 5 through 17 does not, by itself, insure that a mental health problem exists at this time. A "yes" response raises only the possibility of a current problem, which is why a consult with a mental health specialist is strongly recommended.

Mental Health Screening Form-III

Instructions: In this program, we help people with all their problems, not just their addictions. This commitment includes helping people with emotional problems. Our staff is ready to help you to deal with any emotional problems you may have, but we can do this only if we are aware of the problems. Any information you provide to us on this form will be kept in strict confidence. It will not be released to any outside person or agency without your permission. If you do not know how to answer these questions, ask the staff member giving you this form for guidance. Please note, each item refers to your entire life history, not just your current situation, this is why each question begins– "Have you ever . ."

1. Have you ever talked to a psychiatrist, psychologist, therapist, social worker, or counselor about an emotional problem? **YES   NO**

2. Have you ever felt you needed help with your emotional problems, or have you had people tell you that you should get help for your emotional problems? **YES   NO**

3. Have you ever been advised to take medication for anxiety, depression, hearing voices, or for any other emotional problem? **YES   NO**

4. Have you ever been seen in a psychiatric emergency room or been hospitalized for psychiatric reasons? **YES   NO**

5. Have you ever heard voices no one else could hear or seen objects or things which others could not see? **YES   NO**

6. (a) Have you ever been depressed for weeks at a time, lost interest or pleasure in most activities, had trouble concentrating and making decisions, or thought about killing yourself? **YES   NO**

   (b) Did you ever attempt to kill yourself? **YES   NO**

7. Have you ever had nightmares or flashbacks as a result of being involved in some traumatic/terrible event? For example, warfare, gang fights, fire, domestic violence, rape, incest, car accident, being shot or stabbed? **YES   NO**

8. Have you ever experienced any strong fears? For example, of heights, insects, animals, dirt, attending social events, being in a crowd, being alone, being in places where it may be hard to escape or get help? **YES   NO**

9. Have you ever given in to an aggressive urge or impulse, on more than one occasion, that resulted in serious harm to others or led to the destruction of property? **YES   NO**

10. Have you ever felt that people had something against you, without them necessarily saying so, or that someone or some group may be trying to influence your thoughts or behavior? **YES   NO**

11. Have you ever experienced any emotional problems associated with your sexual interests, your sexual activities, or your choice of sexual partner? **YES   NO**

12. Was there ever a period in your life when you spent a lot of time thinking and worrying about gaining weight, becoming fat, or controlling your eating? For example, by repeatedly dieting or fasting, engaging in much exercise to compensate for binge eating, taking enemas, or forcing yourself to throw up? **YES   NO**

13. Have you ever had a period of time when you were so full of energy and your ideas came very rapidly, when you talked nearly non-stop, when you moved quickly from one activity to another, when you needed little sleep, and believed you could do almost anything? **YES   NO**

14. Have you ever had spells or attacks when you suddenly felt anxious, frightened, uneasy to the extent that you began sweating, your heart began to beat rapidly, you were shaking or trembling, your stomach was upset, you felt dizzy or unsteady, as if you would faint? **YES   NO**

15. Have you ever had a persistent, lasting thought or impulse to do something over and over that caused you considerable distress and interfered with normal routines, work, or your social relations? Examples would include repeatedly counting things, checking and rechecking on things you had done, washing and rewashing your hands, praying, or maintaining a very rigid schedule of daily activities from which you could not deviate. **YES   NO**

16. Have you ever lost considerable sums of money through gambling or had problems at work, in school, with your family and friends as a result of your gambling? **YES   NO**

17. Have you ever been told by teachers, guidance counselors, or others that you have a special learning problem? **YES   NO**

Print Client's Name: _____

Program to which client will be assigned: _____

Name of Admissions Counselor: _____   Date: _____

Reviewer's Comments:

_____

_____

_____

_____

Total Score: _____ (each yes = 1 pt.)

Source: Carroll & McGinley, 2000. This material may be reproduced or copied, in its entirety, without permission.

Key Concepts and Terms

construct	naturalistic inquiry	scientific theory
content analysis	postpositivism	social science
focus group	positivism	statistics
iterative process	qualitative	
measurement	quantitative	

CHAPTER THREE

MEASUREMENT

In this chapter we will

- Explore the concept of measurement.
- Describe the different levels of measurement.
- Examine the relation between levels of measurement and the construction of individual items.

In the first chapter we defined an instrument as "a mechanism for measuring phenomena." Key to that definition is its reference to measurement. *Measurement* provides a *systematic process for categorizing and quantifying attributes and characteristics of the things that we observe, experience, or report.* To measure something we assign values, such as numbers (or symbols), and ensure that there is a logical and systematic relationship between the values and what they represent as well as between and among the values themselves (Sarle, 1995). This definition applies to all things that we want to measure, whether they are physical attributes such as size, weight, or time or psychological and social attributes such as opinions, attitudes, and beliefs.

For example, artists' brushes come in a variety of sizes and shapes. The sizes of round brushes are numbered from 0000, the very shortest and thinnest, to 24, the longest and fullest. Each increase in number indicates an increase in size of about one-thirty-second of an inch in both length and thickness. This simple description tells us a lot about measurement. In this case, brush sizes form a continuum from small to large, and a numbering system has been created to categorize size. Because we are using a standard scale, fractions of an inch, we know there is an equal interval between each brush size. Finally, again because we are using a standard scale, we can create an instrument, such as a ruler, to provide consistent measurements.

In this and the next chapter, we will examine the concept of measurement and the attributes of measurement important in developing an effective instrument. Many of the items that you will create for your instrument will present a series of values for the respondent or rater to consider and chose from. The relationship *between these values* is referred to as the *level of measurement*.

Levels of Measurement

Standardized systems of measurement have not always existed. In earlier times the length of a *foot* could quite literally be the king's shoe size. Or imagine going to a marketplace where different merchants used different sets of weights to measure out goods and determine their prices. It was not until the late 1700s that the metric system, one of the first systematic and standardized approaches to measurement, was introduced. For a system of measurement to become standardized, there must be agreement on the units of measurement. The unit of measurement for a kilogram, for example, is a block of platinum and iridium that is kept in a vault at the Bureau of International Weights and Measures outside of Paris. The standard for the unit of measurement we call a meter is the distance light travels in 1/299,792,458 of a second (Strauss, 1995).

A system of measurement embodies a relationship between values and what they represent, such as the designation of inches and feet to measure height or distance, of pounds and ounces to measure weight, and minutes and hours to measure time. From this example you can see that one property of measurement is that the values should be mutually exclusive; inches cannot be used to measure time and pounds cannot be used to measure height. However, values can be combined for measurement, as time and distance, for example, are combined as a measure of speed. An interesting aspect of measurement is that some attributes we want to measure, such as time or attitudes and opinions, cannot be directly observed. Instead, we automatically think of the measurement device, such as a clock or questionnaire.[1]

A system of measurement will also feature a relationship between and among values themselves. For example, the distance, or interval, between the one-inch and two-inch marks on a yardstick is the same as the one between the seven- and

TABLE 3.1: LEVELS OF MEASUREMENT.

Level of Measurement	Definition
Nominal	Numbers are assigned to objects or categories, without having numerical meaning. That is, numbers are used as labels. *Example:* Categories of marital status: (1) married, (2) single, (3) divorced, (4) separated.
Ordinal	Objects of a set are rank ordered on an operationally defined attribute. There is no fixed, measurable interval between one number and another number on the scale. *Example:* An intensity scale of 1 = Never, 2 = Sometimes, 3 = Often, 4 = Always.
Interval	Numerically equal distances, or interval scales, represent equal distances among attributes. *Example:* Height in feet and inches.
Ratio	Ratio scales have an absolute zero point. At zero there is a complete absence of the attribute. *Example:* Income in dollars.

eight-inch marks. This also holds true for the markings on a clock, bathroom scale, or speedometer, and knowing that these values are equally distant helps us when we change measurement devices, exchanging the hands on an analogue clock for the screen on a digital clock, for instance.

As we said earlier, the relationship between and among the values in a set is referred to as level of measurement. Measures are classified into four levels: *nominal, ordinal, interval,* and *ratio* (see Table 3.1). Each level contains certain properties that influence the types of calculations we make with its measures. Knowledge of the properties associated with each level of measurement is important for understanding the type of information being gathered by an instrument and what we can and cannot do when analyzing and interpreting that information.

Nominal Level

Values at the *nominal level* of measurement can be named and placed into categories, but they cannot be ordered. For example, we can separate individuals into groups or categories based on eye color: brown, blue, green, or hazel.

We can even assign a number for each eye color: brown $= 1$, blue $= 2$, green $= 3$, and hazel $= 4$. However, the numbers here serve only as place markers; green does not have a greater value than blue. Another example of a nominal response format is the choice between two (dichotomous) values, such as *male* or *female, yes* or *no*, or *true* or *false*.[2]

A characteristic of a good categorical measure is that the values are mutually exclusive—they do not overlap. This is obvious for eye color, but may not be for other categories. For example, in a list of religious preferences that includes Jewish, Muslim, Protestant, Methodist, and Christian, the choices are not exclusive because a Methodist is a type of Protestant, and both are Christians. An individual given these choices would have difficulty selecting just one.

Because the numbers function only as labels, care must be taken when analyzing nominal data. As labels, the numbers serve to simplify the process of categorizing and tallying the results. For example, we can report the frequency with which these eye colors occur: perhaps 1 (brown) $= 20$; 2 (blue) $= 14$; 3 (green) $= 10$; and 4 (hazel) $= 17$. The numbers we have associated with the eye colors are used solely for coding; they have no numerical value; we could just as easily label the colors with letters (A, B, C, and D). It is important to recognize that here we can order attributes based on the number of responses, putting brown first because there are twenty occurrences, but that is different from ordering the attribute—eye color—itself. Therefore we can report the mode or most frequently appearing eye color, which would be brown, but we cannot report a mean or average, as we do not have common units of measure.

Ordinal Level

At the ordinal level of measurement, values can be placed into categories that are rank ordered or rated along a continuum, such as from high to low.[3] For example, educators might be asked to list the teaching approaches they use in order of *least used* to *most used*. As with nominal level values, the response alternatives can be labeled with numbers: 1 = least used, 2 = sometimes, 3 = occasionally, 4 = frequently, and 5 = most used. Although these items have values that range from low (1) to high (5), it is important to realize that the numbers do not have equal intervals between them as do the numbers on a yardstick; that is, an item that is rated a 5 is not five times as "distant" as an item rated 1; the distance, or interval, between 2 and 3 may not be equal to the distance between 4 and 5. In part, this is because we cannot be sure that all the people using an instrument share the same definition of such terms as *never, sometimes, occasionally, usually,* or *frequently*. For this reason most social scientists classify a rating response scale as an ordinal measure (for example, Streiner & Norman, 1995; Kane, 1997).

Ordinal data can be ranked, and we can use descriptive statistics, such as frequency distributions, percentages, and the mode and median; the mean or average is not an appropriate measure of a response scale for an *individual item*. Although we cannot compute the average for individual items, for most instruments we are interested in collecting aggregate data, and the mean of a *set of responses* can be calculated and is often reported. For example, suppose we ask the following question on a customer satisfaction survey and obtain responses from 100 respondents.

	0 Not sure	1 Not at all	2 Very little	3 Somewhat	4 Very much
Employees of this organization listened to my concerns.	❏	❏	❏	❏	❏

The first respondent rates the item 3, the second rates it 4, the third rates it 4, and so on. We can then calculate the average of the 100 responses for this item and for all of the other items in the questionnaire. Let's suppose that the average for this item is 3.65. What exactly does this mean? We would probably say that "on average," customers were somewhat to very much satisfied with this attribute of service.

Interval Level

Interval measures have a fixed range, or *distance*, between one point and another. Perhaps the best example of the use of the interval level of measurement is a Celsius or Fahrenheit thermometer, where the interval between 30 and 40 degrees is equal to the interval between 60 and 70 degrees. Because the intervals between degrees are equal, a number of analytical operations can be performed, such as computing the average or mean—in this case a mean temperature. However, interval level data is not a proportion—in this case, 60 degrees Fahrenheit is not twice as warm as 30 degrees. Consequently, we should not perform statistical operations based on proportions or ratios.

Ratio Level

Finally, the ratio level of measurement has equal intervals *and* provides for an absolute zero point, that is, the complete absence of a value. Examples of ratio level data are age and income. One person can be twice as old or have three times the income as another. Certain types of questionnaire items will produce data at the ratio level, such as an item that attempts to measure the frequency of an occurrence, asking, for example, "How many times in the past two years have you been charged with speeding?"

❑ 0 ❑ 1 ❑ 2 ❑ 3 ❑ 4 ❑ 5

The presence of a zero does not guarantee that a response set is a ratio level measure. The customer satisfaction question, for example, has a response alternative *labeled* zero, but the response scale is at the ordinal level of measurement. Additionally, many behavioral and psychometric instruments make use of response scales like this: 0 = not present, 1 = mild, 2 = moderate, 3 = severe, 4 = very severe. Although the lowest value is given the rating of zero, these indicators can only be ranked, and we cannot be sure that there are equal intervals between them. We could just as easily assign the numbers 1 to 5 to these ratings. In this case the response scale is at the ordinal level of measurement. Or consider an item that asks the respondent to indicate the number of times he or she has eaten at restaurants in the past year: None, 1–5 times, 6–10 times, 11–15 times, 16–20 times, 21 to 25 times. Although the numbers are at equal intervals and there is a zero point, we have clustered the responses into categories, which can be ranked at best. Therefore this information would be at the ordinal and not ratio level of measurement.

Level of Measurement and Item Construction

Let's see how the level of measurement influences the construction of items. Suppose your boss asks you to conduct an inventory of computer equipment in your work environment. She wants you to determine whether the equipment is at its assigned location. After thinking about the project you come up with an instrument that uses the following structure. Fortunately the first three bits of information (item, ID number, and assigned location) are available on a computer printout.

NAME OF ITEM (SUCH AS COMPUTER, MONITOR, PRINTER, AND SO ON)	ITEM ID (THE 7-DIGIT IDENTIFI-CATION NUMBER ASSIGNED TO THIS ITEM)	ASSIGNED LOCATION (ROOM NUMBER)	ITEM WAS FOUND AT ITS ASSIGNED LOCATION	ITEM WAS FOUND, BUT NOT AT ITS ASSIGNED LOCATION	ITEM WAS NOT FOUND	COMMENTS
Pro-logic 2.5 GHZ computer	5490461	Room 87	Yes			
Pro-printer 85 laser printer	6279948	Room 87		Yes		Found in room 88
Pro-technology flatbed scanner	5238712	Room 88	Yes			

Because your organization has been thinking about upgrading software, you realize this would also be a good time to solicit information to support the decision-making process. So with your boss's approval you develop another instrument to measure aspects of user satisfaction with the software currently installed. Because this instrument will be evaluative, many of the items use a rating format:

	1 Poor	2 Fair	3 Good	4 Excellent
How would you rate your skill level in using X-Pro Word Processing software?	❑	❑	❑	❑
Given your job duties, to what extent does X-Pro Word Processing software meet your needs?	❑	❑	❑	❑

Here we see how the purpose of the instrument helps to define how items are constructed. In the first instrument you only need to categorize the responses, and so they are at the nominal level of measurement. The second instrument includes items where the responses are rated and therefore are at the ordinal level of measurement.

It has been observed that "good measures can help turn abstract ideas into important, relevant findings, while poor measures render invalid seemingly meaningful findings" (Welch & Comer, 2001, p. 38). Even though you may not consciously be thinking of an item's level of measurement when you are creating that item, you should consider levels of measurement as you refine your instrument and plan for the analysis of your data. You might, for example, decide to change the format of a question to produce data more suitable to a particular form of analysis. For example, Babbie (1990) points out that although age is a ratio level measure, for purposes of your study you might be interested only in grouping people by categories such as baby boomer, yuppie, and so forth, which would produce nominal level information.

More Examples of Levels of Measurement

The following items are taken from several aggression assessment instruments to illustrate the various ways that questions are posed, the response alternatives associated with the item, and the level of measurement of the response scale.

Item	Response Set/Scale	Level of Measurement
Within the past 30 days, have you become violent while under the influence of alcohol or drugs?	❑ Yes ❑ No	Nominal
When this child is teased or threatened, he or she gets angry easily.	1. Never true 2. Rarely true 3. Sometimes true 4. Usually true 5. Almost always true	Ordinal
I hit back when someone hit me first.	No opportunity Never 1 or 2 times 3 or 4 times 5 or more times	Ordinal
I teased students to make them angry.	Number of times: 0 1 2 3 4 5 6	Ratio

Source: Dahlberg, Toal, & Behrens, 1998. The various instruments from which these items are taken are in the public domain and may be used without payment of a fee or royalty.

Finally, keep in mind that nominal and ordinal data may not provide the level of precision needed for making high-stakes decisions, such as determining a client's eligibility for services or retaining or firing an employee. In such cases, decisions should be based on multiple factors and should not solely rely on the data produced by one instrument.

Summary

Measurement is a systematic process for categorizing and quantifying the attributes we want to study. Measurement properties such as level of measurement influence how we format items and the type of data an item will produce. In the physical sciences the levels of measurement are often exact units, such as inches, grams, or seconds. In the social sciences the levels of measurement are less precise; for example, they often reflect only categories (nominal) or categories that can be ranked (ordinal). Less frequent are those measures that are at equal intervals (interval) or that include a value of absolute zero (ratio). Level of measurement is an important consideration when constructing items and thinking about the data the instrument will produce and how it will be analyzed.

Instrument 3.A: Data Extraction Form

Instrument 3.A was developed to facilitate extraction of data from existing medical records as part of a study examining drug and alcohol use among adolescents receiving inpatient treatment. The investigators were interested in a number of relationships, such as drug and alcohol use and family structure. as well as drug and alcohol use in relation to clinical diagnosis of mental health problems.

The original instrument is twelve pages long and has over sixty-five items. The sample of items presented here reflects a variety of formats producing data at different levels of measurement. For example, item 1, age at admission, is a ratio level measure; item 3 presents the rater with a dichotomous response set at the nominal level; and item 10 uses a scaled response set at the ordinal level. Although most of the items offer selection items (predetermined responses), some, such as items 1 and 9, are fill in the blank. Level of measurement was an important consideration during the development of the instrument because the investigators were also thinking about what they would do with the data once they obtained them, including how they would need to organize the data for statistical analysis.

Three investigators worked as a team to design the instrument. They had to agree on the definition for each indicator. For example, on item 2, the investigators could have listed several specific languages but chose instead to provide just two options. For item 6, the investigators had to identify a sufficient number of options to cover the possibilities while ensuring that these options were mutually exclusive.

As with observational instruments, when more than one person will be extracting data you must ensure consistency between the raters. In this case, to reduce ambiguity the individuals who would be extracting the data were included in the development of the instrument.

INSTRUMENT 3.A: DATA EXTRACTION FORM.

Adolescents with Co-Occurring Disorders
Data Extraction Form

Facility: ○ A ○ B   **Study ID No: (001-999):**____   **Chart Reviewer I.D. No:**____

DEMOGRAPHICS

1. Age at Admission (in years):____ **2. First Language:** ○ English ○ Other____

3. Sex: ○ Male ○ Female

4. Primary Referral Source:
- ○ JDR/Circuit Court
- ○ CSB
- ○ Social Services
- ○ Private Physician
- ○ School
- ○ Hospital

5. Please circle number of previous acute-care psychiatric admissions:

0   1   2   3   4   5   6   7   8   9 or more

FAMILY STRUCTURE

6. Biological Parents Marital Status:
- ○ Married ○ Divorced ○ Separated ○ Widowed
- ○ Never Married/not living together   ○ Never Married/living together
- ○ Deceased   ○ Not Documented

SUBSTANCE USE

7. Tobacco: ○ Yes   ○ No   ○ Not Documented *(if yes, complete table below)*

Level of Reported Use:

○ Never ○ Once or twice ○ Less than once a month ○ At least once a month
○ Once a week ○ Daily

Question		Not Documented
Youngest age client reportedly used *tobacco*		
Highest number of days used in any 30 day period		
Highest quantity used during any single episode of use		

8. Has client received substance abuse treatment at any time prior to this admission?

○ Yes   ○ No   Not Documented *(If yes, check all that apply in question 8A, if no skip 8A)*

8A. ○ Outpatient   ○ Residential <3 months   ○ Residential >3 months
         ○ Juvenile drug court ○ Other (specify)   ○ Not documented

DSM IV-TR DIAGNOSIS

9. Axis I substance related disorders identified at *admission* (include rule outs, provisional, and by history diagnoses):

Substance Use Related Disorder	DSM IV-TR Code

10. Axis IV: Psychosocial and Environmental Stressors

Stressor (Problem With):	Mild	Moderate	Severe	Severity Not Specified
Not specified, *only severity noted*				
Primary support group				
Social environment				
Educational				
Housing				
Access to health care				
Legal system/crime				
Other				

Endnotes

1. Another aspect of measurement is that indicators may be culturally bound. For example, we use inches and feet in the United States whereas much of the rest of the world uses centimeters and meters.
2. Although Sarle (1995) observes that binary variables "are at least at the interval level. If the variable connotes presence or absence or if there is some distinguishing feature of one category, a binary variable may be at the ratio or absolute level" (p. 5). This is a reminder that social scientists do not always agree on even the most fundamental concepts.
3. Values, or variables, may also be classified as *discrete* or *continuous*. Discrete variables can be placed only into categories (for example, eye color, race, or political affiliation). Continuous variables can assume any value along a continuum (for example, grade in school, height, or income level).

Key Concepts and Terms

interval level	measurement	ordinal level
level of measurement	nominal level	ratio level

CHAPTER FOUR

INSTRUMENT CONSTRUCTION, VALIDITY, AND RELIABILITY

In this chapter we will

- Describe the concepts of validity and reliability.
- Identify a number of ways to demonstrate that an instrument is producing valid and reliable information.
- Explore the implications of misusing or misrepresenting data derived from an instrument.

Artist David Hockney has an interesting theory. He believes that Renaissance painters were able to create photo-realistic paintings by using mirrors and optical devices to project an image onto a canvas. He suggests that the strong lighting and contrast in some Renaissance paintings reflects the use of devices that required a lot of illumination. This is a controversial idea because scholars are not sure the appropriate technology existed at that time. However, if correct, it could explain why as early as the fifteenth century, artists were able to create such accurate and vivid portraits (Hockney, 2001).

Realistic painting attempts to capture an image as accurately and faithfully as possible. As an instrument designer you face a similar challenge—because instruments are used to measure both objective and subjective phenomena, it is important that they provide information that is trustworthy and credible. If an instrument fails to do this, then everything that comes afterward, including the data analysis and the findings presentation will be suspect. As the computer industry adage says, "Garbage in, garbage out."

In this chapter we will examine two concepts applied to ensure an instrument provides credible and accurate information. *Validity* refers to the ability of an instrument to measure what you intend it to measure, and *reliability* speaks to the consistency of your measurement. These concepts are closely related. Suppose that you use this item stem on a job satisfaction survey, "I get a feeling of personal satisfaction from my work," and the respondent is expected to rate the item on a scale of *strongly disagree* to *strongly agree*. If the item is valid, it will be a good, or strong, measure of job satisfaction. If the item is reliable, a respondent will provide a consistent response across time and settings—for example, rating the item the same way on two different occasions.

Validity

Suppose you have been asked to complete a questionnaire that attempts to measure a personal attribute, such as your leadership style. Now imagine an item that asks about your personal health. You would probably scratch your head and wonder what that has to do with leadership style. You might be offended or wonder about the instrument design. Similar though perhaps less obvious problems arise anytime we craft items intended to obtain information about one thing and instead measure something else. For example, a challenge for the developers of psychometric instruments is differentiating and measuring affective states such as depression and anxiety, which may manifest with similar behaviors.

Validity[1] describes the extent to which we measure what we purport to measure. An instrument is or is not intrinsically valid, as validity is a characteristic of the responses. Consequently, it is important to pretest the instrument to obtain preliminary data that can be used to assess validity.

Validity exists along a continuum. The greater the evidence that an instrument is producing valid results, the greater the likelihood that we will obtain the information we need: "Hence, validity is a matter of degree. It is not a simple either-or, all-or-none question of *valid* or *invalid*. It is an attribute that exists along a continuum, from high to low, in varying degrees. It is inferred, or judged from existing evidence, not measured or calculated directly" (Worthen, Borg, & White, 1993, p. 180).

There are several ways to conceptualize and categorize validity. As we will see, assessing validity is often a matter of judgment. It is important to keep in mind that although we can distinguish types of validity, they are all means of answering the same question: Are we measuring what we purport to measure?

Face Validity

Face validity is the degree to which an instrument *appears* to be an appropriate measure for obtaining the desired information, particularly from the perspective of a potential respondent. Suppose you have designed an instrument to measure health behavior, and one of the items asks respondents to indicate if they are smokers and, if so, about how many cigarettes a day they smoke. On its "face," this item appears to relate directly to health behavior and therefore would produce a valid response. Although face validity is often criticized as a less rigorous approach than others to assessing validity, it can provide useful information about the entire instrument and the degree to which it is meeting its intended purpose.

Construct Validity

Many concepts we are interested in, such as safety, intelligence, creativity, or patriotism, are not directly observable or measurable. Social scientists refer to these abstractions as *constructs,* and a major concern is the degree to which an instrument actually measures them. One of the challenges associated with *construct validity* is ensuring that instrument designers and respondents have a shared definition of the construct. Leadership, for example, may have more than one definition, such as an ability to motivate people, to direct people, or to facilitate change in people. If you want to develop an instrument to measure leadership, you will have to be specific in defining the attributes of leadership you are examining. At times our entire understanding of a construct can change. In the 1960s and 1970s, psychiatrist Thomas Szasz argued that mental illness was not so much a physical disease as a sociological process (see, for example, Szasz, 1973). For those agreeing with Szasz, it meant an entirely different way was needed to measure and understand mental illness. (Contemporary models suggest that mental illness is influenced by both physical and environmental processes.) When the meaning and our understanding of a construct can change over time, an instrument designed to measure the construct at one point in time may not provide valid measures at another time.

Because we cannot observe a construct directly, we have to find tangible ways to measure it, a process referred to as *operationalization.* We might operationalize appendicitis, for example, through observed or reported symptoms, such as dull pain in the lower-right abdomen, loss of appetite, nausea, and fever. Because other disorders, such as irritable bowel syndrome, share some of these symptoms, the more factors, or variables, we can associate with the concept of appendicitis the more we will differentiate it and the more valid our measurement (and diagnosis) will be.

Of course appendicitis is not only a concept but also an actual disorder, and once the appendix has been removed, there is physical evidence of the problem.

Operationalizing constructs in the social sciences may not be as straightforward. For example, some of the characteristics associated with depression are loss of energy, feelings of worthlessness, difficulty concentrating, and weight loss. Whereas changes in weight can be directly measured, worthlessness is itself a construct, and so we are faced with the challenge of demonstrating evidence for the validity of one construct by using another construct.[2]

The "T" Test

Ask a group of participants to write the letter "T" on a sheet of paper as many times as they can in one minute. Next, ask them to count the number of T's and plot the distribution on a chart. Then ask them what the T-Test measures.

Most groups can generate at least ten separate concepts that this activity may be attempting to measure, such as eye-hand coordination, dexterity, creativity, competitiveness, anxiety, ability to follow directions, quickness, compulsiveness, achievement need, and T-making behavior.

This activity demonstrates the difficulty of associating an overt behavior with an underlying construct. As an instrument designer, how would you demonstrate the construct validity of this test?

Source: Adapted from Reilly, 1973.

A threat to validity and hence to the data we obtain from an instrument occurs when respondents or raters interpret an item in their own way and respond to that interpretation. To study the impact of misunderstanding or misinterpreting items, Philip Gendall (1994) used an existing questionnaire but added questions about the respondent's understanding of certain items. Respondents were asked if they agreed or disagreed with a statement about people with AIDS and a statement about compulsory military training for young, unemployed people. After each one they were asked, "In your own words, exactly what did you think that statement meant and how did you arrive at your answer?" (p. 2). In regard to the AIDS question, Gendall found that respondents not only had different interpretations of the meaning of the statement but had also created personal definitions of who was meant by people who have AIDS. In other words, both the respondent's interpretation of the question as a whole and his or her understanding of the constituent parts influenced that person's ability to provide a valid response:

> For the majority of the 160 respondents who did not (or could not) explain what the AIDS statement meant, the reason was that they were more concerned with justifying their answer than explaining it. Many of these respondents had disagreed with the statement earlier in the interview and in doing so had taken

the opportunity to express their strong disapproval of homosexuals, drug users and sexually promiscuous people. In other words, these respondents had deliberately reinterpreted the question to allow them to express their own opinion, and for them the "correct" meaning of the question was irrelevant. This conclusion was confirmed when these respondents were asked who they thought was meant by people who had AIDS. Many of them admitted that they had confined their judgment to those they disapproved of [Gendall, 1994, p. 5].

Construct validity also involves *convergent validity* and *discriminant validity*. Convergent validity refers to the relationship between measures of constructs that should be strongly related, such as depression and feelings of worthlessness. Discriminant validity refers to the relationship between the measures of constructs that should not be strongly related to each other, such as depression and feelings of happiness. To demonstrate the construct validity of your instrument you will want to demonstrate *both* convergent and discriminant validity. Demonstrating only one or the other tells just half the story.

Content Validity

Content validity is the degree to which an instrument is representative of the topic and process being investigated. Suppose you are investigating at-risk behaviors among teenagers and plan to administer a survey questionnaire. To demonstrate content validity the instrument should address the full range of at-risk behaviors, those typically identified by experts and discussed in research literature. If it asks about alcohol and drug use and sexual behavior but not about illegal behavior such as shoplifting, then it may not be addressing the full domain of at-risk behaviors.

Note that in assessing content validity you are attempting to identify as many factors as possible that operationalize the construct. In some cases this number may be somewhat finite. In others it may be difficult to identify all the factors related to the construct, or you may have so many factors it is not possible to include all of them in the instrument. In the latter case, you may want content experts to rate the importance of these factors to help you determine which are most relevant to the focus of your study.

Criterion Validity

Criterion validity involves making a comparison between a measure and an external standard. Suppose you want to measure and predict how well someone recovering from a stroke can function independently or the level of assistance required. The first step would be to operationalize the concept of independent functioning by identifying activities of daily living, such as tying one's shoes, getting dressed, brushing one's teeth, and bed making, which would serve as the assessment criteria. Items would then be constructed to attempt to measure the individual's ability to meet these criteria. One way of assessing criterion validity would be to compare individuals' scores on the instrument to their actual performances. Criterion validity could also be determined by comparing the results obtained from your instrument to results from another instrument that attempts to measure the same construct using the same criteria. If there is a strong relationship, then you can say that your instrument displays criterion validity.

Evidence of criterion validity should be obtained for any instruments that measure performance, such as behavior rating scales and psychometric instruments. This is particularly true if you want an instrument to predict future behavior, such as how disabled individuals will perform as a result of receiving physical therapy.

Predictive Validity

Predictive validity exists when you can use an instrument or measure to predict the results of one variable from another variable. The classic example is the correlation between SAT scores and grade point average (GPA). Because there is a correlation, we can predict that students with a high GPA will also score highly on the SAT. If there is a strong relationship or correlation between the scores on your instrument and another instrument intended to measure the same criterion, your instrument would be said to evidence *concurrent validity*.

Multicultural Validity

Some social scientists also contend that instrument developers should consider *multicultural validity* (for example, Kirkhart, 1995), meaning that an instrument measures what it purports to measure as understood by an audience of a particular culture. For example, a multiculturally valid instrument will use language appropriate to its intended audience. This might require translation into a foreign language or checking that phrases and connotations will not be misunderstood by respondents. Whether we refer to such considerations as multicultural validity or as being sensitive to the needs of the instrument's audience, they reflect good practice.

Demonstrating instrument validity is important to you as the developer because this information can be used to refine and improve the instrument. If feedback from pretesting suggests the instrument is not producing valid results, then items should be reworded or deleted. It is also important to describe your pretesting in supporting documentation, so that potential users can answer their questions about the instrument's validity. For example, Grisso and Underwood

(2004, p. 12) suggest that users consider the following criteria when selecting an instrument:

- An instrument should not be selected if no research exists on the degree of its reliability or validity when administered to its intended target audience.
- Instruments that provide evidence of reliability and validity with the intended target audience are preferable to those that do not.
- The greater the consequences and importance of the decisions to be made, the higher the standard that should be applied in judging whether an instrument has an acceptable degree of reliability and validity.

Additional Help for Selecting an Instrument

For over half a century the Buros Institute of Mental Measurements has promoted "meaningful and appropriate test [that is, instrument] selection, utilization, and practice. The Buros Institute encourages improved test development and measurement research through thoughtful, critical analysis of measurement instruments and the promotion of an open dialogue regarding contemporary measurement issues" (Buros Institute of Mental Measurements, 2007). One of Buros's main functions is to provide potential users with information for deciding whether an instrument is appropriate for their population and setting or can be used for comparison, as in assessing criterion validity.

The Buros Institute publishes the *Mental Measurements Yearbook* and *Tests in Print,* which provide systematic instrument review and evaluation and are available in print, from the Buros Test Reviews on Line database, and from many college and university libraries. Reviews include instrument descriptions (including purpose, audience, and content details), publication information, validity and reliability evidence, and strengths and weaknesses assessments, Buros reviews provide examples of what might be considered when pretesting an instrument and a format for presenting evidence of validity and reliability.

You may view a sample review, including a discussion of the approaches used to demonstrate validity and reliability, at http://www.unl.edu/buros/bimm/html/reviewsample.html.

Demonstrating Evidence for Validity

Artists frequently sketch their subjects from many different angles prior to committing to a pose. Pretesting is a similar process that allows you to check the validity, reliability, and utility of an instrument prior to administering it to your target audience. Chapter Six examines the actual process of pretesting in detail; this section focuses on ways that pretesting can provide information for revising and improving your instrument and hence its validity.

There are essentially two types of approaches for assessing instrument validity: qualitative and quantitative. *Qualitative* approaches are evaluative. One of the most effective is to review research literature about the topic of interest. This process will help you define the topic (its themes and content) and can provide evidence that the instrument is measuring these constructs and not something else.

Another approach is to have topic experts review the instrument, using their judgment to identify ways to define and operationalize the construct and indicating whether they believe each item appears to measure what it is intended to measure. For example, researchers were interested in measuring attitudes among psychiatric hospital staff who were subject to the aggressive behaviors of patients. An early version of the instrument did not clearly define the term *aggression*, so respondents were not sure how to interpret items; did aggression refer to verbal threats, nonverbal gestures, a slight push or shove, or assaultive behaviors resulting in injury? In response to feedback from potential users and content experts, designers added the study's definition of aggression to the survey introduction. During a review process, reviewers may also find poorly worded items likely to compromise instrument reliability or prevent valid results.

A third qualitative approach is to develop a *table of specifications,* a means to identify the topic variables, or factors. This can be accomplished deductively or inductively. A *deductive* approach works from the general to the specific. You begin by stating the construct to be examined and then identify the ways it can be operationalized. This in turn suggests specific items. Recording this information in a table, or matrix, gives you a graphic view of the links between topic and items. For example, if your instrument is assessing depression, your table of specifications would include behaviors associated with this affective state, such as withdrawal, feelings of worthlessness, fatigue, and weight loss. This in turn would suggest such specific items as, Have you experienced a change of weight in the past ninety days? (For an example of a table of specifications see Table 5.3 in Chapter Five.)

An *inductive* approach works from the specific, such as finite items, to broader generalizations, such as the underlying construct. You might create a list of the variables associated with the construct and then ask a content expert to match the items you have created to the appropriate variable. The stronger the match, the more likely the item is to be a valid measure.

Quantitative approaches are typically based on measuring the strength of the association between your instrument and another measure of the same construct. Convergent and discriminant validity are ascertained by comparing the results from your instrument to results from existing instruments. For example, when pretesting your instrument you could also administer instruments that tap into related and different constructs. If you were developing an instrument to assess depression, you could also administer an instrument that measures self-worth and another that measures happiness. You would then compare the results by using a statistical measure of association (such as the Pearson product-moment correlation coefficient), which will produce a number (decimal) ranging from −1.00 to +1.00. The closer the number is to 1.00 the stronger the relationship (we will examine this in greater detail in the section on reliability).

Another quantitative approach is to pretest items with the aid of a series of vignettes, as described at the end of this chapter with the example of Instrument 4.B.

Item analysis is the primary quantitative approach for demonstrating validity. A valid item should be a good measure of what it is intended to measure and not of something else. The basic process for conducting item analysis is to demonstrate a relationship between individual items, such as item 1 and item 2, then item 1 and item 3, and so on, until all possible pairings are exhausted. (Keep in mind that you have to administer the instrument to obtain the data needed to do this analysis.) We can also compare the correlation between individual items and the total correlation for all of the items. The stronger the correlations, the more likely it is that the items are measuring the underlying construct. This is the basis for scaling (discussed in Chapter Eleven). Item analysis is also used to estimate the reliability of responses within an instrument; when used for that purpose it is referred to as *internal consistency reliability*.

An alternative approach is *factor analysis*, which also uses correlations to identify common factors that influence a set of measures and individual factors that are unique to each item: "This model proposes that each observed response is influenced partially by underlying common factors and partially by underlying unique factors. The strength of the link between each factor and each measure varies, such that a given factor influences some measures more than others" (DeCoster, 1998, p. 1).

The common factors are underlying constructs, so as with scaling, the stronger the correlations, the more likely it is that the items are good measures of the construct. DeCoster (1998) notes that exploratory factor analysis is often used to "(1) identify the nature of constructs underlying responses in a specific content area, (2) determine what sets of items 'hang together' in a questionnaire, and (3) demonstrate the dimensionality of a measurement scale [where] researchers wish to develop scales that respond to a single characteristic" (p. 2).

Item analysis is based on the assumption that the items are "essentially equivalent measures" of an underlying construct. Another approach, *item response theory* (IRT) "assumes that items are not necessarily equivalent, and, in fact, each individual item taps different degrees or levels of the underlying attribute" (Aday & Cornelius, 2006, p.74). IRT can also produce information about the difficulty of an item given the ability that a respondent brings to the construct being measured (Baker, 2001), and therefore IRT is often applied to the analysis of instruments that use hierarchical items, such as a developmental inventory where it is anticipated that an individual must be able to complete one task before moving to another.

Item analysis is conducted during the pretesting phase of instrument construction and requires a sufficiently large data set. You will need to administer the instrument to 50 to 100 or more respondents if it is a self-report questionnaire or collect data on 50 to 100 or more cases if it is an observer or rater instrument. Also, given the number of calculations involved, the computations require statistical software.

The purpose of this section has been to introduce you to approaches for demonstrating evidence of validity. For the steps for carrying out each technique, we suggest obtaining additional resources, such as Baker's *The Basics of Item Response Theory* (2001), which is available as a free download on the Internet. For approaches needing considerable computation, obtain the assistance of a statistician to do the analysis. Realistically, it may not be feasible for you to use some of these approaches. You need to consider what resources are available and how best to make use of them. Sufficient time, a large enough audience to pretest the instrument, and content experts may not be readily available. However, you may be able to ask coworkers or colleagues to review the instrument and provide feedback on the instrument's face validity. If you cannot administer a complementary instrument you can at least compare instruments to see if the items address the same variables. Regardless of the method, you should plan to invest some time demonstrating validity as part of the instrument construction process.

Reliability

In order to establish a standard for time, the U.S. Naval Observatory in Washington, DC, has developed a system of clocks accurate within 2 nanoseconds per day, which is equivalent to the loss of one second in 1,400,000 years! Clock calibration is ensured by a system that automatically compares some seventy cesium clocks, distributed in over twenty environmentally controlled clock vaults, every 100 seconds. This calibration system has resulted in a time standard so reliable and stable that it does not vary more than 100 picoseconds (0.0000000001) per day (U.S. Naval Observatory, 1999).

In the social sciences we neither work with instruments that produce such precision nor do we operate in such controlled conditions. Instead, we use measurement instruments that produce data subject to a wide variety of influences. For example, we may conduct an opinion poll about a political leader one day, hear about a scandal the next day, and conduct the same poll on the third day with quite different results. Nonetheless, like the scientists at the Naval Observatory, you have the responsibility to construct an instrument that reduces the chance of error and increases the likelihood that your data are reliable.

Reliability is the extent to which an instrument produces the same information at a given time or over a period of time. Some synonyms for reliability are stable, dependable, repeatable, consistent, constant, and regular. Suppose that in a classroom of fifteen students, each is given a tape measure and asked to calculate the height of their classmates within a quarter of an inch. In all likelihood there will be some variation. Measurement theory tells us that the height of each student (the observed score) will be composed of two parts, the student's actual height and an error component. Some error is random and unpredictable; variations in the way some students hold the tape or make a judgment about the height could produce random error. Other error is systematic; a flaw in the material the tape measure is made of would affect all the students in their measurement task. One way to reduce error is to calibrate or adjust the instrument and then take repeated readings to determine if the problem has been corrected. Or we could train the students in order to reduce variation in their judgments. A similar process is used with the paper-and-pencil instruments we use in the social sciences. For example, we might conduct several administrations of a questionnaire and then compare the results.

When discussing reliability, we may be thinking in terms of the instrument itself; however this is somewhat off target. We ascertain instrument reliability, like validity, from the *results* obtained by administering a particular instrument. This means that an instrument is or is not intrinsically reliable. Additionally, the units of measurement we use in our instruments, such as nominal and ordinal level response scales (Chapter Three), may not be as precise as the units of measurement in the physical sciences, such as inches or pounds.

The reliability of the results we obtain may be influenced by a number of factors. For example, between the first and second administrations of a questionnaire, events may occur that influence the way respondents complete items. Items that are ambiguous or unclear may produce different responses across respondents. The mood of an individual respondent could also influence how he or she responds to an item at any given time. Nonetheless, if the instrument is reliable, *an observer or respondent should interpret the meaning of items the same way each time it is administered*. To address some of these problems we can try to standardize the administration conditions and procedures, administering the instrument at the same time of day as previously or allowing only a brief interval between administrations to minimize the possible influence of external events.

Assessing reliability is an important component of instrument construction because it provides information about the stability of the results being obtained. For that reason, whenever you develop a questionnaire, you should plan to measure the reliability of the data. We will examine a number of ways to assess and ultimately improve reliability in the next section, as the procedures differ for self-report and rater-completed instruments.

Methods for Establishing Evidence for Reliability

In this section we present several methods for obtaining evidence to demonstrate data reliability. Some of these approaches are somewhat informal; others require some calculation. All are implemented after you have completed a draft of the instrument and pretested it, thereby producing data that can be used for analysis.

Eyeballing

Eyeballing is one of the more informal methods of determining the consistency of questionnaire items. You administer the instrument twice to the same group of people in a relatively short period of time to see if their responses remain the same. Eyeballing can be done when you have reason to assume that responses have not changed since the first administration. You determine the consistency of individual items simply by looking at each item and determining the extent to which the respondents made the same or similar responses on both the first and second administrations.

Percentage and Proportion of Agreement

Percentage of agreement is an approach that can be used with discrete data (*yes* or *no*, *male* or *female*, and so on) and that with some variation can be applied to data produced from continuous variables such as rating scales. As with many of the statistical approaches used to assess reliability, the results will be a number ranging from -1.0 to $+1.0$. The closer the number is to 1.0 the less likely it is that the results are due to random error.

Assume that you ask students the following question one week after their class ended and again two weeks after it ended. You could then set up a *contingency table* tabulating the results:

Would you recommend this class to other students?   Yes   No

Time 2

Yes   No

In this table

Cell a represents those respondents who said *yes* at time 1 and *yes* at time 2.

Cell d represents those respondents who said *no* at time 1 and *no* at time 2.

Cell b represents those respondents who said *yes* at time 1 and *no* at time 2.

Cell c represents respondents who said *no* at time 1 and *yes* at time 2.

In other words the people counted in cells a and d did not change their minds between administrations of the questionnaire, whereas those counted in cells b and c did. A measure of agreement can be calculated using the following formula:

$$\frac{a + d}{a + b + c + d} = \%\ \text{of agreement.}$$

For example, if we substitute sample numbers for the letters, we can say:

If $a = 12$, $b = 1$, $c = 3$, and $d = 4$,

then $(a + d) = 16$ and $(a + b + c + d) = 20$.

And we can apply the formula to come up with the following results:

$16 \div 20 = .80$, or $(.80 \times 100)$ 80%.

In this example, the percentage of agreement, which is a measure of reliability, is 80 percent. The value you obtain is a measure of how consistent your items were over time, and individual item information can indicate which of the items are consistent over time and which are not. This information can help you to identify external factors that might be influencing consistency and causing respondents to change responses to an item over time. This latter information may then help you to make the decision either to reword the item or to exclude it from the questionnaire.

With some variation this procedure can also be used for determining the *proportion of agreement* for rating scale items. In the following table assume that each *number* corresponds to a response choice for a rating scale item. Each *lowercase letter* then represents the value of the cases of agreement. For example, if an individual responded *strongly agreed* (response choice 1) during both the first and second administrations of a questionnaire, that would be recorded in cell a.

Response choice #:	1	2	3	4	5
Response choice:	Strongly agree	Agree	No opinion	Disagree	Strongly disagree

Time 1

	Response Choice #	1	2	3	4	5
	1	a	b	c	d	e
	2	b	a	b	c	d
Time 2	3	c	b	a	b	c
	4	d	c	b	a	b
	5	e	d	c	b	a

If you want to obtain a measure of those who did not change their response over time, apply the values to the following formula (the symbol Σ means the "sum of"; for example, Σa signifies all the *a*'s added together):

$$\frac{\Sigma a}{\Sigma a + \Sigma b + \Sigma c + \Sigma d + \Sigma e} = \% \text{ of agreement.}$$

The advantage of using the *proportion of agreement* is that it is a quantitative indicator that is fairly simple to calculate. As we will see, other statistical methods can be applied to measure the consistency of response, but they are more complicated and, depending on the purpose of your survey, may be more than is necessary to demonstrate reliability.

Approaches Using a Statistical Test of Correlation

Other approaches for demonstrating evidence of reliability make use of a statistical test of correlation that is a measure of association. Suppose that during pretesting we administer the same questionnaire to the same group on two occasions several days or weeks apart. We expect the responses to be the same or similar. We can then compute the correlation to measure the strength of the relationship between the two sets of data. We can apply a statistical formula (such as the Pearson product-moment correlation coefficient), and the result will be a number (decimal) ranging from −1.0 to +1.0. The closer the number is to 1.0 the stronger the relationship. The closer the number is to 0, the weaker the relationship.[3] If two variables increase or decrease in value together we say there is a *positive* correlation; an example of a positive correlation with an increase in value is that between age and height in children. An example of a positive correlation with a decrease in value is that between caloric intake and weight. A *negative* correlation occurs when the value of one variable increases while the other decreases, as with the age of a computer and its resale value (as its age increases its value decreases).

Because numerous factors influence responses, particularly in questionnaires assessing opinions and beliefs, you should be cautious when interpreting the correlation coefficient you derive. Typically, a correlation of .80 or higher is considered to demonstrate a strong relationship. When applied to tests of reliability, this means that the responses are stable across time, circumstances, and respondents. The squared value of the correlation coefficient is called the *coefficient of determination,* and it suggests the extent to which the responses are stable, rather than being due to other factors, such as random error. For example, a correlation of .80 when squared produces a value of 0.64, or 64 percent, which suggests that 64 percent of the relationship is due to the variable of interest and that 36 percent is due to other factors.

The following are some approaches, using variations of the correlation formula, that can be used to calculate a statistic reflecting reliability. We will not describe how to make these calculations, as the amount of data you will need to analyze will in all likelihood require the use of a computer and statistical software. However, we do want to indicate briefly the circumstances in which these statistical tests are typically applied.

Test-Retest Reliability. The approach for establishing *test-retest reliability* is similar to the eyeballing and the proportion of agreement approaches. You pretest the questionnaire with the same group on two separate occasions, expecting only minor variations in responses. One of the problems associated with this approach concerns the time between administrations. If the interval is brief, respondents may be completing the instrument based on what they remember to be their previous responses. If the interval is long, something could happen to influence respondents and how they rate items. This is particularly true for attitude questionnaires, where a significant event can change a respondent's opinions. For some psychometric instruments that examine "very unstable traits, such as moods that can be expected to fluctuate, the test-retest method of estimating reliability should be avoided altogether, for this method assumes that the trait remains constant during the interval over which retesting occurs" (Worthen, Borg, & White, 1993, p. 148).

Parallel Forms Reliability. Another approach looks at *parallel forms reliability*. It involves administering two equivalent forms of the questionnaire to the same group on two separate occasions. *Equivalent* means that both instruments measure the same constructs and the same content domain. Of course this means creating two versions of your instrument, which can be a time-consuming process. If you have created a large item pool, you may be able to find in it a number of items that are similar in content but not in wording. And as with the test-retest approach, you will need to be aware of external events.

You should also be aware that changing item wording or format could contribute to reducing the reliability (and validity) level found when applying this approach. In one study of item wording, researchers found that "while it is possible to write the same question in a number of ways, simply changing one word may change the whole meaning of the question" (Gendall & Hoek, 1990, p. 25). The same concerns arise when you change the format, such as using rating scales in one instrument and rank order in the parallel form. These findings should remind us that evidence of reliability is not always evidence of validity.

Internal Consistency Reliability. Examining internal consistency allows you to compare results across and among items within a single instrument and to do so with only one administration. An important caveat about tests of internal consistency reliability is that they *apply only to multi-item scales* (because this approach assumes that all the items are measures of the same construct) and not to items that function as independent measures, as in Instrument 2.A, the political opinion poll, where taking one item out or adding an item should not influence how respondents rate the other questions. Here are three methods for testing internal consistency:

- *Average inter-item and average item-total correlation.* A multi-item scale consists of items believed to have a strong relationship to an underlying construct. The stronger the relationship, measured as a correlation statistic, between individual items and between individual items and the value of all the items taken together, the stronger the evidence that the items are good measures of the construct. (For information about multi-item scales see Chapter Eleven.) Suppose your instrument makes use of a response scale with values ranging from 0 to 4, and you pretest it with a sample of 25 respondents. The average score for item 1 is 3.25, for item 2 it is 2.78, and so on. The *inter-item correlation* is calculated by comparing these averages to each other, item 1 to item 2, item 1 to item 3, item 1 to item 4, and so on. Once you have calculated a correlation for every possible pairing, you add up all the correlations and compute their average (thank goodness for computers). To calculate the *item-total correlation*, you compute the correlation between each item and the total score for the instrument. One advantage of this approach is that you can use the correlation values to identify weak items (that is, weak measures of the construct). These items can be removed from the instrument and the correlations recalculated.

- *Split-half method.* Based on comparing equal numbers of items within the same instrument, this approach is typically used to assess the reliability of tests (rather than questionnaires and other instruments whose items may differ considerably in context and format). To make a meaningful comparison, you randomly split all the instrument items into two sets, ensuring that the items in the first set measure the same construct as the items in the second set do. There are a number of ways to divide an instrument into comparable halves; you can compare even to odd items or in, for example, a forty-item instrument, the first twenty items to the last twenty. However, there is no guarantee that correlations derived from the first approach will correspond to correlations derived from the second. In the 1930s, Kuder and Richardson developed five formulas (KR_2, KR_8, KR_{14}, KR_{20}, and KR_{21}) for estimating all possible split-half method correlations. Using the Kuder-Richardson reliability estimates is an efficient and systematic method of calculating all possible split-half correlations without actually going through all the steps. However, this method is appropriate only for instruments intended to measure a single construct. Additionally, the KR_{20} and KR_{21} formulas can be applied only to instruments that use dichotomous items (such as *yes* or *no*, agree or disagree) (Worthen, Borg, & White, 1993).

- *Cronbach's alpha.* Assuming that all items are measuring the same thing (and that could be quite an assumption), you can randomly split the items into two sets as described earlier, pretest the instrument, and compute the correlation between these sets. Put all the items back, randomly split them into two sets again, readminister the instrument, and compute the correlation between these sets. Now, put all the items back and do it again, then again, then again. After you have computed all the possible split-half correlations (a number that will vary based on the number of items in your instrument) calculate the average of all the correlations. That is the premise of Cronbach's alpha, which is computed by a statistical formula rather than by pretesting repeatedly. This will provide a more accurate measure of reliability than a single administration using the split-half methodology.

Interrater and Intrarater Reliability

Interrater reliability methods are used for assessing reliability when more than one independent observer will be collecting the data. For example, you may have developed a personnel evaluation that will be used by different supervisors and you want to ensure consistency among those raters. Or you might have an instrument raters will be using to extract data from records (archival data). To ensure you are obtaining accurate information, you should plan to check the reliability of the data recorders. *Intrarater reliability* is similar to test-retest reliability, as it is a means for assessing consistency when an independent observer uses the same instrument at different times.

Interrater (Interobserver) Reliability

When an instrument is to be completed by two or more independent observers, their scores can be compared and the percentage of agreement calculated. A low percentage suggests that the raters interpreted the items differently or obtained different observations of the same event. The simplest way to derive a numerical score representing the percentage of agreement is to calculate a frequency ratio (divide the results obtained from one observer by the results obtained from the second observer) and then convert the ratio to a percentage (multiply by 100) (Kazdin, 1982): Smaller total ÷ Larger total × 100. For example, suppose that on a twenty-five item checklist, one observer obtains a score of 17 and the other a score of 19 on the same items. We would place the numbers into the formula and obtain the following results:

Frequency ratio: $17 \div 19 = .89$.

Expressed as percentage: $.89 \times 100 = 89\%$.

The resulting number indicates that the two observers agreed 89 percent of the time and disagreed 11 percent of the time. This information can then be used to determine whether problems exist in item interpretation (that is, whether items need to be rewritten for clarity) or whether further rater training is needed to improve the rate at which raters agree in their responses.

In addition to the frequency ratio, the correlation coefficient (such as the Pearson product-moment correlation coefficient) can be computed using the data sets obtained from two or more independent observers. As noted earlier, because this may involve large data sets, correlations are typically determined with computer software.

Several factors can influence the percentage of agreement between independent raters (Kazdin, 1982), particularly in the completion of observation instruments such as behavior rating scales. The following factors should be addressed to enhance the integrity of the rating process:

- *Reactivity* may occur when raters are aware that they are themselves being observed and checked. Typically, reliability indexes increase when this is the case, so this reactivity may not need to be corrected, as the goal of checking for interrater reliability is to increase the percentage of agreement.
- *Observer drift* occurs when the raters begin to interpret and apply item definitions differently over time. This can be controlled through training and by bringing the observers together to compare how they are carrying out the rating process and to receive feedback about the accuracy of their ratings.
- *Observer expectancies* may occur when an observer anticipates a change in what is being measured. If a rater anticipates, for example, that a program will reduce the incidence of off-task behaviors among children diagnosed with attention deficit disorder that may influence how he or she rates the behaviors. To reduce the possibility that this will occur, it is important to control the information you provide to the observer about the program, person, or treatment being studied.
- *Observation complexity* occurs when the observer is required to rate a multitude of responses or behaviors. As the number of elements to be rated increases, particularly if they occur within a specific time frame, the likelihood of errors increases. In part this can be corrected as you are pretesting the instrument; you can ensure that it is not too complex. Additional training, as with observer drift, can also reduce problems obtaining interrater reliability.

When the scores of two or more raters agree, there is always the possibility that they do so by chance. To address this issue, Jacob Cohen (1960) developed a correlational statistic that takes into account chance agreement. Like other correlations, Cohen's kappa produces a value from −1.0 to +1.0. Because chance variation is accounted for, Kappa produces a stronger measure of interrater reliability than percentage of agreement. Although Cohen's kappa can be calculated manually (see for example Stemler, 2001), most statistical software includes this function, making it fairly simple to compute.

Cohen's kappa is a statistical test for nominal level data. For example, observers document whether a specific behavior occurred (*yes* or *no*) during a designated time frame. Or raters may be extracting from records data that are categorical, such as living situation or level of education (elementary, middle, high school, and so on). If they are collecting continuous data, such as actual years in school, you could convert it back to these categories in order to use Cohen's kappa.

As noted, a correlational statistical can be computed for any two variables, and it will produce a value ranging from -1.0 to $+1.0$. If the variables are at the ordinal level of measurement you can use the Spearman rank order correlation or the Kendall rank order correlation. If the variables are at the interval or ratio level of measurement then you can use Pearson's product-moment correlation. Most introductory statistics books describe the steps in computing Pearson's correlation and advanced statistics books will explain the other approaches. In addition, popular computer spreadsheets such as Microsoft Excel will calculate Pearson's correlation, and most if not all of the statistical software on the market, such as SPSS or SAS, will calculate the other formulas.

Intrarater (Intra-Observer) Reliability

Intrarater reliability refers to the degree of stability between two or more observations of the same phenomena. For example, we might train observers by having them watch videos and rate what they observe. We would expect the observer to obtain the same or a very similar rating if scoring the same video on more than one occasion. When an instrument is to be completed by a single, independent observer, his or her scores across more than one administration of the instrument can be compared, and the *percentage of agreement* calculated using the same formula given earlier. The same tests used for interrater reliability can be applied for intrarater reliability. As with interrater reliability, differences may indicate ambiguous items or the need for practice on the part of the rater.

An important part of the pretesting phase is determining the reliability of responses. The findings of reliability assessments provide information about respondents' understanding of questionnaire items. If there are significant differences in responses when an instrument is administered on two separate occasions or when parallel forms of an instrument are used, you should determine why these discrepancies occurred. This information can help you in rewording items or designing the instrument.

Several methods exist to obtain a measure of reliability. Unless you have the time and resources to develop multiple forms of your instrument, we suggest that you administer the same instrument to a sample group for pretesting on two separate occasions. Simple methods such as eyeballing the results and determining the proportion of agreement should provide sufficient information to guide your decisions to revise and improve the instrument.

Validity, Reliability, and Decision Making

Social scientists sometimes make a distinction between *basic research* and *applied research*. Typically, the goal of basic research is to further our understanding of human behaviors and relations, whereas applied research typically addresses real-world issues and provides information for problem solving and decision making. A study designed to improve our understanding of organizational culture (the values, beliefs, and attitudes of individuals within an organization) is an example of basic research. A study to examine whether mode of administration—the Web or surface mail—influences survey response rates is an example of applied research. Depending on the study results, this research might well affect pollsters' actual choice of medium. Even when the original purpose of a project was to further understanding, information from that project is often adapted for decision making.

As instrument designers we need to be concerned about how the data produced from an instrument we have constructed are used. Consequently, we need to be assured and we need to assure the users of our data that the instrument is indeed producing valid and reliable results. At a minimum your documentation should describe how you set about demonstrating validity and reliability, both what you did and what you were unable to do because of time and resource limitations. For example, in documenting an employee job satisfaction questionnaire you might explain that the instrument was reviewed by content experts and pretested with a small group of employees and that you were unable to pretest with a larger sample due to the deadline and difficulty accessing staff. If you have developed an instrument that will be completed by observers or raters, describe what you have done to assess interrater reliability and describe the actions taken in response to pretesting to improve reliability.

It is also important to be explicit about the instrument's intended use in regard to target population, object of measurement, and situation, as both validity and reliability are affected by these factors. Alfie Kohn, a critic of standardized testing in education, has pointed out, for example, that SAT scores are a poor indicator for comparing the quality of education across schools systems because what these scores actually tell us is "the characteristics of the group of students who chose to take the test in a given year—or in a given state" (1999, p. 17). In other words the results are valid and consistent for one use in one situation, but not another.

An added concern is that an instrument designed and validated for one purpose and situation might be used for quite another. Suppose that you work for an agency that provides comprehensive human services, including physical rehabilitation, occupational therapy, vocational and mental health counseling, and academic remediation. You have been asked to develop an instrument that can be used to assess an individual's level of functioning in each of these areas to assist in treatment planning and matching services to client needs. However, when another agency adopts your instrument, it uses it to screen clients for access to services; if clients do not meet a predetermined threshold, they are denied services. In this case the instrument you constructed for one purpose is being put to use for another, with significant consequences for clients. To reduce the possibility that an instrument of your design will be misused, you should clearly specify the purpose and conditions for which it was developed and for which pretesting has provided evidence of validity and reliability.

Although we have focused on describing the demonstration of validity and reliability as a cogent process, it is not always so. For example, an instrument designed by one of the authors is being used to assess a mental health organization's progress in changing organizational culture to improve quality of care (Colton, 2004). The results are intended to be an impetus for addressing problems and improving service delivery. Review by content experts has indicated that the items demonstrate face, construct, and content validity. Pretesting has also revealed that raters often strongly disagree in their ratings of how their organization is making headway. As noted, we expect rating instruments to produce a great deal of variation. Therefore, to enhance the use of results for decision making, users of the instrument are encouraged to discuss their ratings and why they agree or disagree. This is helping organizational members to develop a consensus on the meaning of the items and the actions they can take in response to assessment the instrument produces.

Summary

We began this chapter with a comparison to paintings that attempt to portray their subjects as realistically and accurately as possible. During the past fifty years this style of painting has become so advanced the term *photo-realism* has been used to describe the degree of visual accuracy that is possible. In the social sciences, validity and reliability are corresponding concepts. With validity we want to be sure that the instrument measures what it purports to measure. There are a number of ways to think about validity, such as construct, content, and criteria validity; however, these are all facets of the same concept. It is important to pretest your instrument to ensure that it is producing valid results; if not, the instrument will need to be revised.

Print making is an art analogy to the concept of reliability. If you have ever purchased a limited edition print, you will have noticed that it is numbered. A print numbered 23/150, for example, is the twenty-third print out of a run of one hundred and fifty. Each print is duplicated from the same master but each will differ in a small way, therefore each print is still considered one of a kind. Similarly, each time you administer your instrument (the original) the results will vary somewhat, and as in print making, you want to minimize that variation. Therefore you want to assess how well the instrument produces reliable results, and as with validity, if there is a lot of variation, the instrument will need to be revised.

Absolute validity or reliability can never be demonstrated in the social sciences. Instead, we attempt to provide sufficient evidence that our instrument is producing reliable and valid information, and we adjust the instrument to enhance its ability to provide credible and accurate information consistently.

Instrument 4.A: Performance Appraisal

The job performance appraisal form shown as Instrument 4.A is an amalgamation of items taken from several different personnel rating instruments and is meant to represent the types of items and response sets typically used for this process. However, an underlying question is whether any instrument is truly capable of providing a valid and reliable assessment of an individual's job-related performance.

Performance appraisal systems are typically designed for the purpose of providing employees with feedback about their performance so they can strive to continually improve and be productive members of the organization. Performance evaluations may identify an employee's strengths related to job duties and skills; work-related performance that is deficient and in need of improvement; and areas where training and development might enhance knowledge, skills, and abilities. The ultimate goal is to create a productive workforce in which each member can contribute to the best of his or her ability.

Given these lofty goals, you have to wonder why there are so many articles in the human resource journals describing the shortcomings of the employee performance appraisal process and how to improve the process of conducting these appraisals, including the performance instrument itself. Mary Jenkins and the late Tom Coens also wondered about this. After all, organizations have been conducting evaluations and using rating scales to measure job performance for nearly a century. Jenkins and Coens's answer was in some ways quite simple: the constructs and assumptions on which we base performance appraisals are fundamentally flawed; therefore attempts to improve the process are inherently ineffective. And as a result, performance appraisal instruments are essentially unreliable and invalid.

The performance appraisal process is based on the belief that ultimately there must be some way to gauge the effort that employees put forth in fulfilling their duties and working to accomplish the organization's mission. Specifically, it is assumed that

All jobs and job tasks can be articulated, categorized, operationalized, and ultimately measured.

Employees are able to make use of feedback to correct and improve their performance.

To some extent, all employees need to correct or improve their current level of performance.

The organization, primarily through the supervisory chain of command, is responsible for measuring performance and providing feedback.

Those doing the assessment can do so objectively and without bias.

Inspecting individual performance leads to improvement, and improving individual performance improves organization performance.

Employees respond to external reinforcement, therefore the performance appraisal system can be tied to a system of extrinsic rewards (pay increases, bonuses, and the like) in order to motivate and make employees more productive.

"We have asked thousands of people whether these and other appraisal assumptions are reasonable. The response is always the same—*the key underlying assumptions of appraisals are not logical and realistic*" (Coens & Jenkins, 2000, p. 5). The stakes are high if Coens and Jenkins are right, as most organizations use the results of performance appraisals when deciding on salaries, on promotions, and on whether to discipline or retain employees whose performance has been appraised as poor. Imagine how employees would respond if told that a decision to give employee A a 4 percent raise and Employee B a 2 percent raise was based on an unreliable and invalid assessment process. When Coens and Jenkins examined the use of performance appraisals based on some form of rating system or scale, they found that "ratings typically don't provide information that is helpful or reflective of an employee's true status; ratings also undermine commitment and demoralize because nearly everyone expects to be rated highly and have their efforts appreciated" (p. 23). In regard to instrument construction, they make the following observations (pp. 69–70):

Evaluative processes are largely subjective.

Most raters and supervisors consciously want to rate people fairly.

People unknowingly bring perspectives that distort perception and unknown biases when rating other people.

Training and objective formatting can significantly reduce perceptual and evaluative biases and rating errors, but cannot effectively eliminate these problems.

Rating formats that are designed for a single purpose work better than multi-use ratings.

As raters and ratees, people will attempt to manipulate and distort ratings to get predetermined or desired results, often with positive motives in mind (for example, to ensure that an employee is not restricted from receiving a cost of living raise in pay).

Multiple raters may be more reliable than a single rater, especially with a collaborative process and clear criteria, to be applied for a specific purpose.

The system is the greatest influence on individual performance, making it difficult to ascertain any person's specific level of contribution.

The few people who are exceptionally good or bad performers may be distinguishable from others, especially over a few years.

If not performance appraisal, then what? Coens and Jenkins believe that rather than trying to improve an individual's work performance, organizations should focus on the processes that exert a considerable influence on employee effectiveness and should embrace the following new assumptions (p. 42):

An organization, because it is a system, cannot be significantly improved by focusing on individuals.

The choices of commitment and responsibility must be left to individuals if they are to be meaningful and effective.

Less structure and control over the individual employee often will result in greater motivation and productivity.

Employees cannot be *motivated* to perform their best, but conditions of openness and trust can unleash intrinsic motivation, spirit, and heart felt commitment to organization goals.

A focus on improving the overall "system" of the organization yields better results than trying to get employees to improve their individual performance.

Organizations can survive and grow only if they are freely evolving systems, where variation, differentiation, and diversity are valued as pathways to innovation and improvement.

INSTRUMENT 4.A: SAMPLES OF EMPLOYEE EVALUATION FORM ITEMS.

Employee Name: _____ Job Classification: _____

Evaluation Period: From: _____ To: _____ Department: _____

Item	Potential Response Set			
1. Performs work according to job description.	Unacceptable	Needs improvement	Meets expectations	Superior
2. Demonstrates punctuality and begins work as scheduled.	Unacceptable	Needs improvement	Satisfactory	Excellent
3. Accepts guidance willingly.	Strongly disagree	Disagree	Agree	Strongly agree
4. Responds promptly to customer requests.	Never	Sometimes	Most of the time	Always
5. Analyzes problems and develops effective solutions.	Inadequate	Marginally adequate	Adequate	More than adequate
6. Demonstrates ability to handle several responsibilities simultaneously.	Poor	Needs improvement	Meets standards	Exceeds standards
7. Displays a positive, cooperative attitude toward work.	To little or no extent	To some extent	To a moderate extent	To a great extent
8. Expresses self clearly orally and in writing.	Unsatisfactory	Needs improvement	Meets expectations	Exceeds expectations
9. Works well with coworkers.	Unsatisfactory ○	○	○	Satisfactory ○
10. Produces work that is accurate and neat.	1	2	3	4
11. Completes assignments in a timely manner.	Poor ❏	❏	❏	Excellent ❏
12. Initiates work tasks without direction from supervisor.	Rarely	Occasionally	Usually	Frequently

Areas of strength:

_____

_____

Areas of improvement:

_____

_____

Instrument 4.B: Instructor Evaluation

In order to evaluate the validity of Instrument 4.B, a faculty assessment questionnaire, the designer created vignettes describing the behaviors and styles of three hypothetical instructors. Student volunteers were recruited to pretest the instrument by completing a questionnaire for each one of the vignettes. The following table presents vignettes and ratings (average rating and standard deviation) for item 1: "Instructor's expectations in course were made clear." The average rating shows a strong relationship between the item and vignette description that the item is attempting to measure. The vignette for Dr. Blacke describes an instructor who is well organized and who clearly articulates her classroom expectations. Consequently, you would expect the majority of students to rate item 1 as *agree* or *strongly agree,* which is supported by the 4.8 average rating for this item as well as a standard deviation indicating little variation. In the next vignette Dr. White is described as "disorganized and ambiguous regarding how students will be evaluated in the course." As expected, the majority of students rated item 1 *strongly disagree* and *disagree.* The vignette for Dr. Gray is purposely vague about whether this instructor clearly articulates expectations. In this case you would expect students to select *neither agree nor disagree,* which is reflected by the average rating of 3.1. Student ratings of the vignette suggest that item 1 is a good measure of what it intends to measure; that is, it is a valid measure of the construct.

Instructor and Vignette Statement

Item	Dr. Blacke	Dr. White	Dr. Gray
	This instructor is very organized and outlines her expectations of students throughout the course and how they will be evaluated.	The instructor is disorganized when he comes to class and ambiguous regarding how students will be evaluated in the course.	Even though the instructor gives assignments that are interesting and related to topics, students find it difficult to understand the lectures because the instructor tends to "lecture over their heads."
Instructor's expectations in the course were made clear.	Average Rating = 4.8 SD = .38	Average Rating = 1.8 SD = .79	Average Rating = 3.1 SD = 1.00

INSTRUMENT 4.B: INSTRUCTOR EVALUATION.

Please answer the following questions based on your experience in this class during the past semester. This is an anonymous assessment; please do not write your name on the questionnaire. Place a check in the box ☑ that reflects your choice.

	Strongly Agree	Agree	Disagree	Strongly Disagree
1. Instructor's expectations in course were made clear.	❏	❏	❏	❏
2. Content of course was organized in meaningful way.	❏	❏	❏	❏
3. Assignments were challenging.	❏	❏	❏	❏
4. Instructor demonstrated a genuine interest in teaching course.	❏	❏	❏	❏
5. Instructor was sensitive to student needs and interests.	❏	❏	❏	❏
6. I learned a great deal in this course.	❏	❏	❏	❏
7. Overall, this course was worthwhile to me.	❏	❏	❏	❏
8. Overall, the instructor in this course was effective.	❏	❏	❏	❏
9. Content of course included different racial or ethnic perspectives where appropriate.	❏	❏	❏	❏
10. Instructor provided materials (for example, textbooks, articles, handouts) that reflect different racial and ethnic perspectives.	❏	❏	❏	❏

Course Title: _____

Course #: _____   Section #: _____

Semester (check one): ❏ Fall   ❏ Winter   ❏ Spring   ❏ Summer   Year: 2___

CONSTRUCT VALIDITY VIGNETTES

Dr. Blacke

You're a transfer student, and you've been advised to take this course under this instructor because she is popular with the students. The instructor is very organized and outlines her expectations of students throughout the course and how they will be evaluated. The instructor really enjoys teaching this particular course and tries to make the assignments interesting and practical. The instructor also tries to present different perspectives on various topics taught in the course. She addresses the differences between men, women, and minorities as they relate to sensitive topics in the course. She is also eager to help students out of class as well as in class. You take the course and find that you really like the instructor and the course.

Dr. White

You've been told by your adviser that you needed to take this course because it's a required course in your major. You really don't want to take the course nor do you want to take it under this instructor. You've heard students say negative things about the course and the instructor, but you have no choice because all the other sections were full except this one. The instructor seems to be more involved in doing research than in trying to nurture students' academic growth. The instructor is disorganized when he comes to class and ambiguous regarding how students will be evaluated in the course. The instructor comes in and lectures and immediately heads back to the office to continue his research. The assignments are sporadic, and students get frustrated because the assignments never seem to add any meaning to the course. The instructor doesn't make any attempt to present various perspectives to students. You take the course and find that you really don't like the instructor or the course.

Dr. Gray

You and your adviser discussed the courses you needed to take in order to graduate. Your adviser told you that you've taken all of the required courses and that you can take electives for the hours. You decided to take this course because the subject is of interest to you and because you wanted to learn more about the subject. You take the course and find that you really like it; however, for some reason you don't really like the instructor. It may be that even though the instructor gives assignments that are interesting and related to the topic(s) she is discussing in class, students find it difficult to understand the lectures because the instructor tends to sometimes "lecture over their heads." Another reason why you might dislike the instructor is the instructor's inability to relate to students, and the instructor's resistance to accepting and presenting viewpoints other than her own. For example, the instructor tends to ignore women and minority groups who have their hands up to answer or ask questions.

Endnotes

1. This may also be referred to as *measurement validity* or *instrument validity*, to differentiate it from issues of validity associated with the research design, referred to as *internal validity* and *external validity*. Internal validity is the extent to which the research design rules out alternative explanations of the results. External validity is the extent to which the results of the study can be generalized beyond the study's objects, persons, or settings. Instrument validity, internal validity, and external validity are all part of the same continuum.

2. This is not necessarily a bad thing. The relationship between one construct and another and their combined relationship to an underlying theory is referred as the *nomological net*. It is believed that by conceptualizing these relationships, you improve the basis for operationalizing measures of the construct.

3. In reality we always anticipate some variation because a perfect correlation will produce a value of 0 and not +1 or −1. In other words, if you administer the same instrument to the same individuals at different times and all the individuals produce the same ratings for all of the items, there is no variation.

Key Concepts and Terms

Cohen's kappa

concurrent validity

construct validity

content validity

convergent validity

criterion validity

Cronbach's alpha

deductive approach

discriminant validity

face validity

factor analysis

inductive approach

internal consistency reliability

interrater reliability

intrarater reliability

item analysis

item response theory

multicultural validity

operationalization

parallel forms reliability

percentage of agreement

predictive validity

proportion of agreement

qualitative assessment

quantitative assessment

reliability

split-half method

table of specifications

test-retest reliability

valid

validity

PART TWO

APPLICATION

CHAPTER FIVE

PURPOSEFUL CREATIVITY

First Steps in the Development of an Instrument

In this chapter we will

- Explain how articulating the purpose of your study influences the development of an instrument.
- Describe approaches for focusing your study.
- Identify approaches for developing items for an instrument.

Imagine an artist looking at a blank canvas. She has a choice of medium (oil, acrylic, watercolor, or mixed media), subjects (landscape, still-life, portraiture, and so forth), and styles (such as cubism, pop art, impressionism, or expressionism) to choose from. Two artists can look at the same subject and, given their different approaches as well as their individual talent and vision, produce very different paintings.

Now consider your situation. You need to obtain information, and after considering various approaches, you have chosen to use a survey. Obviously, you have in mind the information you want to obtain, so it may appear to be a contradiction when we now suggest that you reflect on the purpose of your study. Like the artist, while you may have selected a subject, there are still many considerations to be made about the methodology and actual content of the instrument. Just as a painter must consider how objects will be composed and what style to employ, without taking some thoughtful steps at the beginning of this process, you may construct a questionnaire that does not fulfill its purpose. For example, after your survey has been developed and administered, it is very exasperating to identify items that with more forethought would, and should, have been included.

In this chapter we will examine some preliminary steps you can follow to help ensure that your instrument will focus on the right things and to identify the items to include. It is also important during this phase of instrument construction to identify your own beliefs and biases, which may be reflected in the instrument, intentionally or unintentionally. For example, your beliefs and opinions may influence the way that statements are worded and, ultimately, the way that respondents reply to the item. This chapter also presents some practical approaches for developing questionnaire items. This is primarily a brainstorming phase in which item stems are created as you begin to visualize the realm of items you may want to include in the questionnaire.

Articulating the Purpose of the Study and the Focus of the Instrument

Instruments provide information so we can better understand a subject and make better decisions. Using an instrument in a study is an activity you may perform for an academic project, an aspect of your work, or scholarly research. Specifying the purpose of the study helps you to identify the themes you want to study, the methodology you might use, the type of instrument to design, and ultimately, the items to include. For your first step, we suggest you construct a one-to-two-page written summary that articulates the purpose of the study. This *reflective paper* can help you formulate your ideas and objectives. In constructing this *statement of purpose*, it is important to reflect on the rationale for the project and what you propose to achieve. Additionally, you can give this statement to others to obtain feedback and recommendations for crafting the questionnaire. Your statement of purpose may be revised several times, with each iteration more clearly and succinctly specifying the objectives of the study. In the end this *iterative process* should produce a summation of your thoughts and goals that can guide you in the development of the project and design of the instrument. Although the idea of writing a purpose statement might seem at first like an unnecessary exercise, let's examine how this process clarifies and directs the manner in which you construct the instrument.

It Focuses the Study Purpose, the Methodology, and Ultimately the Type of Instrument

There are a number of reasons why we might conduct a study, such as the need to provide information for decision making or to further our understanding of some phenomenon. Often information is requested by external stakeholders. Consider a principal who wants to assess the amount of time students spend in reading activities. This information may be needed because a school division curriculum specialist is assessing a new reading program or a state education administrator is preparing a grant application. Alternatively, the request for this information may have come from a researcher at a state university who wants to know if there is a relationship between the amount of time children spend reading in the classroom and their scores on standardized tests. In this case the information will likely be published and used to expand knowledge of educational practice, although the study results might ultimately inform others' decision making too. For example, another principal may later request similar information about his or her students as part of a quality improvement process based on the article this researcher publishes. Typically, we are interested in subjects that may be difficult to directly observe and measure. It is important to articulate these constructs so that the purpose of the study can be honed to a manageable size. Take, for example, a psychologist in a mental health clinic who wants to investigate the effectiveness of treatment. The psychologist first lists questions that might lead to defining this *effectiveness:*

- What particular treatment approach is suggested for this client?
- What clinical outcome is anticipated as a result of this client's participating in this particular treatment approach?
- How often was this particular intervention offered?
- How did the client make use of this particular treatment approach?
- What aspects of the client's level of functioning or degree of symptomatology influenced treatment?
- Is this treatment approach more effective in reducing symptoms or increasing function, or both, as compared to other approaches?
- What factors enhanced or limited the client's access to this treatment intervention?
- What is the unit cost for providing this particular treatment approach?
- Is this treatment approach more cost effective than other treatment approaches?
- Was the client satisfied with the treatment process?
- Did treatment accomplish the results that the provider had intended and that the client sought?
- In what ways could we have improved treatment for this client?
- In what ways can we enhance the quality of this particular intervention?
- In what ways can we enhance the delivery of this intervention?

As a result of constructing this list, the psychologist has identified fourteen separate questions, each of which could be examined by one or more methods, research designs, and ultimately, instruments, such as a checklist, behavior rating scale, psychometric instrument, or survey questionnaire. Unless the psychologist is part of a large research team, with considerable resources, it is unlikely that all these questions can be addressed. However, by articulating the topic (treatment effectiveness) and then considering the different ways the topic can be examined, the psychologist can identify those questions that would be the most informative to the mental health clinic staff.

In addition, if the psychologist decides to assess client satisfaction with treatment, that will suggest survey research methods, the use of focus groups, and the use of individual interviews. If the psychologist decides to gather data about clinical outcomes, an instrument might be designed to be administered before and after treatment and to measure changes in functioning or acuity of illness. Each approach will influence the design of the instrument as well as the specific items to include.

You may also find yourself formulating the questions you want to ask, or think you want to ask, before you decide on a methodology. This is a "what came first, the chicken or the egg" issue, and it may not really matter. Thinking about a methodology will certainly help you get to the next stage of thinking about the questions. However, formulating questions may lead you toward a particular methodology. For example, asking clients if individual therapy has been helpful and in what way it has helped suggests employing client interviews or conducting a survey. A study based on observing clients or one using an experimental design would not provide the desired information.

Focusing the purpose of your study also helps you to identify the environment in which the instrument should be designed to operate. Using a survey will indicate that you need to develop a sampling strategy, using mail or telephone, for example, whereas use of a behavior rating scale might suggest implementation in a natural setting, such as school, clinic, or home.

It Specifies Underlying Constructs

At first glance, instruments often appear just to be tools for information gathering: How often do you use this product? Have you purchased from this store before? Do you plan to use this service again? However, underlying these questions are more important themes: customer satisfaction, loyalty, and intentions. In some cases you might not think about these themes as you develop your questionnaire. In other situations, they may be the rationale for conducting the study and may have a strong influence on the design of the instrument.

As we noted in Chapter Four, a construct is something that cannot be directly observed or measured. Constructs must be *operationalized;* that is, they must be put into language that allows researchers to observe and measure attributes that represent the construct. Suppose the psychologist in the mental health clinic wants to use a questionnaire as a diagnostic screening instrument for clients entering the clinic for treatment. One construct of interest is depression, which cannot be directly observed. However, a number of behaviors associated with depression are measurable, including level of energy, loss of sleep, and change in appetite. A series of questions assessing these variables could produce a depression scale that could identify clients who are demonstrating the behaviors associated with the construct of depression.

Whenever possible it is helpful and important to articulate the underlying concepts you are interested in studying. If you are developing an instrument to gather what you believe is just factual information, try to consider what is motivating you to collect this information and how the information will be used. Later in this chapter we will describe how to develop a table of specifications that can help you identify constructs, specify construct attributes, and articulate specific questionnaire items.

It Articulates the Object of Measurement

Once you have articulated and focused the topic, you will need to define for yourself and others what you will measure and what the units of analysis will be. For the psychologist who is interested in measuring the effectiveness of treatment, it might be important to define the types of interventions that will be evaluated, such as group therapy, individual therapy, and family counseling. Each form of therapy may require a different form of instrument or set of questionnaire items to assess treatment effectiveness. Additionally, the psychologist will need to articulate who will provide information. Are the respondents the patients, the service providers, or both? If the psychologist is interested in obtaining information about client satisfaction with services, the assumption is that clients will be the respondents. However, in some cases it may be the client's caretaker, such as a family member, who is able to provide an informed response. And if the psychologist can use existing information, such as medical record data, the object of measurement might be a thing rather than a person.

Social scientists also make a distinction between studies that focus on individual cases and studies that attempt to elicit broad principles that can be generalized across groups or populations. *Idiographic* approaches are designed to obtain information about specific cases; that is, the results are confined to a defined setting or time. *Nomothetic* approaches are designed to obtain information about principles and truths that are more universal and can be generalized beyond a singular case or situation. Thinking about how your study will be applied may in turn suggest the methodology and, ultimately, the type of instrument required—for example, a diagnostic questionnaire to provide information about single clients or a survey instrument to gather information from a sample of consumers.

This distinction is also important because the data produced by an instrument designed to collect information about a series of individuals may not be appropriate or valid for making generalizations beyond each individual. Suppose you develop a mental health instrument to support observation of individuals, and it is your intention that the information generated will be used only to provide feedback to each client and for treatment planning. Even though you may eventually collect data from many clients, you cannot assume that you can aggregate those data to make accurate generalizations about the clients as a group. Thinking about the object of measurement can help you clarify whether the data will be used solely for analysis at the individual or at the group level and consequently what the instrument design must consider.

Another way to think about what you want to measure is to consider whether you are interested in understanding *processes* or *outcomes*. In asking, "How often was this particular intervention offered?" the psychologist in our scenario is interested in information about the process of service delivery and in particular information about inputs (the resources needed to deliver a service) and outputs (the tangible products produced or services rendered). As summarized in Table 5.1, questionnaire items that help us to understand a process tend to elicit information about *how much, how often,* and *where* a service is provided. Conversely, the question, "Did treatment accomplish the results that the provider intended and the client sought?" is about *outcomes* (short-term results) and *impacts* (long-term, socially beneficial

TABLE 5.1: PROCESSES AND OUTCOMES.

	Process	Outcome
	Efficiency (doing things right)—productivity	**Effectiveness** (doing the right things)—quality
What to Measure	**Inputs** Resources needed Resources used **Outputs** Services rendered	**Outcomes** Goals and objectives attained **Impacts** Long-term, socially beneficial results
Questions	Did it occur? How often? How much? When? Where?	What was achieved? Did it accomplish what it was supposed to? Does it make a difference?

results). Outcome-oriented questions help to answer questions of effectiveness, such as whether client or program objectives are being attained.

As you can see, the process of articulating the purpose of the study can hone the focus, bringing study goals into clearer view and even suggesting questionnaire items. Let's suppose that our psychologist has decided to assess treatment effectiveness by considering the perspectives of providers and patients. Two separate questionnaires will be developed, one for each population, and where possible the results from these two groups will be compared. This suggests that the two questionnaires should use similar items to measure each construct; for example, both groups might be asked questions about how treatment can be improved. The psychologist then further refines this topic to identify the treatment approach of interest, a process that suggests asking separate questions to address individual, group, and family therapies. Next the psychologist must define the term *improved*, which could refer to such attributes as accessibility to services, helpfulness of staff, timeliness of service delivery, competency of providers, or the availability of information (Martin, 1993). A series of items might be constructed to measure each one of these attributes.

It Communicates Your Intentions to Others

Ultimately, the process that you used to gather information and the information itself may be examined. In order to prepare for these challenges and to ensure that your data is trustworthy (that is, you can demonstrate how you obtained your data and how you accounted for possible errors coming from data collection), it is helpful to share your intentions with others from the outset. In this phase of instrument construction the basic premise for the study and the concepts you want to explore should be tested. Feedback during these preliminary stages can be very helpful in shaping the direction of the study as well as identifying the type of instrument to use and specific items to include.

A written purpose statement is essential for communicating your intent to key stakeholders. Depending on your situation, it can help you communicate your intentions to your faculty adviser, graduate committee, institutional review board (IRB), coworkers and managers, or an outside agency. In addition to helping you disseminate your intentions to others, the printed statement of purpose can elicit feedback about your study. Questions others may pose can be challenging, and given your investment in the project it is only natural to become somewhat defensive in response to some forms of feedback. However, if you accept the comments thoughtfully, you will find you can use some of them to improve and focus your work. This process can also help to identify peers, potential respondents, experts in the field you are studying, and others who through their interest and feedback can assist you during other phases of the study. You might also conduct focus groups with stakeholders, including potential respondents, to obtain feedback (as described in Chapter Six). For example, in our classes, students regularly meet in small groups to critique and make recommendations to help each other develop instruments.

It Suggests How the Instrument Should Be Administered

Defining the purpose of the study helps you identify not only the type of instrument to use but also ways to implement the information-gathering process.

Recall that our psychologist has decided to construct two questionnaires—one for clients and one for treatment providers. In regard to clients the psychologist can examine admission data to obtain a better understanding of who uses services. From that information the format for administering the survey can be determined. By examining service utilization data the psychologist learns that the clinic provides services to over one thousand different clients per year. This suggests the use of a random sampling methodology (discussed in Chapter Thirteen), an approach for obtaining a sample that is representative of all one thousand clients, rather than administering the questionnaire to all of them. The data also provide information about the ages, genders, and diagnoses of clients, which can help the clinic in developing a strategy ensuring that the appropriate attributes are represented in the sample. Conversely, because there are fewer than twenty-five providers—therapists and counselors—the entire population of providers, rather than a sample, can be surveyed. Moreover, the psychologist concludes that it might be just as easy to meet with the providers, individually or in focus groups, to obtain the information being sought. Consequently, the psychologist decides to use a survey approach with clients and an interview approach with providers. As a result of thinking through this process and drafting a statement of purpose, the psychologist needs to construct only one questionnaire.

It Identifies Applicable Standards

In situations where we seek factual information it may be helpful to determine whether standards or criteria related to that information already exist. Knowledge of these standards can help you formulate your questionnaire items. Our psychologist, for example, might be interested in knowing if clients feel the clinic waiting area is large enough to accommodate them comfortably. The clinic administrator advises the psychologist that the local building codes specify the number of square feet necessary for a given number of people in public areas. The psychologist can now consider the actual square footage in the waiting area in relation to the building code requirement, the average number of clients waiting in the lobby, and client responses about comfort on the questionnaire. Additionally, the Health Insurance

Portability and Accountability Act (HIPAA) requires providers to ensure the confidentiality of personal health information. The psychologist will have to determine whether demographic data are considered confidential under this regulation.

In the authors' experience, there are many existing standards that can provide guidance in the development of questionnaire items. One way to identify these standards is to conduct a literature search about your topic. With the advent of the Internet, researching your topic using a key word with one of the many browsers available will likely produce many references. Another source is other questionnaires that have been developed to study your field of interest. The U.S. General Accounting Office (1986) staff describe three ways in which the GAO acquires the standards it uses: "(1) adopt a standard from an authoritative source, (2) ask experts in the substantive field to reach consensus on a standard, or (3) set the standard [ourselves], basing it on a combination of empirical analysis and value judgment" (p. 33).

It Identifies Specific Terms or Vocabulary You Want or Need to Use

To a great extent, instrument construction is about language, about formulating items in such a way that their meaning is clear and unambiguous. You enhance that process when you address the factors we have discussed so far in your statement of purpose. For example, certain terms, technical language, or euphemisms might be familiar to the particular sample you intend to survey even though not to the population as a whole. Similarly, you may need to consider the reading level of your intended respondents. Questionnaires designed for young children often use pictures as well as words.

In designing a questionnaire for clients, our psychologist purposely pretests the vocabulary to ensure that technical terms are not used or are used only minimally. For example, the psychologist might ask clients to rate the effectiveness of the "group that helped you with problem solving and decision making," rather than referring to it as the "cognitive behavior therapy group."

It Helps You Visualize the Instrument from the User's Perspective

You are developing an instrument to obtain information about a topic *you* are interested in or have been commissioned to undertake; you likely have no reason to believe that potential respondents have an equal interest in the subject. It is important therefore to consider how someone might respond to your instrument in terms of its length, completion time, topic sensitivity, administration issues, and relevance. When respondents have no connection with the subject, they are much less likely to complete a questionnaire, and you may find the response rate is so low that you cannot make any decisions from the data you have acquired:

> If there is a single, fundamental principle of questionnaire design, it is that the respondent defines what you can do: the types of questions you can reasonably ask; the types of words you can reasonably use; the concepts you can explore; the methodology you can employ. This is why a survey of doctors, for example, can be, and should be, quite a different proposition to a survey of the general public [Gendall, 1998, p. 29].

This does not mean that respondents define the problem or the research project, design the methodology of inquiry or the instrument. However, it does emphasize the need to take them into consideration. For example, you could interview individuals who are affected by a problem to better understand the problem and articulate your research question. Feedback from these same individuals as you design your study and construct your instrument could help you obtain information that is trustworthy and valid.

Thinking about how the mental health clinic clients might respond to the questionnaire, our psychologist realizes that clients are often sensitive about receiving mental health treatment. Rather than sending out questionnaires labeled with the clinic's name and address, the psychologist decides to ask clients to complete the instrument at the clinic.[1] This could also generate a higher response rate.

This advice applies equally to instruments that will be completed by an observer. If the psychologist in our example was constructing a child development checklist, he or she could involve parents as well as the staff assigned to conduct the observations and implement the instrument.

Researcher as Instrument: Accounting for Personal Bias

As the social sciences developed during the past century, it became abundantly evident that scientists are not the neutral actors tradition has portrayed. We now realize that researchers must account for their biases, values, opinions, and most important, potential influence on the subject of inquiry.

If you believe that you are indeed a detached and objective observer, think again:

> All researchers take sides, or are partisans for one point of view or another. Value-free interpretive research is impossible. This is the case because every researcher brings preconceptions and interpretations to the problem being studied. All scholars are caught in the circle of interpretation. This means that scholars must state beforehand their prior interpretations of the phenomenon

being investigated. Unless these meanings and values are clarified, their effects on subsequent interpretations remain clouded and often misunderstood [Norman Denzin, 1989, as cited in Patton, 1990, p. 476].

One of the most important elements of completing a statement of purpose is the opportunity to consider why you are interested in the topic, what you hope to accomplish by studying the subject, and what you bring to the topic—in both knowledge and attitude. By reflecting on what you have written, you should be able to identify some of your own presumptions and interpretations that might influence your choice of topic and ultimately choice of questionnaire items.

Our psychologist, for example, finds a personal preference for therapies that teach coping skills, such as cognitive behavior therapies, over process-oriented therapies, such as psychoanalysis. Being aware of this preference may help the psychologist to take a balanced approach to writing items about these different treatment interventions.

In conclusion, we strongly recommend that you summarize your thoughts and intentions in a reflective paper, your statement of purpose, addressing the issues discussed here. The value of this exercise is twofold. First, it is an introspective process that can help you think about your project, how it will be conducted, what it will include, and how you will implement it. A number of topics and questions for your questionnaire are likely to begin to surface as you draft this statement. Second, the statement provides a means of sharing your ideas with others and obtaining their feedback, which in turn can help you clarify and focus the project.

Exhibit 5.1 contains our psychologist's statement of purpose and exemplifies the many factors we have discussed. Although your purpose statement should reflect your own unique writing style, try to cover each of the factors we have described. Remember that this is an iterative process and you may need to rewrite the statement several times to clarify and focus the topic. During this process, identify others you would like to share this information with and receive feedback from, including individuals with expertise in the subject area you are studying, individuals who have developed questionnaires, and individuals who might be respondents.

Some artists work on their paintings in stages, with bursts of energy followed by periods of inactivity. While they might not be directly applying paint to canvas, they may continue to think about composition, color, and style. This analogy applies equally to the development of an instrument. For example, sometimes it helps to put the purpose statement aside while you think about the project or seek feedback from others. Over time you will refine the statement to the point that you have a clear sense of direction about creating the instrument.

EXHIBIT 5.1: STATEMENT OF PURPOSE.

As the clinical director of a publicly funded, community mental health clinic, I am interested in knowing if the services we are providing are effective. In particular I would like to know if clients find these services helpful and if providers believe that treatment is producing meaningful change. Having made that statement, I now realize that there are really two parts to this question. The first relates to service delivery: for example, do clients find services accessible and timely or do they have to wait a long time before they are admitted for services? The second question addresses treatment outcomes: if a couple comes into the clinic for marital counseling, does the counseling help to identify and resolve their problems?

Outcome assessment is a "hot" topic nowadays. Clients, therapists, and mental health advocates want to know if treatment produces meaningful results and if it is cost effective. According to the articles I've read, there are a number of ways to evaluate the results of treatment, such as doing testing or completing behavior rating instruments before, during, and at the completion of treatment. I think it would be helpful to meet with the treatment staff of the clinic to discuss how we might accomplish this task, as a project of this magnitude will surely affect their work efforts and could increase their workload. It will not be successful unless we agree that the findings from these evaluations are useful to us as providers.

That brings me back to the first question which is, "How do clients perceive and experience the treatment process?" By asking that question, I hope to obtain the clients' perspective. I would like to be able to answer questions about service delivery, which suggests some way of obtaining clients' *opinions,* and I would like to assess client perceptions about the treatment they receive, which suggests some way of measuring *attitudes.*

This suggests the use of a questionnaire that could determine client needs and ultimately identify ways to improve services. In conjunction with other outcomes measures, a questionnaire could also be used to explore treatment effectiveness. For example, we could include questions that assess a client's perception of his or her problem before and after participating in treatment. The ultimate goal of this endeavor should be to provide clinic personnel with information that could be used to improve service delivery, improve client satisfaction with services, and assess the effectiveness of treatment procedures. If this is to be a successful process, clients and providers should be involved in the development of the questionnaire. The attributes that I think would be of interest include

- Problem(s) that brought the client to the clinic.
- Demographics, such as age, gender, marital status, income range, and occupation.
- Perceptions about the delivery of services, such as ability to obtain an appointment and experience of waiting times and the physical environment.

- Perceptions about financial arrangements. For example, do clients feel comfortable talking to clinic staff about their ability to pay?
- Satisfaction with the therapy received. Note that we may need to develop separate questions for family therapy, individual therapy, and the variety of group sessions we offer.
- Problems in obtaining services or dissatisfaction with services.

I am therefore going to propose that we form two quality improvement committees. The first group will identify measures we can use to evaluate progress before, during, and after treatment. If we cannot find an evaluation instrument that specifically meets our needs, then we may need to consider developing one or contracting with an instrument development specialist. The second group will develop a client satisfaction survey. This group will also be responsible for administering the survey. We may also need to look outside the organization for assistance with this task. The goal of this project should be to improve the delivery and the effectiveness of the services the clinic is providing.

First Steps in Creating Questionnaire Items

In the authors' experience, most books on instrument design focus on the mechanics of writing measurable questionnaire items and formatting the instrument. This book presents that information too, but it also addresses the cognitive-creative process. To some extent, questionnaire items do indeed spring out of thin air. You have already begun to prepare for this activity by writing your statement of purpose, talking to others about your project, reading articles about your topic, and possibly even examining other instruments developed to study this topic. During this process a number of issues and possible questions will have begun to surface.

Conscious thought is often difficult to describe as it cannot be seen and few of us tend to think about thinking or to ask how a thought came into existence in the first place! Psychologists suggest that the creative process occurs in a series of stages: preparation, incubation, inspiration, and verification (Munn, 1966). Although we may not be consciously carrying out this process, internally we are analyzing our ideas, testing them, bringing new information to bear, and synthesizing this information until we are mentally comfortable with the results. A number of approaches have been identified that can enhance this process, such as brainstorming, nominal group technique, and Q methodology. Let's examine some of these approaches and how they might help you formulate specific items.

Conducting a Literature Review

Both prior to initiating the project and while developing the questionnaire, you will be examining articles written about your topic. This literature review serves several purposes:

- Indicates previous research conducted in the area of investigation.
- Stipulates the theories developed to explain the phenomenon.
- Describes methods used to study the topic.

In the social sciences we are often interested in questions related to program or service implementation, program outcome, and policy impact. For example, we might want to know whether lowering the speed limit on interstate highways reduces traffic accidents and fatalities. We might be interested in the academic and social impact of standardized testing in the schools. Or we might want to know if a community mental health clinic provides family therapy as outlined in a program manual. Quite often these concepts are grounded in program theory, an explanation of why things are supposed to work as we believe they should. The *program theory* on which lowering speed limits is based derives from studies that show that drivers have more time to react to changes in highway conditions at slower speeds, and that a positive correlation exists between speed and mortality—the faster you are driving the more likely you are to die in an automobile accident. Consequently, one reason for conducting a literature review is to establish a foundation for understanding the problem we are interested in studying.

In addition to helping you focus your study, the literature review may suggest areas to be addressed in the questionnaire and, ultimately, specific items to include. This could occur in two ways. First, the material in someone else's study may suggest specific items. A human resource manager who decides to use a survey to discover if employees are satisfied with the current company benefits might realize from a literature review that the questions should deal with benefits not currently offered by the company as well as those that are.

Second, an article you read may include examples of appropriate questionnaire items or a study instrument in its entirety. There is nothing wrong with adopting questions from other sources, as long as you realize that you may have to modify the wording to fit your situation. For example, you might find an organizational survey that was used to study employee attitudes about the work environment in a health care setting, and you might see that a number of the items could be revised and used in a survey you plan to conduct in a school system. When you adopt and revise another's work, it is important to reference the original source in your documentation. Additionally, validity and reliability studies completed for the original items will not apply when you modify the wording of items or when you use items in a new situation or setting.

In some cases you may find that specific items or an entire questionnaire, with a few revisions, will fit your study. This could very well be the case if you are conducting a large marketing survey or political poll. Although it is all right to use the work of others for inspiration, if you plan to use an existing item or questionnaire with little or no modification, then you must contact the author(s) of the instrument to obtain permission. In some cases you may have to pay a fee to use the material.

In recent years the use of X-ray technology has enabled art historians to examine the underlying layers of paint on a canvas, and they sometimes find that the artist's original composition is different from the final depiction. Similarly, you may find the links between conducting a literature review and developing an instrument do not form a straightforward process. While researching a topic in the field of mental health, one of the authors reviewed over eighty journal articles and Internet resources. The articles were analyzed for reoccurring themes and elements in these themes with the intent of developing an article for publication. Over time the project bogged down. Many months later the author revisited the list of themes and saw in it the basis for a checklist. Although the article as intended was not written, the checklist was developed, tested, and disseminated to mental health professionals (Colton, 2004).

Making Use of Existing Processes

In some cases preexisting policies, regulations, and procedures may help you determine the type of instrumentation to use or create. For example, approaches for assessing and improving processes and outcomes have been developed for quality improvement initiatives, which have become ubiquitous in many health, education, and human service organizations. And instruments such as questionnaires, checklists, and inventories are often developed to capture data used to monitor processes and identify areas for improvement.

Quality improvement (QI) is defined as a planned approach to achieving better outcomes and transforming organizations by evaluating and improving systems. The plan-do-check-act (PDCA) cycle is an example of a structured approach for carrying out QI activities (McLaughlin & Kaluzny, 1994). In this approach, QI teams are created to identify opportunities for improvement. This may involve construction of an instrument to measure existing processes. Repeated measures are taken to determine if the processes are operating within parameters, and if not, corrections are made to bring each process back to the desired level. Because quality is defined by the customer, questionnaires are often developed and administered to ascertain people's level of satisfaction with services and to ascertain areas where services can be improved.

Brainstorming

Brainstorming is an approach to idea generation and the generation of alternatives. Typically brainstorming is conducted as a group activity, but there is certainly no reason why it cannot be a solitary one as well. Think about your topic and the information you want to know about it. Then begin to write down questions and statements as they come to mind. Do this for as long as you can think of questions. Because brainstorming is a creative process, feel free to wander in many directions, as ideas that appear far-fetched at first may lead to more practical ones. Feel free to generate all types of statements and questions, not just ones you think might fit into some measurable scale. Accept ideas uncritically; if you begin to critique your statements you will shift from a creative process to an analytical one.

After you have completed this process, begin to organize the ideas. Now is the time to begin considering format and wording: Do the statements and questions make sense? Are they ambiguous? Do they provide adequate coverage of the subject? Check to see if you have written more than one version of a statement or question. Variation in wording may mean a question has multiple aspects that need to be addressed with several smaller items. Continue this process until you are comfortable with the items you have created.

Creativity is generally not a continuous process. After you have completed this stage of idea generation, take some time away from the material. Over the next day or two ideas will probably come to you spontaneously either to add details or to change the wording for clarity. During this time you might share your items with others and ask for feedback. Having completed this necessary step, you are now ready to begin the process of formatting your items as either open-ended or closed statements or questions.

Repetitive Why

The classic example of the *repetitive why* process is a young child asking a parent, "Why? . . . Why? . . . Why?" The purpose is to filter from generalities to specifics and to identify appropriate methods to better understand the situation.

The first step is to state your assumption, hypothesis, problem, or understanding of the situation. Next, ask a *why* question. Why do I want to know this? Why is this the current situation? Why does this process work this way? After answering the initial why, ask it again of your answer. Repeat this process several times in order to focus on a specific aspect of the phenomenon you are interested in understanding. For example:

> I want to know if clients receiving outpatient mental health services benefit from treatment.
>
>> *Why?* Because I want to know if I need to modify how I deliver services or provide treatment.
>>
>> *Why?* Because I might be able to match specific treatments and protocols to specific client needs.
>>
>> *Why?* Because clients might recover sooner or demonstrate higher levels of improvement.
>>
>> *Why?* Clients might be able to return to normal life routines, feel better, and demonstrate an improved outlook on life.

This series of questions might suggest using an outcome study or interviews to determine how clients report improvement. This in turn would suggest the type of instrument to design and the questions to ask.

Nominal Group Technique

Brainstorming is the most common method of idea generation. The *nominal group technique* (NGT) builds on the group brainstorming process; it may enhance creativity and therefore the generation of alternatives.

Here are the steps in the NGT:

1. A facilitator (perhaps you) introduces the problem or idea to a small group, typically five to six members and no more than a dozen. Group members brainstorm by writing down all their ideas, without speaking to each other. If using NGT for instrument development, this would be the stage in which group members generate their ideas for items.
2. Each group member shares an idea, which is recorded on a flip chart. After everyone has contributed one idea, the facilitator begins the process again until all the ideas have been recorded. Group members do not critique the ideas, though they may ask for clarification.
3. There are several ways to approach the third step in the process. Each group member can review the list of ideas silently to determine which ideas (or items) he or she feels best reflect the focus of the study (or purpose of the instrument). Or the facilitator can initiate a discussion among group members.

4. Once everyone has had an opportunity to review and reflect on the ideas, the facilitator asks everyone to rank them from most appropriate to the study to least appropriate. The rankings are then recorded on a flip chart.

5. Finally, the results are tabulated to determine which items received the highest ranking, and group members have an opportunity to comment on the selection.

Snowballing or Pyramiding

Snowballing, or *pyramiding*, is another approach to generating ideas in groups. In this approach, group members first generate as many ideas (or items for an instrument) as possible by themselves. Members are then paired together and share their ideas. During this phase there should be considerable give and take as new ideas are generated and the ideas that were generated individually are refined. Next, each group of two is matched with another pair, so that there are now four members in the group to share, generate, and analyze what has been conceptualized up until that point. Depending on the number of individuals involved in the process, more members can be added until everyone has joined into one group.

The advantage of using this technique is that the group members will create a large pool of items and at the same time refine those items. It can be a mentally "exhausting" process, however, given the amount of time and effort people must put into it (Kanji & Asher, 1996).

Delphi Technique

The *Delphi technique* is a method for soliciting the input of content and methodological experts. Because it can be used when group members cannot meet in person. it is helpful when you are working on a project with others at remote sites and when you want to involve participants with a wide range of expertise. To return to our example of the psychologist, he or she could use this technique to obtain feedback from other mental health professionals working at clinics throughout the region and from faculty at a nearby university with expertise in the design and development of instruments.

Using this approach, you would ask a number of colleagues to generate items for a questionnaire. They would send you their written list of items, and in turn you would compile these lists into one list and send it back to the group members. During the second phase, group members analyze the items, and they may add to the list, suggest items for exclusion, or make suggestions for rephrasing particular items. Again they send their recommendations back, and again you compile this information. You may choose to stop at this point and use the information you have, or you may send the compiled information back out for more review and refinement.

You can also use this approach to pretest items when you are the originator. In this case you send items or the first draft of your instrument to a group for review. Then, as before, you use several rounds of review to revise and refine the instrument based on the group members' feedback and recommendations.

Originally, the Delphi technique proved to be rather cumbersome because materials often had to be mailed, and it sometimes took days, weeks, or even months to complete the process. However, with the advent of the Internet, the process can be completed in days using either e-mail or chat rooms, which allow instantaneous exchange of information. One advantage of this approach is that the individuals involved are less likely to be influenced by other group members than they might be if they were meeting in person. Additionally, you may benefit from the contributions of individuals who could not otherwise participate in the process due to time commitments, and distance. As well as being an approach for item generation, the Delphi technique can be a useful process for obtaining peer review of the entire questionnaire prior to sending it out to respondents.

Item Pools and Q Sort

The actual number of items you generate will depend on several factors. For example, you may be attempting to operationalize and measure more than one construct, necessitating multiple items to assess each construct. Depending on the topic of interest, your instrument may consist of fifty or more items. Although lengthy, this may be the only way to adequately obtain the information you require. Additionally, just through the process of idea generation you may have created many more items than you can include in the questionnaire. We suggest that it is desirable to create a large and diverse pool of items to choose from, as it increases the possibility that you can match your informational needs to specific items. Item pools are particularly helpful if you plan to conduct a survey more than once. With the resources of a large item pool you can construct a parallel yet different form of your instrument, or you can include similar yet slightly differently worded items within the same instrument. As discussed previously, this approach is sometimes used to test the reliability and validity of your items, as it allows you to compare the responses to items that attempt to measure the same construct.

At the same time, when you have created many more items than you require, you need a way of determining which items to include, and based on face validity, which are the best for measuring the construct of interest. In addition to some of the methods we have already discussed, such as the nominal group technique, you can use Q sort, an approach to ranking items when there are a large number of them—typically from sixty to ninety. To use Q sort print each of the items on a separate three-by-five-inch card, creating a deck of cards. Then shuffle the deck so the items are distributed randomly. Next, create the criteria on which you want to sort the cards. For example, you might create a scale with these four options: *most definitely include this item, include this item, possibly include this item,* and *definitely do not include this item.* Then have someone (a potential respondent or content expert) sort the deck, placing each card, or item, into one of four piles corresponding to the four criteria. Complete this process with several appropriate individuals. Each person will produce a different Q-sort, reflecting his or her personal perspective of the topic. Tabulating and comparing the results will produce a list of the items that you will most likely want to include in your questionnaire. For an illustration of this process, let's suppose that our tireless psychologist has generated seventy-five items for a questionnaire; however, he or she needs only about half of them. The psychologist asks five colleagues to use Q-sorting to rank items for the questionnaire. Each card with an item has been given a number. The distribution for the first twenty items is shown in Table 5.2.

From this distribution of rankings, it is evident that all four sorters considered some items to be totally unsuitable, for example, items 9, 13, 16, and 19 appear in the row labeled "definitely do not include." Additionally, items 1, 6, and 11 do not appear particularly strong, as they appear in either the "definitely do not include" or "possibly include" rows. In contrast, a number of items appear well suited for the questionnaire; for example, items 2, 3, 4, 7, 8, and 17 appear on all the sorters' choices for either "most definitely include" or "include this item."

A slightly different approach to categorizing the material is to have each sorter select the "best" item and place that card to one side and then select the "worst" item and place it to the other side. Then the sorter picks the next best

TABLE 5.2: Q-SORT DISTRIBUTION.

Criterion	Item Numbers by Sorter			
	1	**2**	**3**	**4**
Most definitely include this item	2,3,5,8,14	2,4,10,11	4,5,7,8,14,	2,3,4,5,8
Include this item	4,7,10,12,17,20	3,7,8,14,17,18	1,2,3,10,11, 17,18,20	1,7,10,12,17,20
Possibly include this item	1,11,15,18,19	1,5,7,12,15,20	6,9,12,19	6,11,14,15,16,18
Definitely do not include this item	6,9,13,16	6,9,13,16,19	13,15,16	9,13,19

and next worst items until the entire pile has been divided. This process is then repeated with the best pile to further weed out items. The final list of items to include would consist of the best items selected by multiple raters. We also examine Q methodology in Chapter Eleven.

Concept Mapping

Concept mapping is a group process, developed by William Trochim (2001), that uses a pictorial display to help participants visualize a topic of interest and organize the stages of implementation. Consequently, it can be an effective approach to focusing a study and identifying approaches for measurement, including the types of instruments that might be needed for assessment.[2]

The concept mapping process has six steps, which incorporate some of the activities we have described previously;

1. *Preparation.* Participants (stakeholders in the process) are identified and take initial steps to focus the topic or project.
2. *Generation.* Group members use brainstorming, nominal group technique, and focus groups to generate statements describing activities related to the project.
3. *Structuring.* Participants sort the statements, using Q-sort or some other rating or ranking process.
4. *Representation.* Participants create visual maps that reflect the relationship between the sorted items. For example, items that are closely related or ranked together will be clustered together on the map. Several maps may be created: for example, one for concepts, one for implementation activities, and another for outcomes.
5. *Interpretation.* The group facilitator works with participants to make sense of the information.
6. *Utilization.* Group members use the concept maps to operationalize programs and develop measures for evaluation.

Operationalizing Constructs

Another approach to generating items is to go back to the original construct and consider how it could be measured. One way to do this is with a *table of specifications,* in which words and phrases associated with various constructs are identified. These words and phrases are then transformed into statements and questions that appear to operationalize the construct.

Table 5.3 is an example of such a table. In this example, we return to the psychologist who has written a statement of purpose (Exhibit 5.1) from which a number of constructs associated with treatment effectiveness have been identified.

TABLE 5.3: TABLE OF SPECIFICATIONS.

Construct	Operationalized	Suggested Item Stems
Accessibility	A. Therapy sessions are scheduled in a timely manner. B. Able to meet with a therapist on short notice.	A. After you contacted the clinic, how long did you have to wait until you were able to meet with a therapist? B.1. If a crisis arose, were you able to meet with your therapist on short notice? B.2. If your therapist was unavailable, were you able to meet with other staff, such as a crisis worker?
Informed	Client is given information about diagnosis, results of evaluation, and recommendations for treatment.	A. To what extent were you informed about the results of testing? B. If you had questions, did your therapist explain things to you using terms that you understood?
Involved	Client is provided opportunity to participate in decision making about treatment.	When you began treatment, did your therapist work with you to develop a treatment plan that addresses your needs?
Responsiveness	A. Staff listen and take into consideration desires of client. B. If the client disagreed with recommended treatment, staff and client jointly explore alternatives.	A. When you first met your therapist, how well did he or she listen to your concerns? B. What treatment procedures were discussed with you?
Utility	A. Client believes that treatment was effective. B. Client can describe how treatment has been helpful.	A. How would you rate the degree to which individual therapy has helped you with your condition/concern ? B. From the following list, please check the ways that you think individual therapy helped? Check all that apply.
Satisfaction	Client would use our services again.	On the following scale, how would you rate your experience with the services provided to you?

They include accessibility (the patient has access to treatment when and where needed); informed, involved, and responsiveness (the patient is an active participant in the treatment process); utility (treatment produces the desired outcomes); and satisfaction (the patient is satisfied with how treatment is provided and the results attained). A construct cannot be observed directly; that is, we cannot see accessibility or utility directly. We can, however, identify measurable characteristics, called *variables*, that represent these constructs.

For example, one of the attributes associated with satisfaction is accessibility—how easy clients find it to avail themselves of treatment services. However, the term *accessibility* may mean different things to different people and also have different meanings in different situations. For some people, accessibility may mean not waiting more than a day or two for an appointment with a therapist. In a crisis situation, however, accessibility may refer to a waiting time of hours or minutes rather than days. For other people, accessibility may mean off-street parking or services within walking distance or convenient public transportation. In the minds of yet other clients, accessibility may mean affordability, as they feel they should not seek services if they cannot afford to pay. Consequently, the construct of accessibility must be further defined and refined to clearly express these alternative meanings. It is important to make these distinctions in order to make sure that items are addressing the concepts and variables the researcher wants to explore.

In a table of specifications, you can stipulate different ways of describing and ultimately measuring a variable. This in turn will suggest how you might phrase items. As reflected in Table 5.3, the psychologist has identified a number of constructs associated with the larger concept of client satisfaction. For example, one aspect of accessibility is timeliness in obtaining a meeting with a therapist. This suggests a questionnaire item eliciting information about waiting times, as well as a possible format for the item, such as an alternative response set (as described in Chapter Nine).

Exercise, Hobbies, Relaxation, and Dreaming

Obviously the development of your instrument must come out of a focused process of thinking about and writing down your purpose and your ideas. However, we want to also suggest that the process can continue and can be enhanced by engaging in other activities that foster creative thinking. For example, during aerobic exercises, such as running, jogging, and walking, the level of endorphins in the brain increases, creating what is known as a *runner's high*. Many individuals report that they think more clearly and experience more spontaneous idea generation when engaged in these physical activities. For others, idea generation may occur when engaged in a hobby. In particular, idea generation seems more fluid when we are alone (that is, not subject to distractions) and our minds are occupied in a pleasurable task.

Studies in the use of relaxation techniques suggest that these activities too can enhance creativity. Activities such as deep breathing, muscle relaxation, guided imagery, yoga, transcendental meditation, and tai chi appear to help us push out the thoughts associated with daily living that may produce stress. As we clear our minds of these details, other thoughts may arise or "float to the surface." If you begin thinking about your project during these periods of deep relaxation, you may find yourself generating many ideas spontaneously. Relaxation appears to also provide a fertile mental environment for processing information and perceiving relationships. Problem solving also appears to be enhanced, and you may find you are able to organize information more lucidly during these periods.

We include dreaming here, as many people state that some of their most creative moments have occurred during dream states. Research suggests that obtaining adequate sleep is essential for creative thinking, sharper memory, and improved problem solving (McCall, 2004), and dreams do appear to allow us to release inhibitions that can impede creativity. However, dreams are often difficult to remember, and unless your project is producing a particular amount of stress, it is unlikely that your dreams will focus on that subject. Still, one never knows, and you may not want to discount ideas that come to you during these periods. The period just before or after waking, when you are in a semiawake stage, is also a fertile time for creative thinking. During this stage it is possible to induce thoughts and still be in a state where your mind is capable of a free flow of ideas.

An important aspect of all of these processes is that you are continuing to ruminate on your statement of purpose and on statements and questions that you have generated for your questionnaire. You might, for example, try to visualize one of your respondents answering a questionnaire item. Will it appear ambiguous, or is it stated succinctly? Will potential respondents be offended by any of the wording? Will the item really capture the information you are interested in, or should it be rewritten? Consider that each time you examine and refine material you have created, the closer it comes to providing the information you really seek.

Summary

The French painter Degas was not limited in his artistic and creative expression. One of his favorite subjects was ballerinas, and he painted them in oils, drew them in pastels, and cast them in bronze. He used his creative talents to visualize these varied works and his technical skills to take them from concept to tangible object.

We contend that instrument construction, like painting, is both a creative and a technical process. In this chapter we have explored the creative side of instrument design, which begins with the development of a statement of purpose. Your work on this statement, like a draft on an artist's sketch pad, is a way of visualizing what you want to accomplish. It clarifies and focuses your efforts. We have also described several creative methods to spawn ideas that will in turn generate statements and questions that will serve as foundations for measurable items. Finally, systematic inquiry, such as a literature review, produces a structured approach to thinking about what you want to know and how that influences the development of your instrument and items.

Instrument 5.A: Employee Questionnaire

In this closing example we discuss how reviewing the literature and meeting with stakeholders to determine their informational needs assisted in the development of a questionnaire (Instrument 5.A).

Organizations that practice quality management routinely seek out the opinions of those who make use of and those who provide their services or products. The information derived from evaluating employee perceptions of working conditions can be used to assess needs, to improve processes and seek solutions to problems where possible—and ultimately to create a workplace where employees can successfully achieve the organization's goals and mission.

One of the authors assisted an organization in the development of a questionnaire to assess employee perceptions of working conditions and environment. After pretesting, the final version of this instrument included fifty closed-ended items using a Likert scale and one open-ended question.

To construct the questionnaire, the author met with the agency head to determine his informational needs and also examined the literature on workplace quality. Organization survey instruments in the public domain were identified and served as a resource for creating an item pool. Specific items were then modified and selected based on their relevance to information that management was interested in obtaining. The approach also used two theories of organization behavior as a framework, Herzberg's motivation-hygiene theory (Steers & Porter, 1983) and the Gallup Organization's study of "great workplaces" (Buckingham & Coffman, 1999). This framework, outlined in the following lists, assisted in constructing the instrument and in analyzing the data within a theoretical context.

Motivation-hygiene theory. Steers and Porter (1983) found that employees respond to motivation factors in different ways. Intrinsic motivators tend to make employees satisfied with their work and work environment. Enhancing motivation factors, through such approaches as job redesign and matching interests and skills to work tasks, can increase job satisfaction. Hygiene factors are things that employees dislike about their work and work environment. Addressing these factors may make the employees less dissatisfied, but it does not enhance their overall satisfaction with the job. For example, if employees are given a pay raise, they may no longer be dissatisfied, but they may not be more satisfied with their work or the contribution they are able to make. According to Herzberg, to enhance job satisfaction, organizations have to deal with the job content: challenge, opportunity, responsibility, recognition, personal growth, and so on.

Motivation (Satisfiers)	Hygiene (Dissatisfiers)
• Company and administrative policies • Supervision • Work conditions • Salary • Interpersonal relations	• Achievement • Recognition • Work itself • Responsibility • Advancement

• *Great workplace study.* Some years ago the Gallup Organization initiated a multi-year research project to try to define what makes for a great workplace (Buckingham & Coffman, 1999). It was important that the organizations studied were producing positive outcomes for their business. Therefore the study looked at organizations that were able to demonstrate results in four areas: employee retention, customer satisfaction, productivity, and profitability. The researchers found that there are no great companies; there are only great workgroups. This finding supports the notion that teamwork is important. In other words, people derive considerable personal and professional satisfaction from their work as a result of the relationships they have with coworkers and their ability to accomplish results working as a member of a team. In turn, that satisfaction translates into better work performance outcomes. The researchers also found twelve dimensions that consistently describe a great workgroup for the individual:

1. I know what is expected of me at work.
2. I have the materials and equipment I need to do my work right.
3. At work, I have the opportunity to do what I do best every day.
4. In the last 7 days, I have received recognition or praise for doing good work.
5. My supervisor, or someone at work, seems to care about me as a person.
6. There is someone at work who encourages my development.
7. At work, my opinions seem to count.
8. The mission/purpose of my company makes me feel my job is important.
9. My associates (fellow employees) are committed to doing quality work.

10. I have a best friend at work.
11. In the last six months, someone at work has talked to me about my progress.
12. This last year, I have had opportunities at work to learn and grow.

After the survey was administered, analysis of the data indicated that from the perspective of motivation-hygiene theory, the work itself could be rewarding and fulfilling. Consistent with the Gallup study findings, employees overwhelmingly identified staff relationships as an important part of working at in the organization. For example, in response to the open-ended question, one employee noted that a "sense of family" existed, and many employees commented on the friendly environment. Staff felt supported by their coworkers, identified themselves as being a part of a team, and felt that team members worked well together to provide quality services. Having the framework of these two theories, or models, of organizational behavior helped the author in focusing the purpose of the study, designing the instrument, analyzing the data, and reporting the study findings.

INSTRUMENT 5.A: EMPLOYEE QUESTIONNAIRE.

Dear Fellow Employee:

From time to time it is helpful to evaluate our organization. For that reason, I want to encourage you to complete the attached questionnaire. The findings from this survey will help us understand how we perceive our working environment and working conditions. Where possible, we can use this information to improve processes and seek solutions to problems.

It takes 10–15 minutes to complete the questionnaire. If possible, it helps to find a place free from distractions. Please fill in each oval completely with a dark pencil or pen.

As with any survey, the response rate helps to determine if the results are reliable and useful. For example, we cannot be sure if the results are an accurate reflection of most employees' beliefs and opinions if only a third of the staff complete the questionnaire. Therefore, please take a few minutes to complete the survey.

Once we have tallied the data, we will post the results on the agency's intranet. Thank you for participating in this process.

Sincerely,

Agency Director

Employee Survey

The purpose of this survey is to allow agency employees an opportunity to comment on current working conditions. For each statement, please indicate whether you agree or disagree by darkening each oval completely. This is an anonymous questionnaire. **DO NOT** write your name on this document.

Item	Strongly Disagree	Mostly Disagree	Mostly Agree	Strongly Agree	Not Sure
1. I am confident in the leadership of this agency.	○	○	○	○	○
2. I am proud to be an employee of this agency.	○	○	○	○	○
3. Temperatures in the building are comfortable.	○	○	○	○	○
4. I clearly understand the agency's organizational structure.	○	○	○	○	○
5. I receive the training I need to do my job well.	○	○	○	○	○
6. I see myself working at the agency for at least the next two years.	○	○	○	○	○
7. I feel comfortable in discussing problems with the agency director.	○	○	○	○	○
8. Parking is adequate.	○	○	○	○	○
9. I have a say in decisions and actions that impact my work.	○	○	○	○	○
10. I usually hear about important changes from my supervisor rather than secondhand (rumors or coworkers).	○	○	○	○	○
11. I would recommend the agency as a good place to work.	○	○	○	○	○
12. I feel that the contribution I make is valued.	○	○	○	○	○
13. It is safe to express my opinion to my immediate supervisor.	○	○	○	○	○
14. Opportunities are provided for staff to help improve working conditions at this agency.	○	○	○	○	○
15. My job is interesting to me.	○	○	○	○	○
16. I consider my workload reasonable.	○	○	○	○	○
17. I can depend on my coworkers.	○	○	○	○	○
18. I am given sufficient latitude to do my job.	○	○	○	○	○

19. I have adequate time to complete most tasks assigned to me.	O	O	O	O	O
20. Managers/supervisors are flexible in scheduling work hours.	O	O	O	O	O
21. I know what is expected of me at work.	O	O	O	O	O
22. I have the necessary materials and equipment to do my job.	O	O	O	O	O
23. I feel safe working at this agency.	O	O	O	O	O
24. Management is good at seeking long-term solutions, rather than just patching or making "quick fixes" to problems.	O	O	O	O	O
25. My department/team periodically takes time to rethink the way we do things.	O	O	O	O	O
26. I am satisfied with the response I get from my supervisor when I ask for assistance or help with a problem.	O	O	O	O	O
27. Conflict between staff affects the services we provide.	O	O	O	O	O
28. The building is free of obnoxious odors.	O	O	O	O	O
29. Policies and procedures are applied consistently among employees.	O	O	O	O	O
30. I am in a position that is a good fit for me.	O	O	O	O	O
31. I get a feeling of personal satisfaction from my work at this agency.	O	O	O	O	O
32. Communication between top management (director and department heads) and employees is good.	O	O	O	O	O
33. My immediate supervisor distributes the work fairly.	O	O	O	O	O
34. My department/treatment team works well together.	O	O	O	O	O
35. The supervision I receive from my immediate supervisor helps me accomplish my duties.	O	O	O	O	O
36. Agency management does a good job of addressing problems.	O	O	O	O	O
37. The director and department heads are highly visible.	O	O	O	O	O
38. I have received adequate training on the use information technology that I use for my job at this agency.	O	O	O	O	O

39. Agency management responds to problems in a timely manner.	○	○	○	○	○
40. I am encouraged to be innovative in my work.	○	○	○	○	○
41. There is a climate that supports and recognizes the importance of learning.	○	○	○	○	○
42. I have a coworker I can confide in.	○	○	○	○	○
43. I am able to perform my duties with a minimum of supervision.	○	○	○	○	○
44. My immediate supervisor acknowledges good job performance on a regular basis.	○	○	○	○	○
45. I am kept informed of new policies or changes to existing policies and procedures.	○	○	○	○	○
46. The duties and responsibilities of my position were clearly explained to me when I started my job.	○	○	○	○	○
47. My coworkers work as a team to get things done.	○	○	○	○	○
48. I am aware of the agency's mission.	○	○	○	○	○
49. I am satisfied with my current schedule/ work hours.	○	○	○	○	○
50. I believe that management will try to resolve concerns raised by this survey.	○	○	○	○	○

Additional comments:

Please complete by Friday, January XX, 20XX. Thank you for participating in this survey.

Endnotes

1. Computer terminals and small desktop units are now being marketed that allow data to be recorded and analyzed electronically. Instead of a paper-and-pencil form, these computerized survey instruments have an LED or LCD screen. They take the respondent through a menu of choices, and selections are made by using a simple numeric keypad. The unit stores the data until they can be downloaded into a computer for analysis, or it may be connected directly to a mainframe computer hundreds or thousands of miles away.

2. For an in-depth explanation of concept mapping and how it has been used, visit William Trochim's Web site: http://www.socialresearchmethods.net.

Key Concepts and Terms

brainstorming

concept mapping

Delphi technique

idiographic approach

input

item pool

literature review

nominal group technique

nomothetic approach

operationalization

outcome

output

process

program theory

pyramiding

Q-methodology

Q-sort

repetitive why

snowballing

table of specifications

variable

CHAPTER SIX

PRETESTING

In this chapter we will

- Illustrate problems that can occur when administering an instrument and that can be addressed through pretesting.
- Explain how pretesting helps you focus the purpose of your study and the selection of an instrument.
- Describe how to pretest during the development phase to address potential problems that might appear later.
- Describe how to pilot-test the instrument to address problems that might occur during administration.

Instrument construction is an iterative process as it involves constant revision and refinement. To turn to our art metaphor, N. C. Wyeth, the noted American illustrator, always had several paintings in various stages of completion. Some were just drawings on canvas, awaiting the application of paint; others were closer to completion. Like many painters, Wyeth often went back to a painting to make corrections and improvements. Through each reworking the painting came nearer to his vision of what it should look like and what it should convey. Ultimately, Wyeth, as a creative artist, had to reach a point at which he was satisfied with his product and ready to share it with others.

In this chapter we describe the activities that make it likely that your instrument will fulfill its designated purpose and unlikely that respondents or raters will misunderstand it, possibly making the data you collect difficult to interpret or use. These actions are collectively referred to as *pretesting* (also referred to as *field testing* and *pilot testing*). You will want to know if the items and the instructions make sense, are unambiguous, and are understandable by those who will complete them; for example, pretesting can determine whether items are complex, are wordy, or incorporate inappropriate language. Once you determine how long it takes respondents to complete your instrument, you can make decisions about its length and format. Pretesting also produces data you can use to demonstrate validity and reliability, which ultimately helps you ascertain whether the instrument is producing the desired information.

Unlike an artist, who often works alone with little input from others, during the process of developing and pretesting the instrument you should obtain input from a variety of stakeholders, such as the individuals who commissioned the study, content experts, and potential respondents. Even Wyeth, who completed works of art for his personal satisfaction, more often produced paintings on commission and had to appease those who were paying for his artwork. In addition, your findings might be used to determine whether a product or service should be marketed, whether a program should continue to receive funding, or whether an individual is eligible to receive financial support. In any of these situations the information obtained through an instrument of your design may play a large part in a decision-making process with implications for yourself and others. The instrument must also stand up to external scrutiny. For example, if you are a student developing a questionnaire for an academic research project, your professors will want to know how rigorously you followed established guidelines for instrument construction.

Pretesting should be conducted throughout the instrument construction process: as you are formulating the purpose of the project and the instrument needed for data collection, while you are creating individual items, and after you have organized the items into a complete instrument. Although this pretesting adds to the time it takes to develop an instrument, it provides valuable information about instrument utility and the trustworthiness of the information produced, and it will lead you to correct errors that might otherwise cause problems during the final administration.

Where Problems Are Likely to Occur

Studies have identified a variety of ways in which respondents and observers may fail to understand and respond as instrument designers intend. For example, for a study of respondent understanding of item wording, Belson (1981) created a questionnaire with a variety of problematic items. He noted that "during the initial administration of them, a watch was kept for any expression of difficulty or uncertainty on the part of the respondent. There was virtually no such evidence. On the other hand, the subsequent testing of the 29 questions provided abundant evidence that each had in fact been subject to a great deal of misunderstanding" (p. 5). And as discussed in Chapter Four, a study by Gendall (1994) revealed that some respondents to a questionnaire on a sensitive subject (AIDS) acknowledged that they *purposely* reinterpreted a question and that for them the intended meaning of the item was irrelevant. Therefore we should not take users' perceptions of a study for granted, nor can we simply assume that an instrument will produce the information we seek.

Thus problems can occur in response to conditions intrinsic to the respondent or rater as well as factors related to instrument design. The respondent or rater must have a reading level adequate for the instrument's language and terminology and he or she must have sufficient cognitive abilities and experience to make sense of any graphic symbols used. Beyond basic literacy, the respondent must be able to comprehend and interpret the meaning of the item as intended. He or she may also be called on to bring prior experience, personal judgment, and memory of information to bear in answering an item, which may result in variability and opportunities for error.

Following are some issues the respondent or rater brings to the process that you should take into consideration when designing and pretesting an instrument (Foddy, 1993; U.S. General Accounting Office, 1986):

- Responses may be affected by the limitations of human memory, such as the amount of time that has elapsed between events and the amount of competing information that has been presented to a respondent. Respondents may skip an item when they cannot remember the requested information, or worse, they might fabricate a response, producing invalid results. For example, in a study where people were asked the same factual questions eight to ten days apart, it was found that 10 percent of them changed their age by a year or more between interviews (a result not due to all of them having had birthdays in the interim) (Palmer, 1943).
- The relationship between what respondents say they do and how they actually behave is not always strong. For example, people polled about whom they intend to vote for in the next election may subsequently either vote for another candidate or not vote at all.
- Respondents' attitudes, beliefs, opinions, habits, and interests often seem extraordinarily unstable. In one study (Gritching, 1986), 17 percent of respondents changed their position during the course of the interview.

- Answers to earlier questions can affect respondents' answers to later questions. Respondents may try to make answers congruent with responses to previous items even though the result may not be what a respondent really believes.
- Respondents may often answer questions when they actually know very little about the topic. One study (Schuman & Presser, 1981) found that 25 percent of respondents rated items *don't know* when that option was provided but gave a substantive response when the *don't know* option was removed.
- The cultural context in which a question is presented often has an impact on the way respondents interpret and answer it. Moreover, researchers are not always be aware of cultural issues that are present or should be accounted for in their instrument design.
- Rather than describing their actual beliefs and behaviors, respondents may choose responses that make them look good to others or that reflect their own biased perception of themselves. For example, a manager may rate his or her skills highly whereas subordinates may offer an altogether different assessment. The influence of *social desirability* may result in overreporting of socially acceptable behavior and underreporting of socially undesirable behavior (behaviors that might be construed as illegal, unethical, or immoral).

In addition to the effects of these factors that respondents and raters bring to the process, factors associated with instrument design and format can lead to problems that can be identified and corrected during the pretesting phase. These problems might involve wording, syntax, format of the item stem and response set, order of items within the instrument, and clarity of instructions. For example, words may convey more than your intended meaning to your respondents. Although you might assume that instrument raters or respondents will understand your meaning, this is not always a given. Consider an item that asks respondents to evaluate spanking as a means of disciplining a child. To some the term may suggest a slap on the hands when a toddler tries to touch a hot stove, whereas to others the term may convey stricter forms of discipline, such as spanking with a belt. The meaning of any word lies within the respondent as much as within the instrument constructor.

A related problem is that respondents may not bring the same meaning that you do to the terminology in the response set. Does *always* mean every time or almost every time? Does *never* mean not at all or fewer than two times? Or they may find the choices inadequate, as described in the case at the end of this chapter. Here are some additional factors related to instrument design (Foddy, 1993; U.S. General Accounting Office, 1986):

- Small changes in wording sometimes produce major changes in the distribution of responses. For example, changing a positive statement to a negative statement may result in a different response. A more typical example is changing the context in which a question is posed. In a 2003 poll conducted by the Gallup Organization, 74 percent of respondents said they favored the death penalty. However, this rate decreased to 53 percent when respondents were given a choice between the death penalty and imprisonment without the possibility of parole (Newport, 2004, p. 225).
- Changing the order in which response options are presented sometimes affects respondents' choices. Sometimes this is accidental; for example, if a respondent anticipates a Likert scale that flows from *strongly agree* to *strongly disagree*, he or she may select the first option even when the scale has been reversed and *strongly disagree* is presented first.
- The item format may affect how the respondent answers the question. Responses to open-ended questions may be quite different from responses to selection items addressing the same content.
- Problems with navigating the instrument may lead respondents to skip an item, resulting in missing data.
- Questions that respondents find embarrassing, threatening, or highly personal, such as questions about sexual activity or medical conditions, can result in low response rates. Respondents may also be reluctant to reveal personal information, such as financial information, sometimes worrying that it might be stolen or misused.
- Respondents may skip items they feel are irrelevant to the topic explored in the questionnaire. (This is one reason to assess the content validity.)
- Items that require the respondent or rater to make computations, search for information, or otherwise spend a considerable amount of time coming up with a response can result in low response rates, as can instruments that are (or appear) lengthy.

Given this list of potential problems the challenge of creating a workable instrument may appear daunting. This is why pretesting is an essential aspect of instrument construction, as it provides an opportunity to identify and correct these problems prior to administering the instrument. Pretesting is a continuous process that begins when you are conceptualizing the project, continues throughout the development phase, and concludes just prior to administering the instrument. Over time a number of approaches have been developed to facilitate pretesting to improve the quality of our instruments and to minimize the possibility that respondents will have difficulty completing them.

Initial Pretesting: Focusing the Study

As discussed in the previous chapter, it is important to obtain agreement on the purpose of the study early on, as articulating the purpose can sharpen your thinking about the concepts you want to address, and that in turn can guide you toward particular methods of data collection and analysis and ultimately the type of instrument needed. This stage of pretesting also helps you to establish construct validity as you are defining the variables of interest. In this stage you should, as described in Chapter Five, complete a literature review, discuss the project with the people who will use the information, and also discuss it with potential respondents. This section focuses in more detail on the process of gathering feedback from the potential information users and respondents.

Individual Interviews and Focus Groups

Individual interviews and focus groups are the two methods that can be used to narrow the purpose of a study and to gain feedback while developing a draft of the instrument. For example, if you are to conduct a program evaluation, you could meet with program staff individually to determine their information needs and involve them in deciding on the program aspects to be evaluated. By using open-ended questions you can solicit information on a broad number of topics and obtain in-depth and thoughtful responses. You will also obtain more personal accounts of the situation. The disadvantages are that interviews can be lengthy and take considerable time to conduct, you may be limited in the number of people you can meet with, and interviews produce a lot of information in the form of notes or recordings, which must then be analyzed.

The other approach would be to use a focus group. A focus group is composed of seven to ten individuals who typically are unknown to each other but who share common characteristics relevant to the topic of interest. The classic use of a focus group is to test new products with potential customers. Focus groups are also often created when an organization is conducting a needs assessment that might lead to a new program; in this case the group might include both potential program users and program providers.

The advantages of using a focus group are that you obtain multiple perspectives; the group process engenders spontaneity, discussion, and feedback.; the facilitator can interact directly with participants and probe as needed; and the process can be efficient and cost effective. Disadvantages are the time it may take to get the group organized and arrange the meeting, the possibility that group will produce a large amount of information of which only a small segment is relevant to the project, and the need for a facilitator who is competent in leading and managing groups. Group members may ramble, may be shy and fail to actively participate, or may attempt to dominate the discussion. The group leader must have the skills to keep all members on task, engaged in the discussion, and respectful of others. (If you are acting as the group moderator or facilitator, you may find yourself actively thinking during the group process about the information that is being shared and how it might shape the study. This can make it difficult to concentrate on the process of leading the group, so you may want to have a co-facilitator.)

When conducting the focus group, the facilitator should clarify the group's purpose for the participants and establish ground rules, especially rules that ensure individuals are allowed to express themselves without being interrupted. The key to obtaining useful information is to use open-ended questions. This gives participants an opportunity to reflect on an issue and then provide feedback based on their personal knowledge and experience. The facilitator should ensure that all group members who wish to are given an opportunity to join each discussion; this might mean pausing—for five, ten, or fifteen seconds or longer before moving on. Facilitators will also need to use a number of other group techniques, such as repeating or reframing a response (putting it into their own words) to obtain clarity and ensure that there is shared meaning. Although there need be no time limit per se, most focus groups last forty-five minutes to an hour, or until the facilitator recognizes that group members are fatigued by the process.

During the group process it is helpful for the facilitator to occasionally summarize what has been discussed. It may also be helpful at the end of the session to write some of the main ideas and recommendations on a blackboard or flipchart and ask the group to reflect on this material. It is important to make a record of the group meeting so that you have documentation to refer back to. This might take the form of notes or, as Fowler (1995) suggests, videotapes or audiotapes of the session. (Be sure to obtain written permission from all participants whenever an audiovisual device is used to create a record.)

After concluding the focus group, review your notes or recordings, reflect on the feedback, and continue to share your thoughts and ideas about the study with others.

Review by Content Area Experts

During this phase you can enhance content validity by reviewing the project with program staff, colleagues, stakeholders, and evaluators who can serve as content experts. Ask them to identify attributes representative of the topic of interest. Use this feedback to develop an exhaustive list of ways the topic can be operationalized and to determine the extent that the instrument taps into the domain(s) of interest. You can also use this information to prepare a table of specifications, as described in Chapter Five. The table of specifications should derive from your literature review, knowledge of the subject, and feedback from content experts.

Continue to Obtain Feedback and Revise the Project If Necessary

This is the stage in which you should draft a one-page summary of your project to share with others, as recommended in Chapter Five. As we have been emphasizing, this process of clarifying the purpose and focus of the study also helps you conceptualize the types of questions that you may need to ask. For example, if you plan to conduct a longitudinal study, where data will be collected repeatedly over an extended period of time, you will want to be sure that you use the same item, with exactly the same wording, for each administration. The Gallup Organization, for example, has done this with its item about supporting or opposing the death penalty, which has kept the same wording since it was first posed in the 1930s. By asking the same question repeatedly, Gallup has found that public opinion has changed over time. Gallup has also asked the same president job approval rating question for over fifty years. The results indicate that presidents, regardless of political party, average a 55 percent approval rating most of the time, a figure that changes primarily when there are major national and world events (Newport, 2004).

Pretesting During Development

One of the ways an artist ensures that a painting is balanced is to look at the initial composition in a mirror. The reversed image makes it easier to see distortions, which the artist can then correct before moving forward with the painting. Similarly, it is in your development stage that you can use feedback to refine the preliminary drafts of your instrument. During this phase, you will share the initial draft with others, including those who will make use of the information provided by the instrument. This stage of pretesting has been referred to as *pre-field testing* (American Statistical Association, 1997) and as *laboratory testing* (DeMaio, Rothgeb, & Hess, 1998), as it may involve review of individual items without the context of a formatted instrument, or an early draft of your instrument before the formatting and relative locations of items are determined.

It is not uncommon for a workgroup to develop an instrument. A workgroup provides a setting for the exchange of ideas and allows you to obtain rapid feedback from coworkers. However, it is also important during this phase of development to ensure that you are also seeking the advice and consultation of individuals who are not members of the workgroup, such as stakeholders and content experts.

At this juncture it is also important to retain copies of each version of the instrument so that you have a record of all changes. We recommend that you keep notes, maintain a record of all correspondence, and possibly keep a journal of the process. This will become a history of the development of the instrument, allowing you to report on the changes made and to have an overview of instrument progress. Journaling is useful because it encourages you to document not only factual transactions but your emotional response as well, making instrument construction a learning process. For example, reviewing a project journal several years after the project has concluded, you might find that you were frustrated by a particular part of the process and with that insight you may be able to circumvent the same problem in developing a new instrument.

Specific reviewing activities during the development stage include the following.

Read and Reread the Items and Read the Items Aloud

You should be the first and principal reviewer of your work. Continually rereading items and reading them aloud can help you identify problems in wording, sentence structure, and the like. For example, as you read an item aloud you may find that it does not flow coherently or that a technical term makes it difficult to comprehend an intended meaning. This is also the time when you should be comparing your items to the guidelines for item construction presented in Chapters Eight, Nine, Ten, and Eleven. As you follow this practice, you will find yourself continually refining the wording and structure of each item.

Review by Content Area Experts

You should continue to check with individuals who are knowledgeable about your topic and who can tell you how well the items tap into that subject area. They may suggest item wording and comment on how relevant an item is to the topic of interest, perhaps suggesting items to add and items to exclude.

Review by Instrument Construction Experts

Individuals with expertise in instrument construction might be faculty at research centers, staff at private polling organizations, management consultants, evaluators, and individuals who have taken classes in instrument construction and survey research design. They can provide feedback about the construction of individual items as well as the organization and design of the entire instrument.

Review by Individuals with Expertise in Writing

English is a complex language with many formal rules associated with spelling and grammar. Language problems can be reduced by having someone with expertise in writing review the instrument, such as a teacher of English or a copyeditor. If you use word processing software to develop your instrument, make use of the thesaurus and the grammar and spell-checking features.

Review by Potential Users

Potential respondents who participate in this review should reflect the target audience for your instrument. If you are developing a political poll, then anyone of voting age could serve as a reviewer. If your questionnaire will be administered to elementary school teachers, then you will want to limit the review to that population. Potential observers can readily identify problems they might have putting an instrument designed for them into use. One of the authors worked with a group using archival data to examine the relationship between substance abuse and mental illness among hospitalized juveniles. The caseworkers who would be extracting the data were also part of the process of constructing and pretesting the instrument and defining the terminology to be used, and this involvement enhanced their interrater reliability.

We suggest that you use focus groups and interviews in this instrument development phase, as you did in pretesting the study purpose. Here are some specific helpful techniques:

Focus groups can be very effective during the initial phase of instrument construction (Czaja, 1998). One useful approach is to provide a draft of the instrument for group members to review and discuss *prior* to meeting with you. Also, Fowler (1995) points out that focus group composition is a consideration at this stage. If your instrument will be administered to elementary school teachers, for example, you will need to consider the grade levels addressed; whether public or private schools, or both, will be covered; and whether school administrators should be involved (that is, will the teachers you invite be comfortable or guarded in providing responses if an administrator is present). An advantage of using focus groups is that members will often volunteer information with little or no prompting, and feedback from one participant may trigger suggestions from others. Focus groups can provide meaningful development information at a number of levels, including the wording of items and whether the items were easy or difficult to understand. If participants do not bring it up on their own, they should be queried about the response sets and problems they might have had using them in relation to the items. If they question you about why you are conducting the study and what you hope to achieve, take it as an opportunity to continue to focus the purpose and function of the study and the instrument you are creating.

Intensive individual or cognitive interviewing can take several forms at this stage. One approach is to administer a draft of the instrument and have the respondent or reviewer make notes as he or she completes it. Then, *after* the individual has completed the entire instrument, use those notes as the basis for a discussion and review. Another approach is to present each item separately to individual respondents, asking them to "think aloud and verbalize their thought process as they interpret the survey questions and formulate their answers" (DeMaio et al., 1998, p. 52). Another approach is to have the individual read the entire questionnaire aloud as you compare what he or she reads to what is printed. Omissions (of words, phrases, or even entire sentences, such as instructions that users might skip), alterations, and additions might change your meaning and intent. It is important to ask the respondent or reviewer about these changes in wording, as they may indicate difficulty with the instrument or verbal problems that occur naturally when reading aloud (Gerber & Wellens, 1995).

During these individual interviews, you might sit quietly allowing the respondent to reflect and think aloud or you can ask probing questions to stimulate discussion. DeMaio et al. (1998) suggest holding twenty or slightly fewer interviews; however, in our experience this is not always possible. Depending on the availability of others to review your work, you may even ask a work colleague, a spouse, or a personal acquaintance to serve as a reviewer.

As you examine the instrument and its items with reviewers your primary focus should be on how well they understood the items; for example, did they interpret the meaning of words, phrases, and items as you intended? Also, did they identify any spelling or grammatical errors or have difficulty with the way a sentence was constructed, finding it too wordy, for example? This is also a good time to check the fit between items and response choices, as reviewers can tell you if they had difficulty responding to an item because of the response alternatives provided. For example, Schwarz (1999, 2001) noted that the format of a frequency scale can influence a respondent's estimate of the frequency of his or her own behavior. When respondents were presented with a low-frequency scale (up to one-half hour to more than two-and-a-half hours) to estimate the number of hours they viewed television, only 16.2 percent indicated they watched television for more than two-and-a-half hours. However, when presented with a high-frequency scale (up to two-and-a-half hours to more than four-and-a-half hours), 37.5 percent of respondents indicated they watched more than two-and-a-half hours of television. Thus it is important to pretest how the response scale might influence respondents' judgment and selections.

Also, if your instrument draft is relatively complete, with a purpose statement, instructions, and so forth, then reviewers may be able to provide preliminary feedback about how easy it was to understand the directions, how well items flowed from one to another, and whether the order of the questions influenced their responses.

Pretesting and analyzing the feedback can be a satisfying and enlightening process, comparable to unraveling a mystery. You are interested in learning how individuals make sense of the questions you are posing and what problems they have using the instrument so that you can improve its quality and utility. Some researchers have even made this quest the focus of their careers. Studies they, and others, have conducted have produced information that has led to the guidelines we are presenting in this book.

Pilot-Testing the Instrument

Ultimately, you will want to try out your instrument under the same conditions you plan to use for the formal administration. This gives you an opportunity to observe the time it takes to complete the instrument, problems with interrater reliability, the influence of environmental conditions, and any problems respondents continue to have with item wording and format. If you plan to use a mail survey, you could mail the questionnaire to a small sample. This will tell you about the average time it takes to prepare and mail the questionnaire and for respondents to complete it and mail it back to you. If the instrument will be available on the Internet, then you will want to explore how the technology helps or hinders the respondent in completing the instrument. If the instrument is to be completed by independent raters, pretesting can identify problems raters might experience under real-life conditions.

As in the laboratory stage of pretesting, during this phase you will want to talk to respondents or raters who have pilot-tested the instrument. This involves a structured approach to interviewing and debriefing. The first step is to have respondents or raters complete the questionnaire; raters should pilot-test the instrument in the environment in which it is intended to be used. For example, if the instrument is designed for teacher observation of students, then it should be field-tested in a classroom setting.

Note that we have referred to respondents and raters in the plural as you will want to have more than one reviewer. The actual number will depend on the type of instrument and the resources available to you. For a questionnaire that will eventually be administered to a sample numbering in the hundreds or thousands, you will want twenty to fifty individuals (possibly more) for pretesting. If you have constructed an observation instrument that will be completed by ten or fewer raters, then you should try to meet with all ten. Although there are no hard and fast rules, obviously the more feedback you can obtain, given available resources, the more information you have to work with during this pilot-test phase of instrument construction.

In addition to using the interviews for feedback, you can consider the completed instruments themselves as artifacts for analysis. You should review each document for erasures, scratched out responses, and uncompleted items, all of which might indicate difficulty in comprehending an item's meaning or format. For example, you might find that some respondents have written in "NA" because they felt that was the best alternative even though it was not one of the choices. This type of information also introduces a direction for questioning during the debriefing process.

Exhibit 6.1 presents a series of questions that should be addressed when debriefing respondents or raters after they have completed the instrument. As in the development stage of pretesting, you will want to know if people had problems understanding the meaning of items; however, in this phase you should also solicit suggestions for improving the instrument in its totality and for resolving problems with instrument administration and completion. For example, if the questionnaire was posted on the Internet, did respondents have any problems accessing the Web site or moving through the instrument? Regardless of mode of administration, you should also seek feedback about the instrument's organization and flow, such as the order of items and placement of instructions.

EXHIBIT 6.1: QUESTIONS TO ADDRESS WHEN PILOT-TESTING THE QUESTIONNAIRE.

Administer a copy of the questionnaire to an individual or small group of reviewers, who may be colleagues, personal friends, students, potential respondents, and the like. Allow each reviewer as much time as he or she needs to complete the instrument. When the reviewer has finished, obtain answers to the following questions:

- Was each set of directions clear (that is, the general directions at the beginning of the questionnaire and any subsequent directions provided in the body of the instrument)?
- Were there any spelling or grammatical problems? Were any items difficult to read due to sentence length, choice of words, or special terminology?

- How did the reviewer interpret each item? What did each question mean to them?
- Did the reviewer experience problems with the item format(s), or does the reviewer have suggestions for alternative formats?
- Were the response alternatives appropriate to each item?
- What problems did the reviewer encounter as a result of the organization of the instrument, such as how items flowed?
- On average, how long did it take to complete? What was the longest time and what was the shortest time it took to complete the instrument?
- For Web-based instruments, did the respondent encounter any problems accessing the instrument from a computer or navigating the instrument once it was accessed?
- Did any of the reviewers express concern about the length of the instrument, or did they report problems with fatigue due to the time it took to complete?
- What was the reviewer's overall reaction to the questionnaire?
- Did they have any concerns about confidentiality or how the questionnaire would be used?
- Did they have any other concerns?
- What suggestions do they have for making the questionnaire or individual items easier to understand and complete?

After reviewing the responses, answer the following questions for yourself:

- What would you like to change about your questionnaire?
- How might you change it?

Although a realistic landscape painting may evoke different moods and feelings from different observers, we would expect these observers to agree on the subject matter. This analogy applies to instrument construction at this stage of pretesting as we would expect different responses to an item but agreement across respondents on what the item means. However, what should we make of the item that evokes a broad range of responses? Does this mean that it is poorly worded and being misinterpreted? Although that possibility exists and should be explored as part of the pretesting process, it is important to keep in mind that for many instruments, such as polls and surveys, response variation is not only expected, it is desirable, as a range of responses can provide a broader and deeper understanding of respondents' perceptions and attitudes: "Patterns of differences in responses obtained by researchers when humans are asked about a subject—based on variations in question wording and so forth—are meaningful and provide a valuable basis for understanding the phenomenon under consideration. The task of the researcher is to describe and then understand the implications of these differential patterns of response and to use them as the basis for deriving the best possible depictions of where the public stands on the issues under consideration" (Newport, 2004, p. 240).

Formal pretesting also produces data, which can then be analyzed for evidence of validity and reliability. For example, you could calculate a correlation coefficient to produce evidence of construct validity or you could compute a measure of inter-rater reliability that would help in identifying problems independent raters have in completing the instrument consistently. Here are reminders of some actions you can take during this stage of pretesting to demonstrate that your instrument is producing reliable and valid information (review Chapter Four for more detail):

Obtain evidence of reliability. Reliability is established by administering the questionnaire to a sample of respondents or raters. You can assess the proportion of agreement over time by administering the instrument to a single group at different times or to two different groups. With the data produced by this process, calculate the proportion of agreement to determine the stability of the items over time. When items show changes over time, interview the respondents or raters to determine the cause. It may be that there is a legitimate reason for these changes and that rather than having unreliable items, you have gained validity information. For an observation instrument assess the percentage of agreement by using multiple raters and determining the stability of items between raters. Lack of agreement may indicate misunderstandings about items or the data collection process. Eliminate or modify items with insufficient stability coefficients, that is, where the percentage or proportion of agreement is low.

Establish evidence of face validity as you interview users. Once you have completed the interviews, organizing the results in a table or other appropriate form can help you and other decision makers determine if the items solicit and obtain the information you and they are seeking.

Obtain evidence of content validity from individuals with expertise in the subject matter being examined. For example, you could create a bank of items and have content experts review and rank the items they believe are most reflective of the topic of interest.

Obtain evidence of criterion validity by comparing responses to your items with responses to similar items on similar instruments or other data sources. For example, to demonstrate criterion validity for demographic information, you could compare that information to such other sources as personnel or student rosters. You will also need to ensure that the data from this second source is accurate! To demonstrate criterion validity for items, you could identify another instrument that attempts to measure the same constructs as your instrument and compare the responses on your instrument to responses on the alternative instrument, which must itself be reliable and valid. If the alternative source corroborates the data from your instrument, you have provided evidence of criterion validity. If there are discrepancies, you should identify the reason for them and decide whether they suggest the need to revise your instrument.

Obtain evidence of construct validity by making comparisons to see if your measures perform the way you expect them to. Use *convergent validity* (comparing the construct of interest with similar constructs to see if they perform in the same manner) and *divergent, or discriminant, validity* (assessing how well the construct of interest differs from dissimilar constructs). Another approach for demonstrating construct validity using data from pretesting is to develop an hypothesis about how reviewers should respond to the items. Identify situations in which different groups of respondents might answer the items differently. Administer the instrument to the different groups and then analyze the results to see if the items operate according to the hypothesis. For example, imagine that respondents might answer items on a health and fitness survey differently based on gender and age. If that hypothesis is accurate, the responses obtained during pretesting should differ based on those attributes. Yet another approach is to create written or video vignettes that illustrate different responses to individual items, as described in Chapter Four. For example, individuals being trained to administer the Child and Adolescent Functional Assessment Scale (Hodges, 1996) complete ratings based on vignettes describing a youngster's social supports (family, school, community), peer relationships, and social and mental health concerns. Their ratings can then be compared to the ratings that the instrument developer has determined are the preferred responses to the vignette information. This form of pretesting can provide you with information about both validity and reliability. Because there is a preferred response, you learn whether the instrument is operating according to the underlying construct. The level of agreement in scoring items (between raters or between raters and the vignette, or both) can provide evidence of interrater reliability. And when you discuss the process with the raters you can learn about the clarity of items, the ease or difficulty of completing the instrument, and the time it takes to administer it.

Finally, it is important to document and to share with others the activities you have carried out to pretest the instrument and the steps taken to enhance reliability and validity. The following principles describe what matters most when providing evidence of those efforts:

- The validity and stability of the results over time provides insights into what you are actually measuring. Changing items to make them behave as you expect them to is a natural part of the process.
- The amount of evidence needed to support the reliability or validity of an instrument is relative. Obviously, the more the better, within your time and

resource limitations. Also, the more important the decisions to be made based on the data, the greater the amount of reliability and validity information that should be provided.

- The reliability and validity information, regardless of the method used to obtain that information, should be made available to decision makers so that they too can judge the value, usefulness, and trustworthiness of the data.
- If some items perform better than others in terms of reliability and validity, then that information should also be shared in the final presentation of the data.
- Most important, the instrument and the results obtained should make sense not only to the instrument designer but also to decision makers, users of the instrument, and respondents.

Summary

The Norwegian artist Edvard Munch (1863–1944) is best known for his expressionist painting *The Scream*. To prepare for this painting, Munch first completed the same subject in a variety of other media, including pencil and lithography. Consequently, there are many variations of *The Scream* for art enthusiasts to study to see how the final rendition evolved. Instrument designers should be prepared to follow a similar process of development, one involving pretesting to correct problems and improve the quality of the instrument as well as to establish evidence of reliability and validity. You should anticipate the need to pretest throughout the instrument construction process—establishing the purpose of your study, developing the instrument, and preparing it for administration—to make sure that you are on the correct path for accomplishing your project goals.

Pretesting involves checking individual items and the instrument in its entirety to ensure that all will fulfill their intended purpose. By pretesting, the instrument designer can

- Identify and correct items that are unclear, poorly phrased, or too complex.
- Identify and correct instructions that are difficult to comprehend and follow.
- Identify problems in administration, such as the length of time it takes to administer or complete the instrument or to access it from a computer.
- Produce evidence to support reliability and validity.

Finally, pretesting is a systematic process of inquiry and therefore in part a scientific endeavor. It is also a humanistic process. For example, it may take technical skills to compute the proportion of agreement or a correlation coefficient and it takes interpersonal and communication skills to coordinate and lead focus groups and conduct individual debriefings.

Instrument 6.A: Failure to Pretest

In recent years, there has been a national effort to reduce or eliminate the use of restrictive treatment interventions, such as seclusion and restraint, in mental health settings. In the case described here, the management of a publicly funded psychiatric hospital wanted to obtain information that might help in attaining that goal. To determine if there was indeed a problem, management developed a checklist (Instrument 6.A) that was to be used to audit medical record documentation of restrictive interventions.

The instrument is titled the Quality Assurance and Improvement Review Checklist; this name is printed in bold ink in the center of the page. Does the title convey the purpose of the instrument? We suggest that an alternative title could be developed to better describe the instrument, such as Restrictive Treatment Measures: Medical Record Audit.

The demographic section consists of five parts: unit (hospital ward), date of (chart) review, clinical record number, name of reviewer, and the date of the event (the date that the seclusion or restraint occurred as reported on the chart in the clinical record). The instrument consists of an eight-item checklist, which provides for a *yes* or *no* response. Although no instructions are given, it is fair to assume that raters would circle the appropriate response. Mental health technicians were assigned to use the instrument to review charts and rate compliance. Staff were not provided training, as the instrument appeared to be clear and unambiguous. The instrument was distributed without pretesting.

Although this appears to be a simple and straightforward instrument to administer, a number of problems arose in its use, which could have been prevented through pretesting. The most significant problem was the lack of a *not applicable* response. In some cases a *no* response would suggest that the criterion had not been met, when in reality the employee had difficulty applying the criterion to the specific situation found on the chart, such as when alternative interventions were listed but not described in depth. Given this conflict the psychiatric technicians assigned to complete the audits would write in "NA," "Not sure," or "?" when they believed a *yes* or *no* response did not fit. Another problem arose from the fact that one item (item 8) monitored physician compliance with hospital policy. This item proved awkward for the psychiatric technicians, as it placed them in the position of evaluating the quality of a physician's written orders. Item 8 is also an example of a *double-barreled* question, as it really asks two questions and respondents may be uncertain which one they should evaluate. Because instructions were not developed for the instrument and staff were not provided training prior to conducting the chart audits, it was subsequently determined that individual employees interpreted the items differently, resulting in a high degree of variation in their ratings, that is, a lack of interrater reliability.

A number of problems were also identified regarding the implementation process. First, hospital management was notified of problems with the auditing process, including the difficulty in interpreting items and the lack of consistency between raters. Despite this feedback, the instrument was not revised, and it continued to be used for nearly two years. Second, hospital management used aggregate data produced by these checklists to compare the performance of treatment units in the use of these interventions. This tended to create tension between management and treatment staff, particularly as there were questions about the accuracy of the data produced by the instrument.

A number of steps could have been taken early in the process to improve the quality and utility of this instrument and the data collection process. In retrospect it is unclear if the instrument really suited management's intended purpose, which was to reduce the use of restrictive interventions. Writing a statement of purpose (Chapter Five) might have clarified for management the appropriate methods to attain that objective. Second, the instrument was not pretested, resulting in

INSTRUMENT 6.A: CHECKLIST FOR A MEDICAL RECORD AUDIT.

Quality Assurance and Improvement Review Checklist

Unit _____ Date of Review _____ Clinical Record # _____

Reviewer _____   Date of Event _____

1. Are statements about the intervention clear and descriptive?	YES	NO
2. Is there an explanation of preventive alternatives attempted?	YES	NO
3. Is there documentation of pertinent antecedent events?	YES	NO
4. Does documentation support that the procedure was the least restrictive?	YES	NO
5. Does the documentation meet criteria in hospital policy #101 or #102?	YES	NO
6. Does documentation include descriptive statements regarding follow-up interventions used to instruct or counsel the patient?	YES	NO
7. Is there a treatment plan incorporating the use of this procedure?	YES	NO
8. Is the physician's order specific to the event and is it time related?	YES	NO

difficulty with administering it and with obtaining consistent results across raters. As we have been emphasizing, an important step is to have the instrument reviewed and to be receptive to feedback. However, even though provided this information, the instrument designer did not revise the checklist. Fortunately, the object of measurement was medical records and not individuals, so that decisions made based on information produced by this instrument did not have a negative impact on clients. Ultimately, management recognized the instrument's shortcomings and alternative methods for addressing this topic were developed.

Key Concepts and Terms

construct validity	focus group	pretesting
criterion validity	interview	reliability
face validity	literature review	social desirability
field testing	pilot testing	

CHAPTER SEVEN

THE STRUCTURE AND FORMAT OF SELECTION ITEMS

In this chapter we will

- Explain how a selection item works.
- Describe the properties of common formats for constructing selection items, including numerical, graphic, and Likert response scales.

Artists often make use of the *rule of thirds* to compose a painting. The artist draws two vertical lines, dividing the canvas into three equally sized columns. Then he or she draws two horizontal lines to divide the canvas into three equally sized rows. The canvas is now divided into nine equally sized rectangles or squares. The simplest way of applying the rule of thirds is to position the subject where two of the lines intersect or partway between one of the intersections and the center. This produces a more pleasing composition than having the subject exactly in the center.

Much of what we do in instrument construction is based on composition: how we compose individual items and how we arrange multiple items to create the instrument. The term *format* refers to how an item or part of an item is organized and presented. Formatting may influence how a respondent or rater completes an item. Formatting is also an important component in the construction of some multi-item scales where the order of the response set influences the choices the respondent makes and how the item is scored.

When we create a selection item we determine in advance how the item will be organized and what alternatives the respondent or rater will have to pick from. For example, if you ask someone for directions there are a number of ways he or she can structure the response. He or she may use landmarks ("Turn right after the first stoplight and then left at the 7-Eleven") or the names of roads or highways ("Take a left onto Elm and then two blocks to the I-95 turnoff"). The same holds true with rating items. Although you may have a basic question you want to ask, the manner in which you format it can affect how it is completed. The format you chose will be based on a number of factors, including prior experience (yours and the respondent's), how well the format fits your information needs, and feedback from pretesting. You might try more than one format as you pretest the instrument and find that respondents have more difficulty with one than another. In this chapter we will describe a number of rating item formats. We will begin with a discussion of response sets, or scales, and then move into the different ways that you can organize and present items with scales.

Response Alternatives, or Scales

An instrument composed of items that ask users to rate their response is, in our extensive observation, one of the most common approaches to constructing a questionnaire such as a marketing survey or political poll. Rating scales are also the predominant format in use in behavior rating instruments, inventories, and checklists. A *scale* is composed of a series of values placed along a continuum, such as the tonal values that create a musical scale. For social science instruments the values are typically response alternatives, and we use the term *rating scale* when we ask users to select an alternative along the continuum, with an instruction such as, "Rate the following on a scale of 1 to 5." A typical rating item is made up of two parts, a *stem* and a response set, or *scale* (you may also use the terms *choices* or *alternatives* for the response set). The stem serves as the stimulus for, or elicits, the response and may be written as a word, phrase, sentence, or paragraph. The response set is a series of categories (which may or may not be numerical), from which the respondent selects one. As we noted in Chapter Three, the response scales for rating items that measure attitudes, opinions, and beliefs provide ordinal level data.

When you use a rating scale, you are making these assumptions:

- The attribute can be scaled along some continuum. For example, an item asking respondents to rate the effectiveness of a training workshop assumes that *effectiveness* can be scaled (for example, from *ineffective* to *highly effective*).

- The continuum is isomorphic to an internal continuum of the respondent's. In other words, the continuum is intrinsic to that individual. If the trait to be rated is greenness and if the rating is to be made on a scale between blue and yellow, then a person who is color-blind will lack a continuum on which to rate the trait.
- The respondent can consistently discriminate between continuum levels. You need sufficient gradation to capture differences along the scale's continuum. At the same time the response set values should be sufficiently exclusive that the user can easily distinguish between them. For example, even though the intervals may not be mathematically proportional, the respondent can differentiate between a 2 and a 3 on a scale of 1 to 5.

Rating scales are formatted in a number of ways. For example, the response set may be composed of word indicators (such as *never, seldom, occasionally,* and *always*), it may be represented solely by numbers or by graphics (pictures, symbols, or a line that indicates change in intensity), or it may be presented along a continuum that is anchored by a word or phrase at each end; we will present examples of each of these approaches in this chapter.

In some cases it may be necessary to include a definition or descriptive statement to clarify the meaning of a response alternative. Consider an item written to measure a behavior, such as a child's temper tantrums, where the response scale is 0 = *not present,* 1 = *mild,* 2 = *moderate,* 3 = *severe.* The *severity* of the temper tantrum could be a measure of intensity (*loud, out of control,* and *not responding to verbal interventions*), frequency (*once a day, twice a day, three times a day,* or *four or more times a day*), or duration (*less than hour, an hour, more than an hour*). Consequently, a descriptive statement may need to accompany each response alternative to instruct the rater. In the following example the descriptors indicate that severity is being measured by behavior intensity.

EXAMPLE

Frustration

0	1	2	3
Not present. Behavior was not observed.	*Mild.* Gives up easily on tasks when the task appears to be demanding. May express frustration by cursing, stomping feet, or leaving activity.	*Moderate.* May initially refuse and therefore require encouragement to engage in a demanding activity. May externalize frustration through attempts to escape the situation or through acting out or aggression toward objects.	*Severe.* Is very avoidant of demanding activities. May externalize frustration through attempts to escape the situation or through acting out or aggression toward objects or others.

A scale must be appropriate to the item's purpose. For example, using a scale running from *strongly disagree* to *strongly agree* would obviously be inappropriate for the item in the previous example. When the scale associated with an item is not appropriate, then it will likely produce results that are not valid.

You can present the response scale to the user of your instrument in a number of ways. You can orient it horizontally or vertically (as a list). You can associate numbers with the alternatives and have the respondent circle the chosen number. You can use a box ❑ and have the respondent place a check in the box. Instruments mounted on Web sites also make use of buttons; when a choice is made, a dot appears in the center of the selected button.

$$\bigcirc\bigcirc\bigcirc\odot\bigcirc$$

Factors that influence presentation include the amount of space available to work in, such as the size of the paper or the amount of computer screen that is visible, the size and style of the fonts and symbols you can use, and feedback during pretesting. For example, respondents might say that an item is easier to follow and mark when the response alternatives are listed across the page rather than down the page.

Fink (1995) identifies five response set categories: *endorsement* (also called *agreement*), *frequency, intensity, influence,* and *comparison.* A response scale must be associated with its item so that the alternatives are appropriate for that item. If the stem asks the respondent to form an opinion—if it says, for example, "The local school system is doing a good job of educating children"—an appropriate and associated response set might be an endorsement scale of *strongly agree* to *strongly disagree.* A response set based on intensity, such as *mild* to *severe*, would not be appropriate to that item. The correct match between stem and response scale is typically evident; however, you may not be able to determine the best fit until you have pretested the item. For example, if you were to use a frequency scale (such as *never, sometimes, frequently,* or *always*) with that school system opinion item, it might appear to match initially, but individuals pretesting the instrument might tell you it is awkward to use and difficult to apply. So that you do not have to reinvent the wheel, Exhibit 7.1 contains lists of commonly used response scales culled from a variety of instruments.

EXHIBIT 7.1: RESPONSE SET ALTERNATIVES FOR RATING SCALES.

Fink (1995) suggests that there are five types of response sets: *endorsement* (also called *agreement*), *frequency, intensity, influence,* and *comparison.* The following lists contain frequently used response sets, organized by these categories.

Endorsement

Definitely true
True
Unsure
False
Definitely false

Strongly disagree
Disagree

Not sure
Mostly agree
Strongly agree

On a scale of 1 to 9 where:
1 = Don't agree [to]
9 = Totally agree

Always no
Mostly no
Mostly yes
Always yes

Very dissatisfied
Somewhat dissatisfied
Both satisfied & dissatisfied
Somewhat satisfied
Very satisfied

Harmful
No help
Moderate help
Very helpful
Uncertain

Very unimportant
Somewhat unimportant
Somewhat important
Very important

More than adequate
Generally adequate
Of marginal adequacy
Inadequate
Very inadequate

Extremely unwelcome
Somewhat unwelcome
Somewhat welcome
Extremely welcome

Minimal commitment
Modest commitment
Significant commitment
Heavy commitment

Definitely yes
Probably yes
Uncertain
Probably no
Definitely no

Trust them a lot
Trust them some
Trust them only a little
Trust them not at all

Very difficult
Difficult
Unsure
Easy
Very easy

One of the worst
Less than average
Average
More than average
One of the best

To little or no extent
To some extent
To a moderate extent
To a great extent
To a very great extent

Yes
No

Agree
Disagree

True
False

Good
Not good

FREQUENCY

Never
Rarely
Sometimes
Frequently
Always

Very little
Some
Quite a bit
Very much

Most of the time
Some of the time
Hardly ever
Never

Typical
Rare
Absent

Every year
Every few years
Almost never
Never

Never
Once a year
Every few months
Every few weeks
Once a week
Several times a week
Daily

One a scale of 1 to 9 where:
1 = Almost never [to]
9 = Almost always

On a scale of 1 to 5 where:
1 = Never happens [to]
5 = Happens often (or happens a great deal)

On a scale of 1 to 9 where:
1 = Not at all [to]
9 = A great deal

On a scale of 1 to 5 where:
1 = Never utilized [to]
5 = Utilized very often

Not present

Slight or occasional

Marked or repeated

Uncertain

Far too much

Too much

About right

Too little

Far too little

A great deal

Somewhat

Little

Not at all

Always

Never

Highest possible

Lowest possible

INTENSITY (SEVERITY)

On a scale of 1 to 4 where:

1 = Functioning well

2 = Mild impairment

3 = Moderate impairment

4 = Severe impairment

None

Very mild

Mild

Moderate

Severe

Very poor

Poor

Adequate

Good

Optimal

Very relaxed

Relaxed

Neither relaxed nor tense

Anxious

Very anxious

Maximum risk

Moderate risk

Minimum risk

No risk

None

Very low

Low

Moderate

High

Very high

On a scale of 1 to 5 where

1 = No difficulty [to]

5 = Extreme difficulty

Very active

Active

Somewhat active

Not active

Poor

Fair

Good

Excellent

High

Low

Painful

Painless

INFLUENCE

Not a problem
Small problem   Fair
Moderate problem   Unfair
Big/large problem

COMPARISON

Much more than others
Somewhat more than others
About the same as others
Somewhat less than others
Much less than others

Numerical Scales

A numerical scale presents the respondent with a stem, and he or she responds by selecting an answer from alternatives ordered along a continuum. These response alternatives may be written descriptions or may be indicated by a letter or number. They are referred to as numerical scales because the respondent chooses from a "number of categories" (Judd, Smith, & Kidder, 1991). Numerals may or may not be associated with the response alternatives, and when they are used, they are placeholders; the response scale produces data of either a nominal or an ordinal nature. The choice of one numerical format over another depends largely on the preferences of the instrument designer, who has knowledge about the potential respondents and about the total organization of the instrument. Following are examples of an item stem formatted with a variety of numerical scales:

EXAMPLES

Assume that you have been instructed to develop an instrument to determine teachers' perceptions of in-service training. One of the variables of interest is the teachers' opinion of text readability.
A. Rate the readability of the text compared with other textbooks you have read. (Check one)

❑	❑	❑	❑	❑
Very difficult to read	Difficult to read	About average to read	Easy to read	Very easy to read

B. Rate the readability of the text compared with other textbooks you have read. (Check one)

❑   ❑   ❑   ❑   ❑
1   2   3   4   5

C. Rate the readability of the text compared with other textbooks you have read. (Check one)

❑   ❑   ❑   ❑   ❑
Very difficult   About average   Very easy
to read   to read   to read

D. Rate the readability of the text compared with other textbooks you have read. (Check one)

———— a. Very difficult to read
———— b. Difficult to read
———— c. About average to read
———— d. Easy to read
———— e. Very easy to read

E. Rate the readability of the text compared with other textbooks you have read. (Check one)

[ ]   [ ]   [ ]   [ ]   [ ]
Very difficult   Very easy
to read   to read

F. Rate the readability of the text compared with other textbooks you have read. (Check one)

————   ————   ————   ————   ————
Very difficult   Very easy
to read   to read

Note that each of these response sets is essentially the same: a continuum with five reference points. The points at the ends of the continuum are referred to as *anchors*. These response sets read from left to right, with *very difficult to read* at the beginning and *very easy to read* at the end. In example A a descriptor is provided for each response, whereas in example B only numbers are used. By convention, response scales are ordered from low to high. However, in example B it is possible that a respondent could associate the larger number with *harder* and the lower number with *easier*. In this case descriptors or anchors should be used to ensure that the respondent understands in which direction the items should be rated.

The Juster Purchase Probability Scale (Exhibit 7.2) further illustrates the variety of approaches for formatting a numerical scale. Use of this scale is limited to the field of marketing research, as it is specifically designed to measure consumer intentions to purchase a product. As part of the original research, the instrument developer, F. Thomas Juster, compared responses to an 11-point and a 3-point response scale and found that the 11-point scale was more sensitive and therefore a better predictor of consumer purchasing decisions (Wharton School, 2004).[1]

EXHIBIT 7.2: JUSTER PURCHASE PROBABILITY SCALE.

Indicator	Likelihood
10 – Certain, practically certain	99 in 100
9 – Almost sure	9 in 10
8 – Very probable	8 in 10
7 – Probable	7 in 10
6 – Good possibility	6 in 10
5 – Fairly good possibility	5 in 10
4 – Fair possibility	4 in 10
3 – Some possibility	3 in 10
2 – Slight possibility	2 in 10
1 – Very slight possibility	1 in 10
0 – No chance, almost no chance	1 in 100

The researcher administers the Juster Purchase Probability Scale by asking a respondent if he or she plans to purchase a specific item within a projected time frame. For example, "What is the likelihood that you will purchase a new television within the next month?" If the answer to the question is greater than zero, then the respondent is asked more specific questions. In this example he or she could be asked about the prospect of purchasing a particular brand of television and then about the type of television. An individual question (item) is asked about each brand or type, such as, "How likely are you to purchase a Sony?" Research has demonstrated that this scale can help predict future buying decisions better than other variables (such as a consumer's socio-economic status) and demographic factors (such as age) (Brennan & Esslemont, 1998).

Graphic Scales

A graphic scales is a rating scale with a stem and a response set consisting of a printed line on which the respondent designates his or her response. The line acts as a visual guide for the respondent and infers that the distances between the choices are all equal (although because this is ordinal data, we know that this inference does not always hold true).

EXAMPLES

A. Rate the readability of the text compared with other textbooks you have read. (Place a checkmark in the space between two slash marks)

_____   _____   _____   _____   _____
  Very   Difficult   About   Easy to   Very easy
difficult   to read   average   read   to read
to read

B. Place an X along the line to rate the readability of the text compared with other textbooks you have read.

_____

Very difficult   About average   Very easy

C. On a scale of one to ten, rate the readability of the text compared with other textbooks you have read. Circle the number that reflects your rating.

  1   2   3   4   5   6   7   8   9   10
Very   Very
difficult   easy

D. Place an X along the line to indicate the readability of the text compared with other textbooks you have read.

☹_____☺
Very difficult   Very easy
to read   to read

The Visual Analog Scale (VAS) is a variant of a graphic scale in which the indicators are indeed at an interval level and, some would contend, a ratio level, as there is a zero value. The VAS is used extensively in the health care field, primarily as a measure to assess pain although it has been adapted to other uses, including treatment of addiction. When used to assess level of pain, a line is drawn or printed exactly 10 cm (100 mm) in length, and the respondent is asked to place a mark on the line to indicate the degree of pain he or she is experiencing. Then a ruler is used to measure the exact distance from the anchor (0) to determine the level of pain. Consequently, this response scale provides a very precise measurement: 100 possible place settings at equal intervals. (Due to variation in the printing process the line shown here is representative and may not be exactly 10 cm long.)

EXAMPLE

0   100
no pain   worst imaginable pain

The VAS may be more sensitive to variations in pain than response alternatives where the respondent has only five or six choices, and this makes it a good choice to use before and after an intervention, such as before and after physical therapy or medication. Also, a patient may remember rating the pretreatment level of pain as a 4 on a 6-point response scale; he or she is less likely to remember the exact pretreatment VAS mark (DeVellis, 1991).[2] Nonetheless, the VAS has limitations. If the line is not exactly 10 cm in length (owing to variations caused by the reproduction process), then measurement will be unreliable, particularly when line length varies across two or more administrations. And given the minuteness of the indicators (millimeters), it might be somewhat of a pain (pun intended) to actually measure the response. Additionally, although there are equal intervals, the rating process is of course highly subjective as individuals' response to a given level of pain varies (DeVellis, 1991).

Likert Response Scale

Just as artists have favorite, well-worn paintbrushes, social scientists probably select the *Likert* (pronounced lick-ert) *scale* most frequently when choosing a rating scale format. A Likert item is composed of a stem (word, phrase, or sentence) followed by an endorsement scale running from *strongly disagree* to *strongly agree*.

EXAMPLE

The textbook for this course is very easy to read compared with other textbooks I have read.

❏	❏	❏	❏	❏
Strongly disagree	Disagree	Undecided	Agree	Strongly agree

Although there are no rules or standards for the direction in which the scale should progress (that is, you are not required to place *strongly agree* at, say, the end of the response set), response order may influence how the respondent rates the item.[3] *Primacy effects* occur when the first alternative to appear in a response set has a higher likelihood of being selected. Conversely, a *recency effect* occurs when respondents are presented with a list of items, and they recall the last–and therefore most recent–items presented to them. In one study, different forms of a course evaluation questionnaire were presented to medical students. The questionnaires that presented a positive rating (*strongly agree*) on the left side of the scale had more positive ratings and less variance, suggesting that the order in which the response alternatives were presented did influence the respondents' selections (Albanese, Prucha, Barnet, & Gjerde, 1997). By tradition, the Likert scale usually begins with strongly disagree, so that when numbers are associated with each indicator they increase in intensity from 1 to 5 (reading left to right). Additionally, there is no requirement that the response scale have a neutral choice, such as *undecided*. However, if a neutral choice is used, it is placed in the middle and given the middle value, such as 3 in a scale of 1 to 5 or 0 if the scale goes from -2 to $+2$.

EXAMPLE

I believe the President is doing a good job of leading the country.

Strongly Disagree	Disagree	Undecided	Agree	Strongly Agree
1	2	3	4	5

or

Strongly Disagree	Disagree	Undecided	Agree	Strongly Agree
-2	-1	0	$+1$	$+2$

Items may be worded either positively or negatively: for example, "I feel that this organization values its employees," or, "Employees of this organization do not feel valued." Depending on the instrument, its purpose, and the intended audience, you may find that it is best to be consistent with a negative or positive tone throughout the instrument. If the tone changes from item to item, you will need to reverse score some items (explained in Chapter Eleven). Additionally, the tone of the stem has the potential to influence the respondent's rating, and you should be aware of these possibilities as you pretest the instrument.

Following are three ways to display a Likert response scale:

EXAMPLES

A. Decreasing intensity, left to right:

❑	❑	❑	❑	❑
Strongly agree	Agree	Undecided	Disagree	Strongly disagree

B. Increasing intensity, left to right (traditional approach):

❑	❑	❑	❑	❑
SD	D	U	A	SA

C. Increasing and decreasing intensity, top to bottom:

❑ Strongly agree   ❑ Strongly disagree
❑ Agree   ❑ Disagree
❑ Undecided   ❑ Undecided
❑ Disagree   ❑ Agree
❑ Strongly disagree   ❑ Strongly agree

One of the advantages of using a Likert scale is familiarity, as many if not most rating items that measure endorsement, or agreement, make use of this format. Multiple Likert items are often used to create scales that produce a numerical score, and we will explore that process in more detail in Chapter Eleven, which discusses scale construction.

Summary

Comparing Pablo Picasso's early works to his later paintings is an exercise in watching the development and maturity of an artist. Although best known for his Cubist paintings, where images are distorted and abstract, Picasso was a gifted draftsman who learned in the classical style and who was influenced by the Impressionist movement at the beginning of his career. . . . In addition to displaying a progression in style, Picasso also chose a variety of subjects to paint, from portraits to landscapes. Consequently, there is a great deal of variety and differentiation in his body of work, which makes his paintings unique and easily discernable from one another.

This chapter has also addressed variety—the different ways that selection, or rating, items and response scales can be structured, which can influence how questions are posed and responded to. Each format presented in this chapter provides a singular approach to collecting and measuring data. The challenge to you as instrument designer is to identify the format that is the most effective for capturing the data you need. Being knowledgeable about the different formats can help you make decisions about the design and presentation of the instrument. This is accomplished by thinking about the purpose of the instrument as well as by pretesting to see what works.

Instrument 7.A: A Large-Scale Survey Using Rating Scales

In 1998, the governor of Virginia commissioned the Survey and Evaluation Research Laboratory of Virginia Commonwealth University to develop a survey of public employees. There was an interest in reforming personnel practices and procedures and a concern that policies under a previous administration had led to demoralization among the public workforce. In the cover letter to public employees, the governor articulated the purpose of the survey: "As I have stated repeatedly since my inauguration, I am keenly interested in your concerns about our State government in general and your personal experience as an employee. You are the backbone of Virginia's government, and as such you know what works well and what areas need improvement. In order to make meaningful change, I need your cooperation" (Office of the Governor, Commonwealth of Virginia, 1998).

The Virginia State Employee Survey, 1998, is a two-page survey form, printed on one sheet of paper, front and back. The title is centered and printed in capital letters at the top of the page. This is followed by a statement on anonymity and then by instructions for completing the survey. The first section of the survey consists of eighty-two items using a Likert format that includes the response choice *don't know*. Each item is numbered. Each item is unidimensional, that is, presents only one concept. It is evident that multiple items are being used to measure a topic. For example, items 2, 10, 11, 18, 31, and 39 address the issue of promotion opportunities. A number of related questions obtain information about pay, benefits, training, and workplace conditions. The number 8 was probably assigned to *don't know* responses, in preparation for statistical analysis where values greater than presented in the response set are used for alternative responses, such as a *don't know* response and unknown or missing values.

This employee survey consists of items that measure attitudes and beliefs. Items use many qualifying terms, such as: "I *generally* feel . . .," "I *frequently* feel . . .," "I am *usually* . . .," and "I *sometimes* . . ." The terminology also features many words that describe a state of being, such as *confident, satisfied, appreciated, respected,* and *valued.*

Although the primary format is rating scales, four open-ended questions are included, items 83 to 86, and respondents are encouraged to expand on their answers on a separate sheet of paper if needed. The last section consists of fourteen demographic items, which are clearly labeled as such. These items employ an alternative response set format, which we will discuss in Chapter Nine. Finally, it is worth noting that to fit all these items on two 8½-by-11-inch pages, the original type size was quite small.

The Virginia State Employee Survey is a job satisfaction survey and is a good example of the use of rating scales to measure opinions and beliefs. The purpose of the instrument is clearly defined in the cover letter, and the findings of the survey have been made available through a state agency Web site. Item construction conforms to the guidelines presented in this chapter.

The survey was mailed out to 143,377 state employees, and 45,598 completed surveys were returned. With this response rate the results cannot be generalized to the entire population of state employees; however, as the developers of the instrument note, "the large number of respondents, the general similarity of the respondents' demographics with demographics known for classified employees, and the patterns of response all lend credence to the results" ("Employees Respond," 1999, p. 2).

The fact that the instrument was developed by a survey lab located in a public university lends credibility to the instrument design. However, public documents (for example, the narrative summary for this survey) do not indicate how the instrument was pretested and what steps were taken to assess instrument validity and reliability.

INSTRUMENT 7.A: LARGE-SCALE EMPLOYEE SATISFACTION SURVEY.

THIS IS AN ANONYMOUS QUESTIONNAIRE. DO **NOT** PUT YOUR NAME ON THIS DOCUMENT.

For each of the following statements, please indicate if you agree or disagree by circling the appropriate number. This survey will be used to better understand the views of the State's work force. It is very important that you give answers that describe current conditions. If you work in a university, please consider your university as the "agency."

	STRONGLY DISAGREE	DISAGREE	AGREE	STRONGLY AGREE	DON'T KNOW
1. State policies and procedures for employees makes sense to me.	1	2	3	4	8
2. Employees are usually promoted based on performance.	1	2	3	4	8
3. I am confident in the leadership at my agency.	1	2	3	4	8
4. If I do a good job, I think I should get more money.	1	2	3	4	8
5. I am satisfied with my retirement plan.	1	2	3	4	8
6. It is important to me to feel appreciated at work.	1	2	3	4	8
7. Employees are usually respected as individuals at my agency.	1	2	3	4	8
8. Fear of losing benefits has kept me from looking for another job.	1	2	3	4	8
9. I generally feel informed about changes that affect me.	1	2	3	4	8
10. Hard work is usually rewarded in my agency.	1	2	3	4	8

11. I am aware of promotion opportunities.	1	2	3	4	8
12. Overall, I believe my employee evaluation system is fair.	1	2	3	4	8
13. I am paid adequately for my responsibilities.	1	2	3	4	8
14. I am proud to be a State employee.	1	2	3	4	8
15. I am satisfied with my health insurance plan.	1	2	3	4	8
16. I am usually treated with respect at my workplace.	1	2	3	4	8
17. Employees have equal access to job-related training opportunities.	1	2	3	4	8
18. I have the opportunity to progress within the State system.	1	2	3	4	8
19. I have adequate technology to do my job.	1	2	3	4	8
20. There is generally no discrimination shown at my agency.	1	2	3	4	8
21. I am paid at an appropriate level for my qualifications.	1	2	3	4	8
22. I feel I am well prepared to do my job.	1	2	3	4	8
23. I frequently feel stress in my job.	1	2	3	4	8
24. I believe that rewards are given fairly where I work.	1	2	3	4	8
25. I get the training I need to do my job well.	1	2	3	4	8
26. I know people in my agency that don't do their share of the work.	1	2	3	4	8
27. The relationship between management and employees is good.	1	2	3	4	8
28. My supervisor takes a personal interest in helping me get ahead at my job.	1	2	3	4	8
29. There are people to whom I can go for help when I have work-related problems.	1	2	3	4	8
30. I can leave work to take care of personal matters if I need to.	1	2	3	4	8
31. I have the opportunity to learn skills that will improve my chances for promotion.	1	2	3	4	8
32. I usually have the equipment I need to do my job well.	1	2	3	4	8
33. My agency offers flextime or alternative schedules.	1	2	3	4	8
34. You have to know the right people to get ahead in the State system.	1	2	3	4	8
35. I know where to go for information related to benefits.	1	2	3	4	8

36. I know where to go to get the information that I need to do my job.	1	2	3	4	8
37. I think the State's Fraud, Waste and Abuse Hotline saves the State money.	1	2	3	4	8
38. I receive enough recognition for the work that I do.	1	2	3	4	8
39. I have the opportunity to advance within my agency.	1	2	3	4	8
40. I sometimes doubt the truth about what management tells me.	1	2	3	4	8
41. I think of my benefits as part of my earnings.	1	2	3	4	8
42. I understand the services offered by the State Employees' Assistance Program.	1	2	3	4	8
43. I usually hear about important changes through rumors rather than management communication.	1	2	3	4	8
44. I would recommend my agency as a good place to work.	1	2	3	4	8
45. I would like more flexibility in my benefit options.	1	2	3	4	8
46. I feel I am valued at work.	1	2	3	4	8
47. Computers are a good way for the State to get information to me.	1	2	3	4	8
48. If I do a good job I have a better chance of getting ahead.	1	2	3	4	8
49. I understand how my retirement benefits are calculated.	1	2	3	4	8
50. It is easy to get answers to questions about personnel policies.	1	2	3	4	8
51. It's safe to say what I think at my job.	1	2	3	4	8
52. It takes too long to hire someone when a position becomes vacant.	1	2	3	4	8
53. My agency offers enough training opportunities.	1	2	3	4	8
54. I usually know in plenty of time when important things happen.	1	2	3	4	8
55. My job description matches my job duties.	1	2	3	4	8
56. I would recommend the State as a good place to work.	1	2	3	4	8
57. My job is interesting to me.	1	2	3	4	8
58. My work-related concerns are generally handled to my satisfaction.	1	2	3	4	8
59. People generally feel appreciated where I work.	1	2	3	4	8
60. My agency has a genuine concern for safety.	1	2	3	4	8

61. My agency is a place where individuals with disabilities can work comfortably.	1	2	3	4	8
62. I am told if I have done a particularly good job.	1	2	3	4	8
63. Policies and procedures are usually applied equally to all employees.	1	2	3	4	8
64. Procedures necessary to do my job often involve unnecessary steps.	1	2	3	4	8
65. The benefits package that I receive is not as good as most available in the private sector.	1	2	3	4	8
66. The current pay system has a positive affect on employee productivity.	1	2	3	4	8
67. The grievance process available to me is a fair way to resolve disputes between employees and management.	1	2	3	4	8
68. Personnel procedures make it difficult to get rid of poorly performing employees.	1	2	3	4	8
69. The information that I have received about employee benefits is easy to understand.	1	2	3	4	8
70. The meetings that I have with my co-workers and supervisor help me to get my job done.	1	2	3	4	8
71. I am paid appropriately for the work-related experience that I have.	1	2	3	4	8
72. The State's Employee Suggestion Program saves the State money.	1	2	3	4	8
73. The State should be more flexible in personnel matters.	1	2	3	4	8
74. I like my benefits package.	1	2	3	4	8
75. The State's communications keep me up-to-date.	1	2	3	4	8
76. The State provides a way for me to get confidential help when I have personal problems that affect my work.	1	2	3	4	8
77. My agency offers flexible working arrangements.	1	2	3	4	8
78. When discussing problems or complaints, I feel that I am treated seriously.	1	2	3	4	8
79. I worry about losing my job.	1	2	3	4	8
80. There is too much paperwork involved in doing my job.	1	2	3	4	8
81. I get a feeling of personal satisfaction from my work.	1	2	3	4	8
82. I read most of the State's newsletters that I receive.	1	2	3	4	8

Please use additional paper for the following questions if necessary.

83. What do you think is the most important action that should be taken to improve the quality of work life for State government employees?

84. What do you think is the best thing about working for the State?

85. What do you think is the worst thing about working for the State?

86. What is one thing that can be done to make State government run more efficiently?

DEMOGRAPHIC INFORMATION: The information you provide below will be grouped with answers received from other employees and will NOT be used to identify you. Smaller agencies of 25 or fewer employees automatically will be grouped to maintain confidentiality.

87. Type of employee:
    - ❑ Wage (check one):
        - ❑ Adjunct faculty
        - ❑ Hourly, not student
        - ❑ Student employee/
          Grad Assist.
    - ❑ Salary/Contract

88. Do you work full or part-time?
    - ❑ Full-time
    - ❑ Part-time

89. Total years you've worked for the State
    - ❑ Less than 2 years
    - ❑ 2–4 years
    - ❑ 5–9 years
    - ❑ 10–14
    - ❑ 15–20
    - ❑ More than 20

90. Zip code at work: _____

91. My usual work schedule:
    ❏ Days
    ❏ Evenings
    ❏ Nights
    ❏ Rotating schedule
    ❏ Weekends only

92. Do you supervise staff at your workplace?
    ❏ Yes
    ❏ No

93. What is the highest level of education that you completed?
    ❏ Less than high school
    ❏ High school or GED equivalent
    ❏ Associate Degree
    ❏ College Degree
    ❏ Master's Degree or higher

94. Your State grade level
    ❏ Grades 1–3
    ❏ Grades 4–8
    ❏ Grades 9–12
    ❏ Grade 13 and above
    ❏ Not a graded position
    ❏ Faculty/Adjunct
    ❏ Don't Know

95. Your annual State pay
    ❏ Under $10,000
    ❏ $10–19,999
    ❏ $20–29,999
    ❏ $30–39,999
    ❏ $40–49,999
    ❏ $50,000 or more

96. Agency Code: (please refer to yellow code sheet enclosed):

    ____ ____ ____

97. Your age:
    ❏ Under 25
    ❏ 25–34 years
    ❏ 35–44 years
    ❏ 45–54 years
    ❏ 55 or over

98. Do you have a disability?
    ❏ Yes
    ❏ No

99. Your race:
    ❏ African-American
    ❏ Asian, Pacific Islander
    ❏ American Indian
    ❏ Hispanic
    ❏ White 0
    ❏ Other

100. Your sex
    ❏ Female
    ❏ Male

THANK YOU FOR YOUR HELP!

Instrument 7.B: An Assessment Instrument Using Graphic Scales

The Brief Situational Confidence Questionnaire (Sobell, 1999) assesses an individual's ability to resist use of alcohol under a variety of situations, such as when stressed, when urges appear, or during social activities. Each of the eight items presents the respondent with a statement beginning with "I feel," a description of the situation, and the instruction to place an X on the line to indicate his or her level of resistance. To facilitate accurate marking of the graphic scale, the questionnaire includes an example illustrating how to rate each item. Each item uses the same anchors: *not at all confident* and *100% totally confident.*

With a graphic scale it is difficult to assign a number to the location where the respondent places his or her mark. Therefore this instrument does not produce a total score for the eight items. Instead, a practitioner, such as a substance abuse counselor, uses the marked scales to determine the individual's situations of most resistance and least resistance to using alcohol. This information can then be incorporated into the individual's treatment process.

INSTRUMENT 7.B: BRIEF SITUATIONAL CONFIDENCE QUESTIONNAIRE.

Brief Situational Confidence Questionnaire

Name: _____ Date: _____

Listed below are eight types of situations in which some people experience an alcohol or drug problem. Imagine yourself as you are right now in each of the following types of situations. Indicate on the scale provided how confident you are right now that you will be able to resist drinking heavily or resist the urge to use your primary drug in each situation by placing an "X" along the line, from 0% "Not at all confident" to 100% "Totally confident" as in the example below.

I feel ...

```
        |————————X——————————————————————————|
       0%                                  100%
  Not at all confident            Totally confident
```

Right now I would be able to resist the urge to drink heavily or use my primary drug in situations involving . . .

1. UNPLEASANT EMOTIONS (e.g., If I were depressed about things in general; if everything were going badly for me).

    I feel . . .

```
        |————————————————————————————————————|
       0%                                  100%
  Not at all confident            Totally confident
```

2. **PHYSICAL DISCOMFORT** (e.g., If I were to have trouble sleeping; if I felt jumpy and physically tense).

   I feel . . .

   0%   100%
   Not at all confident   Totally confident

3. **PLEASANT EMOTIONS** (e.g., If something good happened and I felt like celebrating; if everything were going well).

   I feel . . .

   0%   100%
   Not at all confident   Totally confident

4. **TESTING CONTROL OVER MY USE OF ALCOHOL OR DRUGS** (e.g., If I were to start to believe that alcohol or drugs were no longer a problem for me; if I felt confident that I could handle drugs or several drinks).

   I feel . . .

   0%   100%
   Not at all confident   Totally confident

5. **URGES AND TEMPTATIONS** (e.g., If I suddenly had an urge to drink or use drugs; if I were in a situation where I had often used drugs or drank heavily).

   I feel . . .

   0%   100%
   Not at all confident   Totally confident

6. **CONFLICT WITH OTHERS** (e.g., If I had an argument with a friend; if I were not getting along well with others at work).

   I feel . . .

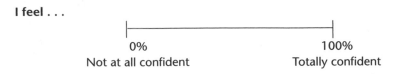

   0%   100%
   Not at all confident   Totally confident

7. **SOCIAL PRESSURE TO USE** (e.g., If someone were to pressure me to "be a good sport" and drink or use drugs with him; if I were invited to someone's home and he offered me a drink or drugs).

I feel ...

0%
Not at all confident

100%
Totally confident

8. **PLEASANT TIMES WITH OTHERS** (e.g., If I wanted to celebrate with a friend; if I were enjoying myself at a party and wanted to feel even better).

I feel . . .

0%
Not at all confident

100%
Totally confident

Source: Sobell, 1999, pp. 204–205. Reprinted with permission of the author.

Endnotes

1. Notice that in the construction of this scale, a likelihood factor has been included that is proportional, suggesting that the items are at the interval level of measurement, such as 3 in 10, 4 in 10, and so on. However, the two anchors are not proportional to the rest of the scale; 99 in 100 is not proportional to the response alternatives that follow it—9 in 10, 8 in 10, and so on.

2. Several studies have examined the precision of the VAS. For example, there must be at least a 13 mm difference in ratings between VAS administrations to represent a clinically significant reduction in pain. Additionally, the more pain that a patient experiences, the greater the degree of change that is needed to reflect a clinically significant change (Sadovsky, 2002).

3. In a client satisfaction questionnaire one of the authors assisted in developing, a Likert response scale was used with *strongly agree* presented first in the list. Moreover, the items were numbered from 1 to 5, so that *strongly agree* corresponded to 1 and *strongly disagree* to 5. When tallying the results, it soon became evident that some respondents were circling 5 when they strongly agreed with the item. This was verified by comparing responses to open-ended questions with responses to the paired selection item. Given this finding, the questionnaire was revised to correct the problem. Another alternative would have been to delete the numbers and have the respondents check or circle the appropriate words.

Key Concepts and Terms

comparison response set

endorsement response set

format

frequency response set

graphic scale

influence response set

intensity response set

Likert scale

numerical scale

primacy effect

rating scale

recency effect

response alternative

response set

stem

CHAPTER EIGHT

GUIDELINES FOR WRITING SELECTION ITEMS

In this chapter we will

- Present guidelines for creating selection items of all types.
- Present guidelines for creating rating scales based on response sets of endorsement, frequency, and intensity.

In Chapter Five we examined creative and technical processes that will help you focus your study and generate questionnaire items. In the early stage of instrument construction, items are often expressed as declarative statements or open-ended questions. During the next phase of instrument construction you will want to format them so they will produce measurable responses. Returning to our painting analogy, your instrument has been sketched on the canvas and is now ready for the application of paint. However, you must begin to decide on the brush strokes—how to convert the ideas and questions that you formulated during the brainstorming process into measurable items.

In the construction of any instrument, various types of items can and should be used, depending on the information to be gathered and the intended use of data gained from a particular item. In this and the next chapter we will examine approaches for constructing *selection items*, where you establish the choices for the respondent. Selection items may use rating scales, alternative response sets (where you select one alternative from a list or check all that apply), or ranking. This format allows you to present the information concisely and produces measurable data that can be tallied and the results systematically analyzed. For example, if you need information about respondents' annual gross income, you can provide alternatives that list income in ranges, such as (1) less than $25,000, (2) $25,000 to $34,499, (3) $35,000 to $39,999, and so on. However, limiting respondents to these choices also limits the scope of the information you can obtain. If that is a concern, then you may want to consider using an open-ended question, asking the respondent, for example, to provide the exact amount given on his or her income tax return.

We begin this chapter with a description of the writing factors, such as sentence length or word choice, that can influence how an individual responds. Then we present guiding principles for constructing selection items that make use of rating scales. Research into instrument design can assist all of us to write items that measure what we intend them to measure, for example, by reducing errors due to respondents' not completely comprehending the meaning or purpose of an item statement. We encourage you to refer to these guidelines as you begin the formal process of structuring each item in your instrument.

Writing Items: Preliminary Considerations

Unlike viewers of an abstract painting, who bring their personal interpretations to the artwork, users of a survey instrument will, ideally, all have the same understanding of each survey item. Therefore, before you consider an item's final format, such as a graphic or numerical scale, you should examine your statements and questions to determine if they are clear, unambiguous, reasonable, and concise.

Sentence Length

Because your goal is to have respondents complete all questionnaire items and because you do not want to confuse respondents, it is important to consider the length of the item stem. Problems arise when an item contains too much information for a respondent to take in easily and ultimately comprehend (Redline, Dillman, Carley-Baxter, & Creecy, 2003). Respondents may even skip an item that appears long-winded and wordy. There are several ways to assess whether a statement is too long. You can have several people read the item and describe their impression of the meaning and of sentence length. You can also count the number of words in the item. The first sentence in this paragraph tries to convey several ideas and accomplishes this in thirty-one words. The third sentence conveys only one concept and does so succinctly in only eleven words. You will be attempting to convey one concept in each questionnaire item. You should do it with just a few words.

Original: Depending on the availability of resources, my supervisor provides me with the opportunity to attend training that can help me do my job better and which is relevant to my job duties.

Rewrite: Management supports training that is job relevant.

Too Many Concepts

Multiple concepts or subjects result in what are sometimes called *double-barreled* items. If a question says, "Do you believe that the automobile sales tax should be repealed or do you believe that the tax on food should be reduced?" the respondent may not know which concept to address. Although this question was meant to solicit a response about taxes, it ended up asking about two distinct subjects—the car tax and the food tax. It offers two different response choices—one to repeal a tax and the other to reduce another tax. A similar problem exists in the example displayed earlier: is the item soliciting information about the relationship between training and job performance or training and its relevance to job duties? One way to resolve this problem is to create two or more separate items. Notice that in the following examples, the way the item has been rewritten also suggests the way the response should be formatted.

Original: Do you buy frozen microwavable food and if so, how many of these items do you purchase each week?

Rewrite: About how many frozen, microwavable food items do you purchase each week?

❑ 0–4   ❑ 5–9   ❑ 10–14   ❑ 15–19   ❑ 20–24   ❑ 25 or more

Original: Indicate the extent to which you agree with the following statement by circling the corresponding number:

The automobile sales tax should be repealed and the tax on food should be reduced.

Strongly Disagree	Disagree	Undecided	Agree	Strongly Agree
1	2	3	4	5

Rewrite: Indicate the extent to which you agree with the following statements by circling the corresponding number:

	Strongly Disagree	Disagree	Undecided	Agree	Strongly Agree
1. The automobile sales tax should be repealed	1	2	3	4	5
2. The tax on food should be reduced	1	2	3	4	5

Note that this is different from offering the respondent a choice about a topic that is the only topic in the stem:

Do you favor or oppose repeal of the estate tax?

❑ Favor repeal of the estate tax   ❑ Oppose repeal of the estate tax

Terminology

An important consideration in item construction is vocabulary. Problems with terminology occur when the words used are overly technical for the intended population, have multiple meanings that might confuse respondents, or contain abstract references that are unclear or misleading.

It is important to identify your target audience and consider whether certain terms might be overly technical for them. A health care questionnaire, for example, might ask respondents if they have ever been diagnosed with "whooping cough," rather than referring to this diagnosis more formally as "pertussis." Because we often work in environments that have their own jargon, it is important to have individuals from other settings review our instruments. These reviewers can help us identify terms that may be singular to a particular profession or subject area. This guidance holds true for abbreviations as well, as abbreviations are also often unique to a particular group or setting. In the following example, LEA might stand for "law enforcement agency" or "local educational agency" and the correct choice is not evident from the context. If you intend to represent a term by an abbreviation throughout your instrument, be sure to introduce and define the term first, before abbreviating it.

EXAMPLE

	Strongly Disagree	Disagree	Undecided	Agree	Strongly Agree
Given increased gang activity in the local community and schools, LEAs should receive additional funding	1	2	3	4	5

When words may convey more than one meaning, it is important to define them in the context of the statement. For example, in common usage the term *affect* means to have an influence on something or someone, whereas in the field of psychology this word refers to an emotional state; a patient might be said to "present with a flat affect." Careful review of your items will help you determine whether you have used words that appear ambiguous to respondents.

Finally, respondents or raters may misconstrue the meaning of abstract words, particularly words that describe constructs rather than the behaviors or attributes that operationalize those constructs. Suppose you want to use an instrument to assess the extent of disruptive student behaviors in the classroom. The term *disruptive behaviors* may connote a broad array of activities to teachers, such as talking too loudly, not following directions, talking to peers during instruction, passing notes between peers, or fighting. One way to address this problem is to work with content experts and stakeholders to define your terms operationally and also to observe for possible misunderstandings during pretesting.

Readability and Literacy Level

A related issue is the literacy level of your potential respondents or raters. Because respondents read the items (rather than having the items read to them), it is important to consider this literacy or reading level. Literacy assumes comprehension: the individual can not only say the word but also has an internal definition of it and can combine it with other words into meaningful sentences. Limitations may be due to a number of factors, including age, cognitive functioning and disabilities, life experience, education, and native language. Reading capabilities may also be affected by physical limitations such as eye diseases.

A study by Gerber and Wellens (1995) indicates that individuals with limited reading skills may misread words in a questionnaire, resulting in incorrect or incomplete answers. For example, on one instrument individuals with reading problems saw the term *county/parish* and misread it as *country*, resulting in a response of "United States of America" or "America"; one individual could not read the words at all and left the item blank. These individuals have problems not only with comprehension but also with instrument structure and format. For example, they may have difficulty maneuvering through an instrument when their response to an item leads to a prompt asking them to skip to another section.

Comprehension problems may also occur when you use words above your respondents' reading level. Even when you do not know respondents' typical level, you can choose words that are more common and less difficult for most individuals to understand, such as *begin* instead of *initiate*, *live* instead of *reside*, or *explain* instead of *elucidate*.

It is therefore important to take the reading skills of potential users into consideration when wording and structuring items. Pretesting will help you assess if there are problems with terminology, if intended respondents will have a problem with the reading level of the instrument, or if age or infirmities necessitate that the instrument be read aloud to respondents.

Typical Problems in Crafting Items

To determine the types of problems that tend to occur when constructing items, Belson (1981, pp. 23–31) analyzed 2,180 questions from an array of instruments. Listed here by frequency of occurrence, these problems reflect the typical problems that can be avoided by following the guidelines in this chapter.

1. Presenting two questions as one
2. Putting a lot of meaningful words in a short space, where each contributes an element of meaning necessary for understanding the question
3. Concluding with a qualifying clause or phrase: for example, "Have you bought any chocolates in the last 7 days, not counting today?"
4. Using multiple ideas or subjects in a single question
5. Using difficult and unfamiliar words
6. Using one or more instructions in the body of the item
7. Starting with language meant to soften a question's impact ("Would you mind telling me how old you are?")
8. Using difficult phrases
9. Using conditional or hypothetical clauses (for example, beginning items with "suppose..." or "if...")
10. Making a question dependent on another item, without which it does not make sense

11. Using a negative element in a question ("Is there any reason why you are not using brand X?")
12. Inverting sentences.
13. Using the words "if any" or "if at all"
14. Making questions very long
15. Using both the present and the past tense in a sentence
16. Using both the singular and the plural in a sentence

Background Information

In order to understand the meaning and purpose of an item or items, you may need to include background information: for example, "The United States Constitution now prevents any foreign-born person from being elected president. Would you favor or oppose a constitutional amendment that would allow a U.S. citizen born in another country to be elected president?" The explanatory sentence is needed to provide context to the question itself. In some cases you may need to explain terms you're using: "The following items relate to disruptive classroom behavior, which for the purposes of this study means arguing loudly with peers or the teacher or engaging in physical fighting." Without this explanation the respondent can define disruptive classroom behavior in any way, with the result that there is no shared meaning and answers are less meaningful. Background information should always precede the question.

These points also apply to background information needed for response sections, as it is important to provide consistency in formatting the response choices. For example, if you ask respondents or raters to rank order items from 1 to 10, be sure to indicate whether 1 reflects the lowest or the highest value. It is sometimes helpful to include an example: "Rank these 10 household items by how often you use them each day; giving the rank of 1 to the item you use the most."

Sufficiency of Response Choices

As you write some items the wording will suggest the format and response choices you want to offer. Now is the time to ensure that you are being inclusive and have not left possible response alternatives out. Think of the times that you have been frustrated in completing a survey because the answer you wanted to provide was not an option among the choices presented to you. A good way to test this is to ask the question of several people and then ask them to name as many response choices as they can think of. This will help you establish the alternative responses to include in the item.

Original: In what type of dwelling do you now reside:

❏ House   ❏ Apartment   ❏ Other

Rewrite: In what type of dwelling do you now reside:

❏ Detached House   ❏ Townhouse   ❏ Apartment   ❏ Mobile home
❏ Motel   ❏ Rooming house   ❏ Other, not specified

Sensitive Questions

Sensitive questions are those that solicit information that is personal or makes the respondent uncomfortable or embarrassed. In some cases, respondents may be fearful that a response could result in a consequence (Hossini & Armacost, 1993). For example, they may not respond to questions about behaviors commonly considered illegal. When possible, sensitive questions should be avoided. However, some surveys are specifically designed to assess sensitive subjects, such as sexual behavior or issues related to health. In these cases, special consideration needs to be given to both the items and sampling methods. Sometimes we may pose a question that at first seems harmless but that turns out to be sensitive when considered from the point of view of potential respondents. For example, some individuals may be uncomfortable about reporting income levels. We suggest that unless the information is vital to your study, you avoid sensitive items. If you are unsure about sensitivity, check with potential respondents before including such items in the final version of the questionnaire.

EXAMPLE

Original: Was this child born out-of-wedlock?   ❏ Yes   ❏ No

Rewrite: What was your marital status when your last child was born?

❏ Married   ❏ Separated   ❏ Divorced   ❏ Widowed   ❏ Unmarried

Management of Socially Desirable Responses

Socially desirable responses are more likely to occur when sensitive questions are asked. That is, respondents may answer an item, intentionally or unintentionally, in a way that presents them in the best light rather than reflecting their actual beliefs or behaviors.[1] If you are designing a questionnaire that will tap into sensitive topics, you should plan to assess the likelihood that an item will produce a socially desirable response. At a minimum you could have content experts review the items and rate their potential for eliciting a socially desirable response. Or you could have prospective respondents rate each item and then interview them to learn why certain items are perceived as potentially producing a socially desirable response. You could also compare responses made during pretesting to known data, if available. For example, if you are administering to high school students a questionnaire that includes items on drug and alcohol use, you could compare the students' responses to data from the Youth Risk Behavior Survey (see Instrument 8.A and the accompanying discussion for more information) that the students might have taken earlier in the year.

One of the traditional ways of checking for social desirability is to administer a social desirability scale with your questionnaire. One of the most frequently used instruments is the Crowne-Marlowe Social Desirability Scale (Crowne & Marlowe, 1960), a thirty-three-item questionnaire that includes such items as, "I'm always willing to admit it when I make a mistake." The instrument has been normed so that you can compare an individual's response to the expected response. In addition, studies have demonstrated that responses on this scale correlate with other measures of mental health. Nonetheless, recent studies suggest that this instrument is not a strong predictor of social bias, and therefore users should be cautious in using, interpreting, and applying the results from this instrument (Johnson & Fendrich, 2002).

If you believe that sensitive items might produce socially desirable responses there are several things you can do when you administer the instrument to address the problem. Perhaps the most effective is to assure respondents of confidentiality (at a minimum) or (preferably) anonymity. Confidentiality ensures that identifying information is not made available to anyone other than those conducting the study and that there is a mechanism to protect the information. For example, as the principle investigator you might maintain a code book that allows you to associate a set of data with a particular participant. Without the code book, however, there would be no way to connect an individual to his or her data.

With anonymity the respondents are guaranteed that there is no way to trace their response back to them. In one study, college students completed measures of self-consciousness, social anxiety, self-esteem, and social desirability under anonymous and nonanonymous conditions. The researcher found that participants reported lower social anxiety and social desirability and higher self-esteem when they completed the instruments under the anonymous conditions. Similar results (lower social anxiety and so forth) were obtained for Web-based versus paper-and-pencil instruments (Joinson, 1999).

Biased Items

A biased item is one whose wording, inadvertently or purposely, influences the respondent to respond in a particular manner. An item may become biased in several different ways. First, the tone of the words or structure of the statement could influence respondents. Consider a survey sent to gun owners that includes this question, "Do you support laws now being proposed by liberals in Congress to require mandatory registration of firearms?" Here the term *liberal* is used pejoratively and is linked to the issue of gun registration.

Another way to insert bias is to present only one side of an argument or position. Suppose that the previous question is restated as follows: "Do you oppose gun control legislation?" Given the target audience of gun owners, this wording may be more likely to elicit a positive than negative response. An alternative would be to restate it as, "What is your current position on gun control legislation?" (Obviously, the response choices would then have to change from *yes* or *no* to *I favor gun control legislation* or *I oppose gun control legislation.*)

EXAMPLE

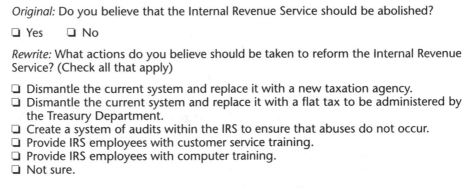

Original: Do you believe that the Internal Revenue Service should be abolished?

❏ Yes   ❏ No

Rewrite: What actions do you believe should be taken to reform the Internal Revenue Service? (Check all that apply)

❏ Dismantle the current system and replace it with a new taxation agency.
❏ Dismantle the current system and replace it with a flat tax to be administered by the Treasury Department.
❏ Create a system of audits within the IRS to ensure that abuses do not occur.
❏ Provide IRS employees with customer service training.
❏ Provide IRS employees with computer training.
❏ Not sure.

The way response alternatives are presented can also create bias, as some studies suggest that when many choices are offered, respondents are more likely to select from the beginning of the list (referred to as a *primacy effect*). For example, a questionnaire was developed with Likert scales containing five, six, or seven options. Respondents were more likely to chose *strongly agree* when it was presented as the first choice in the seven-option scale than when it was presented first in the five-item scale (Albanese et al., 1997). Conversely, when a long list of options is read aloud to respondents, they are more likely to remember and select one of the last alternatives presented to them (referred to as a *recency effect*) (Foddy, 1993). You should be able to detect and correct either of these problems during pretesting.

Bias can also be introduced by the way the item is structured grammatically, choice of words (terminology), or even the length of the statement, so it may seem nearly impossible to write an unbiased item. Fortunately, studies indicate that varying the wording of an item does not make a significant difference in how it is rated, as long as the *meaning* of the statement does not change. "This is reassuring for questionnaire designers, because their task would be impossible if every change in question wording, no matter how small, produced a different question" (Gendall & Hoek, 1990, p. 3). However, when a wording change taps into a new construct or emotional response, there can be a significant difference in how the item is rated: So how do you address the question of bias? You guessed it—pretesting: "The only way to develop a comprehensive and reliable set of rules for question design is to systematically test alternative forms, sequences and wording variations in a variety of situations" (Gendall & Hoek, 1990, p. 3).

Multicultural Considerations

The controversy was not new. Since the first intelligence tests were developed in the early twentieth century, results suggested that differences could be detected between racial and national groups, with whites of Western European ancestry scoring higher than Eastern Europeans, Asians, and black Africans. The debate was rekindled with the publication of *The Bell Curve* (Hernstein & Murray, 1995), which claimed to present new data to support this contention. However, the book also spawned counterarguments that questioned the validity of these data, as well as the authors' findings and assumptions (see, for example, Fraser, 1995).

Critics of intelligence tests believe the language and content of these tests are so rooted in white, middle-class culture that they systematically deprive nonwhite respondents of an equal opportunity to succeed with them. The language may have complexities or use terminology unfamiliar to some groups. Additionally, the situations and examples presented may be alien to certain respondents' life experiences. This raises a fundamental question: do these tests really measure intelligence (that is, are they valid), or are they measuring other constructs, such as experience, educational opportunity, and socioeconomic status?

These are fundamental questions that should be addressed whenever you design an instrument to measure any construct. An instrument has a cultural bias if it has content that adversely affects a group's ability to respond. Additionally, an instrument is culturally insensitive if it portrays any groups in a negative, stereotypical, or undesirable light. Hambleton and Rodgers (1995) suggest that during the pretesting process, instrument developers ask and answer the following questions to reduce opportunities for bias and to become aware of culturally sensitive items:

- Do items give a positive representation of the designated subgroups of interest (DSI)?
- Are items balanced in terms of being equally familiar to every DSI?
- Are members of DSI highly visible and positively portrayed in a wide range of traditional and nontraditional roles?
- Are DSI represented at least in proportion to their incidence in the general population?
- Are DSI referred to in the same way as others with respect to the use of first names and titles?
- Is there an equal balance of proper names? Ethnic groups? Roles for both sexes? Settings?
- Have all groups had the opportunity to become acquainted with the vocabulary?
- Do items contain content that is different for or unfamiliar to different DSI?
- Will members of DSI respond to items correctly or incorrectly for the wrong reasons?
- Do items reflect information unlikely to be within respondents' educational background? Do items contain language that has different or unfamiliar meanings for DSI?
- Are items free of difficult vocabulary?
- Are items free of group-specific language, vocabulary, or pronouns?
- Do items contain clues that facilitate the performance of one group over another?
- Are there ambiguities in the instructions, item stems, or response sets?
- Do the explanations respondents must understand to successfully complete items tend to differentially confuse DSI members?

As we suggested earlier, it is important for you to understand your own beliefs, values, and prejudices. This, along with pretesting, will help you recognize biased or culturally insensitive items.

Guidelines for Rating Scale Development

The following section supplies you with guidelines and recommendations for writing effective rating items. Recall that a rating item is made up of two parts, a stem and a response set, or scale. The stem serves as the stimulus; it elicits the response, and it may be written as a word, phrase, sentence, or paragraph. The response set, or scale, is a series of categories (which may or may not be numerical) from which the respondent selects one.

Write Unidimensional Stems

The stems of rating scale items should be unidimensional. This means that only one attribute or trait should be described in the stem. The opposite approach, a double-barreled question, confuses the respondent, who is not sure what part of the item to rate. In the previous chapter we gave an example of a Likert item that measures textbook readability: "The textbook for this course is very easy to read compared with other textbooks I have read." In this case, readability is limited to a comparison of one textbook to other textbooks. This eliminates the possibility that a respondent will compare the readability of the textbook to the readability of other types of printed matter. It also allows the person reviewing the data to make a straightforward interpretation. For examples of double-barreled items and ways to resolve them, review the section "Too Many Concepts" at the beginning of this chapter.

Write Unidimensional Response Sets

The response sets for rating scales should be unidimensional. This criterion is closely related to the previous one. You can ensure that a response set is unidimensional by writing it so it refers only to the attribute described in the stem. The unidimensionality of the stem and the unidimensionality of the response set should be considered jointly for each rating scale item.

Tie the Response Set to the Stem

The response set should be logically tied to the stem. In the following example the stem asks the respondent to rate the readability of a text; however, the response set is logically inconsistent with that request. It is ambiguous and does not fit well with the stem, as the stem asks about readability and the response set refers to *frequency.*

EXAMPLE

The textbook for this course is very easy to read compared with other textbooks I have read.

❏	❏	❏	❏	❏
Very often	Often	Don't know	Infrequently	Very infrequently

Obviously, this response set should be rewritten so that it is logically related to the stem. The stem is asking for level of agreement, so a response set of *strongly agree* to *strongly disagree* would fit.

Make the Stem Specific to the User's Needs

The level of specificity of the stem item should match the user's needs. For example, if the purpose of an item is to determine generally how a teacher is performing, the item could be phrased: "Rate the overall effectiveness of the instructor." However, if the purpose of the instrument is to provide feedback to individual teachers concerning their abilities in various teaching activities, the information gathered by this general item would not be particularly useful. A series of items assessing various teaching activities would likely prove more informative. These items might address abilities to plan, work individually with children, lead discussions, lecture, and grade papers, to note just a few.

Include Directions and Examples

Directions for using any specific type of rating scale should be included, along with appropriate examples. We have probably all had the unfortunate experience of trying to complete a questionnaire that asked for ratings along a certain continuum, without specifying how those ratings should be made:

Now that you have had a chance to examine a free sample, how do you rate our magazine?

I hate it   I love it

Here the actual rating task is unclear. Should you place an X on or between the lines? If so, what does an X in the middle space mean? Should you circle one of the oblique lines? If you place an X between the oblique lines, the response scale offers five choices, but if you circle one of the oblique lines, it offers six. The designer has created essentially two scales, obfuscating the process of analysis. He or she has a clear idea of the appropriate response but has not made that clear to the respondent. To ensure that all respondents know how to respond appropriately, the designer should provide explicit directions on rating procedures and then provide an example. Let's look at the readability examples again to clarify this point. Obviously, slightly different directions are in order for each scale.

EXAMPLES

1. Rate the following items by placing an X in the appropriate box above each item. For example, if you feel that the textbook for this course is as readable as comparable textbooks, you would rate the following item by placing an X in the box labeled "about average to read," as shown below.

Rate the readability of the textbook for this course compared with other textbooks you have read.

❑	❑	☒	❑	❑
Very difficult to read	Difficult to read	About average to read	Easy to read	Very easy to read

2. In the following set of items, you are to rate each item by placing an X over the set of words which best describes your feelings. For example, if you feel the textbook for this course is more readable than comparable textbooks, your response would look like this:

Rate the readability of the textbook for this course compared with other textbooks you have read.

___________________**X**_________\\

Very difficult to read	Difficult to read	About average to read	Easy to read	Very easy to read

3. In the following set of items you are to rate each item by placing an X in the appropriate space. As you will note, only the extreme ends of the scale are marked. Your task, therefore, is to consider each item on a seven-point continuum, decide which line on the continuum corresponds with your feelings, and place an X on that line. For example, if you feel that the textbook for this course is a little more difficult than average, your response would look like this:

Rate the readability of the textbook for this course compared with other textbooks you have read.

Very difficult to read _____ _____ **X**_____ _____ _____ _____ _____ Very easy to read

4. In the following set of items you are to decide whether or not you strongly agree (SA), agree (A), are undecided (U), disagree (D), or strongly disagree (SD) with each of the statements listed, and indicate your preference by circling the appropriate letters. For example, if you agree with the statement that the textbook for this course is one of the more readable you have encountered, you would circle "A" as shown below.

The textbook is very easy to read compared with other textbooks I have read.

    SD   D   U   Ⓐ   SA

To the extent possible, provide one set of directions and one response format for a series of items. It can quickly become confusing if you move from one item format to another, forcing the respondent to concentrate on the method of answering each question rather than on the content. The following example demonstrates one way of organizing a series of questions that use the same response set.

For the following items, indicate the extent to which you disagree or agree with each statement by placing an X in the appropriate box.

	Strongly Disagree	Disagree	No Opinion	Agree	Strongly Agree
Management provides financial support for in-service training.	❑	❑	❑	❑	❑
My workgroup works effectively to accomplish results.	❑	❑	❑	❑	❑
Management in this organization is receptive to new ideas.	❑	❑	❑	❑	❑
I feel comfortable asking my supervisor for assistance.	❑	❑	❑	❑	❑

This example also suggests the type of statements you might make in order to ensure that respondents make the correct type of response. The importance of such directions cannot be overemphasized, because the quality of the data resulting from any questionnaire or item depends on the extent to which the respondent understands how to complete it. Directions, in general, should be as brief and concise as possible. The language should be appropriate to your respondents' needs. If you are *sure* that your respondents are familiar with the type of rating scale you are using, examples may not be necessary; however, spelling out the directions for any set of similar items is probably advisable.

Use Language Appropriate to the Respondent

The language used in rating scale stems and responses should be adapted to respondents' abilities. As we noted earlier, it is important to check your statements for readability, use of technical language, and use of sensitive wording. In some instruments, such as those for children, you may even want to use graphics to assist in comprehension, and sometimes item stems will need to be read aloud.

Color in the group of circles that best describes how you feel when you go to school:

Select an Easily Understood Scale Format

The rating scale format selected should be easily understood by all of the respondents. Pretest for appropriateness if necessary, administering instrument items with several types of scales to a sample of your target audience. After they have experimented with these scales, ask them which format they felt most comfortable with and which one best allowed them to express their opinions. This procedure, although time consuming, will ensure better, more valid results in the final analysis.

Write to Avoid Biased Responses

Rating scale items should be written so as not to elicit biased responses. The respondent should not be led to think that certain responses are preferred over others. Here's an example of a poorly written item:

Rate the extent to which you enjoyed the immoral movie *Lolita*.

❏	❏	❏	❏	❏
One of the worst I have seen				One of the best I have seen

Clearly, the bias in the stem suggests that a person should rate this item low rather than high. A quick perusal of item stems by a colleague or other qualified person should help you to eliminate this problem.

Write All Items in the Same Order

Items should all be written in the same direction. As we have mentioned, an area of great interest to researchers is whether the order, or direction, of stems and response sets has an effect on the way respondents complete items (see, for example, Chan, 1991; Barnette, 1999; Friedman & Friedman, 1994). For example, you have the choice of phrasing the *stem* in a positive or negative direction: it can say, "I am satisfied with my retirement benefits," or "I am not satisfied with my retirement benefits." Additionally, you can order the *response set* from *strongly agree* (SA) to *strongly disagree* (SD) or, conversely, from *SD* to *SA*. And as you compile the items within the instrument it is possible to mix the order of item stems and response sets.

Our recommendation to write all items in the same order is our most controversial guideline, because many researchers argue that by having all positive or negative poles similarly situated on the page, you run the risk of *patterned* responses. That is, the respondent may simply mark all items in the same way without thinking about them individually or may tend to select the first choice in the response set (the primacy effect). However, the attempt to prevent these patterns by sometimes reversing the response anchors can be very confusing to respondents and may invalidate their responses. For example, one study found that preadolescent students had difficulty responding to items when the order of the response alternatives was mixed and that this difficulty was correlated to reading level (Marsh, 1986). However, Barnette (1999) administered four versions of a twenty-item survey and did not observe a primacy effect: "there is no evidence that the directionality of Likert response alternatives should be a concern in the design of at least some types of surveys. A primacy effect was not observed in this experiment. This indicates that at least sometimes it may not make any difference which direction is used as related to the technical adequacy and stability of the results obtained" (pp. 5–6).

We have found that mixing the order of items is rarely necessary when an instrument is designed for a specific audience that has an interest in the topic, as they tend to read each item carefully and are thoughtful about their responses. Therefore, it is important to know your intended audience and, through pretesting, to examine the impact of maintaining one direction or mixing directions of stems and response sets. Our guidance is to use positively worded stems whenever possible and to maintain the direction of the stems and response sets within the instrument. In particular, if you must have both positive and negative stems, the response set should remain in the same direction throughout to reduce the risk that respondents will select a rating that does not actually reflect their choice and/or will become fatigued and not complete the instrument. Yet there will always be exceptions, and you will find the best fit by pretesting the instrument. For example, you can identify patterned responses based on directionality by interviewing your pilot participants after they have completed a draft of the instrument.

Potential bias may also be counteracted by structuring the rating scale items in such a way that response sets are specific to only one question, so that response sets and stem make up a single entity (see Figure 8.1 for an example). Arranging stems and response sets into a single graphic display is also useful when response sets are the same across items. If you establish that your respondents do not respond similarly to items (through either a small pretest of the scales or previous administrations), then you might choose a matrix format as displayed in Figure 8.2. The primary advantage of this format is its use of space; that is, maximal information can be obtained in minimal space.

If you are concerned that selections might be biased when the response sets are all written in the same direction, you can intersperse negatively with positively slanted stems, *while keeping the response sets in the same direction.* This is particularly appropriate with summative scales (described in Chapter Eleven). In the example at the bottom of page 192, the stem wording differs by one word; in the first statement the textbook is described as the "most" readable and in the second it is described as

FIGURE 8.1: EXAMPLES OF RESPONSE SETS WRITTEN IN THE SAME DIRECTION.

The following questionnaire items were developed to measure student perceptions of teacher performance. Notice that each stem describes a different performance trait and each response set is different to fit with its stem. However, all the items move in a positive to negative direction, which assists the respondent in completing the questionnaire.

Interest in subject

❏   ❏   ❏   ❏   ❏

Always interested   Sometimes interested   Never interested

Availability to students

❏   ❏   ❏   ❏   ❏

Always available   Sometimes available   Never available

Fairness in grading

❏   ❏   ❏   ❏   ❏

Absolutely fair and impartial to all   Shows occasional partiality   Constantly shows partiality

Presentation of subject matter

❏   ❏   ❏   ❏   ❏

Clear   Unclear

Personal appearance

❏   ❏   ❏   ❏   ❏

Always well groomed, clothes neat and clean   Somewhat untidy at times   Slovenly, clothes untidy and ill-kept

Stimulates intellectual curiosity

❏   ❏   ❏   ❏   ❏

Inspires students to independent effort   Occasionally inspiring   Destroys interest in subject, makes subject uninteresting

the "least" readable. You would expect that someone who strongly agrees that it is the most readable would also strongly disagree that it is the least readable. So, you might want to use both items, placed at different points in the instrument, to check whether respondents are consistent in their responses. If not, you will want to find

FIGURE 8.2: MATRIX LAYOUT FOR A RATING SCALE.

Matrix Configuration

Rate your instructor on the following attributes, from below average to above average, by circling the appropriate number.

	Way below average				Way above average
Interest in subject	1	2	3	4	5
Sympathetic attitude toward students	1	2	3	4	5
Fairness in grading	1	2	3	4	5
Presentation of subject matter	1	2	3	4	5
Personal appearance	1	2	3	4	5
Stimulating intellectual curiosity	1	2	3	4	5

Alternative Configuration

Rate your instructor on each of the attributes below by placing the appropriate number on the space provided.

1 = way below average
2 = below average
3 = average
4 = above average
5 = way above average

_____ 1. Interest in subject
_____ 2. Sympathetic attitude toward students
_____ 3. Fairness in grading
_____ 4. Presentation of subject matter
_____ 5. Personal appearance
_____ 6. Stimulating intellectual curiosity

out why they are inconsistent; for example, is the instrument too long and respondents experience fatigue, or are they perhaps not taking enough time to carefully read and consider each item?

EXAMPLE

This textbook is one of the most readable I have encountered.

❏ | ❏ | ❏ | ❏ | ❏
Strongly disagree | Disagree | No opinion | Agree | Strongly agree

This textbook is one of the least readable I have encountered.

❏ | ❏ | ❏ | ❏ | ❏
Strongly disagree | Disagree | No opinion | Agree | Strongly agree

Avoid Global Terms in Response Sets

Avoid using global terms in response sets. Global terms ask respondents to rate things in terms of best or worst, all of the time or none of the time, and high score or low score. The major problem with using global terms is that the interpretation lies with each respondent. For example, if an instrument designer was interested in how often the respondents went to the movies, he or she could ask the question in the following ways:

How often do you go to the movies?

❏	❏	❏	❏	❏
Never attend	Infrequently	Sometimes	Often	Regularly attend

A better way to elicit information on this variable is to use a categorical scale:

How often do you go to the movies?

❏	❏	❏	❏	❏
Never	Once or twice a year	Once a month	Once a week	More than once a week

By asking the question in the latter way you are helping to ensure that every person is using the same continuum for responding, and in addition, you are getting information that is more easily interpreted.

FIGURE 8.3: DIFFICULTIES ASSOCIATED WITH USING ABSTRACT TERMS FOR RESPONSE CHOICES.

Is there a difference between *rarely* and *seldom*? Does *sometimes* mean less than 50% of the time, about 50% of the time, or more than 50 % of the time? Would your answer to the above questions change depending on the question being asked?

Response scales that make use of global terms may result in considerable variation between respondents. For the following word or term indicate the percent of time—0% to 100%—you think an event happens. Ask an acquaintance to do the same and then compare your estimates.

_____ Almost never		_____ Once in a while	
_____ About as often as not		_____ Rarely	
_____ Frequently		_____ Rather often	
_____ Generally		_____ Seldom	
_____ Hardly ever		_____ Sometimes	
_____ Never		_____ Usually	
_____ Not often		_____ Usually not	
_____ Now and then		_____ Very seldom	
_____ Occasionally		_____ Very often	
_____ Often			

Use Three to Seven Categories in Rating Scales

Rating scales should include from three to seven categories. In deciding on the number of response categories, it is important to consider the trait being rated, the extent to which individual categories can be identified, and the ability of respondents to discriminate between alternatives (see the sidebar "How Many Categories"). At times a limited number of alternatives may be desirable, such as *yes, no, not sure.* At other times, item stems may suggest a more extensive range. Research on rating scales has demonstrated conflicting findings. Matell and Jacoby (1971) suggest that the number of categories selected does not change the results. However, a study by Munshi (1990) found that a Likert item with seven options provides better discrimination than a response set with five alternatives.

How Many Categories?

Behavior rating scales are typically based on some measure of *severity*. However, there is no standard for the number of response alternatives. As displayed in these examples, the wording of the response set and the number of alternatives are dependent on the information contained in the stem.

❏	❏	❏	❏	❏
No Behavior	Mild	Moderate	Severe	Information is Unavailable

Source: Lyons, 1998.

❏	❏	❏	❏	❏
No Difficulty	A Little Difficulty	Moderate Difficulty	Quite a Bit of Difficulty	Extreme Difficulty

Source: McLean Hospital, 1999.

❏	❏	❏	❏	❏	❏	❏
Not Present	Very Mild	Mild	Moderate	Mod.– Severe	Severe	Extremely Severe

Source: Overall & Pfefferbaum, 1998.

❏	❏	❏	❏	❏	❏	❏
Absent	Slight	Mild	Moderate	Marked	Severe	Extreme

Source: Derogatis, 1992.

❏	❏	❏	❏	❏	❏	❏	❏	❏
No Problem	Less than Slight Problem	Slight Problem	Slight to Moderate Problem	Moderate Problem	Moderate to Severe Problem	Severe Problem	Severe to Extreme Problem	Extreme Problem

Source: Ward et al., 1997.

In choosing the number of response choices, it is particularly important to consider the respondent. Is it possible for the respondent to make the discrimination demanded? In a study of how people perceive nonverbal communication, observers were asked to view a videotape and rate the *emotional content* of a person's facial expressions. The rating system consisted of a twenty-one-point scale that ranged from *extremely negative* to *extremely positive* (Mullen et al., 1986). Use of a scale this large ensured that the raters could discriminate minor changes in expression. However, it also raises the possibility that this level of discrimination created results that might have been otherwise undetectable and therefore not significant. For example, if the researchers had not discerned a difference with the twenty-one-point scale during pretesting, would they have continued to increase the number of options until they did detect a difference?

In addition to ensuring that people can discriminate between choices, you must consider that people can process and remember only limited amounts of information, and those limits may influence how they respond to multiple items. One study (Miller, 1956) suggests that humans have difficulty working with more than seven *unidimensional* bits of information. For example, when presented with tones of different pitches, people have little difficulty distinguishing between four or five levels of pitch but become confused when presented with greater numbers. Subjects were able to differentiate a much greater number of colors, however, because color has two dimensions—hue and saturation—that assist with the task. One of the ways this plays out is through the primacy effect: "The longer the list, the more likely the first answer becomes a standard for comparison; the more alternatives given, the greater likelihood of stronger competition between alternatives given later in the list; and the longer the list, the greater cognitive cost of optimizing rather than satisficing" (Evaland & Sekely, 2005).

For most rating items, we believe a minimum of three and a maximum of seven alternatives is typically a sufficient number to allow respondents to discriminate between the options. For instruments that will be presented orally, consider limiting the number of choices to less than seven, as respondents may not remember all the choices and may tend to select from among the last presented. Ultimately, as we said earlier, the number of response categories to offer will depend on the topic of interest, the intended audience, and administration issues. If you believe more than seven alternatives are necessary to enhance discrimination, you should pretest with several formats of the instrument.

Assign Numerical Values When Appropriate

Assign numerical values to the response scale when they are needed for data analysis. Logistically, response categories that measure frequency typically form a *unipolar* scale

(Spector, 1992), where they move from low to high value (as in a response set scaled from *never* to *frequently*).[2] In this case the appropriate response scale is 0 to 5 or 1 to 7 and so forth. In contrast, intensity scales form a *bipolar* scale, where there are low values (*strongly disagree*), possibly a neutral position (*undecided*), and high values (*strongly agree*). Both unipolar and bipolar scales can be coded sequentially from 1 to 5; however, with a bipolar scale you can also use both positive and negative values, such as -2, -1, 0, $+1$, and $+2$.

There is some indication that the number sequence can influence respondents' choices. Researchers have found that a linear sequence (1 to 5) can produce a response pattern that is different from the pattern for a bipolar series (-2 to $+2$): "It appears that subjects perceive the negative-evaluation side of the scale as being more negative when there are negative numbers on that side rather than positive numbers" (Amoo & Friedman, 2001, p. 5). If you plan to use the numbers to create an aggregate score, as in the development of a multi-item scale (see Chapter Eleven), you would be wise to pretest alternate versions of the instrument using the different numbering sequences. Conversely, if the numbers are primarily placeholders or if you are using a frequency scale, you can number the choices from low to high or not assign numerical values at all. For example, the items in political polls tap into a variety of constructs, and therefore the response sets are typically not numbered.

Allow "Not Applicable" When Appropriate

Allow respondents to choose not applicable *when appropriate.* Because respondents may not have had the opportunity to form perceptions about specific traits being assessed by the questionnaire, a *not applicable* response should be available. For example, if you were assessing a set of training workshops on various dimensions, including clarity of presentation, materials, and use of audiovisual equipment and if the presenters in workshops A and B used audiovisual equipment but the workshop C presenter did not, then your instrument should be designed so that it does not force the workshop C participants to rate the effectiveness of audiovisual materials.

Similarly, instruments completed by an observer or rater may need an *information not available* response option, particularly when the information is a criterion for ruling an attribute in or out. Consideration should be given to the numerical value you assign to this alternative, as can be seen in the following examples. Each one uses the same numerical scale but with a different response set. Although the initial choice is coded 0 in each case, there is clearly a difference in the alternative associated with that category.

Examples

	0	1	2	3	4
Problems falling asleep:	No difficulty	Some difficulty	Moderate amount of difficulty	A lot of difficulty	Extreme difficulty

	0	1	2	3	4
Problems falling asleep:	No information available	Mild	Moderate	Severe	Very severe

Offer an Even or Odd Number of Categories and a Middle Choice as Appropriate

Assess the need for providing an even or an odd number of categories and whether to offer a middle choice. Related to deciding on the number of categories is deciding whether to use an even or an odd number of alternatives. This is more of an issue for bipolar scales, where a middle choice could indicate an indecisive position. The advantage of an even number of categories is that the respondent must be either positive or negative about the attribute and cannot be noncommittal. This is similar to a forced-choice question on a test, as the respondent must commit to one position or another.

Example (even)

❏   ❏   ❏   ❏

Very difficult   Difficult   Easy   Very easy

The advantage of using an odd number of categories is that the respondent has the option of being in the middle if he or she chooses.

Example (odd)

Very difficult   ❏   ❏   ❏   ❏   ❏   ❏   ❏   Very easy

A middle position exists when you provide a respondent with an option exactly halfway between two contrasting positions on a bipolar response scale. It differs from a *not applicable* or *don't know* alternative because it represents a legitimate intermediate viewpoint. The following are examples of different response scales containing a middle position:

Endorsement:	The worst	Bad	*Average*	Good	The best
Frequency:	Far too little	Too little	*About right*	Too much	Far too much
Intensity:	Very tense	Tense	*Neither tense nor relaxed*	Relaxed	Very relaxed

No clear-cut guideline exists for using an odd or even number of alternatives, as this depends on the purpose of your study and how you need to structure items to capture information. However, it is very important to pretest the items, as the number of response choices may bias how an item is rated. For example, when respondents who have not formed an opinion on a topic face a question that offers no middle position, they must decide either to skip it (resulting in missing data) or to make a selection that does not represent their point of view (resulting in incorrect data).

We recommend use of a midpoint when it provides the respondent with a necessary alternative and when it will provide meaningful data. If you are unsure, the best solution is to pretest two forms of your instrument—with and without scale midpoints—and then interview the respondents to determine if and how the midpoints made a difference. Although the research is mixed, some studies suggest that retaining the middle value does not unduly influence the respondent from selecting a more decisive alternative but that omitting the middle value may actually increase random selection of other alternatives (O'Muircheartaigh, Krosnick, & Helic, 2000). Further, a study by Presser and Schuman (1978) found that when limited to just three choices, respondents were more likely to choose the middle position, but when presented with five alternatives they were less likely to select it. This suggests that providing respondents with more options in the response set (for example, five to seven) may make it less likely that they will select the midpoint unless it is what they really believe represents their position.

Consider a Neutral Choice

Also consider offering a neutral choice. A neutral choice exists when you provide a noncommittal position, such as *undecided, unsure,* or *no opinion.* It is sometimes confused with a middle position because it is typically placed at the halfway point on a bipolar response scale; however, it can also be placed at the beginning or end of the response set.

Whether to provide a neutral choice is another debated topic in the questionnaire design literature. On the one hand it is considered a legitimate alternative because respondents may not have fully formed an opinion about the topic. Depriving them of this option may force them to take a position that does not reflect their actual belief or lack of knowledge, and therefore can skew the data. On the other hand there is a concern that respondents will tend to select an *undecided* or *unsure* response rather than make a commitment, that they will sidestep making a decision when they could and should make it.

The research on this topic is mixed because a neutral alternative may be influenced by the survey setting, topic, and audience. For example, one study found that education, age, and gender influenced selection of a *don't know* alternative, as did having "less knowledge about the topic, less interest in the topic, less exposure to information about the topic, and less perceived competence at understanding the topic" (O'Muircheartaigh et al., 2000, p. 23). Another study found that a *no opinion* alternative was "most common among respondents low in education, when respondents voted secretly, when questions were asked late in the survey, and when respondents devoted little effort to answering questions" (Krosnick et al., 2002, p. 396).

Our guidance is to consider your audience and the information you need. A case will illustrate this point. During the 1980s, health care providers became increasingly aware that smoking and the provision of health services do not mix. One of the authors served on a team assigned to determine how ready hospital employees were to become part of a nonsmoking organization. Some of the options being considered included banning smoking in designated areas in hospital buildings, banning smoking throughout the buildings, banning smoking on the grounds, banning smoking by patients at all times or at designated times, banning smoking by employees, and so forth. An employee questionnaire was developed and administered to all personnel. The pace at which the organization could implement these changes would depend on the amount of acceptance or resistance. The team decided that it was important to know whether employees held a strong conviction one way or another or whether they were straddling the fence on these issues; therefore respondents were provided an *unsure* option.

Public opinion polls typically provide a neutral choice because pollsters are interested in identifying the percentage of respondents who do not hold a strong position as well as the percentage of those who do. The items in Instrument 2.A were adapted from numerous polls and you will notice that all make use of a three-point scale with a neutral option. You can also format your questions to provide information about respondents' knowledge of the topic or to provide a middle position. For example, the alternative *I don't know enough to answer* is different from both *unsure* and *no opinion*. Some studies indicate that when both an undecided and a middle position are provided, the number of neutral responses decreases (Foddy, 1993). Finally, some instruments, such as employee evaluation forms, are not suited for a neutral point. In rating an employee on how well he or she works as a team member, an *unsure* option might reflect more on the supervisor (suggesting that the supervisor does not have a accurate judgment of the employee's abilities) than on the supervisee. In other words, if respondents have reason to be knowledgeable about the topic, a neutral choice is probably not necessary or useful and may encourage noncommittal responses. However, if you believe respondents have reason not to have formed an opinion, it is appropriate to provide them with an *unsure* or *undecided* alternative (Fowler, 1995).

Summary

The most frequently used format for creating questionnaire items is the rating scale, and the purpose of this chapter has been to provide you with guidelines that will help you create items that accurately frame your question. We have purposely used the term *guidelines*, rather than *standards* or *rules*, to describe the information presented in this chapter, as you may find that you need to adapt the formats suggested here to accommodate a particular situation or audience. For example, you may find that a Likert scale with nine response categories best meets your particular needs, rather than one with the recommended three to seven (and typically five) categories.

This is where the art of instrument construction begins. It is important to follow the guidelines, but they are not hard-and-fast rules. Pretesting for the most effective wording, number of options, and so forth, will help you, as the instrument developer, to decide what works best.

Instrument 8.A: Writing Sensitive Questions

The Youth Risk Behavior Survey (YRBS) was developed by the National Centers for Disease Control and Prevention (CDC) as part of a nationwide program to monitor the prevalence of major risk behaviors among American youths. The survey is administered through school systems to students in grades 9 through 12. It gathers information about students' nutrition, tobacco use, alcohol and drug use, physical exercise, safety practices, injuries, and sexual behaviors or practices related to AIDS, sexually transmitted diseases, and pregnancies. Communities can compare their results to national norms to identify needs for services and programs or for revising educational curriculums.

The YRBS, high school form, is a thirteen-page, ninety-nine-item questionnaire. To illustrate questions of a sensitive nature, we have included the first ten demographic items and the ten questions about cocaine and other drug use in Instrument 8.A. The first page of the survey consists of the title, introduction, and instructions. In the school district where we observed the YRBS being used, a "parent notification letter" was sent home with students prior to administering the survey. This letter was to be signed by a parent only if the parent did *not* grant permission for the child to participate in the survey. To facilitate scoring and tallying results, responses are made on a separate "answer sheet" by filling in ovals with a No. 2 pencil. The sheets are then scanned by a high-speed optical mark recognition scanner and the data stored in a database.

This survey asks many questions of a sensitive nature, including questions about behaviors that are illegal. For that reason students are instructed not to sign the survey, so as not to incriminate themselves. Anonymity is an approach often used to obtain a high response rate when a questionnaire attempts to measure behaviors in sensitive areas. However, it is also important to consider if and how the demographic information might compromise that level of confidentiality. For example, with some effort, the information provided in the first ten demographic items on the YRBS could be used to identify individuals fitting a specific profile, particularly where the sample size is small.

When developing instruments to produce information that will be used by individuals other than yourself, it is important to be clear about who will "own" these data (we will examine this issue in more detail in Chapter Fifteen). This should be documented in writing, as part of a legal contract, to ensure that the data and data sources (that is, the completed questionnaires) are not made available to entities that could misuse them. In the case of the YRBS, parents were ensured that the "survey procedures have been designed to protect your child's privacy and to allow for anonymous participation." However, the cover letter did not describe how the data would be handled or released. Ultimately, your integrity as researcher and instrument designer will be compromised if information you are responsible for is misused.

The ten YRBS questions on drug use attempt to measure behaviors and not attitudes; these are selection items that ask about frequency of use and that make use of alternative response sets (Chapter Nine) and not rating scales. Each item is written clearly and concisely. Items specifically address usage by drug type, including cocaine, heroin, steroids, and methamphetamines. The instrument designers cannot be faulted for their directness, given the sensitive nature of the topic.

The Youth Risk Behavior Survey also conveys a message about the importance of defining the purpose of your study. On the one hand, many items are related to a healthy life style. For example, the nutrition questions seek information about the frequency of eating vegetables, fruits, and dairy products. On the other hand, a number of items specifically address at-risk and illegal behaviors. The duality of the instrument tends to obscure its purpose and may raise questions about who will use the results and how that information will be applied.

Instrument 8.B: Biased Language

George Lakoff is a linguist who is interested in how politicians frame issues and use language. For example, the term *tax relief* connotes that taxation is onerous and thus something we need relief from. The term can be used to support one side of an argument, such as support for tax cuts, without presenting the other side, such as paying for national defense, education, and public health (Lakoff, 2004).

The following questionnaire was developed for a member of the U.S. House of Representatives (Goodlatte, 1998) and suggests the sort of framing that seems likely to bias respondents' answers. (The response rate as a percentage is provided for each option.) For example, the question about affirmative action (item 5) produced the following results:

Should the federal government grant hiring, contracting, or educational preferences or quotas on the basis of race or gender?

(a) Yes (5%)   (b) No (95%)

This item illustrates the use of biased language. The meaning of the term *quotas* is quite different from the meaning of *preferences*, as *quotas* infers assigned numbers. For example, organizations may implement policies that give preferences to various groups, such as veterans, minorities, the handicapped, or people with special, work-related skills. This is quite different from a government regulation that requires organizations to hire a predetermined number of individuals. Because the terms have different meanings, it is difficult to know which of the terms each respondent used to rate the item.

As we will examine in Chapter Thirteen, the method for collecting data can also create a form of bias. Because bias has been introduced here through the framing of items and by the process of administration, the results of this survey cannot be considered reliable or representative of voters in the congressional district where it was used.

INSTRUMENT 8.A: YOUTH RISK BEHAVIOR SURVEY (SAMPLE ITEMS).

This survey is about health behavior. It has been developed so you can tell us what you do that may affect your health. The information you give will be used to develop better health education for young people like yourself.

DO NOT write your name on this survey. The answers you give will be private. No one will know what you write. Answer the questions based on what you really do.

Completing the survey is voluntary. Whether or not you answer the questions will not affect your grade in this class. If you are not comfortable answering a question, just leave it blank.

The questions that ask about your background will be used only to describe the types of students completing this survey. The information will not be used to find out your name. No names will ever be reported.

Make sure to read every question. Fill in the ovals completely. When you are finished, follow the instructions of the person giving you the survey.

Thank you very much for your help.

DEMOGRAPHICS:

1. How old are you?
   1. 12 years old or younger
   2. 13 years old
   3. 14 years old
   4. 15 years old
   5. 16 years old
   6. 17 years old
   7. 18 years old

2. What is your sex?
   1. Female
   2. Male

3. In what grade are you?
   1. 9th grade
   2. 10th grade
   3. 11th grade
   4. 12th grade
   5. Ungraded or other grade

4. How do you describe yourself? (Select one or more responses.)
   1. American Indian or Alaskan Native
   2. Asian
   3. Black or African American
   4. Hispanic or Latino
   5. Native Hawaiian or Other Pacific Islander
   6. White

5. Do you receive free or reduced lunch at school?
   1. Yes
   2. No

6. In the home where you spend the most time, who are the adults who are the most responsible for you?
   1. Mother and Father
   2. Mother
   3. Father
   4. Grandparents
   5. Foster Parents
   6. Step-Parents
   7. Other Adult Relatives
   8. Other

7. How tall are you without your shoes on?
   1. Under 4′8″
   2. 4′8″ to 4′11″
   3. 5′ to 5′2″
   4. 5′3″ to 5′5″
   5. 5′6″ to 5′8″
   6. 5′9″ to 6′
   7. Over 6′1″

8. How much do you weigh without your shoes on?
   1. Less than 65 pounds
   2. 66–90 pounds
   3. 91–115 pounds
   4. 116–140 pounds
   5. 141–165 pounds
   6. 166–180 pounds
   7. 181–205 pounds
   8. Greater than 206 pounds

9. Who/what most influences your decisions and behavior?

   1. Family

   2. Friends and peers

   3. School teachers/counselors/ nurses

   4. Religious leaders

   5. TV/newspaper/magazine

   6. Other

   7. Not sure

10. How often do you attend religious services?

   1. Never

   2. Rarely

   3. Once or twice a month

   4. About once a week or more

The Next 10 Questions Ask about Cocaine and other Drugs:

54. During your life, how many times have you used **any** form of cocaine, including powder, crack, or free-base?

   1. 0 times

   2. 1 or 2 times

   3. 3 to 9 times

   4. 10 to 19 times

   5. 20 to 39 times

   6. 40 or more times

55. During the past 30 days, how many times did you use **any** form of cocaine, including powder, crack or freebase?

   1. 0 times

   2. 1 or 2 times

   3. 3 to 9 times

   4. 10 to 19 times

   5. 20 to 39 times

   6. 40 or more times

56. During your life, how many times have you sniffed glue, breathed the contents of aerosol spray cans, or inhaled any paints or sprays to get high?

   1. 0 times

   2. 1 or 2 times

   3. 3 to 9 times

   4. 10 to 19 times

   5. 20 to 39 times

   6. 40 or more times

57. During the past 30 days, how many times have you sniffed glue, breathed the contents of aerosol spray cans, or inhaled any paints or sprays to get high?

   1. 0 times

   2. 1 or 2 times

   3. 3 to 9 times

   4. 10 to 19 times

   5. 20 to 39 times

   6. 40 or more times

58. During your life, how many times have you used **heroin** (also called smack, junk, or China White)?

   1. 0 times

   2. 1 or 2 times

   3. 3 to 9 times

   4. 10 to 19 times

   5. 20 to 39 times

   6. 40 or more times

59. During your life, how many times have you used **methamphetamines** (also called speed, crystal, crank, or ice)?

    1. 0 times
    2. 1 or 2 times
    3. 3 to 9 times
    4. 10 to 19 times
    5. 20 to 39 times
    6. 40 or more times

60. During your life, how many times have you taken **steroid pills or shots** without a doctor's prescription?

    1. 0 times
    2. 1 or 2 times
    3. 3 to 9 times
    4. 10 to 19 times
    5. 20 to 39 times
    6. 40 or more times

61. During your life, how many times have you used a needle to inject any illegal drug into your body?

    1. 0 times
    2. 1 time
    3. 2 or more times

62. During the past 12 months, has anyone offered, sold or given you an illegal drug on school property?

    1. Yes
    2. No

63. How old were you when you tried any form of illegal drug (excluding tobacco and alcohol) for the first time?

    1. I have never tried an illegal drug
    2. 8 years old or younger
    3. 9 or 10 years old
    4. 11 or 12 years old
    5. 13 or 14 years old
    6. 15 or 16 years old
    7. 17 years old or older

INSTRUMENT 8.B: RESULTS OF THE 1998 CONGRESSIONAL QUESTIONNAIRE.

Earlier this year, I included a survey with my *Congressional Report* to learn your views on several important issues facing our country. I am very pleased with the response, as nearly 20,000 folks took the time to complete the survey and return it to my office. Below are the survey results. Next to each answer, in parentheses, is the percentage of folks who indicated that response. For example, for Question 1, 44 percent of those responding believe that moral decline is the number one problem facing the United States. Thank you to all those who participated.

1. What do you consider to be the number one problem facing the United States?

    (a) Education (12%)   (b) Economy (5%)   (c) Crime (11%)

    (d) IRS/Tax System (17%) (e) Moral Decline (44%) (e) Other (12%)

(*Continued*)

2. Regarding federal spending, since 1995, the Congress has cut:

   (a) Too much (6%)   (b) Not enough (78%)   (c) The right amount (16%)

3. Regarding changing federal income taxes, which of the following is closest to your views?

   (a) Replace the current federal income tax with a flat tax (40%)

   (b) Replace the current federal income tax with a national sales tax (20%)

   (c) Modify the current federal income tax (35%)

   (d) Leave the federal income tax as is (5%)

4. Should the IRS be:

   (a) Abolished (27%)   (b) Dramatically changed (66%)   (c) Left as is (6%)

5. Should the government grant hiring, contracting, or educational preferences or quotas on the basis of race or gender?

   (a) Yes (5%)   (b) No (95%)

6. Should the federal government have unrestricted access to information and communications transmitted by individuals and businesses over the Internet?

   (a) Yes (15%)   (b) No (85%)

7. Should Congress continue investigating the current presidential campaign and administration's fundraising activities?

   (a) Yes (59%)   (b) No (41%)

8. U.S. troops have been in Bosnia for two years. What do you think should be done?

   (a) Pull the troops out now and let European powers work it out (55%)

   (b) Continue U.S. involvement indefinitely (15%)

   (c) Allow the troops to stay up to a year longer (30%)

9. Which statement more closely reflects your views on education?

   (a) The federal government should be given more control over our children's education (5%)

   (b) Educational decisions should be kept at the state and local level (95%)

10. Do you consider your personal beliefs to be:

    (a) Conservative (50%)   (b) Moderate (47%)   (c) Liberal (3%)

Endnotes

1. Respondents may also provide *socially undesirable* responses: for example, a substance-abusing client who does not want to participate in treatment might exaggerate behaviors that are not tolerated by a rehabilitation program.

2. The higher the number the greater the intensity, whether the intensity is positive (from worst to best) or negative (from pain free to intense pain). For example, on the Symptoms Distress Scale the value of 5 is given to the most stressful health problems. In the following example, also notice that the more intense symptomatology is placed on the left-hand side of the response scale (Hinds, Schum, & Srivastava, 2004).

Please put a circle around the number that most closely measures how well you sleep last night.

Couldn't have been worse   5   4   3   2   1   A perfect night

Key Concepts and Terms

appropriate language	primacy effect	sensitive question
biased item	readability	socially desirable response
bipolar scale	recency effect	unidimensionality
middle option	response set	unipolar scale
neutral option	selection item	

CHAPTER NINE

SELECTION ITEMS

Alternative Formats

In this chapter we will

- Present guidelines for creating selection items using alternative response sets.
- Describe the process of rank ordering and guidelines for creating items that ask respondents to rank their responses.

In this chapter we continue to present information about several approaches to constructing items where you, as instrument developer, provide the response sets. These approaches are scales that use alternative response sets and response alternatives that are ranked rather than rated. An example of rating using an alternative response scale is asking respondents to select the year's best picture out of a list of five motion pictures. Alternatively, you could use the process of ranking to determine the best picture; instead of asking respondents to select just one response, you would ask respondents to rank their preferences from one to five and determine the "winner" as the movie given the highest rank by the majority of respondents. The advantage of this approach is that it also provides information about the second most-liked movie, the third, and so on.

As in the previous chapter, we will define and describe each type of item format, provide guidelines for constructing each item, and explain how to analyze and report findings produced by these alternative item formats. Making use of these additional formats can support effective decision making by helping you obtain the exact information you seek.

Alternative Response Scales

In this section we use the term *alternative response scales,* or *alternative response sets,* to describe scales that offer alternatives to the more familiar scales of agreement, frequency, or intensity. For example, demographic items, such as questions about age, gender, educational level, cultural background, and socioeconomic status, often make use of alternative response scales.

Alternative response scales may consist of items that are clearly related, thus forming a continuum, or they may consist of a number of diverse factors, related to the stem of the question but not to each other (see the following examples). Alternative response scales may also take the form of dichotomous items—such as questions eliciting a *yes* or *no* response or asking the respondent's gender, *female* or *male*—and check-all-that-apply items.

EXAMPLES

Responses Related to Each Other and to the Stem

What is your professional rank?

❑ Full Professor
❑ Associate Professor
❑ Assistant Professor
❑ Instructor
❑ Adjunct Faculty
❑ Other

Responses Unrelated to Each Other But All Related to the Stem

Which of the following hobbies do you currently pursue?

❑ Bird watching
❑ Camping or hiking
❑ Cars or car repairs
❑ Flying
❑ Model trains/planes/cars
❑ Photography

Alternative Response Scale Used to Obtain Factual Information

How many hours a week do you spend reading—including newspapers, magazines, and books? (Check one)

❑ Less than 1 hour
❑ More than 1 hour, but less than 3 hours
❑ More than 3 hours, but less than 5 hours
❑ More than 5 hours, but less than 7 hours
❑ More than 7 hours

Alternative Response Scale Used to Measure Attitudes and Beliefs

Regarding the federal income tax, what actions do you believe Congress should take? (Check one)

❑ Replace the current income tax with a flat tax.
❑ Replace the current income tax with a national sales tax.
❑ Reduce all tax brackets by 10%.
❑ Leave the system as it is.
❑ No opinion.

Before considering specific criteria for writing this type of item, it is important to understand some general points. First, the purpose of these alternative formats for selection items is to elicit information from the respondents through a predetermined response set. As the instrument designer, you will have considered beforehand whether to use an open-ended question or a response set. For example, you might ask for a respondent's job classification with an open-ended question, or you might create a list of job classifications. An open-ended question might obtain a broader range of responses; the disadvantage is that this broad range could be difficult to categorize. One advantage of using an alternative response set that limits choices can be that the results can be easily analyzed. If you decide to limit respondents' choices, your next task is to determine what the choices in the response set will be. In the previous example using academic ranks, the respondents are limited to six alternatives. As with all items in which you provide the choices, this narrowed focus can also turn to a disadvantage. Pretesting is essential to ensure that you have included all the likely response choices for each item.

An alternative response set may be relatively cumbersome if the question you are asking can be fully answered with one number. For example, you could ask respondents to indicate the number of children they have by circling a number on a response set (1, 2, 3, 4, 5 or more), or you could obtain the information perhaps more easily by asking an open-ended question such as, "Indicate the number of children currently living in this household ————." Consequently, it is important to weigh both the benefits and limitations of using an alternative response set rather than an open-ended item.

Second, alternative response scales are an effective approach when differences between choices are qualitative and not just quantitative, as in the previous example asking about hobbies. And these qualitatively different choices are particularly useful when all or most of the response categories are known. This provides the added advantage of ensuring that all respondents can select from the same set of response categories.

Now let's consider the guidelines for developing alternative response sets.

State Items Clearly

The stem and responses should be stated clearly and unambiguously. It is important to check that each item is not worded in such a way that different respondents are likely to interpret it differently. One way to accomplish this is to read the item aloud, because even when you do not *see* a problem, you may *hear* that a word has more than one meaning in the context of the statement. Another way to check for lack of clarity is to have several different people read each item and then explain to you what they think the item or specific words mean. If their understanding is different from what you intended, then you should rewrite the item.

Ensure Language Is Appropriate

Item language should be appropriate to the respondents. As we discussed in Chapter Eight, it is important to check your statements for readability, unnecessarily technical language, and unintentionally sensitive wording. In particular, if a response set is used to collect demographic data, such as race, ethnicity, marital status, or income, be sure that gathering this information is absolutely essential and that items are carefully worded. Individuals may not answer questions when they are uncomfortable with the terminology used: for example, researchers asking about race need to be aware that during the 1960s and 1970s the term *black* replaced the term *Negro* in common usage and that for the past twenty years the term *African American* has been widely used in addition to black.

Write Stems Unidimensionally

The item stem should be stated unidimensionally. As noted in the previous chapter, this means that only one attribute or trait should be described in the stem. Consider the following example of a *double-barreled* item, which may be almost impossible to answer as a respondent's answer to the two-part stem may not match any of the paired answers shown in the response set. The way to correct this, of course, is to create two separate items.

EXAMPLE

Original: Identify your position and salary:

❑ Administrator ($50,000–$100,000 annually)
❑ Teacher ($25,000–$50,000 annually)
❑ Teacher's aide ($10,000–$20,000 annually)

Rewrite

1. Indicate your current position with this school system:
   - ❑ Administrator—Central Office
   - ❑ School administrator
   - ❑ Classroom teacher
   - ❑ Teaching assistant
   - ❑ Teacher's aide
   - ❑ Other

2. Indicate your current annual salary from employment with this school system:
   - ❑ Less than $15,000
   - ❑ $15,001–$20,000
   - ❑ $20,001–$30,000
   - ❑ $30,001–$40,000
   - ❑ $40,001–$50,000
   - ❑ $50,001 or more

Make Choices Exhaustive

The response set should be exhaustive, identifying all possible choices. For example, if you were surveying personnel at a local elementary school and wanted to know their job levels, you might write this selection item:

Identify your position:

❑ Administrator   ❑ Teacher   ❑ Teacher's aide

You will not, however, have written an exhaustive item because there is no choice for the school counselor, clerical support staff, or nurse to check. You can and should avoid this problem by identifying the most likely choices (by researching your subject and pretesting) and offering an *other* or *miscellaneous* category:

Identify your position.

❑ Administrator	❑ Counselor
❑ Teacher	❑ Secretary
❑ Teacher's aide	❑ Other (please specify) ———————

By including the *other* category you make the item applicable to all respondents, and if you ask respondents to *please specify*, you find out who or what these *other* categories include. This latter information can be of particular benefit both in qualifying results and in constructing similar items in the future.

A related challenge for the instrument designer is ensuring that the response set is meaningful to the respondent. Studies have demonstrated that the alternatives you choose may "influence respondents' own frequency estimates and judgments, as well as respondents' interpretation of the question" (Schwarz & Oyserman,

2001, p. 146). For example, if your item uses the term *teacher's aide* but some respondents work in a school system that uses the term *teaching assistant,* they may be unsure whether the job duties are the same and the job titles interchangeable. Once again, it is important to pretest items with potential users to ensure that the response choices provide a meaningful set of the attributes for respondents as well as providing you with the data you are looking for.

Make Choices Exclusive

The response categories should be mutually exclusive. They should not overlap to the extent that people cannot easily select the appropriate one. Overlapping seems to occur most often with numerical categories.

EXAMPLE

Original: How much time do you spend in lesson planning during the average week? (check one)

❏ 0–1 hours
❏ 1–3 hours
❏ 3 or more hours

The teachers who estimate either 1 hour or 3 hours face a selection dilemma here. Moreover, if they tend to select the longer duration, a systematic distortion of the data will result. You have a couple of methods available for ensuring mutual exclusiveness in numerical choices. First, you can avoid using selection items with numerical categories and use open-ended items instead. Second, if you do use numerical response categories, check carefully that you have written categories in which limits do not overlap. Here is one way to correct the previous example:

Rewrite: How much time do you spend in lesson planning during the week? (check one)

❏ Less than 1 hour
❏ Between 1 and 3 hours
❏ More than 3 hours

In addition to numerical categories, the groupings we use to describe demographic factors may raise exclusivity difficulties. As our society becomes more pluralistic, it is becoming increasingly difficult to classify people by narrowly defined categories, such as *married, separated, divorced,* or *single.* An individual having a "live-in partner" might not feel that these choices fit her situation; an individual who is divorced and has not remarried may not be sure if he should check *divorced* or *single.* Pretesting may help in creating the mutually exclusive categories required, such as *divorced—not remarried, single—never married,* and the like.

Provide Directions

Respondents should be given directions. It is important to be clear about what you want the respondent to do when presented with an item. For example, checking all that apply is a decidedly different activity from the activity of selecting one response. If the directions are not specified and the respondent selects just one when you wanted him or her to check all that apply, you may lose useful information.

Put Choices in a Logical Order

Responses should be logically ordered. You might order a response set alphabetically, by level of importance, by status, or by quality. In an example used earlier, college faculty were listed by tenure—from full professor to adjunct, whereas hobbies were listed alphabetically. Level of income, age, length of employment, and other quantitative categories are typically presented from lowest to highest. Although you may not be consciously thinking about the order of the alternatives as you are developing an item, it is important to return to the item at some point to order the choices in a logical sequence.

Check-All-That-Apply Response Sets

When using a *check-all-that-apply* response set, you present the individual with an array of choices for simultaneous review and selection. However, unlike the purpose of other alternative response sets, the purpose of a check- (or mark-) all-that-apply option is not to discriminate but to be inclusive. For example, based on your pretesting you may find that multiple options can be relevant to individuals and that forcing a respondent or rater to select just one or to rank them by importance excludes meaningful data. Using a check-all-that-apply format also allows users to select alternatives without having to judge their importance in relationship to each other. In this way, a check-all-that-apply item is similar to a dichotomous choice, as the alternative is either included or excluded. Check-all-that-apply items can be developed to obtain factual information as well as to capture opinions and attitudes.

EXAMPLES

A. Which of the following educational approaches do you use? Please check all that apply.

———— Lectures
———— Experiential exercises
———— Group discussion
———— Individual student presentations
———— Guest lecturers/presenters
———— Case study analysis

B. What steps do you believe the federal government should take to make the United States more energy independent? Please check all that apply. ☑

☐ Raise the gasoline tax.
☐ Provide incentives for oil exploration.
☐ Provide tax breaks for energy efficiency.
☐ Enforce better automobile fuel economy.
☐ Provide incentives for alternative fuels.
☐ Nothing, it is not a government responsibility.

Because the user is not being asked to discriminate between options, the list can be considerably longer than the lists for other alternative response sets or ranking alternatives. It is assumed that the respondent will read and consider each option independently of the others and select only those he or she agrees with, and therefore not find it too burdensome to consider twelve to fifteen alternatives. We say "assumed" because there is some evidence that respondents are more likely to choose the options at the beginning of a list presented in writing (a primacy effect) and to select the last options on a list when presented orally, as during a telephone survey (a recency effect) (Dillman, Smyth, Christian, & Stern, 2004; Mooney & Carlson, 1996).

The guidelines we presented earlier for alternative response scales apply equally to check-all-that-apply items. In particular it is important to state the alternatives unambiguously and to use terminology users will understand. In the examples just given, will a teacher know what is meant by *experiential exercises*? Will respondents wonder whether *tax breaks for energy efficiency* applies just to automobiles or to other situations as well, such as home building? Most important, through your pretesting you should be able to present a fairly exhaustive list of alternatives. Because the goal is inclusion, limiting the number of choices could affect the depth and range of information you obtain.

Dichotomous Response Sets

Some questions may be best expressed with only two response categories. Dichotomous response sets create forced-choice items, as the respondent must choose one over the other alternative. In addition to items requiring *yes* or *no* response categories, you might, for example, ask respondents to choose between two candidates for public office or two positions on public policy: for example, If the election were held today whom would you vote for: McNamara or Keats. This puts the information out in a concise form that is unambiguous and easy to tally. Dichotomous items are also useful for rating instruments where the observer is asked to indicate the presence or absence of a behavior without looking for subtleties. The advantage of dichotomous questions is efficiency and clarity; however, care must be taken to avoid introducing bias by, for example, emphasizing one option over another.

You can also use dichotomous *yes* or *no* and *if … then* questions to direct inquiry within the body of a questionnaire and to lead the respondent through a series of related items. The advantage of this approach is that it allows the user to move through the instrument efficiently by skipping those sections that do not apply—this is particularly useful if the instrument is lengthy.

EXAMPLE

Are you currently employed?   ❑ Yes   ❑ No

If your response to this question was no, please complete the next three items. If your response was yes, please skip those items and proceed to item number fifteen.

1. If not employed, how long have you been out of work?
   ❑ Less than six months   ❑ Six months to a year   ❑ More than a year

2. If unemployed for more than a year, how many times have you applied for work in the past year?
   ❑ Less than 20   ❑ 21–30   ❑ 31–40   ❑ 41–50   ❑ More than 50

3. During the past six months have you received vocational counseling to assist you in applying for work?
   ❑ Yes   ❑ No

However, you should be judicious in using this approach as it also creates opportunities for respondents to lose their place, inadvertently skip items that should be completed, or take a longer time than anticipated to complete the questionnaire because they are double-checking to be sure they haven't missed something or skipped too much. It is also human nature to read questions one is directed to skip; consequently, using *yes* or *no* items in this way may not actually increase administration efficiency. Use of dichotomous statements to direct the user should be carefully checked during the pretesting phase to ensure that these items produce the desired benefits without creating potential pitfalls.

You might also use *yes* or *no* responses to reduce the possibility that respondents will omit information, as may happen with a check-all-that-apply format. This approach may also reduce primacy effects—placing more weight on the first alternatives presented in a list. When presented in a *yes* or *no* response format, options must be considered and responded to individually rather than as a set (Sudman & Bradburn, 1982).

EXAMPLES

Alternative Response Set

Which of the following values do you agree with? Check all that apply.

☐ Getting ahead financially
☐ Being tolerant of others
☐ Obeying the law
☐ Pursuing an education
☐ Working hard
☐ Being honest
☐ Helping others
☐ Respecting another's property
☐ Respecting one's parents
☐ Participating in civic activities

Dichotomous Response Set

Which of the following statements do you agree with? Indicate by checking each statement either Yes or No.

Value	Yes	No
Getting ahead financially		
Being tolerant of others		
Obeying the law		
Pursuing an education		
Working hard		
Being honest		
Helping others		
Respecting another's property		
Respecting one's parents		
Participating in civic activities		

Many of the guidelines discussed earlier apply to dichotomous items also. The following two guidelines will also be helpful when preparing these items.

Consider Expanding the Choices

Consider adding other *and* not applicable *choices to* yes *or* no *items.* Although a dichotomous response is limited by definition to two choices, the situation may call for more alternatives. The discussion of Instrument 6.A in Chapter Six offers a good example of a situation where an additional alternative was needed to capture information that did not easily fit into a response set limited to *yes* or *no*. Indeed, some raters using that instrument wrote in "not applicable" rather than selecting a *yes* or *no* response.

Consider the Audience When Asking About Demographics

Be sensitive to prospective audiences when using demographic items, such as questions about gender. Although the majority of respondents are unlikely to have a problem with the traditional response choices of *male* or *female* (or *female* or *male*), some populations might take offense that an *other* category is not provided. For example, individuals who are undergoing sex change surgery would not feel that the response choices are adequate. As with other demographic items, be sure that the information is absolutely essential to the questionnaire.

Rank-Ordered Response Sets

Judged art exhibits give viewers an opportunity to contrast the "Best in Show" against the recipients of second-, third-, and fourth-place awards. We can view and compare all of the paintings, which may suggest what the judge was thinking when he or she was evaluating the artwork. Similarly, the method of rank ordering is a popular and practical approach for obtaining information because it allows a respondent to judge a large number of potential responses in reference to one another at one time. In other words, all the response choices are present for simultaneous observation and consideration. A certain number of choices are presented to the respondent, who ranks them from highest to lowest based upon the standard or guidelines provided. This provides more information than a rating in which the respondent records a single choice without reference to the other presented alternatives.

There are generally two approaches to creating rank-ordered items. Ranking by preference asks for respondents' personal choice. Judging paintings by how well we liked the way they looked, movies by how well we enjoyed viewing them, and cakes in a baking contest by how well they tasted are examples of ranking by preference. Conversely, we may need to choose less personal criteria on which to base our rankings. In selecting a new car we might base our comparison on specifications such as miles per gallon of gas, safety features, and horsepower. Rankings of colleges and the "best towns to live in" are criterion based, and some of these measures are highly controversial because their validity and meaningfulness can be questioned. For example, among the criteria used to rank colleges are reputation in the academic community, faculty pay, class size, and alumni giving. This would tend to put Ivy League colleges at the top, and so it is no surprise that in 1998, MIT and Harvard, Princeton, Yale, Stanford, Duke, and Johns Hopkins Universities were ranked in the top ten (Associated Press, 1999).

From a measurement perspective, ranking provides information about the order of and relationship between selections; however, it does not provide information about the size of the interval between the choices. It may indicate that you liked one movie more than another, but not how much more you liked it. This is because rank, whether preference or criterion based, is ultimately internal to the individual doing the ranking.

Simple rank ordering involves tabulating the responses for each item and reporting the results in the form of a frequency table. When two or more items produce the same number of responses, the ranking is divided. Consequently the number of rankings will not always equal the total number of items. For example, the project manager for a children's mental health treatment center would like to determine staff preferences for in-service training. She makes a list of eleven relevant areas and asks staff to rank them by assigning the number 1 to the area they believe they need training in the most and the number 11 to the area they need training in the least. Twenty-five employees are queried, producing the following frequencies and rankings:

Item #	Area	Frequency	Ranking
11	Parent training techniques	22	1
4	Self-help skills	20	2.5
8	Discipline	20	2.5
1	Cognitive development	17	3
2	Language development	16	4
9	Assessing child development	15	5
3	Motor development	14	6
5	Social and emotional development	12	7
10	Individual programming	11	8
6	Perceptual development	8	9
7	Verbal stimulation	3	10

In this example, twenty-two respondents ranked alternative 11 (parent training techniques) as their top or number one choice. Alternatives 4 and 8 were selected by twenty respondents. When scores are tied, the average rank of the two should be reported. For example, based on the sequence in which they originally appeared, alternative 4 would be ranked second and alternative 8 would be ranked third; however, the average of their rankings $(2 + 3)$ is 2.5, and that is what is reported.

Follow these guidelines for the development of ranking items.

State Items Clearly

State each item unambiguously. As in the construction of other item formats, both the stem and the response choices must be stated clearly and succinctly. Use terminology that is understood by respondents, and pretest by having others read for comprehension.

Offer Enough Choices

Provide an exhaustive yet not overwhelming list of choices to rank. If the list is large, respondents may have difficulty keeping track of the alternatives. If the list is small, you may not have included all of the response choices appropriate to the item. Although there are no firm rules, we suggest that you limit the number of alternatives to between eight and twelve. If you have identified five to seven response choices, you may want to consider another format, such as an alternative response scale. If your list exceeds twelve, you may want to divide the item into two parts or even two separate items.

Create Associated Categories

The response choices for each item should form a category, being associated by theme, concept, or attribute, and yet be mutually exclusive, showing enough differentiation that a hierarchy can be established. In the following example, the concept is supervisory training; however each alternative addresses a different topic.

EXAMPLE

To best meet management needs for continuing education, please rank the topic that you believe would most help you carry out your job, then the next most important topic, and so on. Rank the items by placing a number in the blank in front of the item, with number 1 being the most important, number 2 the next most important, and so on to number 8, the least important.

———— Mastering time management skills
———— Counseling employees about personal issues

———— Correcting work performance problems
———— Addressing sexual harassment in the workplace
———— Understanding employee benefit programs and options
———— Developing quality improvement work teams
———— Improving technical writing skills
———— Improving public speaking skills

Give Directions

Provide instructions about the order of ranking. By convention, the most important item is ranked number 1; however, instructions must be provided to explain whether you want items ranked in descending or ascending order: for example, "Rank the following ten items, with item number 1 being the most important and item number 10 being the least important." In addition, the instructions should indicate where and how the items should be ranked. The following instructions, for example, were developed to provide guidance in completing an item that will be scored by optical mark recognition software.

EXAMPLE

How would you rank the following in regard to the amount of time you would like instruction to be provided to your child? (1st = most time spent, 8th = least time spent). Use each ranking only once; for example, do not rank two or more items as 4th. Please check the box that corresponds to your chosen ranking.

	1st	2nd	3rd	4th	5th	6th	7th	8th
Academics—physical sciences (physics, geology, biology)	❑	❑	❑	❑	❑	❑	❑	❑
Academics—social sciences (history, geography, psychology)	❑	❑	❑	❑	❑	❑	❑	❑
Academics—language arts (English, drama, public speaking)	❑	❑	❑	❑	❑	❑	❑	❑
Creative arts (dance, music, art, photography)	❑	❑	❑	❑	❑	❑	❑	❑
Vocational subjects (home economics, computer basics)	❑	❑	❑	❑	❑	❑	❑	❑
Vocational training (auto mechanics, carpentry, electronics)	❑	❑	❑	❑	❑	❑	❑	❑
Health and physical education (gym, health education)	❑	❑	❑	❑	❑	❑	❑	❑
Extracurricular activities (drama club, band, choir, sports)	❑	❑	❑	❑	❑	❑	❑	❑

Summary

Vincent van Gogh's paintings are instantly recognizable due to his use of large, vibrant brush strokes. In contrast, Salvador Dali used a more subtle style that resulted in paintings of an almost photographic quality. Like artistic techniques the approaches introduced in this chapter—alternative response sets and rank order—provide you with additional approaches to collecting and measuring information. The use of these item formats is dependent on the information you are trying to obtain and the circumstances in which the data will be collected. Ideas about which item format best meets your needs will occur as you plan your study. Then pretesting will help you assess whether that item format produces the desired information.

Instrument 9.A: Records Audit Checklist

This checklist displayed in Instrument 9.A was designed for auditing medical records and is typical of alternative response sets used in checklists and inventories. (The actual document is two pages long and has more items.) The instrument includes a title and three demographic items—record number, date of audit, and name of person completing the audit. The checklist was developed by a medical records supervisor to be used by other medical records personnel; therefore instructions were not deemed necessary. The first column is for the item in the medical record that will be audited. The second column is for the name of the person responsible for completing that particular piece of documentation, in case he or she needs to contacted for a signature.

The third column is formatted as a dichotomous response set (*present* or *absent*), with an additional selection for *not applicable*, to be used when a chart contains required documents that do not need the signature of hospital staff. The fourth column is organized as a simple alternative response set with just three alternatives. Staff felt they needed the last option (*not in chart at time of review*) because they did not consider a chart audit to be complete if a document was required but not in the chart at the time the audit was performed. Marking this option ensured that medical records personnel would return to the record to complete the audit at a later time.

INSTRUMENT 9.A: MEDICAL RECORD AUDIT CHECKLIST.

Record No. _____   Date of audit_____

Individual completing this audit _____

Item	Name of Individual Responsible for Completing this Documentation	Presence or Absence of Staff Signature (Check One)	Status
Psychiatric evaluation		❑ Present ❑ Absent ❑ Not applicable	❑ Completed ❑ Not completed ❑ Not in chart at time of review
Psychological evaluation		❑ Present ❑ Absent ❑ Not applicable	❑ Completed ❑ Not completed ❑ Not in chart at time of review
Social work evaluation		❑ Present ❑ Absent ❑ Not applicable	❑ Completed ❑ Not completed ❑ Not in chart at time of review
Educational evaluation		❑ Present ❑ Absent ❑ Not applicable	❑ Completed ❑ Not completed ❑ Not in chart at time of review
Nursing evaluation		❑ Present ❑ Absent ❑ Not applicable	❑ Completed ❑ Not completed ❑ Not in chart at time of review
Neurological assessment		❑ Present ❑ Absent ❑ Not applicable	❑ Completed ❑ Not completed ❑ Not in chart at time of review
Master treatment plan		❑ Present ❑ Absent ❑ Not applicable	❑ Completed ❑ Not completed ❑ Not in chart at time of review
Daily treatment note		❑ Present ❑ Absent ❑ Not applicable	❑ Completed ❑ Not completed ❑ Not in chart at time of review
Discharge plan		❑ Present ❑ Absent ❑ Not applicable	❑ Completed ❑ Not completed ❑ Not in chart at time of review
Discharge summary		❑ Present ❑ Absent ❑ Not applicable	❑ Completed ❑ Not completed ❑ Not in chart at time of review

Instrument 9.B: A Marketing Survey

Retailers are often interested in obtaining consumers' reactions to a product. This information can be used to modify or improve the product and to plan marketing strategies. From cars to computers, vendors are increasingly enclosing marketing surveys with their merchandise. For example, the following instrument was inserted between the pages of the book that was the object of the survey. It was originally printed on a postage-paid, 5.5-by-7-inch card, with the return address printed on the opposite side.

This is a brief and succinct instrument, designed to collect information for marketing rather than for product improvement. The first four items are demographic, and the next five ask for purchasing information. Only the last item, an open-ended question, gives the consumer an opportunity to comment on the quality of the product. The first nine items use alternative response sets to capture factual information, and this instrument is a good example of how this item format is often used.

INSTRUMENT 9.B: MARKETING SURVEY.

Your Comments About (*Name of Text*) Are Important to Us!

We'd like to hear from you. Please take a moment to complete the following questions and mail this card back to us. Thank you!

1. Gender: ❑ Male ❑ Female

2. Age: ❑ Under 35 ❑ 35–45 ❑ 46–60 ❑ Over 60

3. Occupation: _____ _____

4. Annual household income:
   - ❑ Under $15,000 ❑ $15,000–29,900 ❑ $30,000–49,999
   - ❑ $50,000–$74,999 ❑ $75,000–99,999 ❑ $100,000 and over

5. How did you hear about this book?
   - ❑ Advertising ❑ News article ❑ Friend/relative
   - ❑ Healthcare professional
   - ❑ Other _____

6. How did you get your copy?
   - ❑ Gift ❑ Purchased in bookstore
   - ❑ Ordered from direct-mail offer ❑ Purchased in store other than a bookstore
   - ❑ Ordered from 800 number seen on TV
   - ❑ Ordered from 800 number seen in newspaper/magazine
   - ❑ Other _____

7. What influenced you to purchase this book? (Check all that apply)
   - ❑ Interest in your health ❑ Recommendation of a friend/relative
   - ❑ Bookstore representative ❑ Advertising
   - ❑ Recommendation of a healthcare professional
   - ❑ Concern for an elderly relative's health
   - ❑ Interest in child's health
   - ❑ Other _____

8. Did you see any in-store promotional materials on this book?
   - ❑ Yes ❑ No

9. What time of year did you buy it?
   - ❑ Spring ❑ Summer ❑ Autumn ❑ Winter

10. Please share with us your comments about the book.

Key Concepts and Terms

appropriate language	dichotomous question	rank-ordered response set
alternative response scale	dichotomous response set	ranking by preference
alternative response set	exhaustive response set	unidimensionality
check-all-that-apply response set	mutually exclusive categories	
criterion-based ranking	rank order	

CHAPTER TEN

SUPPLY ITEMS

Open-Ended Questions

In this chapter we will

- Compare and contrast the use of selection and supply items (open-ended questions).
- Present guidelines for writing supply items.
- Explain content analysis—an approach for making sense of responses to supply items.

Imagine going to an art gallery where all the pictures are painted in the same style. After a while you would probably yearn to see something varied and unique. We have chosen to use artistic expression as an analogy to instrument construction as the processes have many parallels, and without variation the results in either endeavor can be very unfulfilling. In this chapter we continue our presentation of item formats by examining the use of open-ended questions.

Open-ended questions are also referred to as *supply items* or *qualitative measures*. This format differs significantly from the types of items previously discussed, as the respondent must produce a response rather select one from a set provided by the instrument designer. Because the response is supplied by the respondent, supply items are made up only of stems. Although an open-ended item can be used to obtain finite, factual information, it is also effective when the response domain is unknown or when in-depth information about a specific subject is sought. It is particularly useful in eliciting respondents' feelings, suggestions, or explanations of events. For example, you might ask people to describe the strengths and weaknesses of an educational curriculum or ask them what they would do to improve a social program. Compared to data from selection items, the data gathered from opened-ended items can render much more detail and much richer descriptions, primarily because the respondent or observer is able to answer in his or her own words and is not limited to predetermined choices.

This rich and thick description is one of the primary assets of supply items, whether they are the primary means of obtaining information or are coupled with selection items. Consider surveys that ask questions about sensitive social issues, such as abortion, gun control, welfare reform, or racial quotas. Although questions can be designed to address many of the factors involved, rating scales, alternative response sets, or rank-ordered items may not be able to capture all of a respondent's thoughts and feelings about these complex issues. In contrast, open-ended questions can be designed that allow respondents to diverge from a direct line of inquiry. As they do so they may provide information above and beyond what can be obtained through selection items.

Open-ended responses may also be more efficient to use than selection items, particularly when you are finding it difficult to limit the size of a response set. You could, for example, present a list of thirty to forty job titles and ask respondents to find the title that most closely matches their current position. The advantage is that by limiting answers to a predetermined response set, you will facilitate tabulation of your results. However, you can gain administration efficiency by offering a simple fill-in-the-blank question to obtain the same information: for example,

What is your current occupation? _____

There are two basic disadvantages to using open-ended items. First, it may be harder to obtain responses. For example, respondents may not want to spend the time needed to carefully think through and phrase an adequate response. Second, supply items tend to produce a great many diverse responses, which may be difficult to organize. Aggregating these data for analysis can also be extremely time consuming. When you develop a response set, such as a list of occupations, you have, as instrument designer, also established the definition and criteria for each occupation. In contrast, when you ask an open-ended question, you must then deal with the respondent's perception of how the question should be answered. You may get a job title ("secretary"), or a description ("I do word processing"), or a social role ("administrative assistant"). Consequently, there may be very little consistency in the responses you receive. For this reason, we will spend some time in this chapter discussing the analysis of qualitative data.

Considerable forethought must also be given to creating supply items, as the choice of wording is likely to affect the information you obtain. Consider these two similar statements: "What do you believe are the reasons your marriage failed?" and, "Why are you divorced?" The first question suggests that there may be any number of factors that contributed to the termination of the marriage. However, the phrasing of the second question carries with it connotations that may make the respondent defensive or more likely to blame the spouse.

Open-ended questions may be directed or nondirected. A *directed* question attempts to follow a specific line of inquiry and asks for a response to a specific topic or area of interest: for example, "List ten factors that influenced your decision to become a teacher." Directed questions are useful when you want to obtain a broad range of information that might be difficult to capture using response sets. Short-answer, fill-in-the-blank items (such as, "How many children are currently living in this household?____") are also directed items. And some stems that appear to be directed open-ended questions in reality are not. For example, the question, "How were things at work today?" will probably produce only a dichotomous response—either "good" or "bad."

Nondirected items allow you to broaden the range of inquiry. "Why did you become a teacher?" is a nondirected question. Obviously, however, the response may go in multiple directions.

Whether directed or undirected, open-ended questions will produce information that may need to be summarized and reported in ways other than a frequency table or graph.

Guidelines for Constructing Supply Items

If you follow the guidelines presented in Chapter Eight, you will be well on your way to developing focused and concise open-ended items for your questionnaire. However, there are some additional considerations when writing supply items.

Pay Attention to Sentence Length

Write items that are concise and direct. Although this general rule still holds true for open-ended questions, it is also possible to construct items containing more than one sentence in order to place the question in context, explain the rationale for the question, and ensure that the respondent comprehends the intended meaning.

EXAMPLE

> There is currently a great deal of concern over the cost of health care. However, Congress and the President have been unable to develop a consensus about a national approach for funding health care. What is your opinion about a federally funded program for health care insurance for all Americans?

Avoid Having Too Many Concepts

Present only one concept in each question or statement. Separate items should be developed for each related question. For instance, you might follow up on the question in the previous example with questions addressing the topic of a national health care program.

EXAMPLE

> If the government were to sponsor a national health care program, what services would you like to see included?
>
> What services do you believe should be excluded from a national health care program?
>
> If you are currently a health provider, what impact do you think a national health care program would have on your practice?

Use Appropriate Terminology

Review items to ensure that you are not using terms respondents may not recognize. Avoid acronyms that may be common in your setting but not clearly understood by all respondents. Additionally, it may be helpful to define any special terms you use. For example, *national health care program* is likely to have different meanings to different people. It could refer to a system of socialized medicine in which practitioners, such as doctors and nurses, work for and are paid by a federal agency. National health care also could refer to what is called a "single payer system." In this system, everyone pays a health care tax similar to Medicare, but the government contracts with privately owned insurance companies to manage the system.

EXAMPLE

> Congress is considering a national health care program based on a single health care tax. This tax will replace the current tax for Medicare and would replace employer-provided health benefits. Instead, you would be provided access to all health services, which would be managed by your regional health maintenance organization (HMO). What is your opinion about this proposal?

Consider Question Tone

Think about whether to word open-ended items positively, negatively, neutrally, or in a combined format. Some research suggests that the tone of the wording in the item influences the quality and tone of the wording of the response. For example, a study by Gendall, Menelaou, and Brennan (1996) suggested that negatively worded items tended to produce negative responses, positively worded items tended to produce positive responses, and neutral wording more neutral responses. Brennan (1997) found that positively and negatively worded items produced lengthier responses than neutral wording did, though the difference did not appear to be statistically significant. Gendall's study had suggested that negatively worded items generated more ideas, and Brennan's research confirmed this. However, all these researchers caution that these results are tentative. At best, Gendall notes, "researchers need to be aware that the cue they provide will influence the type of responses they receive" (p. 6). This suggests not only being conscious of the tone of your items but also pretesting to determine whether question tone is influencing your respondents' answers.

EXAMPLES

Positive: What aspects of Nectar body lotion did you like?

Negative: Do you have any objections or concerns about Nectar body lotion?

Neutral: What is your opinion of Nectar body lotion?

Combined: What did you like about Nectar body lotion, and what did you dislike about this product?

Be Alert to Sensitive Subjects and to Bias

As with selection items, address sensitive issues with care, and avoid language and structure that might bias responses. At the same time, open-ended questions do allow instrument designers more opportunities in question writing and respondents more latitude in providing information. Consequently, open-ended questions, particularly when nondirective, can be quite useful for obtaining opinions about sensitive subjects. The following examples deal with a sensitive subject that could evoke strong feelings. The wording of example A suggests an underlying bias against assisted suicide, whereas example B attempts to present both sides of this controversial topic.

EXAMPLES

A. Assisted suicide is the practice of helping a terminally ill patient end his or her life. The Bible clearly indicates that this is not morally acceptable behavior. What is your opinion about this subject?

B. Assisted suicide is the practice of helping a terminally ill patient end his or her life. Some view this as the ultimate expression of freedom of choice, while others feel that there is never an occasion in which taking one's own life is morally acceptable. What is your opinion about this subject?

Describe the Units of Interest Where Necessary

In writing fill-in supply items, specify appropriate units wherever possible. You might, for example, be interested in the average number of hours students spend studying per week or their height and weight, hours spent working, or monthly or weekly wages. In writing items to elicit this type of information, it is important to name the unit of measurement with which respondents should answer. For example, in surveying full-time graduate students to determine how much time they spend working at outside jobs, you might ask, "How much time do you spend working at jobs not directly related to your studies?"

However, this question, as it stands, invites all sorts of responses, such as, "about 10 hours per week," "only on the weekends," "full-time during the summer," "about 2 hours per day," and "one week out of four." If your purpose in asking the question is to get answers comparable across respondents (perhaps in order to relate the amount of time spent working with some other variable, such as academic success), it is essential to set some delimiters. Here is a better item:

During the academic year, what is the average number of hours per week that you spend working at jobs that are not a part of your coursework?

————Hours per week

Data that are comparable across respondents allow statistical aggregation and easier interpretation when they are analyzed.

A further example reveals a different aspect of the problem. In a survey of college administrators, a question was asked about the amount of money formally allocated at their institutions for volunteer activities. A perusal of the results showed these sorts of answers: "Less than 0," "$866," "$4,000," "$25," and "around $10,000." How is it possible to reasonably aggregate results like these where the degree of accuracy varies so greatly? We might assume that the person who said "$866" was being accurate to the nearest dollar, although the same assumption should probably not be made about the person who replied "around $10,000." It appears that some administrators answered to the nearest dollar, and the others answered to the nearest thousand dollars. If the purpose of the question is to aggregate data across institutions, it will be necessary not only to state the units, in this case dollars, but also to provide several examples. The revised question could read:

Please specify the amount of money that is formally budgeted to your volunteer programs to the nearest $100. For example, if your budget is between $0 and $49, you would enter 0; if your budget is between $40 and $140, you would enter $100, and so on. If your budget exceeds $1,000, please report it to the nearest hundred dollars.

$————————.

The same type of question could be used to solicit information other than numbers. For example: "Please list the working electrical appliances in your home, such as televisions, radios, computers, toasters, and the like." Although this makes responding to the questionnaire more tedious and assumes a fairly sophisticated respondent, it is absolutely necessary if the resulting data are to be treated meaningfully.

Allow Enough Space for Responses

The questionnaire should offer sufficient space for writing responses. Nothing is more frustrating than trying to squeeze your response into a totally inadequate space. In general the designer should consider the type of response he or she is looking for and provide space accordingly. Remember that some respondents write small, but others write big—if the survey offers lines to write on, do not put them too close together. If you expect respondents to write longer responses to some stems than to others, space should be allocated accordingly. An instruction to provide additional comments on a separate piece of paper is often well received.

Use Formatting to Help the Respondent

Format each item for ease of completion. Whenever possible, use tables, matrices, and graphic design to assist the respondent in providing the information.

EXAMPLE

What is the average daily census in your nursing home, as defined by the following age brackets?

Age Group	Average Daily Census
65 and under	
66–70	
71–75	
76–80	
81–85	
86 and over	

Review Clarity and Meaning

To improve clarity and meaning, consider how an item has been worded. Notice that the slight changes in wording in the following questions might produce different responses:

> A. Do you consider yourself healthy?
> B. In general, would you say that you are a healthy individual?
> C. How would you describe your physical health?
> D. What type of health problems have you experienced in the past year?

The first item is actually a closed question, as it can be answered by either a *yes* or a *no* response. The second item is ambiguous, as there is no indication of how the question defines being healthy. This question also lends itself to a dichotomous rather than an open-ended response. The last two items, however, are actually open-ended questions and therefore are more likely to elicit the desired, albeit different, information. To reduce ambiguity, write each item out several different ways and pretest them with potential respondents. You will likely find that compared to the item you started with, the item you finally decide to use is more concise and more effectively articulates your intended meaning.

Making Sense of Qualitative Data

Like other item formats, open-ended items can be used to obtain factual information or to assess options, attitudes, and beliefs. The previous examples that requested hours of employment outside of studies, amounts of organizational funding, and numbers of patients in various age groups will produce quantitative data that can be aggregated and presented in a frequency table. For example, you could give the percentages of students who report spending 0–10 hours per week working at jobs unrelated to their studies, 11–20 hours per week, and so on.

In contrast, aggregating, organizing, and analyzing data that reflect opinions, attitudes, and beliefs will be more difficult because these responses may not fit into clearly discernable categories. Data produced by open-ended items are referred to as *qualitative*, because each response is unique to a respondent or observer and thus cannot be easily grouped with other responses and tabulated. There are, however, methods you can use to organize this information, identify patterns in the responses, and ultimately aggregate the data. This section discusses content analysis, the primary means of making sense out of large amounts of qualitative information, and how you can conduct a content analysis of your data.

The simplest way to report responses to open-ended items is to list the response and the frequency of its occurrence. For example, if you have asked for specific information, such as income in dollars, you could summarize the responses by category and frequency:

EXAMPLE

Less than $20,000 = 23

$20,001 to $30,000 = 49

$30,001 to $40,000 = 12

$40,001 to $50,000 = 5

More than $50,001 = 3

In some cases, such as when you have a manageable number of responses to open-ended questions, you can just list the responses. For example, if you received ninety responses to a customer satisfaction questionnaire, you could compile a verbatim list of the five most favorable responses and also the five least favorable for comparison. However, if the responses are detailed or more numerous, you may need to use some form of coding to organize, categorize, and analyze the data.

Content analysis may be defined as a systematic, objective, and quantitative procedure for summarizing the content of written, recorded, or published communication. Because you will establish the exact guidelines and criteria for the content analysis procedure you use, your documentation must clearly explain it. This is important, as another person working independently might not come up with the same categories you did for summarizing the data. However, once another person has your established guidelines, he or she should be able to follow the same process you used to analyze the data. Another caveat is that once you have established objective criteria for conducting the analysis, there will still be room for subjective interpretation of the data. Nonetheless, the goal is to obtain consistency between analysts.

To illustrate the factors that must be taken into consideration when doing a content analysis, let's briefly examine two responses to the question, "How would you describe your physical health during the past year?"

Respondent 1: Healthwise this has been a terrible year for me. I started the year with the flu and was laid up in bed for over a week. I was pretty weak after that and wasn't able to return to work for another week. Then, my wife was diagnosed with a kidney stone. She had a lot of tests and finally they put her on some medications that helped dissolve the stone. Then in late August, I fell off the back of my pickup truck and broke my left arm. Fortunately, it was a clean break, but I was in a hard cast for a month and then a soft cast for another six weeks. It's really difficult to sleep when you have to wear a cast. I hope this year will be better.

> *Respondent 2:* I had a bad cold this past winter. I took a lot of vitamin C, but I don't know if that helped any. Other than that, it's been a pretty good year healthwise. I run three to four times a week and I think that's good for my health. I've been able to keep my weight steady and the doctor tells me my blood pressure and cholesterol levels are good. I'd say I was in pretty good health.

In these two answers, we are presented with a wealth of information about each respondent's health, and yet there are considerable differences in the way each respondent answered the question. The first respondent characterized his health by describing illnesses and injuries. The response also diverges from the question, as the respondent describes an illness that his wife experienced. Other than mentioning a cold, the second respondent has characterized his health by describing his lifestyle and specific indicators of wellness. The challenge for the instrument designer is to create a systemic approach for analyzing such responses. For example, we might look for a recurring theme, one that runs through all the responses and can help us make sense of this information. The responses in the example might suggest creating two categories: one centered on wellness and one on illness and injury. An examination of the other responses to the question would help you in determining if those are indeed meaningful categories.

Fortunately, there is a series of steps you can follow in conducting a content analysis of qualitative data, such as those obtained from open-ended items on a questionnaire:

- Identify the universe of content (the content to be analyzed).
- Obtain examples of the content to be analyzed.
- Identify the coding units (by which the content will be divided).
- Specify a category system (into which content will be fitted).
- Apply the selected category system to the individual coded units.
- Revise categories based on application.

Finally, to ensure that your analysis is not arbitrary nor the product of your individual preferences, you will need to check that your category system is reproducible. You might ask someone to conduct an independent analysis of your data, using the categories and coding units you created, to see if this person obtains results similar to yours.

Let's examine each of these content analysis steps in detail.

Identify the Universe of Content

Given the purpose of your questionnaire, you need to consider the type of information that will be generated by the supply items. Although this may seem apparent, trouble will result if care is not taken to identify the specific universe of responses. For example, suppose that you have developed a questionnaire that college students will use to evaluate a course. The questionnaire is divided into three sections, one that evaluates the instructor, one that evaluates resource material, and one that evaluates the learning environment. Finally, assume that some open-ended questions are used in each of those sections. The question you want to ask yourself is, do I want to analyze responses from each section separately, or do I want to aggregate all the responses and analyze them together? Again, this decision is based on your purpose. For example, you might be trying to demonstrate a relationship between the variables assessed in all three sections. You might be asking whether a relationship exists between student evaluations of their instructors and factors such as resource materials and learning environment. In that case you might want to group the responses and analyze this content as one set of information.

The issue of time may also be a factor if you have conducted a survey and received responses over an extended period. Suppose you send out a survey through the mail, and after six weeks you obtain a 65 percent response rate. In order to increase the number of responses, you send the survey out one more time to the 35 percent of respondents who did not mail the questionnaire back the first time. This second phase takes an additional eight weeks to complete and increases the response rate by 15 percent. Given the time differential between mailings, you have in some ways conducted two separate surveys. The question you must address is whether the responses from the two mailings should be analyzed together or separately. The answer depends in part on the questions you asked and in part on the time that elapsed between receiving the first and second sets of responses. For example, if you modified item wording slightly (in response to the answers received from the first mailing), then you should consider the second mailing a separate survey (and universe of content) and analyze those data separately.

If Necessary, Sample the Content to Be Analyzed

Content analysis can be used to examine many forms of qualitative information, such as observation notes, records, and transcripts as well as the responses to open-ended questions on questionnaires. On the one hand, studies involving interviews of individuals may produce lengthy written narratives, dozens or even hundreds of pages in length, and content analysis is typically applied to the entire record. On the other hand, an organization might administer a marketing survey to customers that produces thousands of responses to open-ended items. In this case the organization might want to obtain a sample of responses for analysis (Chapter Thirteen describes sampling techniques).

Identify the Coding Units

Coding units are content subdivisions used for classification. The five coding units usually employed in content analysis are words, themes, characters, items, and space and time measures (Berelson, 1954).

The *word* is typically the smallest unit used in content analysis. An analysis of a question about personal health might produce a number of words describing health or illness. You can use the search feature in word processing software to find specific terms and count how frequently they occur. However, care must be taken with this approach, as a word may have different meanings depending on its context.

The next largest coding unit is the *theme*. In its simplest form a theme may be a simple sentence or single idea. Although the theme is one of the most widely used units of content analysis, it can also be one of the most difficult. When structures other than simple sentences occur in the content, the issue of coding reliability arises. That is, different content analysts subdividing content by theme would probably have some difficulty agreeing where the divisions should be made. The chapter and section headings in a book help to convey how it is organized, whereas the organization of responses to open-ended items may not be as evident.

The third coding unit divides content according to *character* or *person* mentioned. This analysis unit is especially effective when analyzing literary pieces and can also be used for student themes, autobiographies, or diaries. In some situations this approach could be used when analyzing responses to questionnaire items, such as coding unit for each member of a focus group.

Coding by *item* means identifying the whole, natural unit in which the content was initially generated. The natural units for supply-item responses might be sections of interview transcripts, notes in a medical record, or entries in an observer's journal. If you were analyzing responses to open-ended questions by item, any one response would be the coding unit.

The final coding unit is the amount of *space* or *time* that particular content occupies. For example, one might analyze essays by number of pages written, films by the foot or frame, or audiotapes by the minute. This approach to coding has limited application to the analysis of questionnaire items.

The choice of one coding unit of analysis over another depends on the investigator's purpose and category system. Also you need not restrict your analysis to a single coding unit. In many instances it is appropriate to use more than one unit on the same content to get at information for different decisions. In analyzing responses to open-ended questions, for example, it might be useful to classify content by both words and themes. Responses to the question, "How would you describe your physical health?" might result in the use of such terms as *flu, virus, lethargy,* or *sinus headache.* Consequently, these words could be used to identify coding units. The same question might also produce information that could be classified according to themes, such as wellness, illness, and mental health. Choosing the coding unit precedes selecting the category system, but selection of the latter may necessitate changing the former.

Specify a Category System

Category systems can be divided roughly into two kinds: those that deal with *what is being said* (content) and those that deal with *how that content is said* (process). An example of the what-is-said type can be seen in an analysis of responses to the question, "How would you describe your physical health?" That analysis might classify all references to feeling well as one category and all references to illness and disease as another category.

Illustrative of the how-it-is-said analysis is the process of looking at the syntax and grammatical structure of responses. Suppose you decide that your coding units will be words. You could then decide to categorize each of the words according to the part of speech it represents (noun, verb, adjective, and so forth). If you are using audio or video transcripts, you could also develop category systems to analyze vocal intonations or gestures. In the following example, responses to a question about personal health resulted in a number of statements that could be categorized by parts of speech and coded using words:

EXAMPLE

I caught (verb) the flu (noun).

Broke (verb) my arm (noun) two months ago.

Ingested (verb) the wrong (adjective) medication (noun).

Broke out (verb) into hives (noun) after getting (verb) poison ivy (noun).

Had my appendix (noun) removed (verb) about two years ago.

It was the worst (adjective) cold (noun) I can remember having contracted (verb).

I've been cancer-free (adjective) for seven years now.

The best approach to developing your category system is to think about the kinds of questions you are trying to answer through your instrument. The selection of a particular category system is also dependent on the coding unit you have chosen. The following examples show some typical relationships between category systems and coding units:

A. Analysis of responses to questionnaire items to determine respondents' written vocabulary levels.

    Coding unit: Word

    Category system: Number of syllables

    Readability index based on standardized measure

B. Analysis of responses to an open-ended question that asked faculty members to list desirable admission criteria for a special education program.

Coding unit: Item (an individual response in total)

Category system: All the admission criteria listed

C. Analysis of responses to open-ended questions about personal health.

Coding unit: Theme (for example, wellness, illness, or injury)

Category system: Frequency of each subject mentioned

Now that we have reviewed examples of how items might be coded and categorized, we can examine the final steps in the content analysis process.

Apply Categorization System to Coding Units and Revise as Necessary

After the coding units have been identified, the classification system should be applied to each unit separately to help the developer determine the utility of the categories and their definitions. Usually in this process of trying out the system, some categories are redefined, others are eliminated as dysfunctional, and still others are added. The process of testing the categorization system results in a more useful content analysis procedure and ensures better agreement among coders.

For example, assume that you ask the following question as part of a health survey: "How would you describe your physical health during the past year?" You obtain fifty responses, varying in length from a phrase to three paragraphs. You decide that you want to apply a content category system; that is, you are interested in what respondents said rather than how they said it. Specifically, you want to identify the frequency of references to poor health, illness, and disease. As you apply the category and coding system to the responses, you find many references to herbal remedies and nontraditional medicine. Consequently, after trying your original system, you decide to add another category to your analysis.

Once you have tested your category and coding system, it is important to document the definitions and procedures you used. This ensures that you or anyone else who goes over the same data later will be able to use the same format and guidelines, which should produce similar results.

Finally, the most fundamental kinds of data generated are *frequencies* of categories by coding unit. Frequencies can also be used within a content universe to compare numbers of occurrences. An example of this use would be comparing the number of verbs to the number of nouns. One of the particular strengths of content analysis is that the data analyst is able not only to quantify the information but also to interpret the meaning of the quantification more fully than is possible with other measurement procedures. In our health survey example the data might demonstrate that the percentage of references to illness increased with the age of the respondent. This would give those using the information a much better understanding of the impact of the quantitative changes.

Although the purpose of doing a content analysis of responses is to summarize information in a coherent manner, it is also important to remember that open-ended questions allow you to individualize responses and to seek meaning beyond numbers. You can tabulate the number of responses that refer to illness and the adjectives used to describe the severity of the illness. However, you can derive additional meaning by considering an individual's response in its entirety. An individual's response to an open-ended item can provide a richness of depth and breadth not available in a response to a closed question with a limited response set. It provides information within the context of the respondent's life that is not as easily elicited using other item formats. For example, a question about personal health takes on a unique meaning when the respondent describes his or her health within the context of a physical handicap, severe illness, or chronic disease.

Summary

Traditionally, artists paint on linen canvases. At times, however, an artist may feel limited by the typical canvas and may choose other approaches, such as painting a fresco on the side of a building or stretching canvas over hundreds of feet for a panoramic mural. In this chapter we have presented guidelines for developing items that do not limit respondents to a preselected response set and that can greatly expand the amount and type of information you obtain with your questionnaire. An open-ended item, or supply item, can solicit information that is succinct—a number, word, or phrase. Additionally, it can provide an opportunity for respondents or observers to provide a wealth of detail difficult to obtain from scaled items.

Some types of open-ended items produce data that can be presented through frequency tables and histograms. For example, if an item is structured to produce a specific number or word within a designated range, such as income levels or years of education, then the responses can be aggregated and fairly easily categorized.

Content analysis is a method for analyzing responses to open-ended items that do not provide a structured format for those responses. The steps you take in conducting a content analysis of qualitative data are very similar to the steps for the construction of a questionnaire. Once organized by code and category, such as word, item, or theme, the responses can be tabulated and their frequency reported, like the responses to closed items. Additionally, individual responses may provide information that is illuminating in itself and need not be analyzed as aggregated data.

Instrument 10.A: Open-Ended Item Examples and Commentary

Few instruments rely entirely on open-ended items. Instead, many instruments use this format to complement response sets. The items shown and discussed in Instrument 10.A have been selected from a variety of questionnaires to demonstrate the different ways that open-ended items are used. Note that the majority are nondirective, as open-ended questions are typically used to elicit information unlikely to be captured by selection items.

INSTRUMENT 10.A: OPEN-ENDED ITEM EXAMPLES AND COMMENTARY.

From a computer training needs assessment:

Would you be willing to teach a particular computer skill or software, and if so, what would it be?

Comments: This item really contains two questions, one addressing skills and the other software. As with rating scales and alternative response sets, it is preferable that an open-ended item be unidimensional, with only one attribute or trait addressed in the question. However, an open-ended item does provide some leeway, as the respondent can choose to answer one or both of the topics.

From a leisure skills inventory:

What special hobbies do you have?

Comments: Given the array of hobbies that an individual could engage in, it would be difficult to construct an exhaustive list of hobbies. It is not clear what the adjective *special* means, and it is possible that respondents would not answer this question if they believed that their interests did not rise to the level of a special hobby.

From an assessment used by teachers to screen for special mental health and educational services:

What concerns you most about this pupil?

Comments: Although stated briefly, this question is sure to elicit a comprehensive response.

From a student survey of university campus safety:

Are there areas at the University in which you do not feel safe from physical or sexual assault? ❏ Yes ❏ No

If you replied "Yes" please let us know where and at what time you feel unsafe.

Comments: This item uses a dichotomous response set followed by a supply item. Given the size of the campus, it would be difficult to develop an exhaustive list of potential locations (although a map could be included in the instrument).

From a questionnaire about college and private sector collaboration:

> For the open-ended questions, please be as comprehensive as you can, and if necessary, use the back of the page to complete the questions.

> Based on your professional observation, what do you see as the major activities that facilitate successful workforce development partnerships between university continuing education divisions and business and industry?

Comments: In the previous examples, instructions were not provided in regard to the question. Here, directions are included that encourage the respondent to write a thoughtful, comprehensive answer to the question.

From an employee survey about quality of work life and workplace conditions:

> Please indicate your responses to the following statements by writing your answers in the space provided below.

> Describe the work environment that is most conducive to your job performance.

Comments: This item is part of a larger survey, which begins with four demographic items, continues with seventy-two Likert-type items and one multiple-choice item, and ends with four open-ended questions. The open-ended questions allow respondents to comment on workplace conditions that may not have been covered by the rating items.

From another quality of work life survey in a human service agency:

> Please list four things that you believe will improve morale, working conditions, or client care.

Comments: This item appeared at the bottom of the second page of a two-page questionnaire. It was printed in a small box measuring about one inch high by four inches long, with four lines, numbered one through four. It appears that the instrument designer was more interested in fitting the item into the allowable space than in providing respondents with adequate room to provide a comprehensive answer.

From a program evaluation questionnaire:

> How would you describe your group to someone else, such as a patient, parent, or other staff member? What would they see and hear?

Comments: This was one of six items about therapeutic groups in a mental health program. Within the item, the second question reframes the first one, by suggesting a context in which to respond. Interestingly, even though this question provides a lot of leeway for response, the last item on this instrument encouraged further discussion and clarification: "If these questions limit you in responding, please provide additional comments and thoughts."

Instrument 10.B: Behavioral Assessment

Youth violence is a concern being addressed by a number of federal agencies in the United States. In 1998, the Division of Violence Prevention of the Centers for Disease Control and Prevention (CDC) published a compendium of more than 100 instruments for evaluating youth violence prevention programs (Dahlberg, Toal, & Behrens, 1998). To support research and evaluation the CDC has placed the compendium in the public domain; in other words, researchers are free to use these instruments and study their effectiveness.

The instruments are divided into four categories: (1) attitude and belief assessments, (2) psychosocial and cognitive assessments, (3) behavior assessments, and (4) environmental assessments. For each category a table lists the instruments, for each one giving the construct of interest, a brief description, the target audience, reliability and validity information if available, the name of the instrument developer, and the date it was first published.

The instrument presented here (Instrument 10.B) fits in the behavior assessment category. It is described as measuring "the frequency with which respondents have witnessed or been subjects of stealing or property damage" (Dahlberg et al., 1998, p. 147). The target group is African American students aged eight to eighteen. No validity or reliability information is available for this questionnaire. The developer is listed as Dolan, 1989, as adapted by Church, 1994 (two unpublished sources). This instrument makes use of alternative response sets, including *yes* or *no* items (see Chapter Nine), as filters. If the child answers in the affirmative he or she is then presented with an open-ended follow-up question.

An interesting aspect of this questionnaire is that the results can be tallied and a score computed. The higher the score the more likely it is that the child has engaged in stealing and property damage. As we will discuss in the next chapter, when items are added up to produce a score, it is assumed that there is a relationship between and among the items and between the items and the underlying construct the instrument is purporting to measure. Because the strength of the relationship has not been demonstrated (that is, information to support validity or reliability is not present), we should be cautious in interpreting these scores. However, we should not forget that one of the reasons the CDC has made these instruments available is for researchers to use them and in the process determine if they are indeed reliable and valid measures.

INSTRUMENT 10.B: BEHAVIORAL ASSESSMENT.

Delinquent Behavior—High Risk Behavioral Assessment

This assessment measures the frequency with which respondents have witnessed or been subjects of stealing and property damage. Questions are asked during a one-on-one interview.

1. A. Have you witnessed any stealing? ❏ Yes ❏ No

   B. What kinds of things have you seen get stolen?

   _____

   _____

   _____

   C. How often? ❏ Rarely ❏ Occasionally ❏ Regularly,
                  (1–3/year) (1–2/month) (daily or 1–2/week)

   D. Why do you think people steal?

   _____

   _____

   _____

2. A. Have you had things stolen from you? ❏ Yes ❏ No

   B. What kinds of things have been stolen from you?

   C. How often? ❏ Rarely ❏ Occasionally ❏ Regularly
                  (1–3/year) (1–2/month) (daily or 1–2/week)

   D. Why were these things stolen?

   _____

   _____

   _____

3. A. Have you ever stolen from anybody else? ❏ Yes ❏ No

   B. How often? ❏ Rarely ❏ Occasionally ❏ Regularly
                  (1–3/year) (1–2/month) (daily or 1–2/week)

   C. Why did you steal?

   _____

   _____

   _____

4. A. Have you witnessed others damage property? ❑ Yes ❑ No

   B. What was damaged?

_____

_____

_____

   C. How often?   ❑ Rarely   ❑ Occasionally   ❑ Regularly
                      (1–3/year)   (1–2/month)   (daily or 1–2/week)

5. A. What kinds of activities make you feel happy?

_____

_____

_____

   B. How often do you do these activities?

                       ❑ Rarely   ❑ Occasionally   ❑ Regularly
                       (1–3/year)   (1–2/month)   (daily or 1–2/week)

SCORING AND ANALYSIS

The number of "A" items to which the respondent answered "yes" are summed. Then for those respondents who scored at least 1, the frequency is calculated by averaging the answers for the "B" or "C" items (How often?). Point values are assigned as follows:

Rarely = 1
Occasionally = 2
Regularly = 3

A high score indicates a high level of involvement in stealing and property damage.

Key Concepts and Terms

biased item

category system

coding unit

content analysis

negative tone

neutral tone

open-ended question

positive tone

qualitative data

sensitive question

supply item

universe of content

universe of responses

CHAPTER ELEVEN

GUIDELINES FOR CONSTRUCTING MULTI-ITEM SCALES

In this chapter we will

- Describe instruments that use multiple related items to better understand a topic, and discuss how they differ from other instruments in construction.
- Introduce the Semantic Differential Scale and explain how SD items are constructed.
- Describe how to use Q methodology and Q-sorting in constructing multi-item scales.
- Introduce goal attainment scaling, and explain how to construct a GAS.
- Introduce Likert scaling, and explain how to construct a Likert scale.
- Introduce cumulative scales and Thurstone scales, and explain how to construct two Thurstone scales: one using equal appearing intervals and one using paired comparison.

A collage is an artwork with a central theme but composed of mixed media, such as drawings, photographs, and documents. In the realm of instrument construction a *multi-item scale* is similar in that it is composed of interrelated items that attempt to measure an underlying construct. In this chapter we introduce the concept of a scale as an instrument and discuss how it differs from other instruments where items may have a shared focus but function independently of each other.

A unique aspect of a multi-item scale is not only that the items are interrelated but also that the values associated with the response choices can be combined to produce a statistically validated score. If, for example, you have developed an scale to measure self-reliance and it uses Likert type items with values of (1) *strongly disagree* to (5) *strongly agree,* the numbers can be tallied, with higher scores being associated with increased self-reliance.

The following sections describe several multi-item scale formats and explain how to construct different types, including goal attainment, summative, and cumulative scales. This introduction can help you decide if this approach is appropriate to your needs and if you have the time and resources needed to complete the process.

Five Essential Characteristics of Multi-Item Scales

So far our discussion has focused on instruments where the items function as independent measures. Consider the political poll displayed at the end of Chapter Two (Instrument 2.A). Although the developer of this instrument might be interested in how respondents view government activities generally, each item is a separate measure; rating the president's job performance is uniquely different from expressing a belief about prayer in school (and in this instance the sets of response alternatives are different too). As with many questionnaires, each item is a distinct measure—you could delete an item and still obtain considerable information about the topic of interest. For many activities, instruments such as this may provide all the information you want or need for your project.

But now think of a questionnaire you have completed where the items *do* appear to be related. Probably many of you have completed instruments on the topic of team building that ask questions about how well you get along with coworkers, how well team members work together to accomplish work tasks, and so on. Typically, the response set associated with each item produces a score, and the higher the score when all the items are added together, the stronger your view of the cohesiveness of your workgroup. There are times when the relationship between and among items is of critical importance for understanding a social construction, as in this case in which multiple items are used to help people better understand the function of teamwork. This is similar in concept to the television game show *Wheel of Fortune,* where the object is to guess a word or phrase based on the least number of letters presented. The more letters of the alphabet presented, the more evident the word or phrase becomes. Likewise, we can learn more about a construct by using multiple, interrelated items.

When we first used the term *scale* in this book, it referred to the relationship between the values in a response set, that is, we were discussing a *rating scale*. The term *scale* can also mean an instrument made up of multiple items that have a relationship to each other as well as to the concept of interest. A multiple-item scale that is used for measurement has five characteristics. Just as stretching a canvas and putting it on an easel does not make that canvas a painting, the use of a number of items to better understand a topic does not make those items a scale. All five of the following interrelated characteristics must be present before multiple items will function as a scale.

The first characteristic is that *the scale is used to measure the degree to which a certain trait or attribute is present in a person, place, or thing*. Typically, the trait or attribute you are interested in and want to measure or describe is defined in general terms, and these terms are open to interpretation. For example, each of us can define such terms as *happiness, satisfaction, political activism, anxiety*, and *family values* for ourselves. However, these terms may convey different meanings to others. These constructs (or latent variables[1]), cannot be observed or measured directly.

A construct, as we discussed in Chapter Four, is different from a common purpose or theme. All instruments should be designed with a specific purpose in mind. A multi-item scale is developed specifically for the purpose of measuring a construct. Social scientists talk about *operationalizing* a construct when they are describing an approach to measure an attribute representative of the construct.[2] One way we might operationalize the concept of political activism, for example, is by examining a number of *overt behaviors*, such as consistently voting in elections, being an active member of a political party, and making regular donations to support political causes. Our instrument will be designed to measure these behaviors because we believe they function as a measure of political activism. It is also important to recognize that there is more than one way to operationalize a construct. For example, another way to operationalize this construct would be to create an instrument that measures an individual's *perception* of his or her own political activism; in this case items that measure attitudes and opinions would be used to operationalize the construct.

The second defining characteristic of a scale is that it is *composed of multiple items*. As DeVellis (1991) says, *scales*[3] are "collections of items intended to reveal levels of theoretical variables (constructs), not readily observable by direct means" (p. 8). Our instrument will probably require a number of items to assess the variety of behaviors associated with political activism, and if we can demonstrate a strong relationship between the attributes the items are attempting to measure with the underlying concept we will be on the way to creating a "political activism scale."

One way to establish the association between the items and the construct is to measure the strength of the relationships between an item and the rest of the items in the instrument, both individually and collectively. If our political activism scale consists of fifteen items, during pretesting we would compare how respondents answered item 1 to how they answered item 2, then item 1 answers to item 3 answers, and so on. We could also compare item 1 results to the total score for all the other items. As explained in Chapter Four, the stronger the relationship (which is determined through statistical analysis), the more confident we can be that the item is an actual measure of the construct.

At this point you may be thinking that this is a lot of work, and you would be correct. All instruments should be thoughtfully designed and pretested; however, instruments that make use of multi-item scales may require additional activities. You may be able to pretest a questionnaire with a small group of users and acquire sufficient information to support that it is consistently providing trustworthy information. For multi-item scale development, you will need to pretest with a large group of users (perhaps fifty or more) to obtain enough data to support statistical analysis.

The third essential characteristic of a scale is that *each item is an intended, unique measure of the construct;* although items may differ in content and wording, each purports to measure some attribute of the same construct. If you can demonstrate that items are a good measure of the construct of interest, and not another construct, you can also say that they are valid measures. For example, some of the attributes associated with political activism are voting, involvement in a political party, and support of political causes. As noted, the stronger the relationship of an item (and hence the attribute it is attempting to measure) to other items, individually and collectively, the greater the probability that the item is a good measure of the construct. Conversely, if these attributes could also be measures of another construct, such as patriotism (that is, if the attributes for political activism and patriotism are not mutually exclusive), then you cannot guarantee that you have created a scale that is solely a measure of political activism.

The fourth characteristic of a scale is *dimensionality,* which is closely related to the previous three components. One way to approach the concept of dimensionality is to think of a physical attribute such as height, weight, or age. Each of these attributes exists along a single dimension of short to tall, thin to fat, or old to young. Now consider the construct of physical maturation, which incorporates all three of these attributes as well as factors related to motor skills such as coordination. In this case, assessment of physical maturation requires measurement of a multidimensional construct. Another example comes from attempts to operationalize the construct of intelligence. If we want to measure intelligence as a reflection of verbal ability than our scale will likely be unidimensional. However, if we operationalize intelligence to include the ability to reason quantitatively or think creatively, our scale will likely reflect a multidimensional construct (Trochim, 2001). At the same time, keep in mind that individual items should be unidimensional (as discussed in the guidelines in the previous chapters); it is when they are used collectively that they may be used to measure phenomena that are unidimensional or even multidimensional.

Dimensionality is an important aspect of multi-item scaling because "if a series of variables all measure a single general characteristic of an attitude or other construct, the variables should all be highly interrelated" (Judd, Smith, & Kidder, 1991, p. 147). In other words, we expect a strong inter-item correlation when the instrument is tapping into one dimension.

The final essential characteristic of a scale is that *it can produce a numerical value*. For example, you can add the values of the responses together to create a score. In a ten-item questionnaire designed to measure political activism, where the response alternatives for each item are rated from *low* = 1 to *high* = 5, it would be possible to have a total score of 50, which would indicate a very high level of political involvement. These scores are interval level data, so we can also find the mean score for a group of individuals completing our political activism instrument. (Note that dichotomous response scales can be given values and used in multi-item scales as well: for example, 1 = *no* and 2 = *yes*, or 1 = *disagree* and 2 = *agree*.) Because scales produce a numerical value, they involve additional steps in the instrument construction process and considerably more pretesting to ensure that the scores they produce are valid and reliable measures.

This is an important feature of the scaling process, as scores may be used to support decisions having a significant impact or consequence. For example, the score on a job performance evaluation may contribute to the decision to retain or terminate an employee or to grant him or her a raise in pay; the score on a mental health screening instrument may help to determine whether a client receives inpatient or outpatient services. This suggests that there are ethical issues associated with the use of some scales and points to the importance of demonstrating that a scale is indeed a reliable and valid measure.

Thinking about the purpose of your study can help you determine whether you need to construct an instrument that focuses on a common theme with items that function independently of each other or whether you need to study an underlying attribute. If the purpose is to provide multiple measures of the same construct and to produce a numerical value, then you are attempting to create a multi-item scale, and you should take that into consideration as you design your instrument. As the instrument designer, you need to consider which of these objectives are pertinent and whether your items meet these criteria. If meeting any of these objectives is questionable, alternative item types should be considered.

Scale Construction

Multi-item scales can be created in a number of ways. In this section we will introduce several different formats and provide an introduction to constructing a number of different scales, including goal attainment scales; Likert, or summative, scales; and cumulative scales using equal appearing intervals and paired comparison.

Semantic Differential Scale

One of the challenges faced by the developer of an instrument is constructing items that are unambiguous. If users are unclear about an item's intended meaning, the results obtained from that item will be unreliable. Faced with this problem, psychologist Charles E. Osgood examined the issue of the connotations of words in relation to measurement (Osgood, Suci, & Tannenbaum, 1967), ultimately developing the semantic differential. The term *semantic* refers to the meanings that words convey. The purpose of the semantic differential is to assess the meaning of an object or variable to the respondent. As the following example illustrates, it uses pairs of discrete descriptor words or phrases as anchors for its response scales. Each semantic differential response scale represents the continuum of choices between two anchors, which typically name opposing, or bipolar, positions. To construct a Semantic Differential Scale, you identify the topic or concept of interest and then construct the items by selecting a number of related but different pairs of statements or terms that could describe the topic. The respondent then rates each item. Taken together, the ratings create an overall response scale for that respondent.

EXAMPLE

For each pair of terms, place an X on the line at the point that best describes the characteristics of your family.

Family

1. Stable ____:____:____:____:____:____:____ Changeable
2. Cold ____:____:____:____:____:____:____ Hot
3. Strong ____:____:____:____:____:____:____ Weak
4. Incomplete ____:____:____:____:____:____:____ Complete
5. Sober ____:____:____:____:____:____:____ Drunk
6. Soft ____:____:____:____:____:____:____ Hard

7. Insane	____:____:____:____:____:____:____	Sane
8. Bad	____:____:____:____:____:____:____	Good
9. Active	____:____:____:____:____:____:____	Passive
10. Severe	____:____:____:____:____:____:____	Lenient
11. Optimistic	____:____:____:____:____:____:____	Pessimistic
12. Calm	____:____:____:____:____:____:____	Excitable

Through their research, Osgood and his associates identified fifty pairs of adjectives to create fifty bipolar response scales—although you can create your own adjective pairs relevant to your topic (Kerlinger & Lee, 1999). They also found that their response scales tended to cluster into three groups, which they referred to as *factors of judgment*. The first and most commonly occurring factor, *evaluation,* comprises adjective pairs such as *good* and *bad, fresh* and *stale, hot* and *cold.* The second factor, *potency,* addresses adjectives such as *weak* and *strong, rugged* and *delicate.* The third factor, *activity,* is reflected in such adjectives as *active* and *passive, tense* and *relaxed, fast* and *slow.* The response scale formats we considered previously, graphic and numerical scales (Chapter Seven), are unidimensional—they measure responses along a one-dimensional line from low to high, bad to good, weak to strong, and so forth. The semantic differential, in contrast, suggests that topics or concepts can be measured along three dimensions: evaluation, potency, and activity. For example, you might rate the topic of soccer high on evaluation (if you enjoy playing or watching the sport), high on potency (if you think of it as a sport involving strength and endurance), and high on the factor of activity. Conversely, you might rate television high on evaluation, neutral on potency, and low on activity (if it makes you think of a couch potato). Consequently, the Semantic Differential Scale is an approach to measuring a topic through multiple items and dimensions (Emmerson & Neely, 1988; Trochim, 2001).

Let's look again at the previous example. Notice that some of the anchors have negative connotations and others have more positive connotations. Also notice that items do not run consistently from negative to positive, or vice versa. Some of the words with positive connotations, such as *stable, strong,* and *optimistic,* appear on the left-hand side of the list, and others, such as *complete, sane,* and *good,* appear on the right-hand side. It is important that respondents treat each bipolar pair as a separate and distinct choice. Altering the direction of the anchor words is meant to ensure that respondents read each choice carefully before maring their response. But also note that when measuring more than one concept, as in the following example, where *myself* and *sister* are being measured with the same adjective pairs, those pairs should be shown exactly the same way for both concepts.

EXAMPLE

For each statement, circle the mark that best describes how you see each member of your family.

Myself

happy	♦	♦	♦	♦	♦	♦	♦	sad
calm	♦	♦	♦	♦	♦	♦	♦	excitable
lazy	♦	♦	♦	♦	♦	♦	♦	energetic
rational	♦	♦	♦	♦	♦	♦	♦	irrational
friendly	♦	♦	♦	♦	♦	♦	♦	distant
withdrawn	♦	♦	♦	♦	♦	♦	♦	outgoing
thoughtful	♦	♦	♦	♦	♦	♦	♦	impulsive

Sister

happy	♦	♦	♦	♦	♦	♦	♦	sad
calm	♦	♦	♦	♦	♦	♦	♦	excitable
lazy	♦	♦	♦	♦	♦	♦	♦	energetic
rational	♦	♦	♦	♦	♦	♦	♦	irrational
friendly	♦	♦	♦	♦	♦	♦	♦	distant
withdrawn	♦	♦	♦	♦	♦	♦	♦	outgoing
thoughtful	♦	♦	♦	♦	♦	♦	♦	impulsive

Although positive or favorable and negative or unfavorable anchors may appear on either side of the scale, for scoring purposes the most favorable adjective is always given the highest score (often 7) and the least favorable adjective always receives a score of one. To create a score for *an individual*, simply sum all of the scores. To obtain the score for a group, sum the scores for each member and then compute the mean. Because each factor is independent, you can also combine the scores for each factor separately and report separate scores for evaluation, potency, and activity. In other words, you might have a Semantic Differential Scale made up of a stimulus and nine response sets—three reflecting the evaluation factor, three the potency factor, and three the activity factor—and you could report the score the three response sets produce for each factor.

Although Osgood developed the semantic differential using a 7-point response scale, it is also possible to use fewer or more alternatives; Kerlinger and Lee (1999) note that for children five items should suffice. This answer format can also be used for single items in a survey, when there is no desire to construct a multi-item scale, although this would negate the format's ability to produce a score.

One of the challenges in using the semantic differential is understanding the meanings that respondents apply to the adjectives. As Underwood (2000) points out, "the method becomes self-contradictory—it starts from the assumption that people's connotations for a word differ, but has to rely on the assumption that, for certain words at least, they don't.... [H]ow do you know that your 'tense/ relaxed' is the same as my 'tense/relaxed'?" (p. 2).

It may also be difficult for respondents to relate an adjective pair to the word or phrase representing the topic or concept. For example, how are *hot* and *cold* or *wet* and *dry* associated with the concept *polite*? Even though the underlying assumption of the scale is that respondents bring their own meanings to the process, difficulty in relating the stem to the adjectives may make it difficult for respondents to rate the item in a meaningful way.

Finally, it is worth noting that although the Semantic Differential Scale was developed in the 1950s, researchers continue to examine the sensitivity and effectiveness of this approach. For example, with the scale originally developed by Osgood and his associates, respondents are given a topic or concept and asked to rate it with a variety of opposing adjectives along a seven-item scale. However, in a later study, respondents were presented with these three different formats:

Unlabeled

| Adjective | [ ] | [ ] | [ ] | [ ] | [ ] | Adjective |

Numerical

| Adjective | 1 | 2 | 3 | 4 | 5 | Adjective |

Labeled

| Adjective | very | quite | neither/nor | quite | very | Adjective |
| | [ ] | [ ] | [ ] | [ ] | [ ] | |

Using these different formats in a marketing survey, the researcher found that users preferred a labeled response set. But because labels remove some of the respondent's ability to bring a personal interpretation to the response scale, this format negates part of the purpose of the semantic differential.

> On questioning respondents about why they preferred a particular scale in relation to a particular task, it became evident that the majority of participants in the survey wanted definite options (labeling) along the scales to aid them in making a decision. The presence of verbal tags or cues on the labeled semantic differential was seen as offering reassurance and making the task more or less self-explanatory. Precise answers seemed to be important to respondents, and the verbal tags were seen as aiding precision. Economy of effort, an important prerequisite for engendering respondent cooperation in any survey, also appeared to be well served by the labeled semantic differential (Garland, 1990).

Q Methodology and Q-Sorting

Like Charles Osgood, psychologist William Stephenson was interested in the meanings that individuals bring to their assessment of subjective concepts.

Stephenson believed the best way to understand those meanings was to involve potential respondents in the construction of items. For example, through a separate instrument, focus groups, or interviews, individuals can suggest topics and themes that can then form the basis of the stimuli (words, phrases, sentences, or pictures) to be evaluated. In this way the items emerge from the respondent's, rather than the instrument developer's, understanding of the construct. Stephenson's Q methodology involves creating a large pool of items and then, through pretesting with potential users or statistical analysis, or both, identifying the most appropriate items. Even after culling out the weakest and least useful stimuli, the typical Q-sorting process will involve 60 to 120 items. Q methodology is therefore a multistep process and as such can be complex and time consuming to develop.

Q-sorting is the method of arranging the stimuli or items. Typically the stimuli are placed on cards, and the individual is asked to sort the cards according to some criterion: "The Q statements are placed by people in order of agreement (or lack thereof) in relation to one another. The result is a 'scale' that is anchored in the respondent's own subjective reality as opposed to one that is constructed and anchored for the respondent by the researcher" (Grudens-Schuck & Kramer, 2000, p. 1).

This sorting is done in several steps. For example, the individual may be asked to sort the items into two groups, such as *most like my feelings* and *least like my feelings,* or even three groups, such as *agree, disagree,* and *neither agree or disagree.* Then the individual re-sorts each pile. The agree pile might be sorted into *strongly agree, agree,* and *minimally agree;* the disagree pile is similarly sorted. Items that formed the *neither agree nor disagree* pile are re-sorted to see if some can be moved into the *minimally agree* or *minimally disagree* piles. Respondents may also be asked to rank the items in each pile.

Another approach to sorting is to use a Q-sort matrix. For example, an individual might be presented with twenty-nine numbered statements written on individual cards. He or she is asked to sort the cards into three piles along a bipolar scale running from *most unlike my feelings* to *most like my feelings,* with *not unlike or like my feelings* as the middle position. As the individual goes through the sorting process, he or she is asked to record the number of each statement under the appropriate value label. In the following example, the designer has created a matrix that forces the responses to take the shape of an even distribution, although you could create a matrix without a midpoint, with a shorter response scale (for example, from -2 to $+2$), and so on. When completed, the matrix allows visual comparison of the individual's choices and, if administered to a larger sample, comparison of responses between individuals (Brown, 1991).

EXAMPLE

Most UNLIKE my feeling						Most LIKE my feeling		
−4	−3	−2	−1	0	+1	+2	+3	+4
3	14	23	8	17	15	16	21	1
13	19	9	2	27	11	18	25	6
	4	29	12	26	10	7	5	
			24	20	22			
				28				

Source: Amin, 2000.

As you can see, it takes considerable time to perform the process, and for that reason Q methodology is more often used for individual assessment rather than for survey assessments of large groups. Moreover, as we have discussed in previous chapters, researchers have other ways to include potential users in the instrument construction process so as to reflect their needs and interests. However, even if Q methodology is not your first choice for assessment, Q-sorting is a useful approach for selecting items for an instrument (as described in Chapter Five).

Goal Attainment Scaling

Goal attainment scaling, or GAS for short, was developed by Thomas J. Kiresuk and Robert E. Sherman in the late 1960s to measure an individual's progress in changing behavior or learning a task (Smith, 1994). The process was originally designed to evaluate outcomes in mental health treatment but has since been adapted to a variety of other needs and settings, including evaluating goals for individual performance in areas such as physical rehabilitation, special education, and long-term care. Typically, GAS is used in conjunction with a treatment or educational plan that uses goals and objectives as a measure of progress. GAS has also been successfully applied to measuring organizational performance in terms of attaining project goals and to evaluating the effectiveness of programs and services when program objectives have been established.

A well-written performance goal is measurable. For example, a physical therapist might write this goal: "Following twelve sessions of physical therapy, John will be able to raise both arms to shoulder height without the aide of a support." The purpose of evaluation for a goal written in this manner would be to determine whether or not the goal was accomplished. It would not pick up gradations in achievement. In contrast, GAS allows a goal to be subdivided into five levels of attainment, which are scaled from −2 (much less than expected) to +2 (much more than expected).

TABLE 11.1: GOAL ATTAINMENT SCALE.

Level of Attainment	Parental Relationship	Use of Anger Management Self-Help Skills
Much less than expected (–2)	Gets into verbal arguments with his mother more than three times a week. Attempts to hit, kick, or scratch mother during these incidents.	Ignores prompts and needs physical assistance to de-escalate, including therapeutic holds and time-out. When agitated is unable to make use of anger management skills that he has learned.
Somewhat less than expected (–1)	Gets into verbal arguments with mother no more than three times a week. Disagreements remain verbal and do not include physical aggression.	Uses time-out to de-escalate after prompting from his mother or teachers. Responds to verbal prompts without escalating further.
Expected level of outcome (0)	Gets into verbal disagreements with mother no more than once a week.	Initiates self-imposed time-out whenever he becomes upset, so as not to escalate into an argument or aggressive behavior.
Somewhat more than expected (+1)	May have verbal disagreements with mother, but is able to resolve them to both his and his mother's satisfaction.	Uses ten-minute breaks, positive self-talk, and stop-and-think strategies when upset.
Much more than expected (+2)	Is able to state needs without being demanding or initiating disagreements. Resolves problems so that they do not escalate into disagreements or arguments.	Uses mediation and conflict resolution strategies to state needs, negotiate, and get his needs met.
	To be accomplished during the next ten weeks. Review by July 15, 2xxx.	To be accomplished during the next ten weeks. Review by July 15, 2xxx.

The term *scaling* in *goal attainment scaling* refers both to the response scale and to the process of creating a multi-item scale to measure a construct. In some circumstances it may be necessary to develop only one item, with five levels of attainment. However, GAS is typically used to develop several related items, which taken together create a scale. Table 11.1 illustrates how the five levels built into the GAS can provide a more sensitive measure of goal attainment. It displays level goals for a young child who has difficulty self-managing his aggression. Time frames for reviewing goal accomplishment and assessing progress are also established in this example (Cardillo & Choate, 1994).

The following guidelines apply to the development of a Goal Attainment Scale (Smith, 1994):

- *Identify the issue or issues that will be the focus of the intervention.* Ensure that the scale concentrates on those issues that will be the focus of intervention and for which resources are available to support treatment.
- *Translate the selected problems into at least three goals.* Goal setting is typically accomplished with the individual whose performance is expected to change. in order to focus on the important goals and obtain the individual's commitment to work toward goal attainment. (In our example, the therapist, parent, and child would jointly develop additional aggression management goals.)
- *Choose a brief title for each goal.* Make the title succinctly define the purpose. In the previous example, "Use of Anger Management Self-Help Skills" names the goal, and this might be one of several goals under an overall goal such as "Aggression Management."
- *Select an indicator for each goal.* Choose a behavior or affective state (such as the arguing or physical fighting in our example) that can be measured and that represents the goal.
- *Specify the expected level of outcome for the goal.* Have the individuals who set the goal identify a reasonable expectation of performance. This becomes the midpoint of the scale and represents positive progress in addressing the issue or problem.
- *Review the expected level of outcome.* Ensure that it is challenging but attainable, that resources are available to assist the client in attaining it, and that it is consistent with the overall problem and goal to be addressed.
- *Specify the somewhat more and somewhat less than expected levels of outcome.* Once the expected level of outcome is articulated, then envision the steps above and below this level. These steps should also be challenging but attainable.
- *Specify the much more and much less than expected levels of outcome.* Envision the most challenging (but still realistic) levels to attain or to avoid or cease.
- *Do not leave a level blank.* Establish indictors for every level of performance, to ensure that the client clearly understands the expectations for each level.
- *Make levels mutually exclusive.* Ensure that behaviors and performance factors on one level are distinct from those on the next level in either direction. In treatment settings a therapist may have a colleague review the GAS to ensure that the levels are succinct and do not overlap.
- *Ensure that levels form an unbroken continuum.* If the expected outcome for an individual on a weight loss program is shedding eight to twelve pounds in three months, the next level—somewhat more than expected—should pick up where the previous level ended—say, thirteen to seventeen pounds, not twenty to twenty-five pounds.

- *Use language the client understands.* Avoid technical jargon and choose language meaningful to the client (language revealed when the client assists in GAS development).
- *Ensure that indicators are measurable.* Describe each level so that performance can be measured quantitatively or qualitatively. For example, a weight loss program will produce a number (weight), which can be counted and compared to the level of attainment. An aggression management program might look at the ability to use a self-imposed time-out when upset. This indicator does not have to be quantified, but it should be stated so that an independent observer can determine whether or not it has been attained.
- *Indicate a review date.* Always include a projected date by which the goal should be attained. If it is not stated in the body of the GAS, it should appear elsewhere in the instrument, such as below the title or below the GAS table.
- *Repeat these scaling steps for each of the goals under the overall goal.*

The simplest method of scoring Goal Attainment Scales is to add up the scores for each goal. For example, if there were four goals and they received the scores +1, 0, −1, and +2, the total score would be +2 (where the highest possible score is +8 and 0 equals meeting expectations). This would indicate positive overall progress toward goal attainment, as the client met one goal and exceeded the expected level for two others. Individual goal scores may also indicate that a particular goal requires more effort or additional resources or is not realistic. Because performance development and improvement is typically an ongoing process, individual goals may need to be revised, making some levels more or less challenging, for example, or modifying them to support maintenance of goals now successfully achieved.

At times a therapist may need to compare scores from several clients. However, different clients may have different total numbers of goals, and someone who has a total GAS score of 5 with four goals cannot be compared to another individual with a total GAS score of 5 and seven goals. In this situation you need to convert the total GAS to a standard score. Fortunately, conversion tables, such as Table 11.2, have been developed to assist with this process. To use Table 11.2, find a client's total GAS score in the first column. Then find his or her number of goals in the table's column headings. The cell where the row with the GAS score and the column with the number of goals intersect contains the standard score. For example, if an individual has three goals with scores of +1, +1, and 0, the total GAS is +2 and the standard score is 59. Another individual might have five goals with scores of 0, +2, −1, +1, and 0 for a total GAS of +2. However, given the number of goals (five) the standard score for that individual is 56. Consequently, even though both have total GAS scores of +2, the standard score indicates some difference in performance, given the difference in the number of goals.

TABLE 11.2: GOAL ATTAINMENT SCALE CONVERSION TABLE: CONVERTS GAS SCORES TO STANDARD SCORES.

Total GAS Score	Number of Goals					
	1	2	3	4	5	6
−12						19
−11						22
−10					20	24
−9					23	27
−8				21	26	29
−7				25	29	32
−6			23	28	32	35
−5			27	32	35	37
−4		25	32	35	38	40
−3		31	36	39	41	42
−2	30	38	41	43	44	45
−1	40	44	45	46	47	47
0	50	50	50	50	50	50
+1	60	56	55	54	53	53
+2	70	62	59	57	56	55
+3		69	64	61	59	58
+4		75	68	65	62	60
+5			73	68	65	63
+6			77	72	68	65
+7				75	71	68
+8				79	74	71
+9					77	73
+10					80	76
+11						78
+12						81

Source: Mindel & Dangel, 1998. Reprinted with permission of Richard F. Dangel.

Summative (Likert) Scales

Most of us are familiar with instruments that allow tallying the numerical values associated with rating items to produce a total score. For example, there are a number of questionnaires that assess your style of leadership, producing a score that indicates that you are, for example, either people or task oriented. Many instruments have also been designed to assess personal attributes such as locus of control, job satisfaction, self-esteem, and integrity and also opinions and beliefs. Because the numerical values assigned to the response sets can be tallied to produce a score, these instruments are referred to as *summative scales*. Some of these instruments are designed to produce a single score, and others are designed to measure multiple constructs and thus they produce individual or subscores within the totality of the instrument.

A summative scale can be created using some of the rating formats we have discussed so far, such as items using a numerical, graphic, or Likert response scales, and in fact the term *Likert scale* is often used to describe a response set as well as a multiple-item summative scale.

Rensis Likert (1903–1981) studied more than the use of a standard response scale format. A psychologist whose research focused on management and organizational development, Likert conducted his research in scale development during the first half of the twentieth century. The benchmark for social science instrument construction at that time was the intelligence test. Likert was interested in developing attitudinal measures that would have the reliability and validity of measures of cognition. He theorized that attitudes are a reflection of an individual's intrinsic and internal values. Individuals operationalized their values by what they said (verbalization) and how they acted (behavior). An individual might have many attitudes about a subject, some harmonious with each other and some antagonistic. However, Likert believed that if one administered multiple items, an underlying pattern would emerge that could accurately measure the individual's overall attitude toward the subject (*Biographical Dictionary of Management*, 2001).

To test his theory, Likert developed a questionnaire that he administered to undergraduate students (primarily male) at nine colleges and universities. The questionnaire consisted of three parts. The part Likert called the Internationalism Scale attempted to measure attitudes about the role of the United States as a world power. The Negro Scale attempted to measure attitudes about race relationships. The Imperialism Scale addressed questions about the use of force by the United States in its relationship with other countries. The questions in each scale used three formats. One format used a response set of *yes, ?, no;* another used multiple choice; and the third used the now-familiar five-item intensity scale.[4]

Likert used a statistical test (correlational analysis) to examine the strength of the relationship between individual items and between individual items and the scale as a whole. He also found that he could use the number assigned to each response choice (for example, *strongly disapprove* = 1, *strongly approve* = 5,) as a raw score, which could then be tabulated for all the items and could produce a statistic indicating the strength of the measure of attitude. For example, an individual who held a strong belief in the role of the United States as a world leader would produce a high score on the Imperialism Scale and there would be a strong correlation between responses to individual items (Likert, 1932).

There are essentially two ways to use the score produced by a summative, or Likert, scale, and both are based on ranking and comparison. A *criterion-referenced* approach compares an individual's score to an existing criterion. Some employee performance evaluations are scored on predetermined criteria, such as the number of pages an administrative assistance is expected to type in one hour or the number of packages a supply room clerk is expected to handle in a day. Another example is a leadership inventory used to determine leadership style, where the respondent's score is used to determine whether he fits the criteria for being an autocratic, laissez-faire, or participatory leader.

A *norm-referenced* approach compares the score for an individual to the scores for a group. To establish the norm you administer the instrument to a representative sample of users, which will produce a range of scores. This becomes the group norm, the range you can expect for the population of interest, to which you can make comparisons. In developing an instrument to screen for depression, for example, you could pretest the instrument with a sample of individuals who have been diagnosed with the disorder or who have been identified as not having depression. The scores from these two groups will help you determine norms and thus scores that reflect when depression is or is not present. Another example is the developmental inventory, where an individual's age-related development is reflected by a score that can be compared to norms from a sample group, such as the norms for children for walking, talking, and holding a utensil.

The following steps (adapted from DeVellis, 1991; Spector, 1992; Trochim, 2001) outline the process for developing a summative, or Likert, scale:

Step 1. Determine what you want to measure (Chapter Five). This typically involves a literature review to help specify the construct of interest and the factors that can be used to operationalize it. Once you define the construct, have experts review and reach agreement on the definition. It is important to define the construct so that to the extent possible, it can be differentiated from similar but different constructs (for example, differentiate depression from anxiety).

Step 2. Generate items and create an item pool. Trochim (2001) suggests generating 80 to 100 items. DeVellis (1991) notes it is impossible to predict the number that you will need but says you should always prepare more items than you will use. "Thus a 10-item scale might evolve from a 40-item pool" (p. 57).

As you construct items, consider whether they should be negatively or positively worded: for example, "I argue a lot" (negative) or "I get along with others" (positive). Also determine whether you want the scale to be constructed entirely of items worded in the same direction or whether you want to vary item direction. Also follow all the other suggestions in Chapters Seven, Eight, and Nine for constructing well-crafted items.

Step 3. Identify an appropriate response set. Although Likert Scales are associated with Likert response scales of endorsement (*agree – disagree*), you also can use any of the other formats we introduced in Chapter Seven, such as a frequency scale (*always – never*) or intensity scale (*mild – severe; good – poor*).

Also determine whether you want the response set to be unipolar (numbered consecutively from low to high, such as 1 to 5) or bipolar (numbered from negative to positive, such as −2 to +2, with or without a midpoint.

A total (summative) score is calculated by adding the values of the ratings for all the items. If the scale includes bipolar items the total score is calculated by adding positive and negative values; four items with the values of +2, +1, −2, and +1 would result in a total score of +2. If the scale includes both negatively and positively worded items, negatively worded items will need to be reversed scored. For the item "I get along with others" using a Likert response set with five choices (1 to 5), *strongly agree* would be scored 5. However, if you do not reverse score negative items, then a *strongly agree* rating for "I argue a lot" would also receive a score of 5, and the items would cancel each other out. To reverse score items, use the following formula (Spector, 1992):

$$(H + L) - RS = \text{Reverse score.}$$

Where

H = the largest value in the response scale.
L = the lowest value in the response scale.
RS = the respondent's score, or rating.

For example, if you are using a response scale with five choices (1 to 5) and the respondent answers "I argue a lot" by selecting *disagree*, which has a value of 2, putting that information into the formula gives you a reverse score of 4:

$$(5 + 1) - 2 = 4.$$

Step 4. Evaluate the item pool, and select the most appropriate items to use for pilot testing the instrument. As described previously in Chapter Six, this test is typically conducted by a panel of content experts who assess the relationship between each item and the construct of interest. The panel may rate items or use a method such as Q-sorting to select those items they believe are the strongest measures of the construct. Trochim (2001) suggests that the panel rate each item using the following scale:

1 = strongly unfavorable to the concept
2 = somewhat unfavorable to the concept
3 = undecided
4 = somewhat favorable to the concept
5 = strongly favorable to the concept

Step 5. DeVellis (1991) suggests a fifth step to enhance the validity of the scale. including an existing social desirability scale in with your scale, to check how likely it is that respondents are responding to items based on concerns about how they perceive themselves or how they believe others may perceive them. Items from your scale that demonstrate a substantial correlation with the social desirability scale items should probably be deleted.

Step 6. Pretest the scale by administering it to a sample (as described in Chapter Seven). To the extent possible the sample should be representative of the intended population of respondents. Spector (1992) recommends a sample size of 100 to 200 respondents; DeVellis (1991) suggests upward of 300. Pretesting produces the data that will be used to conduct the item analysis in the next step. We recommend that you pretest with as large a sample as is feasible within your resources and that you include the information in your documentation. In lieu of pretesting with a sample group, Trochim suggests using the ratings produced by the panel of judges for the needed data. However, it is important to keep in mind that judges may produce results different from potential respondents' results.

Step 7. Conduct an item analysis to determine which items are most strongly correlated with each other and therefore with the construct. Given the amount of data generated by pretesting the scale, statistical software, such as SPSS or SAS, is required for conducting item analysis.

Two correlations are computed. The item-remainder coefficient is the correlation between the responses to one item and the sum of the responses to the remainder of the items. For example, for a ten-item scale, responses to item 1 are correlated with the sum of the responses to items 2 through 10. Then responses to item 2 are compared to responses to items 1 and 3 through 10, and so on for each item. The items with the strongest or highest correlations should be retained, and those with the lowest correlations should be discarded (Spector, 1992, p. 30).

Next Cronbach's coefficient alpha is computed to provide a measure of internal consistency, or how well items correlate with each other. "Coefficient alpha involves comparison of the variance of a total scale score (sum of all items) with the variances of the individual items" (Spector, 1992, p. 32). Consequently, coefficient alpha provides an alpha score for the entire scale and not just individual items. Spector notes that the widely held rule of thumb is that an alpha of .70 or higher indicates internal consistency (a "perfect" correlation would have an alpha of 1.00). If alpha is below .70, there is a good chance that the items are not tapping into the construct (or latent variable) and that the scale should be revised.

Spector provides data (Table 11.3) to help us understand how the item-remainder coefficient and alpha should be interpreted and used for retaining

TABLE 11.3: ITEM ANALYSIS.

	Item #	Item-Remainder Coefficient	Alpha if Item Removed
First analysis	1	.53	.68
	2	.42	.70
	3	.36	.71
	4	.10	.74
	5	.07	.75
	6	−.41	.80
	7	.37	.71
	8	.11	.79
	9	.55	.68
	10	.42	.70
		alpha = .72	
Second analysis	1	.56	.79
	2	.43	.81
	3	.31	.84
	7	.39	.82
	9	.58	.78
	10	.44	.81
		alpha = .83	

Source: Spector, 1992, p. 33. Reprinted with permission.

and deleting scale items. The column of Table 11.3 titled "Item-Remainder Coefficient" provides the value for each item when correlated with the sum of the remaining items. The higher the number, the stronger the correlation indicating that item should probably be retained. Notice that in the first analysis, items 4, 5, 6, and 8 have low values compared to the other items, suggesting that removing them from the instrument could improve validity.

The last column displays how the alpha value for the entire scale will change when an item is removed. The second analysis, displayed in the lower section of the table shows that the alpha value for the entire scale increases when one deletes the four items with the lowest values (4, 5, 6, and 8). For most of the items, but not item 3, the item-remainder coefficient also increases when the lowest-value items are deleted. Item 3's decrease may be due to any number of factors; for example, it may have been strongly correlated with one of the deleted items and that item's removal may have affected item 3's correlation with the remaining items. This suggests that you might want to compute coefficient alpha again after deleting item 3 (Spector, 1992, p. 35),

Finally, coefficient alpha is influenced by both the magnitude of the correlations and the number of items. For example, the more items you use, the more likely you are to obtain a high coefficient alpha, because you increase the likelihood that some of the items will tap into the construct. As instrument designer, you have a choice to make here. A lengthy scale may be a better measure of the construct but may also be completed by fewer respondents. A shorter instrument might be easier for respondents but may also produce less reliable and valid measures.

As you can see, developing a summative scale has its constraints. Adequate time is necessary to create and test the scale prior to administration, and a fairly large sample is needed for pretesting. Access to a computer to do the number crunching is essential. Defining the purpose and focus of your information needs will help you determine if a summative scale is appropriate for your project. For example, summative scales are typically used in the construction of psychometric instruments to evaluate emotional states or behavioral characteristics where the object of measurement is an individual. Summative scales are also used to create attitude measures that might be used on more than one occasion and with more than one target audience. It might be difficult to justify the time and effort needed to develop a summative scale if you need an instrument for a single project. Nevertheless, it might be a good investment if you are interested in thoroughly measuring an underlying construct and the instrument has potential for more than a one-time use.

Cumulative Scales

A *cumulative scale* uses multiple items to measure an underlying, unidimensional construct. With a cumulative scale, an affirmative answer to an item assumes that the prior responses were also affirmative; when a cumulative scale composed of seven statements is scored, a score of 4 means that the respondent agreed with the first four statements but not the last three: "The items themselves are constructed so that they are cumulative; if you agree with one item, you probably agree with all of the ones above it in the list" (Trochim, 2001, p. 115).

When using a cumulative scale (also known as a Guttman scale, after its developer), the respondent is asked to agree or disagree with each statement. In the process of creating the scale, these statements may be presented in any order, but once the scale has been derived, they should be presented to the respondent in order of intensity.

EXAMPLE

There is little hard evidence demonstrating the health risks of smoking.

One has to smoke for years and years before experiencing any health risks.

There is growing evidence of health risks associated with smoking.

The link between smoking and some health risks has been established.

Research has firmly established that smoking is a major health risk contributing to a high rate of mortality.

The Bogardus Social Distance Scale is a specialized form of Guttman scale developed to measure a respondent's attitude toward members of another ethnic or cultural group. It creates a cumulative pattern, as a response on one item should be dependent on the response to a prior item. In the following example, the level of contact with a member of an ethnic group increases with each statement, hence being comfortable with a member of this group playing with your children infers a willingness to have that person be a neighbor as well.

EXAMPLE

Read each statement below and then place a checkmark (✓) on the blank if you agree with it:

———— I would be comfortable with a (name of an ethnic group, Hispanic, Muslim, Hindu, and so forth) coming into the United States for temporary employment.

———— I would be comfortable with a (name of ethnic group) as my neighbor.

———— I would be comfortable with the child of a (name of ethnic group) playing with my children.

———— I would be comfortable with a (name of ethnic group) becoming a citizen of the United States.

———— I would be comfortable with a (name of ethnic group) marrying my son or daughter.

Developing a cumulative scale involves creating a large item pool, having a panel of judges rate the strength of the relationship between each item and the construct, ordering the items based on these ratings, and conducting a statistical analysis to determine which items are good measures of the construct and which items are not as strong and should probably be deleted. (For a succinct description of this process, we recommend Trochim, 2001, pp. 147–150.)

Given the complexity of their construction process, properly designed cumulative scales are not often used by researchers, although you may come across surveys that appear to use this format but that have not been analyzed to ensure that the necessary scale properties exist.

Thurstone Scales

Psychologist Louis L. Thurstone (1887–1955) was interested in understanding how to measure such attributes as cognition and emotional states. His research lead to the development of three different cumulative scales: the method of equal appearing intervals, the method of successive intervals, and the method of paired comparisons (Trochim, 2001). In this section we will take a look at the first and last approaches.

One of the advantages of multi-items scales is that they can produce a numerical score you can use to assess the strength of the measurement. The method of *equal appearing intervals* is a multistep process that begins by identifying the topic of interest and then formulating a large pool of items—from 100 to 200 items! Next, a panel of judges is asked to rate each item along an 11-point response scale indicating whether the item presents a favorable or unfavorable attitude toward the topic with 1 = a very unfavorable attitude and 11 = a very favorable attitude. It is important that the judges rate the item as a measure of the topic and not whether they agree or disagree with the statement. For example, a judge might rate the following statement as reflecting a favorable attitude toward the topic of the death penalty: "I think the death penalty is appropriate for anyone found guilty of premeditated murder."

Thurstone originally used up to 100 judges, however, it is probably more realistic to find twenty to twenty-five people at a minimum to rate the items. Judges' ratings for each item are added together and the median value (midpoint) is tabulated. This is done for all 100 to 200 items, which even with the assistance of a computer is a time-consuming process. The items are then ranked by their medians, from lowest to highest. When an 11-point response scale is used, the median values can range from 1 to 11, with the statements having the highest median value (its score value) representing the most favorable attitude toward the topic.

The next step is to select items that are at equal intervals across the range of medians. For example, select at least one item from the group of items with a median of 1, one item from those items with a median of 2, and so on. Trochim (2001) notes that in addition to selecting the items based on these values, you should also assess each item to determine which ones make the most sense (to you as the instrument designer) in relation to the topic of interest.

Now that you have selected the items, you administer your questionnaire, using a dichotomous response scale such as *agree* or *disagree,* or *yes* or *no.* Notice that it is the items themselves (that is, their median values) and not the response scale choices, that are at an interval level of measurement. The final step is to add the median values for all items where the respondent has selected agreement (such as *agree* or *yes*). The average of these median values is the total score for the respondent. Let's suppose that on a 10-item questionnaire a respondent rates seven of the items as agree. The medians associated with those seven items are: 8, 9, 7, 10, 8, 8, and 9. The average for those items–8.4–is the respondent's score.

It is obvious that constructing and administering an instrument with the method of equal appearing intervals is complex and time-consuming process. Thurstone's interest as a psychologist was in the development of scales for individual assessment, and for that purpose this can be an effective approach. Consequently, you might consider the method of equal appearing intervals when assessing an individual (self-response or observation instrument), but it is unlikely you would find this a manageable approach for conducting a survey to be administered to a large group.

When the method of *paired comparison* is used, an individual is supplied with a list of statements and must compare each statement with every other statement on the list. There may be a large number of alternative statements; however, the respondent is looking at only two at a time. For example, if the respondent is presented with four statements, he or she will compare and make a selection between statement A and statement B, then between A and C, and then A and D. Having made those comparisons, the respondent then goes to statement B and compares it with C and then with D (remember, the comparison has already been made between A and B). This continues until all possible comparisons have been exhausted.

EXAMPLE

What do you believe are the most important problems your state legislature should address this year?

A. Highway construction

B. High cost of tuition at state colleges and universities

C. Sale of guns by unlicensed gun dealers

D. Limiting marriage to heterosexual couples

Paired comparison is designed to increase a respondent's ability to discriminate between items. As with the method of equal appearing intervals, paired comparison produces interval level data. It too is a time-consuming process, particularly when a large number of respondents produce a considerable amount of data for analysis. Additionally, the process of constructing and analyzing data produced through paired comparison is even more complex than the process for the previous method.

The first step in using paired comparison is to identify the purpose of your study and from that to create a pool of items. In the following example, five items have been identified as indicators of potential problems at a university: (1) increasing tuition, (2) insufficient faculty advising, (3) lack of faculty diversity, (4) inadequate parking, and (5) unfriendly atmosphere. These items can be presented as a list and the respondent instructed to make comparisons as follows (for five items there are ten pairings): 1 to 2, 1 to 3, 1 to 4, 1 to 5; 2 to 3, 2 to 4, 2 to 5; 3 to 4, 3 to 5; 4 to 5. Or the items can be presented in pairs, with each set identified by a letter rather than a number:

EXAMPLE

Below are several sets of statements referring to problem areas at the university. For each pair, check the one that is the most important to you.

A. ——— Increasing tuition
    ——— Insufficient faculty advising
B. ——— Lack of faculty diversity
    ——— Insufficient faculty advising
C. ——— Inadequate parking
    ——— Lack of faculty diversity
D. ——— Lack of faculty diversity
    ——— Increasing tuition
E. ——— Inadequate parking
    ——— Insufficient faculty advising

F. ——— Inadequate parking
    ——— Unfriendly atmosphere
G. ——— Increasing tuition
    ——— Inadequate parking
H. ——— Unfriendly atmosphere
    ——— Insufficient faculty advising
I. ——— Unfriendly atmosphere
    ——— Lack of faculty diversity
J. ——— Unfriendly atmosphere
    ——— Increasing tuition

Follow these guidelines when using the paired comparison approach:

- *Each pair must be mutually exclusive so that the respondent has a clear choice.*
- *Directions should be explicit, with an example of what the task actually requires.* One way to assist respondents with the task is to create an item matrix, as shown in the previous example, to ensure that statements are properly matched and compared. A sample item can also illustrate how to complete the activity.
- *The statements should be placed in random order,* without any suggestion of a hierarchy or ranking.
- *Do not make the number of statements, and thus the pairings, excessive.* The process can become complex and time consuming when too many statements are included. As with rank ordering, once you get above a dozen alternatives, it is best to consider constructing more than one item.

    After each respondent makes his or her choice, a table like the following is used to tabulate the results. For example, if there were five statements, the table would have five rows and five columns in order to make comparisons. Statement sets cannot be compared with themselves—there is no pairing of A to A, for instance—therefore mark the cell where A intersects with A (and B with B, and so on) with an X.

EXAMPLE

		Tuition	Advising	Diversity	Parking	Atmosphere
		A	**B**	**C**	**D**	**E**
Tuition	**A**	X				
Advising	**B**		X			
Diversity	**C**			X		
Parking	**D**				X	
Atmosphere	**E**					X
	Total					

The following table is based on a hypothetical administration involving fifteen respondents and shows how to tally the results. Values are entered by columns; for example twelve respondents chose tuition over advising, nine chose tuition over diversity, and fifteen chose tuition over atmosphere. Moving to next column, eight respondents chose advising over atmosphere, and in the next column we see that ten chose diversity over advising, and so on.

EXAMPLE

		Tuition	Advising	Diversity	Parking	Atmosphere
		A	**B**	**C**	**D**	**E**
Tuition	**A**	X			11	
Advising	**B**	12	X	10	12	
Diversity	**C**	9		X	11	
Parking	**D**				X	
Atmosphere	**E**	15	8	14	15	X
	Total					

The matrix provides for a total of twenty numbers, but we have accounted for only ten (pairs). In the remaining boxes calculate the difference between the number of respondents and each of their choices. For example, nine of the fifteen respondents chose tuition (A) over diversity (C) and we placed the number nine in the cell corresponding to those coordinates (A, C). In the corresponding cell (C, A) place the difference between fifteen and nine ($15 - 9 = 6$). At this stage we can total the columns and rank them. This process creates a frequency matrix:

EXAMPLE

		Tuition	Advising	Diversity	Parking	Atmosphere
		A	**B**	**C**	**D**	**E**
Tuition	**A**	X	3	6	11	0
Advising	**B**	12	X	10	12	7
Diversity	**C**	9	5	X	11	1
Parking	**D**	4	3	4	X	0
Atmosphere	**E**	15	8	14	15	X
	Total	40	19	34	49	8
	Rank	2	4	3	1	5

At this point we have ranked ordinal level data. Among this group of respondents, parking ranks as the most serious problem, followed by rising tuitions, faculty diversity, advising time, and finally atmosphere. However, by converting to interval-level data, we can see just how much the respondents differed.

The first step is to transform the raw scores into percentages, which is accomplished by dividing each score by the number of respondents. The new matrix looks like this:

EXAMPLE

	Tuition	Advising	Diversity	Parking	Atmosphere
	A	**B**	**C**	**D**	**E**
Tuition	X	0.20	0.40	0.73	0.00
Advising	0.80	X	0.67	0.80	0.47
Diversity	0.60	0.33	X	0.73	0.07
Parking	0.27	0.20	0.27	X	0.00
Atmosphere	1.00	0.53	0.93	1.00	X
Total	2.67	1.26	2.27	3.26	0.54
Rank	2.00	4.00	3.00	1.00	5.00

The final step in the conversion process is to look up each of the values in our new matrix in a reference table (Areas Under the Normal Curve, which can be found at the back of most statistics texts). This converts our data to z scores, which always have a mean of 0 and a standard deviation of 1. In a normal distribution, half of the values will be below the mean and half above the mean, therefore values less than .50 have a negative value.

	Tuition	Advising	Diversity	Parking	Atmosphere
	A	**B**	**C**	**D**	**E**
Tuition	X	−0.53	−1.28	0.74	0.00
Advising	0.53	X	0.95	0.53	−1.88
Diversity	1.28	−0.95	X	0.74	−0.18
Parking	−0.74	−0.53	−0.74	X	0.00
Atmosphere	0.34	1.88	0.18	0.34	X
Total	1.4	−0.1	−0.9	2.4	−2.1
Mean	0.35	−0.03	−0.22	0.59	−0.52
Rank	2.0	4.0	3.0	1.0	5.0

Once the new matrix is completed, the sum of each column is computed, as well as the mean. The means provide the scale values of the continuum and when we plot the values on a line, we have a visual depiction of the distance between each rating, as shown here:

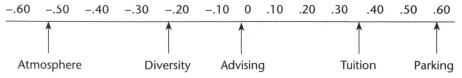

−.60	−.50	−.40	−.30	−.20	−.10	0	.10	.20	.30	.40	.50	.60

Atmosphere   Diversity   Advising   Tuition   Parking

Summary

The term *scale* has two meanings in instrument construction. First, it means a response set where the choices are laid out on a continuum from which the respondent makes a selection. Second, it means an instrument with multiple items that measure an underlying construct and that produce numerical values, or scores, that can be summed to reflect the strength of the measure. We can compare this to the pointillist style of painting, where individual dabs of paint in complementary colors are applied to build up an image. This definition distinguishes between an instrument that is a scale and an instrument that focuses purely on information gathering, with no emphasis on measuring a hypothetical construct. The latter may use multiple items to obtain information about the topic of interest, but these items function independently of each other, and so the instrument does not possess all the properties needed to function as multi-item scales.

You may be interested in examining an underlying construct where the strength of the relationship between and among the items is an indication of the relationship between the items and the construct of interest. As the instrument designer you will then need to consider whether you have the resources necessary to develop a reliable and valid multi-item scale.

Instrument 11.A: Summative Scale

Morris Rosenberg, a professor of sociology at the University of Maryland, was interested in how individuals perceive self-worth. The instrument he developed, the Rosenberg Self-Esteem Scale, is an example of a multi-item summative scale where the values from each item can be tallied to produce a total score. The higher the score the greater the individual's perception of self-worth.

The Rosenberg Self-Esteem Scale is a concise instrument containing only ten items. Notice that items are both positively and negatively worded, with some items connoting high self-esteem and others low self-esteem. Also note that the column numbers associated with the response values are not used for scoring . For example, *strongly agree* appears first in the response scale and is numbered 1, but as described in the scale's "general information" section, *strongly agree*'s value for scoring is 3, on a scale of 0 to 3. Information is also provided about correlations (a measure of reliability that we explored in Chapter Three); these tests indicated that when the scale was administered to the same individuals on two different occasions, the results exhibited a high level of agreement over time.

INSTRUMENT 11.A: ROSENBERG SELF-ESTEEM SCALE.

ROSENBERG SELF-ESTEEM SCALE

General Information for using the Rosenberg Self-Esteem Scale (SES):

- While designed as a Guttman scale, the SES is now commonly scored as a Likert scale. The 10 items are answered on a four point scale ranging from **strongly agree** to **strongly disagree.**
- The original sample for which the scale was developed in the 1960s consisted of 5,024 high school juniors and seniors from 10 randomly selected schools in New York State and was scored as a Guttman scale. The scale generally has high reliability: test-retest correlations are typically in the range of .82 to .88, and Cronbach's alpha for various samples are in the range of .77 to .88. . . . Studies have demonstrated both a unidimensional and a two-factor (self-confidence and self-deprecation) structure to the scale. To obtain norms for a sample similar to your own, you must search the academic literature to find research using similar samples.
- To score the items, assign a value to each of the 10 items as follows:
  - For items 1,2,4,6,7: Strongly Agree = 3, Agree = 2, Disagree = 1, and Strongly Disagree = 0.
  - For items 3,5,8,9,10 (which are reversed in valence, and noted with the asterisks** below): Strongly Agree = 0, Agree = 1, Disagree = 2, and Strongly Disagree = 3.
- The scale ranges from 0–30, with 30 indicating the highest score possible. Other scoring options are possible. For example, you can assign values 1–4 rather than 0–3; then scores will range from 10–40. Some researchers use 5- or 7-point Likert scales, and again, scale ranges would vary based on the addition of "middle" categories of agreement.

Present the scale with the following instructions. *Do not print* the asterisks on the sheet you provide to respondents.

Directions: Below is a list of statements dealing with your general feelings about yourself. If you **Strongly Agree**, circle **SA**. If you **Agree** with the statement circle **A**. If you **Disagree** circle **D**. If you **Strongly Disagree**, circle **SD**.

		1. STRONGLY AGREE	2. AGREE	3. DISAGREE	4. STRONGLY DISAGREE
1.	I feel that I'm a person of worth, at least on an equal plane with others.	SA	A	D	SD
2.	I feel that I have a number of good qualities.	SA	A	D	SD
3.	All in all, I am inclined to feel that I am a failure.**	SA	A	D	SD
4.	I am able to do things as well as most other people.	SA	A	D	SD
5.	I feel I do not have much to be proud of.**	SA	A	D	SD
6.	I take a positive attitude toward myself.	SA	A	D	SD
7.	On the whole, I am satisfied with myself.	SA	A	D	SD
8.	I wish I could have more respect for myself.**	SA	A	D	SD
9.	I certainly feel useless at times.**	SA	A	D	SD
10.	At times I think I am no good at all.**	SA	A	D	SD

Note: The family of the late Morris Rosenberg has given permission for use of the Rosenberg Self-Esteem Scale at no charge when used in conjunction with educational and professional research. Also see the background information at the University of Maryland Web site: http://www.bsos.umd.edu/socy/grad/socpsy_rosenberg.htm.
Source: University of Maryland, Department of Sociology, 2006; Rosenberg, 1989.

Endnotes

1. DeVellis (1991) notes that this is referred to as a latent variable because it is not overt and because the value of what we are measuring may vary rather than being constant. For example, the level of intensity in which an individual engages in political activities (as a measure of activism) can vary over time and from situation to situation.

2. The terminology associated with scales is not always consistent. For example, one text uses the term *questionnaire* to describe instruments that use rating-scale items that function independently of each other and the term *attitude rating scale* to describe instruments that measure a construct (Henerson, Morris, & Fitz-Gibbon, 1987).

3. Social scientists also differentiate *indexes* from *scales*. "A scale differs from an index in that it takes advantage of any intensity structure that might exist among the individual items" (Babbie, 1990, p. 148). Simply put, both indexes and scales use multiple items to operationalize and study the construct; however, a scale is an ordinal measure that provides a means of measuring the relative intensity of responses.

4. Most people associate the term Likert scale with any rating item that uses a response set of *strongly agree, agree, no opinion, disagree,* and *strongly disagree*. Interestingly, when Likert first introduced this item format, he used slightly different wording: *strongly approve, approve, undecided, disapprove,* and *strongly disapprove*. His terminology in the title Negro Scale is of course a reflection of the culture at the time the scale was developed.

Key Concepts and Terms

construct	Guttman scale	Q-sorting
cumulative scale	Likert scale	scale
dimensionality	multi-item scale	scaling
equal appearing intervals	operationalizing	Semantic Differential Scale
factor of judgment	paired comparison	summative scale
frequency matrix	proportional matrix	Thurstone scale
Goal Attainment Scale	Q methodology	

PART THREE

ORGANIZATION AND ADMINISTRATION

CHAPTER TWELVE

ORGANIZING THE INSTRUMENT

In this chapter we will

- Describe the components of an instrument, and provide guidelines for drafting each component, including the title, introductory statement, directions, and demographic section.
- Present guidelines for organizing the different components.
- Explain how to use typography (text styling) to improve organization and presentation.

Composition is the term used in painting to describe how an artist organizes and balances a variety of elements on the canvas. Typically the main effort to organize those elements occurs before the artist ever puts paint to canvas. In contrast, the main effort to organize and format the elements that make up the survey instrument—items, introduction directions, demographic section—typically occurs after the items have been developed.

In this chapter we provide guidelines for designing the various components that make up the questionnaire, such as the title, the purpose statement, the directions, and the like. We then explore the organization of these components. This is an important activity, as the appearance of the questionnaire and the flow of the items will influence the ease with which respondents complete the instrument and the time it will take them to complete it. In turn, the factors of ease and time can have a significant influence on the response rate and reliability.

Title

The first thing a respondent will see is the title of your instrument. It would be nice if people followed the maxim "Don't judge a book by its cover." However, in instrument construction it is all too likely that respondents will indeed judge a questionnaire by its title. The title should convey the purpose of your questionnaire and its intended audience. If the title is wordy or abstract, a respondent may set the questionnaire aside and not complete it. For that reason you should be thoughtful in creating your title. Writing it is usually best done after construction of the entire instrument, so that it can accurately reflect the content and the method of eliciting responses. In writing the title, consider these five criteria:

Reflect instrument content. One way to summarize the purpose of the instrument in the title is to reflect the content of the items. For example, an appropriate title for a questionnaire on political attitudes might be simply Survey of Political Attitudes. Another way to reflect content is to refer to both substantive content and the major type of item. For example, if you develop an instrument for student teachers to assess their teaching skills and all or most of the items feature 5-point rating scales, you might appropriately title it Student Teacher Self-Rating Questionnaire.

Be concise. The title should help the respondent to grasp the scope of the instrument without bogging down in specifics and being distracted from the questionnaire itself. Both of the titles suggested earlier are good examples of succinctness. A wordy, and consequently bad, title for a political attitude survey would be A Survey of Attitudes, Reactions, and Observations of Current Political Parties in the U.S. During the Past Years.

Use easily understood language. Because complex or unrecognizable words or phrases in the title might discourage potential respondents, jargon and acronyms should be eliminated. In general the title should be easy for your target respondents to understand yet informative. Your well-designed instrument may remain unanswered if people are alienated by language in the title.

Avoid potentially offensive or off-putting wording. As with questionnaire items, you must be sensitive to the language you use in the title. This is especially true when your main purpose is to obtain information about such sensitive subjects as income, sexual behavior, or controversial social policy. Additionally, some words may be acceptable in a general context but sensitive in a more specialized one. For example, older respondents might take offense at a survey titled Assessment of Physical Activities Among Geriatric Americans. The term *Americans over age 65* might be less offensive than *geriatric*. Whenever you suspect language might be misconstrued, it is best to obtain the opinions of others, preferably potential respondents.

Place the title appropriately. The title should be the first thing the respondent sees. It should be placed at the top of the page, centered, and preferably in boldface type. If a cover letter or set of instructions precedes the questionnaire, the title should appear on those pages as well. If the questionnaire is lengthy, say three to four pages, place the title at the top of each questionnaire page too.

Introductory Statement

Almost every questionnaire should have an introductory statement informing respondents about the instrument's purpose, confidentiality of respondents' information, use of data, and motivations for completing the questionnaire. This statement usually takes the form of a brief paragraph or two following the title of the instrument or an accompanying cover letter. The introductory statement serves two purposes. First, it prepares the respondents and, one hopes, engages them so they are motivated to complete the instrument. Second, it has been demonstrated that respondents who are invested in the process are more likely to return mail surveys (Odom, 1979).

An introductory statement should be included regardless of mode of administration. For example, if you have created an instrument to be completed by observers or raters, the introductory statement can help them focus on the purpose of the project and the task of rating. Following are important criteria to consider in constructing the introductory statement:

Present a brief summary of the instrument's purpose. This statement will draw on the material you wrote about the purpose and the use of the instrument prior to the actual instruction construction (as described in Chapter Five). Indicating how and by whom the information will be used, it should be concise. It should allow respondents to see what they are getting themselves into, should be straightforward and truthful, and should *not* (intentionally or unintentionally) bias respondents' answers. This summary should also state how the results will be reported and to whom: the results obtained from an instrument designed to support research might be reported in a journal article, for example, whereas a school needs assessment might be reported to the local school board, school administrators, teachers, and taxpayers. If you are summarizing two or more purposes, they should not be inconsistent or contradictory. Inconsistency can lead respondents to acquiesce to the more noncommittal responses, from which little information will result.

Looking at Instrument 12.A, you will see that its introductory paragraph states that the purpose is to provide "an anonymous opportunity to evaluate the course and the instructor." Additionally, "the results will be used to provide a basis for course improvement and overall assessment of the effectiveness of this course." By assuring anonymity, the instrument tries to encourage respondents to provide honest responses, without concern that future interactions with the instructor will be tainted. Still, informing students that their information will be used to judge the instructor's effectiveness could affect responses. For example, if students feel that their responses could affect an individual faculty member's chance for tenure or a salary increase, they may answer differently than they would if they felt their responses would be used only for pointing out weaknesses or strengths in the instructional program.

A side benefit of providing respondents with a description of how the information will be used is that they then have an opportunity to gauge the face validity of the instrument for themselves: does the instrument measure what it purports to measure as described in the title and introduction?

Describe the level of confidentiality. The introduction should explicitly state whether an individual's completed instrument will be used by and made accessible to others or used only as part of an aggregation. Obviously, in certain situations divulging respondents' negative comments or suggestions might have serious repercussions for them, a possibility likely to temper their responses. Furthermore, it is improper, unethical, and in some cases illegal to elicit information for one purpose or situation and then use it for another.

Recall that confidentiality is different from anonymity. Confidentiality means that access to identifying information is limited to specific people and is not disclosed to others. For example, you might ask respondents to supply their names and phone numbers so that you can contact them to obtain clarification. However, when reporting the results, you release only aggregate data and no information about individual respondents is included. This is referred to as *deidentifying* the data. Another approach to confidentiality is to code each survey with a number that corresponds to the respondent's identifying information, and to limit access to that information to, for example, the principal investigator. Others may have access to the data but not to the information about individual respondents. In a truly anonymous survey, no one can connect a completed instrument to a specific respondent, not even those administering the instrument.

The introductory paragraph for Instrument 12.A, for example, states that responses will remain anonymous. Note also that this instrument contains no demographic data, information that might allow an instructor to identify a respondent (an issue discussed in Chapter Five). Without this reassurance, students might be concerned that their comments, if individually identified by an instructor, could affect their grades or rapport with that teacher.

Consider including a motivator. A motivator is something that encourages the respondent to complete the questionnaire, and these incentives can take a variety of forms. Examples of frequently used motivators are promising the respondents a copy of the survey results, offering to put them on a notification list, or otherwise making them feel as though they will have an individual impact on an organization. More expensive motivators include offers of free tickets, money, discounts, or access to generally inaccessible places such as reserved areas of an art museum. One gardening magazine promised a free plant to people completing a 200-item gardening questionnaire. Often outside motivators exist that ensure replies, for example, withholding a person's paycheck or making response a general expectation of the job.[1]

Research tends to support the use of such inducements to increase the response rate. In one study, individuals receiving a $5 check for participating in a survey had a 57.5% response rate whereas those that did not receive the incentive had a 45.5% response rate (Donaldson et al., 1999), and if more respondents reply, the data gathered may better represent the sample or population surveyed. Nonetheless, some question the ethicality of using motivators, particularly financial rewards. The important considerations are, first, can you afford the motivator and, second, could the existence of the motivator bias the responses? For example, if your population of interest is potentially evenly distributed by income, but use of a financial incentive results in a disproportionate number of lower-income individuals responding, the incentive may have skewed the sample.

State how long it takes to complete the instrument. You should have determined during pretesting the average amount of time it takes to complete the instrument, and you can present that number as an estimate: for example, "It should take approximately fifteen minutes to complete this questionnaire." You might be concerned that this estimate will discourage some respondents from filling it out the instrument. However, as Childers and Ferrell (1979) say, "The issue of questionnaire length has been the subject of considerable investigation but with often confusing and conflicting results. It seems logical . . . that response rate would decrease with an increase in questionnaire length. However . . . research to date has failed to support this hypothesis and certain studies have yielded opposite results" (p. 429). A number of later studies have come up with similar conclusions (see Subar et al., 2001), which suggests that multiple factors, in addition to or aside from length of completion time, influence response rate. Our guidance is to be aware of your intended users. For example, if potential respondents are engaged with the topic they may be willing to invest the time it takes to complete a lengthy questionnaire. Pretesting may also suggest the need to revise and possibly reduce the number of items if potential respondents tell you the instrument takes too long to complete. Additionally, we believe that providing this information demonstrates respect for the respondents and the task you are asking them to complete.

Use appropriate language. Here, as in the title and in all other sections of an instrument, the language used should be easily understood by the respondents. This appears obvious but may be difficult to comply with. Lack of knowledge of respondents' reading and comprehension levels may result in introductions, directions and items written at the instrument designer's level. This problem can be easily remedied by administering the questionnaire to a small subsample of respondents and questioning them verbally to see whether their understanding of terms and expressions is congruent with the designer's understanding. Where congruence is lacking, the instrument will not measure what it purports to measure.

Are introductory statements required in all instruments? In many situations the needed information about the issues discussed here is implied. A general guideline in writing introductory paragraphs or cover letters is that if this information is not clearly implied or stated somewhere in the questionnaire package, a statement pertaining to each topic should be provided.

Directions

Directions (also referred to as instructions) serve to explain and clarify as well as to move the respondent through the task of completing the questionnaire in an efficient manner. Directions come in two basic types: those that relate to the total questionnaire and those that are specific to individual sections of it. In Instrument 12.A we see both types.

First, general directions are provided describing how to mark the form, such as using a No. 2 pencil and not an ink or ballpoint pen. However, these instructions do not provide the information needed to complete the first three items (course, instructor, and section number); that information is provided by the instructor.

Then instructions are given with each set of items. On the front of the survey, a different typestyle (all capitals) is used to highlight the directive "ANSWER THIS SIDE FIRST."

On the second page, part of the form is shaded and contains the statement "DO NOT WRITE IN THIS SPACE." To highlight this directive, the words are printed in large capital letters and in a contrasting color.

As is the case with the general introduction, placement of these general directions varies with the structure of the questionnaire. Two appropriate places are at the beginning of the instrument and in the cover letter.

There are several important considerations in writing directions for an instrument. Not all of them will apply to every instrument, but all should be reviewed for appropriateness.

Make directions complete, unambiguous, and concise. If users are unclear about how to complete the instrument, they may choose to skip items or may complete them in a way that is not useful. Therefore it is as important to pretest your instructions as it is to pretest individual items.

Also be aware that readers tend to skim directions. To prevent them from missing vital information, avoid bunching the instructions into one long paragraph. If instructions are more than two or three sentences long, break them into naturally occurring sections, perhaps by theme.

Use appropriate language. Like the rest of the instrument, the directions should use terminology and be at a reading level appropriate to the audience. This is particularly important when an instrument will be completed by children or individuals with cognitive limitations. For example, instructions for young children should be composed of short sentences, with each sentence conveying just one idea.

Tell respondents how to return the completed instrument. If the person who administers the instrument can simply hand it out and tell respondents or raters to return it to her or him when they have completed it, written directions on disposition are not required. However, if the respondent receives the questionnaire in the mail, it must include clear instructions about how to return it. In most cases including a self-addressed, stamped envelope facilitates easy return. Although the envelope adds to the cost of the survey, it generally increases the response rate.

Furthermore, it is a good idea to give respondents a completion deadline: for example, "Your cooperation in returning the completed questionnaire by [date] will be greatly appreciated." You hope that specifying the time will make respondents aware of the importance of returning the questionnaire promptly. Or you might use a more pointed statement: for example, "Only those responses received by October 1st will be used in the data summaries." This approach is particularly effective when the respondent is motivated to respond to a questionnaire because the results of the instrument directly affect him or her. A similar instruction should be included with Web and e-mail surveys. For example you might state that the Web site will be open for use until October 1st, after which access will be denied.

Specify how to fill out an accompanying answer sheet. One of the decisions you will need to make is whether responses should be made directly on the questionnaire or if a separate answer sheet should be provided. Answer sheets can facilitate scoring, particularly when the questionnaire is composed of a large number of items. (Answer sheets are often referred to as *bubble sheets*, as the answer circles covering the sheet resemble bubbles.) If you do supply an answer sheet, also supply instructions for using it: for example, "Use only a No. 2 pencil or black ink." Such instructions are often placed directly on the answer sheet.

Use the general directions to describe how to deal with items that are not applicable. Does the respondent leave items that are not applicable blank, is an appropriate choice provided, or is the respondent expected to respond to all items? Ensuring that all users respond similarly to nonapplicable items makes the results more interpretable and easier to analyze; for example, you might say, "Please rate each item on a scale of *strongly agree* to *strongly disagree*. If the item does not apply to your current situation, please circle *not applicable*."

Decide if a change in item format requires new directions. With one-page questionnaires, where they can easily view the entire document and see format changes coming, respondents may have little or no difficulty shifting from one format to another (from an endorsement scale to a frequency scale, for example). Such changes may also be highlighted by how you organize items on the page. However, with longer instruments or instruments administered through the Internet, users may not be able to take in the entire instrument at once. If such an instrument begins with, say, a page or more of multiple-choice demographic items and then switches to a long list of Likert scale items, instructions should explain how each set of items is to be completed.

Take special care with directions for branching questions. Branching occurs when the questionnaire directs respondents to a new section owing to their response to an item. For example, if respondents answer yes to item 14, they might be directed to skip items 15 through 24 and then proceed to answer items 25 through 32. Studies have shown that as such directions become more complex, respondents are more likely to answer questions they were asked to skip (such as responding to items 15 through 24, an error of commission) or to skip questions that they should have answered (such as items 25 through 32, an error of omission) (Redline, Dillman, & Creecy, 2003).

There are several actions you can take to improve the readability and usability of branching questions. You might use a different font (typeface) and a new color to highlight directions, and you might use graphic symbols such as arrows to help the respondent navigate the instrument. (Redline, 2005). In the following example, a bold typeface and arrows are used to enhance the directions:

Do you use public transportation (bus or subway)?

❑ Yes → **SKIP TO 26**
❑ No—**Proceed to next question** ↓

Another approach is to include a direction with the item that begins a branching sequence. This prepares the respondent for a change and encourages him or her to read the item carefully before proceeding. The following example makes use of both a separate instruction and a different font for that instruction, to make it stand out:

NOTE: Please be prepared to skip to another question, based on your response.

How often do you use public transportation (bus or subway)?

❑ Don't use public transportation → **SKIP TO 26**
❑ Once or twice a week → **SKIP TO 29**
❑ Three to four times a week → **SKIP TO 32**
❑ Daily → **SKIP TO 36**

Demographic Section

In almost every situation, whether a person is developing an instrument for a work-related project or to conduct an evaluation or research study, there will be certain demographic variables that relate to the basic content being examined. The demographic section of a questionnaire provides information about respondents or cases, may determine whether respondents are representative of the population, and helps to establish a context for the responses. In some cases the factual information obtained from the demographic section is the main purpose for the questionnaire.

Although the course feedback survey displayed at the end of this chapter (Instrument 12.A) provides anonymity for respondents, it does include demographic items. The first section solicits the codes for the course title, the instructor, and the section number. Conversely, the Training Needs Assessment: Computer Skills and Abilities (Instrument 12.B) requires the respondent to supply his or her name and job title. This information is used to contact employees about training opportunities that address their assessed needs. In both instruments the demographic variables are the first to be completed. Neither instrument requests information about gender, age, or ethnicity.

Although demographic variables differ according to the type and purpose of the questionnaire, some general guidelines can be followed:

Ask only for demographic variables that will be used to answer specific questions. It is important to get information that will facilitate better understanding of the data. One way to ensure this is to review a standard list of characteristics—such as age, race, sex, years of experience, and class name—that might give better insights into the data. However, all of us are familiar with questionnaires that contain lengthy demographic sections eliciting information that appears unrelated to the apparent overall purpose of the questionnaire. To avoid this problem, you should ask how the information gained from any given demographic item will be used in data analysis. If particulars, comparisons, or relationships cannot be identified, then the item is probably not required.

Basically then, the problem is one of identifying the critical information and making sure that you obtain data on those variables and not unnecessary ones. Gender, age, and race are important demographics for a personal health questionnaire, as they may be relevant to medical conditions and medication use. However, they are less essential to an assessment of an individual's computer training needs (Instrument 12.B).

Ensure that the attributes of interest are unambiguous and clearly defined. In many studies we are interested in the relationship between a demographic factor and responses to items; for example, do women favor a product more than men do, does age relate to an individual's political party affiliation, or do college seniors participate in more extracurricular activities than sophomores do? Analysis of these relations can be compromised if the variables at issue are not clearly defined.

We have already mentioned the difficulty of obtaining consensus for some demographic factors, such as race. For example, a study in the 1960s found that minority youths objected to the term *Negro;* they crossed out the word and replaced it with *black* or *African American.* Another study from that period suggested that whites objected to the terms *white* and *Caucasian* because these terms do not reflect an individual's ethnic origins (Bayer, 1973). Martin, DeMaio, and Campanelli (1990) observe that "despite its familiarity, the concept of race is not a simple one. Racial classifications, both popular and scientific, are based on a mixture of principles and criteria, including national origin, tribal membership, religion, language, minority status, physical characteristics, and behavior. The criteria and categories for racial classification vary among cultures and over time" (p. 552).

As an instrument designer you can do several things to ensure that demographic attributes are consistent and unambiguous: (1) be aware of the purpose of your study and how demographic information will be used; (2) align your definitions with other criteria, such as those used by the U.S. Census Bureau (see the following sidebar) or other researchers in your area of interest; and (3) pretest to identify how potential respondents react to the categories and how that might influence response rates.

A Short History of Defining Race

Race is a social construct and the definition of the term has changed over time and may differ from country to country and group to group. In the mid-1700s, Carl von Linné (Linnaeus) divided humans into four groups: Europeans, Americans, Asiatics, and Africans. In 1775, German anthropologist Johann Blumenbach created a different classification system: Caucasian, Mongolian, Ethiopian, American, and Malay. Witzig (1996) notes that "both von Linné and Blumenbach stated that humans are one species, and the latter remarked on the arbitrary nature of his proposed categories" (p. 675).

In the United States, people were usually categorized as Caucasoid, Mongoloid, and Negroid. In 1977, the U.S. Office of Management and Budget issued Statistical Policy Directive Number 15, which formally recognized four racial categories: American Indian or Alaskan Native, Asian or Pacific Islander, Black, and White. Additionally, two ethnicity categories were created: Hispanic origin and Not of Hispanic origin.

Over time it became necessary to expand these classifications, so in 1997, the Office of Management and Budget revised the definitions of race to include the following categories: American Indian or Alaska Native, Black or African American, native Hawaiian or other Pacific Islander, White, and Some Other Race. Additionally, the OMB guidelines allow an individual to select more than one race (U.S. Census Bureau, 2006).

Nonetheless, because the United States is a pluralistic society, even these categories may not match an individual's perception of her or his racial and ethnic identity. As a result, people may increasingly mark the Some Other Race option, making even these recent designations less useful over time.

Identify the relationship of the respondent to the object of measurement. One important category of demographic data that is sometimes overlooked relates to respondent judgments about others' performance. For example, teachers are often asked questions about students, and principals are asked about teachers. In such situations it is imperative to learn how much contact the respondent has had with the person or thing being rated, and an item in the demographic section should document this information. If a principal is rating a teacher's performance, it is important to know the extent to which the principal has observed this teacher in the classroom. Certainly, data from a principal who has observed the teacher on multiple occasions should be viewed differently from data from a principal who has conducted only one observation or none at all.

Identify demographic items that should be optional. This criterion has specific implications for situations where decisions about individual respondents will be made. For example, if you are using an instrument to screen applicants for an advertised position, equal employment opportunity legislation forbids you from requiring the individual to divulge information about sex, race, or religious preference. Briefly explaining the need for the information and requesting the respondent to provide it can avoid this problem. The following example of such a statement is taken from the Commonwealth of Virginia's public employee application form: "Pursuant to federal regulations, we collect responses to the questions below for record keeping purposes. This information will NOT be kept with your application for employment. Federal law prohibits unlawful discrimination on the basis of race, color, sex, age, national origin, religion, or disability."

Place demographic items at an appropriate point in the instrument. The consensus among most researchers is that demographic items should be located at the end of the instrument. For example, Dillman (2000) and Babbie (1990) believe that placing demographic items at the front disrupts the flow of the instrument and does not allow the user to immediately engage in the task of responding to substantive items. This lack of engagement may reduce the response rate. It is also possible that respondents will be reluctant to complete the instrument if first presented with sensitive items such as questions about income.

Despite these opinions, one study that examined different placements of demographic items—at the beginning and at the end of an instrument sent to social workers—did not detect a difference in response rates (Green, Murphy, & Snyder, 2000). Although the researchers cautioned that the results might have been different with another population.

In our experience the location of demographic items is dependent on the purpose of the instrument and the number of those items. Instruments 12.A and 12.B place their demographic items at the beginning. This is appropriate because they have just a few items, and these items are not sensitive. However, if you need to ask more than three or four demographic questions, we concur with others that the demographic section should be placed at the end of the instrument. And regardless of placement, demographic items should be grouped together.

Ensure that the demographic section does not compromise confidentiality. It is important to consider the context and situation in which your instrument will be administered and how that might affect confidentiality. In a small organization or an organization with a small number of position classifications, an individual could be easily identified if the demographic section asks for job title and just a few other items such as gender, age, race or ethnicity, or income. Imagine a survey of staff in a community mental health agency employing five psychologists. It might be quite easy to identify each psychologist's questionnaire from just two demographic items: the respondent's job title and just one other demographic trait.

Sometimes demographic information need not be requested because it exists in some other form that can be easily associated with the data from the questionnaire. For example, if you were conducting a national survey of deans of student affairs to learn about volunteer activities at their schools, you would probably not have to ask each dean the location of his or her school, the number of pupils enrolled, or the number of graduates. That information could be easily obtained from some other source, such as Barron's *Compact Guide to Colleges* or the National Center for Education Statistics. Obtaining appropriate demographic information from other sources accomplishes at least two purposes. First, you relieve the respondents of a somewhat tedious task, and second, you ensure compatibility of demographic data across your respondents. A survey of graduates of a particular program might be another illustration of this procedure. If the program has kept an up-to-date file on the graduates, demographic information might be taken from this source rather than elicited from the respondents.

Organization and Format of the Instrument

After you have written your items, directions, and demographic section, it is important to put the questionnaire together in a clear, concise final form. Items should flow logically, and the overall appearance should be neat and orderly. Several criteria can be applied in this phase of the instrument's construction.

Group items according to types or content. In formatting your instrument it is best to group items according to some logical criterion. You might group together items that deal with similar content or items that share a format, perhaps grouping rating-scale items together, then rank-ordered items, and then supply items. A logically structured questionnaire or observation instrument is more easily filled out by the user and therefore shows an increased response rate. For example, the items in Instrument 12.A are divided into three groups: (1) demographic items, (2) rating-scale items for course and instructor evaluation, and (3) open-ended items. Each instrument's structure should be decided individually and will depend on the purpose, the variables, and the item type(s) selected. When item sections seem long, it may be appropriate to break them into subsections. Once again, the purpose of this is to make the task of filling out the questionnaire easier for the respondent.

When subsections are grouped by item types, the designer can write directions specific to each subsection and its item format.

There are two basic formats for arranging and displaying items. The first is the *individual display*, in which each statement functions as a separate item with its own set of responses. The response sets do not have to provide the same options. The following example comes from Instrument 2.A (Chapter Two).

EXAMPLE

Do you think the Congress is in touch with what is going on in the country?	❑ In touch	❑ Not in touch	❑ Unsure
Generally speaking, would you say things in this country are heading in the right direction, or are they off on the wrong track?	❑ Right direction	❑ Wrong track	❑ Unsure
Do you think America is ready to elect a woman president, or not?	❑ Ready	❑ Not ready	❑ Unsure
In general, do you believe that members of Congress are honest and trustworthy in their conduct?	❑ Honest	❑ Not honest	❑ Unsure

The second format is a *matrix* (the following example is from Instrument 5.A in Chapter Five; Figure 8.2 in Chapter Eight also contains two examples of a matrix format); the contents of the item stems are different, but the response alternatives are the same. The advantage of the matrix arrangement is that it allows the instrument designer to cover more variables in less space. Its major disadvantage is that it necessitates the use of general terms in the response set, because those terms must be appropriate to a great number of different stems. Furthermore, it may allow respondents to respond to all items in the same fashion rather than to each item individually. For example, a student who likes a teacher might rate the teacher high on all items without reading each one specifically. Generally, the matrix display structure should be used with respondents who are experienced in the use of rating scales. The individual display of items may be best for less knowledgeable groups because it forces respondents to read each item individually and gives them response sets specific to individual items.

EXAMPLE

Item	Strongly Disagree	Mostly Disagree	Mostly Agree	Strongly Agree	Not Sure
1. I am confident in the leadership of this agency.	O	O	O	O	O
2. I am proud to be an employee of this agency.	O	O	O	O	O
3. Temperatures in the building are comfortable.	O	O	O	O	O
4. I clearly understand the agency's organizational structure.	O	O	O	O	O
5. I receive the training I need to do my job well.	O	O	O	O	O

One way to group items visually is to use boxes that clearly delineate where one section of items ends and another begins. The borders in the previous example and in Instrument 12.B at the end of this chapter help the user see where transitions of item formats occur and where the content changes. Additionally, in Instrument 12.B shading has been used to differentiate one item from another and to help the respondent discriminate between items while moving through the questionnaire. Vertical lines can differentiate response alternatives.

Be cognizant of the potential for order effects. Order effects occur when the sequence in which items are presented influences how a respondent answers the item; for example, if you believe your first choice for a response to a question conflicts with your response to a previous item, you may instead select a response that is congruous with the prior item. Suppose the first item in a questionnaire asks you to identify your political ideology as liberal, moderate, or conservative and you select *conservative*. Then, when presented a series of questions about political issues, you may tend to select the responses that reflect a politically conservative perspective.

Order effects can be caused by a number of factors, such as ability to recall information, social desirability, and even age (Knäer, Schwarz, & Fritsch, 2006) and approaches to resolving their influence are still evolving (Smith, 1989). One of the primary methods is to consider how items are organized within the instrument. For example, placing questions of a general nature before items that ask for specific information (such as demographic questions) appears to reduce order effects.

Place selection items before supply items. Following this criterion helps to ensure that respondents do not get discouraged by the more difficult or time-consuming items before they have answered the simpler ones. When the instrument is made up of both selection and supply items the selection items should precede the supply items, because respondents are more likely to check rating scales than they are to fill in open-ended questions, particularly when the latter are phrased as options, such as asking at the end whether respondents would like to make additional comments.

For similar reasons, items that require expressing an opinion should come before items that entail recall of information. Both require some pondering before formulating a response. Supply items that ask for an opinion necessitate thinking about the response and then thinking about how to phrase that response coherently. Items based on recall confront the respondent with the reality that he or she may not accurately remember the information. This may be due to the passage of time or to the fact that the information to be recalled is not important to the respondent (Fowler, 1995). Consequently, the respondent may leave the item blank, and if these types of items are placed at the beginning of the instrument, they could be so off-putting that the respondent may choose not to complete the questionnaire at all.

Print the response headings on each page. When using a matrix format, it is important to print the response headings on each page where respondents must select from scale. This provides continuity and a reference point for respondents as they complete the item. If a subsection of items must overflow onto a new page, be sure to restate the directions and indicate that the subsection is continuing.

Relate instrument length to the respondents and the purpose. As the instrument designer you face a dilemma when deciding how long to make the instrument. You want to get as much information as possible but you also want the greatest response rate. The common assumption is that when respondents see a lengthy questionnaire (with many questions or many pages), they are likely to not even begin the task or to quit before the instrument is completely filled out. This suggests that mode of administration may affect the response rate: a respondent to a mailed survey can see the length before starting, whereas a respondent to a telephone survey may not know how many questions will follow.[2]

However, in a comprehensive review of research on questionnaire length, Bogen (1996) concluded that the results were often contradictory and inconclusive: "Possibly the most noteworthy finding of this literature search is the fact that there is remarkably little sound experimental work to guide the survey practitioner in decisions about survey length. This is particularly true for in-person and phone surveys as well as for effects in longitudinal surveys. There is somewhat more information for mail surveys, though even the results there have been so mixed that it is not clear where the length limits are" (p. 5).

Another concern is that questionnaire length may be related to the likelihood of respondent errors in checking boxes and making selections (respondent fatigue). Complex instrument organization—multiple parts, a variety of item formats, and multiple and branching directions—may also result in fatigue, confusion, and frustration. Item length and complexity (many wordy items or items containing a lot of information) may also influence the respondent's decision on whether to work through the items and ultimately the entire questionnaire. Of course you should never take up respondents' time and energy with questions that you have neither the time nor ability to analyze.

Our guidance is to determine how long it takes potential respondents or raters to complete the instrument during pretesting and to ask if they had concerns about questionnaire organization or length or item complexity. You will gain a better understanding of your respondents' tolerance limit for answering questions, and you can balance that against the minimum amount of information you require. Also consider respondents' investment in the purpose of the study, as there is some evidence that highly motivated respondents tend to answer more questions than those who have no incentives for filling out the instrument (Bogen, 1996).

Instrument length is also a factor in deciding whether to number the items. If the instrument is longer than one or two pages or if it contains branching questions, you will definitely want to number each item. Numbering can also help you keep your place if you must transpose data manually at some point. However, in a short instrument where the items are clearly delineated there is no reason to number each item. In our classes students have observed that instruments often appear less cluttered when the items are not numbered.

Finally, the purpose of the study will substantially influence the type and number of items to include when the instrument is to be completed by an external rater. For example, a job evaluation form should contain only items that are relevant and valid measures of an employee's work performance. Behavior assessment instruments may require frequent observation of only a few (no more than four or five) discrete behaviors. An instrument that required the rater to simultaneously track fifteen to twenty behaviors at fifteen-minute intervals would be nearly impossible to complete and would probably render unreliable data.

Be sure the copies respondents use are clear. All your work to develop a good questionnaire can be negated if the copies respondents use have typographical errors, blurred or unclear reproduction, or a poor layout. Is the title centered, and are the sections clearly delineated? Or does the page appear cluttered due to using a small typestyle or clustering items too close together? The messier the copy, the less likely respondents are to take the instrument seriously, which can ultimately compromise response rates.

Nothing takes the place of a good proofreading, particularly if the instrument has gone through multiple revisions. Although most problems should have been addressed during the pretesting phase, it is not uncommon to make minor misspellings when drafting the final version. And do not depend solely on the spell-checking feature of your word processing software, as it cannot catch wrong-word typos, such as *bee* for *be,* or *I* when you meant to type *In.* Be sure that item stems and response sets are properly aligned, as misalignment can cause difficulty later when you are extracting the data.

Finally, care should be taken to include only content that is essential to the purpose of your study. And content is anything that appears on the page, not just material in an instruction or question. In a discussion on EVALTALK (the listserver of the American Evaluation Association), for example, a contributor described a consumer satisfaction survey that included pictures of smiling employees interacting with smiling customers. The consensus among discussants was that the photos created a bias, encouraging the socially desirable response, a positive rating.

Typography and Instrument Design

We have addressed the topic of readability from the perspective of the functional reading level of users, your choice of words, the syntax of phrases and sentences, and special terminology. However, readability can also be influenced by the presentation of the printed text, that is by the *typography,* the letter style and page arrangement that you select for presenting information. Studies indicate that reading rate and comprehension are influenced by the choice of font and typestyle, the size of the print, the width of a line of text, the height of the letters in relation to the width of the line, the space between the lines, and how text is arranged on the page (Paterson & Tinker, 1940).

Alignment refers to how words are arranged on the page, such as

Left   Centered   Right

Our eyes tend to shift to the left of a printed page because in our culture we read from left to right, so most text lines start on the left. However, titles of documents are often centered, and titles of chapters or subsections are occasionally placed to the right.

Alignment can also be vertical, which as you can see takes up less horizontal space on the page.

Typography

Vertical alignment is a useful tool when you have limited space, such as when the space for the response scale is not very wide:

EXAMPLE

	Strongly Disagree	Disagree	Neither Agree Nor Disagree	Agree	Strongly Agree
Gone with the Wind is one of the ten best motion pictures ever made.					

You will find the tables feature in word processing software very helpful for aligning words. The following response scale has been aligned by applying a table with five equally spaced columns. You can print tables with or without gridlines. We show the following scale both ways: first with the gridlines showing and, second, without the gridlines.

Strongly Agree	Agree	Disagree	Strongly Disagree	No Opinion

Strongly Agree   Agree   Disagree   Strongly Disagree   No Opinion

There are two categories of typeface (or font): *serif*, which has tear-shaped strokes at the ends of the lines making up each letter, and *sans serif*, which lacks these adornments. Examples of serif typefaces are Times Roman and Baskerville. Examples of sans serif typefaces are Arial and Century Gothic. In part, the category of typeface to use is dependent on the size of the letters. If you have a lot of items on a page and must use a small typeface (font size of 10 or smaller), then a sans serif font will probably be more legible. However, text in a serif font tends to flow across the page more easily, so if you can use a larger text and still get everything on the page, then a serif font is preferable.

EXAMPLE

How would you rate your experience working with computers? (Times Roman, font size 12)

How would you rate your experience working with computers? (Arial, font size 9)

Typestyle refers to features added to type, such as **bold,** *italic,* or underline styling or a combination of these enhancements. Varying typestyle is an effective way to set off important information, such as instrument titles or internal headings. The advent of word processing software has added to the basic features that you can use to enhance typestyle; you can now use embossed, **shadow**, and engraved styles and colors. Not all printers recognize these enhancements, so you will have to pretest the *appearance* of your instrument as well.

Another way that you can set off text is to start a sentence or section by changing the size or other attributes of the typeface. As with graphic design, too much variety can be distracting. For this reason it is best to limit your "palette" to two fonts or one font and two typestyles, perhaps one for the title and major headings, and another for the main body of the instrument, including instructions, items, and demographics.

The spacing between letters, words, and lines should be considered part of the design. Desktop publishing software does provide for changing the spacing between letters, referred to as *kerning,* so that more words can be placed on a line. It also allows you to change the spacing between lines while keeping the size of the letters the same. These two features are useful if your instrument is lengthy and you are trying to keep the total number of pages manageable.

EXAMPLE

How would you rate your experience working with computers? (normal)

How would you rate your experience working with computers? (expanded)

How would you rate your experience working with computers? (condensed)

Bulleting highlights important information by inserting a graphic symbol before a line to set it apart from other information:

- Useful symbols include bullets.
- ➤ Useful symbols include arrows.
- ○ Useful symbols include circles.
- ■ Useful symbols include squares.
- ✓ Useful symbols include checkmarks.

One of the ways that we can take advantage of typographical design options is to construct items using multiple formats and pretest them with users. In the following example a question (from a behavior rating scale) is presented in two variations. In the first, the same typestyle is used throughout. In the second, bold print, indenting, and line spacing have been used to differentiate the stem and the response choices. One advantage of the second approach is that the transition from one part of the item to the other is identified for the respondent, allowing him or her to scan and move through the instrument easily and quickly.

Examples

Stereotypical Movements:

1. Not Present—Behavior was not observed.   2. Mild—Occasional repetitive motor activity, such as teeth grinding, wringing hands, or smacking lips.   3. Moderate—Persistent motor activity often appears repetitive and nonproductive such as bowing back and force for no apparent reason.   4. Severe—Repetitive motor activity occurs throughout the day and may interfere with ADLs and/or social communication with others.

Stereotypical Movements:

1. **Not Present**—Behavior was not observed.
2. **Mild**—Occasional repetitive motor activity, such as teeth grinding, wringing hands, or smacking lips.
3. **Moderate**—Persistent motor activity often appears repetitive and nonproductive such as bowing back and force for no apparent reason.
4. **Severe**—Repetitive motor activity occurs throughout the day and may interfere with ADLs and/or social communication with others.

Finally, aspects of graphic design can also be used, such as printing letters in white against a black background or using 3-D text. However, care should be taken when using such effects as they may make the instrument appear "busy," which can be distracting.

Summary

Prior to painting a picture on canvas, an artist will complete a number of rough sketches that help in visualizing the subject and its placement in the painting (pretesting). When painting a person, the artist may first draw the person in a variety of positions—seated, standing, leaning, or lying down—and from a number of angles. In transposing the sketch the artist must also decide how much space the figure will take up on the canvas. For example, the painter may decide that the figure will be placed so far to one side that not all of it will be depicted or the figure could be reduced in size and placed conspicuously in the center. All of these decisions involve composition, which for the viewers of the painting, sets the stage for how their eyes move across the painting and, ultimately, how they make sense of and feel about the subject.

The process of organizing and formatting an instrument is quite similar. Like the artist making preliminary drawings, we develop and pretest items, perhaps trying different formats and response scales as well as varying the order of the items. The next task is to examine the placement of the items, directions, and other components that will form the instrument in its entirety. As noted in Chapter Five, pretesting continues during this phase to ensure that the instrument has an attractive, uncluttered appearance and that items are organized logically. Our goal is to create an instrument that users can complete efficiently, without becoming confused or frustrated. We want to ensure that respondents or raters can complete the instrument accurately and provide valid information, which can enhance response rates. To that end, Exhibit 12.1 provides a checklist that you can use during pretesting to help ensure that the guidelines presented in this chapter are being addressed.

EXHIBIT 12.1: ORGANIZING AND FORMATTING CHECKLIST.

Factors to Address When Organizing and Formatting an Instrument

The following checklist can be used to assess your instrument prior to administration. Items that are not checked may indicate a factor that needs to be addressed and corrected.

TITLE

❑ Reflects the content of the instrument.
❑ Is worded concisely.
❑ Is written in language easily understood by the respondents.
❑ Is not perceived as offensive or off-putting.
❑ Is centered at the top of the document.

INTRODUCTORY STATEMENT

❑ Includes a brief summary of the instrument's purpose.
❑ Contains an appropriate statement concerning the confidentiality of the respondents' information.
❑ Provides a motivator for the respondents.
❑ Specifies the approximate amount of time required to complete the instrument.

DIRECTIONS

❑ Are complete, unambiguous, and concise.
❑ Are written at a language level appropriate to the respondents.
❑ Tell the respondents how to return the instrument once they have completed it.
❑ Specify how the accompanying answer sheet should be filled out.
❑ Instruct the respondents how to deal with items that are not applicable.
❑ Indicate when there is a change in item format.
❑ Are given for all branching questions.

DEMOGRAPHIC SECTION

❑ Is limited to variables that will be used to answer specific questions.
❑ Portrays the relationship of the respondents to the object of measurement.
❑ Allows certain items in to be optional.
❑ Is written to the language level of the respondents.
❑ Is located appropriately for the purpose of the instrument.
❑ Does not compromise confidentiality by making respondents identifiable.

STRUCTURE AND FORMAT

❑ Items are grouped according to item types or similarity of content.
❑ The attributes of interest are unambiguous and clearly defined.
❑ Items are grouped into sections according to ease with which they can be answered.
❑ Length of the instrument is related to respondents and purpose.
❑ Copies of the instrument are clear and easy to read.

Instrument 12.A: Scoring by Scanning

The Course Feedback Survey form (Instrument 12.A) was developed at the University of Virginia to obtain student feedback at the end of the semester. Students typically complete the form during the last class session. A student is asked to distribute the questionnaire, and students are asked to place their

INSTRUMENT 12.A: COURSE SURVEY.

UNIVERSITY OF VIRGINIA
CURRY SCHOOL OF EDUCATION
COURSE FEEDACK SURVEY

| COURSE | INSTRUCTOR | SECTION # |

- **DO NOT use ink or ballpoint pen.**
- **Make each mark heavy and black.**
- **Mark should fill circle completely.**
- **Erase cleanly any mark you wish to change.**
- **Make no stray marks.**

The ONLY correct mark ● ◁ ⟨ USE NO. 2 PENCIL ONLY ⟩

STUDENT-ORIENTED ITEMS

Please answer the following by marking the appropriate circle.

1. ① ②   This course is: (1) Required; (2) Optional.
2. Ⓐ Ⓐ Ⓐ   The grade I am expecting in this course is:
   Ⓑ Ⓑ Ⓑ
   Ⓒ Ⓒ Ⓒ
   Ⓓ Ⓓ Ⓓ
   Ⓕ Ⓢ Ⓤ

This questionnaire provides you with an anonymous opportunity to evaluate this course and the instructor. The results will be used to provide a basis for course improvement and overall assessment of the effectiveness of this course. Please be thoughtful, constructive, and candid in your responses. ANSWER THIS SIDE FIRST.

Items 3 through 13 should be answered according to the following scale: Strongly disagree (SD), Disagree (D), Neutral (N), Agree (A), Strongly Agree (SA).

3. Ⓢ Ⓓ Ⓝ Ⓐ Ⓢ The instructor's expectations in this course were made clear to me.

4. Ⓢ Ⓓ Ⓝ Ⓐ Ⓢ The content of this course was organized in a meaningful way.

5. Ⓢ Ⓓ Ⓝ Ⓐ Ⓢ Assignments were challenging.

6. Ⓢ Ⓓ Ⓝ Ⓐ Ⓢ Assessment of student's progress was appropriate.

7. Ⓢ Ⓓ Ⓝ Ⓐ Ⓢ Feedback from assessment was provided at suitable intervals.

8. Ⓢ Ⓓ Ⓝ Ⓐ Ⓢ The instructor demonstrated a genuine interest in teaching the course.

9. Ⓢ Ⓓ Ⓝ Ⓐ Ⓢ The instructor was sensitive to student needs and interests.

10. Ⓢ Ⓓ Ⓝ Ⓐ Ⓢ I learned a great deal in this course.

11. Ⓢ Ⓓ Ⓝ Ⓐ Ⓢ Overall, this course was worthwhile to me.

12. Ⓢ Ⓓ Ⓝ Ⓐ Ⓢ Overall, the instructor in this course was effective.

13. Ⓢ Ⓓ Ⓝ Ⓐ Ⓢ The course and materials content included different racial or ethnic perspectives where appropriate.

Instructor furnished additional items - optional.

14. Ⓢ Ⓓ Ⓝ Ⓐ Ⓢ
15. Ⓢ Ⓓ Ⓝ Ⓐ Ⓢ
16. Ⓢ Ⓓ Ⓝ Ⓐ Ⓢ

DO NOT WRITE IN THIS SPACE

How would you evaluate the content of this course?

What course learning experiences were most valuable?

What instructor characteristics contributed to the effectiveness of the course?

Was the instructor equally responsive to all students (men, women, different racial or ethnic backgrounds)? Please explain.

Other?

COMPLETED - THANK YOU

Source: Curry School of Education. Reprinted with permission.

completed evaluations into an envelope, which is taken by a student to the office of the department chairman. In this way, confidentiality is maintained. The instrument is designed to be used with a separate answer sheet, which is machine scored. Instructors receive only aggregate data and do not see individual answer sheets or identifying information.

This questionnaire illustrates many of the points about instrument organization and format discussed in this chapter. The title is printed in the left-hand corner, in large, bold serif typeface. The remainder of the instrument is printed in a smaller sans serif font. For ease of data entry, the form (or answer sheet) can be scanned; items are completed by filling in numbered or lettered circles (bubbles). Instructions appear directly after the title, whereas the purpose statement appears before the course rating section. Items 3 through 13 use a Likert scale, which is placed to the left of (before) each item. Every other item is shaded for contrast. A combination of item formats is used, including scales and open-ended responses.

The usefulness and reliability of student evaluations is often debated, as the quality of a course derives from a variety of factors, including the instructor's personality and skills, available resources, and the physical environment, as well as factors the student brings to the situation. For example, one student may find class assignments challenging and illuminating, whereas another might consider the same assignments difficult and boring. Nonetheless, these instruments continue to find favor in most colleges and universities, particularly now that they can be administered confidentially as Web-based evaluations.

Instrument 12.B: Word Processing Software

Instrument 12.B was developed to determine newly hired employees' computer skills. If the results suggest that an employee needs some level of training in conjunction with his or her job duties, the organization pays for the training at a local community college (rather than maintaining the staff and resources to conduct the training in-house).

This instrument was designed using today's highly versatile word processing software. To set the title off, it is printed in bold using a slightly larger font than the text in the body of the instrument. Two typefaces are used: a serif font for item text and a sans serif font for instructional text. The questionnaire was divided into sections using text box and table formatting. The instructions and identifying items were placed in text boxes (in word processing software these boxes can be constructed using the text box command or the table command, creating a 1×1 table, that is, a table consisting of one row and one column). The size of the text

INSTRUMENT 12.B: TRAINING NEEDS ASSESSMENT.

Training Needs Assessment: Computer Skills and Abilities

In order to design and plan training for computer skills, we would like you to complete this needs assessment. It is important that you sign the form so that we can match your level of skill development with the appropriate level of training.	Name: (Please Print) Job Title:

How would you rate your experience working with computers? (circle one)	1 Never used	2 Very limited	3 Moderate	4 Highly experienced
How would you rate your comfort in using computer hardware and software? (circle one)	1 Dislike using computers	2 Use them only to get the job done	3 Very comfortable, enjoy using them	

On a scale of 1 to 4, how would you rate your ability to use the following software? Circle the number that best describes your current level of knowledge, skills and abilities.

	Never Used	Fair	Good	Excellent
Word processing software (for general typing), such as Word or Word Perfect.	1	2	3	4
Spreadsheet software (to manage data and create graphs of your data), such as Excel or Quatro Pro.	1	2	3	4
Database software (for organizing and managing data), such as Microsoft Access.	1	2	3	4
Website development software, such as Front Page or Web Publisher.	1	2	3	4
Desktop publishing software (used to create pamphlets, letterhead, etc.), such as Microsoft Publisher or Quark.	1	2	3	4
Presentation software (to create slide show presentations), such as Powerpoint or Corel Presentations.	1	2	3	4
Graphics software (for drawing, painting, and photo retouching), such as Corel Draw or Photo Shop.	1	2	3	4
Statistical software (for doing statistical calculations), such as SPSS or SAS.	1	2	3	4
Organizational software (calendars, scheduling, etc.), such as Mircrosoft Outlook or Corel Central.	1	2	3	4
Other (please indicate):	1	2	3	4

On a scale of 1 to 4, how would you rate your ability to operate in a Windows environment and use the Internet? Circle the number that best describes your current level of knowledge, skills and abilities.

	Never Used	Fair	Good	Excellent
Open and close documents.	1	2	3	4
Move around using a mouse.	1	2	3	4
Save a document.	1	2	3	4
Fit two or more documents or folders on the screen.	1	2	3	4
Resize a document (make it bigger or smaller)	1	2	3	4
Change the size of the print.	1	2	3	4
Create folders.	1	2	3	4
Search for documents.	1	2	3	4
Copy, cut, and paste within and between documents	1	2	3	4
Customize tool bars.	1	2	3	4
Customize the printing of documents.	1	2	3	4
Log onto the Internet.	1	2	3	4
Move from site to site on the Internet.	1	2	3	4
Find information using a search engine, such as Yahoo.	1	2	3	4
Save and organize favorite Internet sites.	1	2	3	4
Use Email	1	2	3	4

Additional Comments:

Thank you for completing this questionnaire.

Organization Name   Organization Address box can be enlarged or reduced by clicking on the box border and then dragging a corner. The box can be moved by clicking on the border and then dragging the entire box to another location on the page.

Respondents rate their computer skills on a 4-point intensity scale formatted so that the scale definitions appear at the head of each column and the respondent circles a corresponding number. The items have been placed in a table (using the table function in the word processing software), which is outlined by an exterior border; the gridlines between the items and response set have been hidden so that they do not appear when the instrument is printed. However, shading has been used to highlight and visually separate items. The table function is a handy way of organizing items as the size of the rows and columns can be adjusted by dragging the border or by using the table properties menu to adjust the height and width of a cell.

Instrument 12.C: Conflict Resolution Skills Assessment

Instrument 12.C is a needs assessment included in a manual for implementing conflict resolution programs in schools, youth-serving organizations, and community and juvenile justice settings (Crawford & Bodine, 1996, pp. E.1–E.4). The manual was developed for the Office of Juvenile Justice and Delinquency Prevention, U.S. Department of Justice, and the Safe and Drug Free Schools Program, U.S. Department of Education. The instrument is in the public domain and may be copied and used without prior permission from the authors.

This needs assessment is presented as an example of an instrument containing items with several different response alternatives. The majority of the items ask the respondent for a rating, although the response scales differ from item to item. Two of the items ask the respondent to estimate percentage. Consequently, respondents must change their frame of reference from one item to the next. Nonetheless, each stem and its response set are clearly separated from the others and taken together the items flow in a logical order.

This example does not contain a statement of purpose or a statement at the end thanking the respondent; we recommend that this information be included. The one reservation we have about this instrument is that some items are better suited for school personnel to complete, and some are clearly intended for student completion. For example, a student might become frustrated by items 4 and 6, and a teacher or school administrator might feel that item 8 is not relevant. For this reason, we recommend that a *not applicable* alternative be added.

INSTRUMENT 12.C: CONFLICT RESOLUTION SKILLS ASSESSMENT.

Conflict Resolution Needs Assessment

Answer each question by providing the response that most accurately reflects your personal view of your school.

1. I am a: ❏ student   ❏ staff member   ❏ parent   ❏ other

2. Conflicts interfere with the teaching and learning process:

   ❏ often   ❏ sometimes   ❏ rarely

3. Problems between people at this school are caused by:

	often	sometimes	rarely
a. expectation to be competitive	❏	❏	❏
b. intolerance between adults and students	❏	❏	❏
c. intolerance between students	❏	❏	❏
d. poor communication	❏	❏	❏
e. anger and/or frustration	❏	❏	❏
f. rumors	❏	❏	❏
g. problems brought to school from somewhere else	❏	❏	❏

4. Without exceeding 100% as the total, estimate the percentage of problems referred for disciplinary action by the following categories:

   a. between students   _____%
   b. between student and classroom teacher   _____%
   c. between student and other staff members   _____%
   d. between student and school rules   _____%
   e. other   _____%
                                      Total   100%

5. Indicate the types and frequency of conflicts experienced by students in this school:

	often	sometimes	rarely
a. put-downs/insults/teasing	❏	❏	❏
b. threats	❏	❏	❏
c. intolerance of differences	❏	❏	❏
d. loss of property	❏	❏	❏
e. access to groups	❏	❏	❏
f. rumors	❏	❏	❏
g. physical fighting	❏	❏	❏
h. verbal fighting	❏	❏	❏
i. school work	❏	❏	❏
j. other: _____	❏	❏	❏

6. Indicate the effectiveness of each of the following actions in causing a student to change a problem behavior:

	very effective	somewhat effective	not effective
a. time out	❏	❏	❏
b. detention	❏	❏	❏
c. conference with an adult	❏	❏	❏
d. suspension	❏	❏	❏
e. contacting parent(s)	❏	❏	❏
f. expulsion	❏	❏	❏

7. Without exceeding 100% as the total, what percentage of influence do the following groups have in the way the school operates?

a. students   _____%
b. teachers   _____%
c. parents   _____%
d. principals and school administrators   _____%
e. superintendents and district administrators   _____%
f. board of education   _____%
g. other   _____%

                        Total   100%

8. In this school, I am generally:

	most of the time	about one-half of the time	not very often
a. treated fairly	❏	❏	❏
b. treated with respect	❏	❏	❏
c. given equal opportunity	❏	❏	❏
d. treated with compassion	❏	❏	❏
e. accepted	❏	❏	❏

9. I am allowed to solve problems that affect me:

     ❏ nearly always   ❏ sometimes   ❏ hardly ever

10. This school should do a better job teaching students to:

	definitely yes	maybe	definitely no
a. tell another person how I feel	❏	❏	❏
b. disagree without making the person angry	❏	❏	❏
c. respect authority	❏	❏	❏
d. control anger	❏	❏	❏
e. ignore someone who is bothering me	❏	❏	❏
f. solve problems with other students	❏	❏	❏

11. When I need help, I ask for it:

    ❏ nearly always   ❏ sometimes   ❏ hardly ever

12. If I needed help, I think I could get it from:

	definitely yes	maybe	definitely no
a. a parent	❏	❏	❏
b. a brother or sister	❏	❏	❏
c. another family member	❏	❏	❏
d. a teacher	❏	❏	❏
e. a counselor	❏	❏	❏
f. another school staff member	❏	❏	❏
g. another adult	❏	❏	❏
h. another student	❏	❏	❏

13. I think this school has:

    ❏ more problems than most other schools
    ❏ about the same amount of problems as most other schools
    ❏ fewer problems than most other schools

Endnotes

1. Of course the danger here is that respondents might retaliate and not provide honest responses.
2. Surveys administered over the Internet may include page counters, so that the respondent knows how many screens or pages of questions have been completed and how many are left.

Key Concepts and Terms

anonymity	font	statement of purpose
branching question	introductory statement	title
confidentiality	questionnaire organization	typography
demographic section	order effect	typestyle

CHAPTER THIRTEEN

ADMINISTERING THE INSTRUMENT

In this chapter we will

- Provide guidance for administering an instrument that is completed by a rater/observer.
- Provide guidance for administering self-report instruments.

Ultimately a piece of artwork is taken out of the studio and shared with others, perhaps in an art gallery or as an illustration for a book or magazine. Likewise, having constructed and pretested your instrument, you will take it out of the "laboratory" and implement it in the real world.

Although this chapter focusing on administration is near the end of the book, issues related to administration can and do influence the design and structure of the instrument. Therefore you should be thinking about administration issues beginning with the earliest stages of the instrument construction process. For example, knowing how you plan to deliver your questionnaire to a specific target audience can influence your choice of wording, item type, and instrument format. At best we are providing an introduction to the process, and in fact administration of instruments is a field unto itself. Therefore we encourage readers to seek out additional resources, such as Kazdin (1982) for a thorough discussion of using observer, or rater, instruments and Dillman (2000) and Babbie (1990) for excellent descriptions of the processes of survey research.

Administering an instrument is primarily a technical process and can be divided into two broad categories: instruments completed by a rater, or observer, and self-report instruments. For each approach you must consider certain issues to ensure that the data obtained are reliable, usable, and meaningful.

Administering Instruments Completed by a Rater

Many instruments are designed to be used by an external rater, or observer, such as performance evaluations conducted by managers and supervisors, developmental inventories administered by a therapist; interview guidelines used by program evaluators; checklists completed by auditors or accreditation and licensure teams; and behavior checklists used to support research in the social sciences. Regardless of your instrument's intended purpose, you should address the following considerations to successfully implement it:

- Select the setting for observation.
- Select a sampling strategy.
- Train observers.

Site Selection

Although we usually think of an instrument administration setting as a physical environment, it also involves the time of day in which observations will be made, the individuals involved in the process—both raters and those being rated—and relationships between the rater and the object of measurement, be it an organization, individual, or inanimate object. To a large extent, issues related to site selection should have been taken into consideration as you developed your instrument, so that you could tailor it to the particular situation.

Site selection may require obtaining entrance, such as approval to enter an organization to interview employees or to conduct an observational study. It is important to make contact with the organization, to obtain approval and to learn what you might need to do to comply with the organization's policies and procedures. For example, you might want to study student-teacher interactions in a school system where you are not an employee. Initial discussions with school administrators would be followed up in writing, in the form of a letter of agreement or a contract, outlining the scope of the study and agreements about confidentiality; selection of schools, teachers, and students to be observed; data ownership; and how the results of the study will be shared with the school system.

Although entrance is not a problem with an instrument used internally, such as a job performance evaluation, it is still important to administer the instrument in conformance with organization policies, procedures, and objectives. Additionally, if your instrument is to be used in a department other than your own, it may need to be approved by the department manager.

In some cases preexisting agreements may facilitate entrance. Many educational, health, and human service organizations, including school systems, colleges and universities, hospitals, and nursing homes, are licensed and accredited. If you are a member of a survey team administering a checklist as part of an accreditation or licensing process, the organization is typically open to inspection, with (and sometimes without) advance notice.

Studies based on observation or participation of individuals or review of confidential information in records require the *informed consent* of participants (from parents or legal guardians when studying young children). The individuals who gives informed consent agree to participate in your study and are fully informed about procedures and interventions that will be used, their responsibilities as participants, the ways data will be collected and secured, and any risks that might be associated with the process or intervention. If you are going to conduct a study involving people, you should become familiar with participants' rights and the guidelines and regulations that protect participants, such as organizational procedures and state and federal regulations. For example, medical researchers should comply with federal regulations for the protection of human subjects (Protection of Human Subjects, 2001). Additionally, your study will require review and approval by an institutional review board (IRB) if you are administering an instrument as part of a research project.

Additional issues when considering setting involve raters' well-being and ability to do the work properly, time of day, methods of data collection, and the effect of observers on the observed. Unless you are doing clandestine surveillance, there is no reason why raters should be placed in environments that are physically uncomfortable or that hinder their ability to make observations. For example, individuals conducting record audits should have adequate lighting and a place to sit with adequate desk space to open records for inspection. Given current technology the instrument could be created as a word processing or database template so that the auditors can document their observations on a laptop or palmtop computer. It is also important to consider the length of time over which observations will be made, so the opportunities for observers to take care of their physical needs are incorporated into the observation plan. Safety is yet another concern, both for the rater and the people being evaluated. For example, if the task is to complete an inventory of books in a large metropolitan library, it might not be safe to send an individual employee to a dimly lit storage area in the basement of the library without first ensuring that access to the space is controlled. To further enhance staff safety you might plan to have the inventory conducted by two or more employees working as a team. At no time should raters and clients be placed in situations that compromise their physical safety in order to make observation more efficient.

You might also need to think about time of day: for example, do observers need to adjust their personal schedules in order to conduct observations at night? Will observers need adequate daylight to videotape observations? The subject of the observation might be available only at certain times or even seasons: for example, you might be studying student behavior during spring break, or "beach week."

You need to determine whether the data collection and recording will be done directly by people or by automated recording devices. Although we focus here on the observation and collection of data by human beings, there are a number of devices, such as video cameras and traffic counters, that can record and store data, and many of the issues that matter for human observers matter for automated recording devices as well. For example, electronic equipment may fail if the temperature is too hot or cold, if the humidity is too high, or if the lighting is inadequate to capture visual images clearly.

There is an extensive body of literature regarding the influence observers have on those being observed. This relationship was first noticed during studies conducted between 1924 and 1933 at Western Electric's Hawthorne plant in Chicago. Led by Harvard researcher Elton Mayo, the researchers examined how productivity and efficiency were influenced by physical changes in the work environment, assembly processes, and relationships between workers. In perhaps the best-known experiment the researchers created a carefully controlled environment for women who were assembling telephone components. No matter how they modified the working conditions, the assembly workers' output increased. This ultimately led the researchers to the conclusion that their presence had as much influence on the worker's output as the environmental and situational variables that they manipulated (an outcome often referred to as the Hawthorne Effect) (Albanese, 1981).

During the past seventy years the findings coming out of that study have been heatedly debated. For example, did the researchers' presence really influence work output or were the workers reacting to other factors, such as the Great Depression and the fear of losing their jobs? The importance of this to our discussion is that researchers must be aware that people may change their behaviors in response to being observed. Several actions can be taken to mitigate this problem. In most cases it is important to inform people that they are being observed and to explain the purpose of your observations. You can even show them the instrument and explain how the observation will be conducted. If you believe that observers' presence could influence behaviors, then you can try to have observers spend as much time as possible with those being observed so that they become acclimated to the observers' presence and become less guarded.

An alternative approach for reducing observers' possible effects is to make observations in the field. Fieldwork is conducted in the environment where the behavior to be observed normally occurs, such as a client's home or a work setting rather than a laboratory setting. Although the laboratory setting may be more convenient for the researcher, anxiety and reactivity (behavior in response to being observed) might be lessened when the observations occur in a setting that participants find familiar or comfortable.

Unobtrusive observations occur when individuals are unaware they are being observed, such as when observations are made through a two-way mirror. Unobtrusive observation may present ethical problems, and it is important to consider its impact. Typically, it is conducted as part of a research protocol that has been approved by an oversight body, such as a human subjects or institutional review board. At a more pragmatic level, unobtrusive observation is not appropriate when the findings will affect decisions about the individuals or programs being observed. For example, a principal should not base a teacher's performance evaluation on clandestine observations, as this is likely to create an atmosphere of distrust.

The goal of identifying issues related to setting is to conduct your measurements efficiently and effectively, with minimal disruption by the rater and the object of measurement. Some forethought and planning in light of the factors just discussed should facilitate this process.

Sampling

Sampling involves making decisions about *selecting* who and what will be measured. For example, if you have developed a checklist to audit medical charts, you may decide to review every chart, every fifth chart, or every fiftieth chart. Because sampling is often associated with surveys, we will examine this aspect of sampling in more detail in the next section, covering self-report instruments.

When applied to instruments administered by an external rater, sampling also refers to such factors as the frequency and duration of observations and the number of clients to be observed. When we use rater instruments we often want to use the findings to measure a single entity, such as an employee's performance or a specific behavior in a child. Or consider the researcher who wants to study classroom interactions. An instrument is developed that will measure verbal and nonverbal interventions, such as eye contact, physical touch, and verbal redirection of student behavior. The researcher has trained four graduate students who will make classroom observations. The study will be conducted at two middle schools, in one seventh-grade history class and one eighth-grade English class at each school. Consent to participate has been obtained from the students and the students' parents or guardians. To acclimate the students and teachers to their presence, the raters plan to spend at least two weeks in the classroom before using the instrument to formally document their observations.

However, the researcher must still resolve several questions about the observation process. For example, will the observers rate only interactions between the teacher and individual students or will they also rate interactions between the teacher and groups of students? If group interactions are to be counted, both the instrument and observation process must be designed to take this into consideration. For one thing, in situations where multiple individuals in a group are being observed, the sheer number of behaviors may limit observations to whether the behavior did or did not occur, and behavior frequency and duration will not be measured. Another decision regards scheduling the observations. Kazdin (1982) has identified four ways to schedule observations: frequency measures, discrete categorization, interval recording, and duration.

Frequency measures count the number of times an action or behavior occurs within a given time period; for example, an instrument could be created to count the number of times a teacher uses verbal praise to maintain classroom discipline or to tally how frequently a child displays age-appropriate social skills. The behavior must be clearly defined to reduce ambiguity and enhance observer reliability. Additionally, the definition should describe a distinct beginning and ending for the behavior. In other words, the instrument should make it possible to distinguish teacher verbal interventions to maintain classroom discipline from verbal interactions that are a part of classroom instruction, or to tell when children's shouting is an aspect of age-appropriate play rather than of anger.

To provide structure to the process, frequency measures are taken during a predetermined time frame. The observation period could be the duration of the class, such as fifty minutes, or at fixed intervals, such as the first twenty minutes of each hour. An observer counting social behaviors might observe for ten minutes, break for ten minutes, and then observe for ten minutes over the period of one hour. "The rate of response each day can be obtained by dividing the frequency of responses by the number of minutes observed each day. This measure will yield frequency per minute or rate of response, which is comparable for different durations of observation" (Kazdin, 1982, p. 27).

Discrete categorization differs from using frequency measures in that the instrument is designed to measure both occurrences *and* nonoccurrences, that is, to document whether the behavior of interest was present or not present, or performed correctly or incorrectly, within a given time period. If you were interested in measuring verbal praise as a means of maintaining classroom discipline, you would identify, during pretesting, a number of words, phrases, or statements that convey positive recognition. You would then measure the presence and the absence of this verbal praise in response to certain behaviors and situations during fixed intervals, such as fifteen-minute intervals. For example, if a teacher verbally redirects a student by saying, "Please take your seat," does the teacher follow up with "thank you" or some other positive statement when the student displays the desired behavior? Similarly, a checklist for a developmentally delayed child who is being taught to perform activities of daily living such as tying her shoe, toileting, and bathing might measure whether or not a behavior occurred and whether it was executed appropriately.

When you use *interval recording* the focus is on time intervals rather than discrete behaviors. You are interested in whether the behavior did or did not occur during a fixed period of time rather than its frequency. You might design your instrument for observations at five-minute intervals during a fifty-minute class. Regardless of the actual number of times the teacher used verbal praise during each five-minute block of time, it would be recorded as having either occurred or not occurred during that time. A variation of interval recording is time sampling. Rather than making your five-minute observations during one class period, you might spread them out over a longer period, such as the entire school day.

Finally, you might want to base your observations on *duration*. For example, you might be interested in how much time the teacher spends in reinforcing positive classroom behaviors during a fixed interval, as compared to the amount of time spent in classroom instruction.

Given these choices, you can understand why it is important to consider the design of an observer instrument, as the structure and format of the instrument should support the measurement process and will influence how it is administered.

Observer Training

In the fourth chapter we defined interrater reliability and explained how to compute the percentage of agreement (the level of agreement between the ratings of two independent observers). Having constructed and pretested your instrument, you will still need to consider how observers will be prepared and trained to administer the instrument consistently. You should consider this an integral part of the instrument construction process, as improper administration can compromise the validity and reliability of your data and findings and may ultimately adversely affect decisions about individuals, such as academic placement, entrance into a program, and evaluation of work performance.

The most frequently used method of training observers involves vignettes, either written or videotaped. Using vignettes is preferable to training observers in the field, where their activities may be disruptive to programs or clients.

A written vignette might take the form of a brief case history. Each rater individually reads the vignette and then uses that information to score the instrument that is to be administered. The raters then compare their scores and discuss the reasons for any different interpretations of the vignette and their individual ratings. Questions about the meanings of words or items can also be answered at this time, as well as questions about the observation process. This scoring and comparing process is repeated a number of times, until the raters can demonstrate a fairly high level of consistency. Kazdin (1982, p. 73) notes that "traditionally, agreement was regarded as acceptable if it met or surpassed .80 or 80 percent, computed by frequency or point-by-point agreement ratios. Research has shown that many factors contribute to any particular estimate of agreement. Hence, it is not only the quantitative estimate that needs to be evaluated, but also how that estimate was obtained and under what conditions." In other words, even though a high level of agreement is desirable, if you are unable to obtain 80 percent agreement or more, it is important to look at other factors that might be influencing the process, such as problems with the instrument, the observation method, or the training process.

The training program for scoring the Child and Adolescent Assessment Scale (CAFAS) offers an example of using vignettes. The CAFAS assists mental health professionals to evaluate children and adolescents with emotional, behavioral, and substance abuse problems, and the *CAFAS Self-Training Manual* (Hodges, 1996) uses two sets of vignettes to help raters develop their skills. In the first set, six case histories are presented along with completed and scored instruments. Explanations describe how the ratings were obtained, and raters can compare their scores with the scores that the instrument designer has indicated are appropriate for the case. The second set of vignettes contains ten case histories. Raters complete each vignette and then compare and contrast their scores with each other's scores and with an "answer key" of recommended ratings. Consequently, raters have sixteen opportunities to hone their skills in completing the instrument.

Videotaped vignettes are another medium for observer training. Observers view a video of the behaviors or situation that they will rate—it may show a simulated or a real-life situation—and have a chance to practice and sharpen their scoring. The advantage of video vignettes is that observers can go back over a vignette repeatedly to see and discuss the behaviors they are evaluating.

In some situations you may need to provide training on an ongoing basis. For example, if your organization routinely hires or promotes employees into supervisory positions, then you should regularly schedule performance-rating training for these new managers. When you are using a behavior assessment or conducting a research project and have turnover among raters, you will need to recruit and train new raters. In such cases it is important to obtain measures of interrater reliability between your experienced raters and the new recruits, to ensure that you are obtaining consistent measurements. *Observer drift* refers to differences that may occur over time between seasoned raters. For example, the definition of what is to be observed may evolve and change somewhat as individuals internalize and filter their observations. Consequently, if your instrument will be administered over an extended period of time or in different settings, you should plan to retrain experienced observers as well.

In conclusion, it is important to plan the administration of instruments that will be completed by a rater, or observer. This ensures that the work that you put into instrument development is not negated by poor implementation.

Administering Self-Report Instruments

Self-report instruments can be used to obtain information about one individual or entity, such as one person's response to a health status questionnaire. However, self-report instruments are more often used to collect information from and about large groups, as questionnaires used for marketing research, political polls, and organizational surveys do. Although an individual's response to a health status questionnaire can tell us a lot about that one person, analysis of findings from many questionnaires may reveal trends related to health, illness, and disease among all the people that have completed the questionnaire. Because self-report instruments are often used to obtain data that will be aggregated among and across respondents, the following administration considerations should be addressed:

- Sampling methodology
- Method of administration
- Nonresponse bias

Sampling

When we think of a population, we usually have in mind a large number, such as the population of a country, state, or city. However, for many projects your population of interest may be smaller and more finite, such as all employees in a fifty-person business organization, all fifth grade students in a specific elementary school, or the medical records of all patients discharged from a hospital in the past year. Therefore, in many situations it may be practical and desirable to administer your instrument to an entire population. In some situations it may even be feasible to administer an instrument to a very large population. The Virginia State Employee Survey (Instrument 7.A in Chapter Seven), for example, was mailed out to all 143,377 employees on the state payroll. If it is not practical to take measurements from an entire population, then you might want to identify a group that reflects the population characteristics you want to examine, and administer your instrument to that group, which is referred to as a *sample*.

There are two ways to obtain a sample. A *nonprobability* sampling approach (producing a *convenience* sample or *purposive* sample) involves administering the instrument to entities that are readily available. You might stop people as they leave a theater and ask them their opinion of the movie they just watched, for example. However, because the sample would be limited to those individuals who agree to give you their opinion, the responses would certainly not reflect the judgments of all those in attendance, let alone the much wider audience of all viewers who saw the movie locally or nationally. Or perhaps you have responded to an Internet survey asking you to choose your favorite actor, song, or book. Even if 200,000 people respond to the survey, because probability sampling procedures were not used, the results will reflect only the preferences of those 200,000 respondents and not of the public in general.

Nonprobability sampling can be an appropriate approach in many situations. For example, people use purposive sampling when they are primarily interested in the results from an individual, as when doctors ask clients to complete a health status questionnaire each time they visit the doctor's office. The focus here is on differences an individual may report over time, rather than on aggregating data across patients. Similarly, many mental health assessment instruments are administered individually. Benchmarking is a method for comparing an organization to other organizations known to be high performing, and questionnaires may be developed to elicit information from this targeted group. Here you are not interested in how all organizations that provide services or products similar to yours are performing; you are interested only in a specific, nonrepresentative group of high-performing organizations.

Although nonprobability sampling may be adequate for many of the instruments you plan to administer, it has some limitations, particularly when it is used to administer an instrument to a group rather than an individual. For example, many magazines include mail-in questionnaires, and Internet sites are increasingly inviting individuals to complete surveys on line. However, one of the problems associated with this approach is controlling multiple entries. It may be possible for someone to submit more than one copy of a mail-in or Internet questionnaire, thereby skewing the results (equivalent to "stuffing the ballot box" in an election).

Another problem is that the respondents are self-selected; the situation described in Chapter Eight in discussing a survey conducted by a member of Congress (Instrument 8.B). In that case many more of the congressman's constituents identifying themselves as politically conservative or moderate rather than as liberal responded to the survey. But because this sample was self-selected, we have no way of knowing if the respondents are or are not representative of all voters in that congressional district.

You can do several things to address the limitations associated with a non-probability sample. First, be cautious in interpreting the data, as they may be skewed by multiple entries or self-selection. Second, always describe how you administered your instrument and any shortcomings associated with the data collection method. For example, you can state in your report that nonprobability sampling was used and that the responses are limited to those who chose to respond. Finally, as soon as you recognize that you will need to generalize your findings beyond the immediate sample, choose to use probability sampling.

A *probability* sample is constructed in such a way that you can estimate the extent to which the responses obtained from the sample are representative of all members of your population of interest. For example, a political poll might develop a probability sample of 1,200 registered voters from across the country, survey this sample, and then generalize the results to all registered voters (the population of interest), who number in the tens of millions. Or suppose that the CEO of a large, urban hospital has asked you to conduct a survey of employees regarding work-related issues, such as wages, benefits, work schedules, and the like. The population of interest is all 2,200 employees of the hospital, ranging from doctors, nurses, and clinical technicians to housekeepers, food service workers, and maintenance staff. You could of course try to survey the entire population, but suppose that time and resources limit you to a one-time attempt with a smaller sample. The challenge is to design a sampling strategy that adequately represents these diverse occupational groups.

The first step is to determine the sample size. Sample size is based on several factors, including resources and the margin of error you are willing to accept to be able to say that your sample's responses are representative of the responses you would expect if you administered your questionnaire to everyone. In calculating the sample size, you need to specify the *confidence level* and *confidence interval* you are willing to accept. The confidence level indicates how certain you are that the sample is indeed representative. Typically, confidence levels of 90, 95, or 99 percent are selected. A 95 percent confidence level indicates that 95 times out of 100 your sample responded as you would expect if the entire population of interest had completed the survey. The confidence interval is sometimes referred to as the *margin of error*. For example, if you select a confidence interval of 3.0 and

75 percent of your sample rate an item in a certain way (such as strongly agree), you can be confident that your population would have responded in a similar fashion within plus or minus 3 percentage points (72 percent to 78 percent). The confidence interval is related to sample size, so that the smaller the margin of error you are willing to accept, the larger the sample you will need. Let's suppose that due to limited resources you are willing to accept a fairly large margin of error in order to work with a small sample. In our example of a hospital with 2,200 employees, at the 95 percent confidence level and with a confidence interval of 7.5, you can work with a sample of 160 respondents. Sample size can be calculated by using the relevant formula in a statistics book, a statistics software package with that capability, or one of the automated sample size calculators available on the Internet (search using the term *sample size calculator*). It is important to keep in mind that the confidence measures are dependent on your entire sample responding to your survey. In the next section we will examine how to work with the data when the response rate is less than the desired sample size.

The next step is to select a random sample. This means that every individual in the population has an equal chance of being included in the sample and that selecting one individual in no way affects the chance of any other individual to be included in the sample. To obtain a random sample for our example, you could put the names of all 2,200 hospital employees in a hat and pick at random until you have selected 160 names. You could also obtain a list of names from the hospital's human resource department and select every fourteenth name on the list (2,200/160), although neither method will guarantee that the selections are truly random. A better way is to use the functions in spreadsheet or statistical software such as Excel or SPSS; for example, Microsoft Excel has two ways of creating a random sample—the RAND command or the random number process generator. Either of these functions can be accessed using the Help menu (Zimmerman & Icenogle, 1999). Although these and other methods will help you obtain a random sample, it may still not be a truly representative sample. For example, if nursing employees make up 40 percent of the staff but only 20 percent of your sample, you may need to use other approaches to obtain a representative sample.

Additional sampling strategies include using *stratified* random samples and *cluster* samples. For a stratified sample, the population is broken into strata, or classes, by a factor such as gender, age, or income, and then a random sample of each grouping is generated. If personnel records indicate that 65 percent of the hospital's employees are female and 35 percent are male, a stratified random sample based on gender would ensure that your sample was representative of all hospital employees at least on that variable. Cluster sampling breaks large segments of the population into smaller units. For example, the clusters in an organizational survey could be departments, and the number of respondents to be randomly selected would be apportioned so that more respondents are selected from departments having larger numbers of employees, such as the nursing department.

The primary benefit of using nonprobability sampling is ease of access to your sample, whereas the advantage of using a probability sample is the ability to extrapolate your results to a larger population of interest. Your decision on whether to sample or not and, if you decide to sample, on sampling method will be based in part on resources and in part on how you or other decision makers plan to use the results.

Method of Administration

Now that you have decided who will receive the instrument, you will need to select a method of delivering the instrument to potential respondents. The most frequently employed methods are meeting personally with each respondent or using the postal service or e-mail, the telephone, or the computer (the Internet).

A personal meeting requires you or someone you have trained to meet one-to-one with each potential respondent. One advantage of a personal interview is that the interviewer can immediately clarify questions a respondent may have about the instrument or specific items.[1] Personal meetings are usually the method of choice when the instrument is composed of open-ended items, as the interviewer can ask the respondents to clarify or expand on their answers. The disadvantages associated with this approach involve cost, especially if you will be employing multiple interviewers, and time—both the time needed to train interviewers and the time needed to conduct the one-to-one meetings. Obviously, this is not an approach to use if your population or sample is large and your resources are limited.

Perhaps the most frequent means of administering an instrument is through the mail. Mail surveys can be cost effective when the sample size is small (in the hundreds) and when you need to keep track of the distribution process (who received and who returned the questionnaire). One disadvantage is that it may be difficult to obtain a large enough response rate to ensure a representative sample. As Fowler (1988) says, "It is important to realize that samples of data resulting from returns of 20 to 30 percent, which are not uncommon for mail surveys that are not followed up effectively, usually look nothing at all like the sampled populations" (p. 49).

Mailing *time* may be another disadvantage, as several days may elapse between the mailing and delivery dates. This can be problematic when external events have the potential to influence respondents' choices—if, for example, you were to send out a questionnaire about smoking at the same time that the Food and Drug Administration announced approval of a new, highly effective nicotine patch. Additional time is incurred if the respondent sets the questionnaire aside and does not immediately complete and return it. Yet more time is associated with mailing the instrument back. Some of these limitations can be overcome by using e-mail. E-mail provides almost instantaneous dissemination of the instrument, and people may be more likely to read and complete information they receive via e-mail. The disadvantages are that administration is limited to respondents with e-mail capability (we discuss the use of computers further in Chapter Fourteen) and recipients can easily delete the message or may be hesitant to open e-mails with attachments for fear that they contain a computer virus. Researchers are always interested in maximizing response rates, and e-mail would appear to be a promising approach. However, a review of the literature suggests that this medium is seldom used to administer large-scale surveys (a finding that may be due to increased use of Web-based surveys) and that the response rate is not significantly different from the rate for regular mail (Sheehan, 2001).

As with personal meetings, an advantage of obtaining information over the telephone is the ability to answer questions a respondent may have about the instrument and to obtain comprehensive responses to open-ended questions. Telephone interviews can access large samples and special populations across great distances in much less time than it would take to obtain responses to a mailed questionnaire. For example, most nationwide surveys of voters, such as those conducted prior to presidential elections, are conducted by telephone, as that makes them quick to administer and reduces the chance that external events influence responses. As with e-mail, one disadvantage is that you are limited to respondents with the appropriate service. Although virtually every household in the United States has a telephone, this may not be the case in developing countries or in rural regions. Additionally, many people, particularly cell phone users, have unlisted numbers—up to 30 percent of households in the United States according to one study (Newport, 2004)—which makes sampling difficult. A second disadvantage is the need to train interviewers. Like raters completing an instrument, telephone interviewers administering a questionnaire need to do so similarly, as different vocal intonations or phrasings could influence how respondents comprehend the meaning of items.

To overcome the problem of unlisted numbers, pollsters use *random digit dialing*, or RDD. Every area is broken down by a three-number area code, a three-number exchange, and then the four digits of the specific telephone number. There are 10,000 possible numbers for each exchange, as they can range only from 0000 to 9999. Therefore, for each exchange, a computer can select four-digit combinations at random and every possible combination will have the same probability of being selected, whether or not the number is listed. Newport (2004) notes a number of ways that pollsters have refined RDD to increase the likelihood of calling a working residential number rather than a business or discontinued number: "Firms that prepare and market telephone samples also attempt to keep the sampled numbers as close to real residential exchanges as possible by using ways of 'cleaning' or purging nonresidential numbers before the survey interviewers actually begin calling them. In some instances, automatic dialers call every number before it is released to be in a sample in order to eliminate those that the computer picks up as being nonworking" (pp. 179–180).

The size and scope of your project will suggest whether administering the instrument by telephone is within your resources, as it is a process that may require technological support as well as multiple telephone interviewers. If you are engaging in a small study, with a finite target population, such as members of the Parent Teacher Association for your child's school, then telephone interviewing might be an efficient and effective process. However, if you are the primary investigator and there are more than a hundred respondents in your study, you could easily be overwhelmed by the task.

Nonresponse Bias

We have already touched on the concept of nonresponse bias in our discussion of nonprobability sampling, where respondents are self-selected. For example, in the case of the congressional survey, we could not be sure that respondents were representative of all constituents. Nonresponse bias can also occur when you administer an instrument to a population or when you get a low response rate (typically less than 70 percent) from a probability sample. In such situations you cannot be sure that the individuals who did not respond are similar to those who did respond. And if the response rate is very low, between 20 and 30 percent, the respondents are basically self-selected and the effects of random sampling essentially negated (Fowler, 1988).

To understand nonresponse bias, it is important to keep in mind that there is a difference between sample size and response rate. Returning to our example of an organizational survey in a hospital, 160 respondents were needed to obtain a representative sample. However, it is highly unlikely that all 160 people to whom the questionnaire is mailed will complete and return it. If only eighty employees (50 percent of the sample) respond, you cannot be sure that they are really representative, and in fact they may be systematically different from the population of interest.

Nonresponse Bias in the Administration of a Survey

When people are polled about their beliefs and opinions on political issues it is important to ensure that respondents are representative of all potential voters. Therefore, it is essential to use random sampling methodologies when conducting political polls. The congressional survey questionnaire (Instrument 8.B) was published in newspapers as well as mailed to registered voters in the congressman's electoral district; that is, an attempt was made to administer the questionnaire to the entire population of potential voters (Goodlatte, 1998). The congressman received nearly 20,000 responses—roughly 40 percent of the electorate in the district. Although this is a large response rate, we have no way of knowing if the ratings reflect the opinions of all 50,000 potential respondents or if the 60 percent of individuals who did not respond are demographically similar or different from those who did. For example, it is possible that a majority of those not responding hold very different opinions and would rate the items quite differently. Additionally, we have no way of knowing if individuals in either the did-respond or did-not-respond groups under- or overrepresent the entire electorate in terms of gender or ethnic, religious, or racial identity.

Fifty percent of respondents to this 1998 survey identified themselves as conservative, 47 percent as moderate, and only 3 percent as liberal. Because we do not know how all district voters categorize themselves, we cannot tell if this breakdown is representative of the congressman's constituency. Additionally, the administration process did not include safeguards to minimize multiple entries. Consequently, we could infer that the results are biased, as they reflect only the views of those individuals who chose to respond.

There are several actions you can take to minimize the effects of nonresponse bias and the impact it can have on interpreting your study findings. Regardless of the method of administration, it is important to try to maximize the response rate. With mail surveys it may be necessary to mail (or e-mail) reminder notices and, if need be, send out another copy of the questionnaire. For telephone inquiries, you may need to make multiple attempts at contacting the respondents on your list. If, despite these efforts, you obtain a response rate of less than 50 percent (some authorities suggest a minimum of 70 to 75 percent), you will need to be careful in interpreting the results and using them for decision making.

One way to determine whether nonresponse bias is influencing your findings is to compare the results from your first mailing to results from a subsequent mailing (in essence, creating two samples). For example, if only 45 percent of your sample returned the questionnaire, you would resend the instrument to the 55 percent who had not yet responded and then compare the findings from the first and the second mailings. If you found a substantial difference in the way the two sets of respondents completed the questionnaire, you would have evidence that nonresponse bias had indeed influenced your findings. If the findings were similar, then you could conclude that your sample is less likely to be biased.

A slightly different approach is to randomly sample the nonrespondents. In other words, rather than resending the questionnaire to all of the 55 percent who did not respond, create a small random sample of that 55 percent and readminister the instrument to this sample. As before, the more this sample is like the first responders, the more likely it is that both samples are representative of the population of interest.

Another way to assess for nonresponse bias is to compare the makeup of your respondents and of the target population. In the example of the hospital survey, where 65 percent of the employees are female, you would expect the return rate to be stratified in the same proportions as the distribution rate. If 40 percent of the respondents are female and 60 percent male, then you need to question the representativeness of your sample.

It is important to make users and stakeholders aware of your methods and to explain any factors that might influence their understanding of the data. For example, it is important to describe the sampling strategy you used and what you did to maximize the response rate. If you believe that your findings are compromised due to nonresponse bias, then you and stakeholders must be cautious in making use of the data; you may even decide to readminister the instrument, rather than depend on questionable data.

Summary

As with artwork, there comes a time where you need to take your creation into the real world. In this chapter we have described the process of administering an instrument with its intended audience and in its intended setting and situation. The specific process activities reflect the instrument's mode of administration—completed by an observer or by the individual who is the object of the measurement. When the instrument is designed for completion by an observer, you will address issues related to selecting the setting for observation, selecting a sampling strategy, and training the observers. If you have designed a self-report instrument then you will address sampling methodology (administering to an entire population, a nonprobability sample, or a probability sample), method of administration (personal meetings, phone calls, mail, and so on), and nonresponse bias.

Although the primary focus of this book is to assist you in creating a *good* instrument, administration is an important aspect of the instrument construction process, as issues related to delivery and implementation will influence your instrument's design and development. For that reason it is important to address issues related to administration from the onset, integrating them into the instrument construction process.

Instrument 13.A: Behavioral Rating Scale

A review of the literature found that although a number of instruments are designed specifically for the assessment of children and adolescents in behavioral health care settings, they may not provide the type of information treatment teams require for treatment decision making. For example, the majority of these instruments are designed for intake assessment rather than for continuous monitoring to measure the effects of treatment.

In response to this need, one of the authors (Colton, 2003, 2005) developed the Child and Adolescent Inpatient Behavioral Rating Scale. This instrument, which is in the public domain, can be used as a consistent and stable measure to identify trends and patterns and other changes in specified behaviors.

The instrument consists of sixty-four defined behaviors. With the exception of the items measuring eating habits and sleeping patterns, all the items are rated using a scale of severity: 0 = *not present,* 1 = *mild,* 2 = *moderate,* and 3 = *severe.* The items have been grouped thematically: anxiety, depression, communication problems, psychomotor activity, and so on. However, the behaviors to be observed and rated can be selected from across the instrument and do not need to be limited by category.

The primary function of the Child and Adolescent Inpatient Behavioral Rating Scale is to serve as a source for repeated (weekly, daily, shift-to-shift, or hourly) observations. Behaviors the treatment team wishes to monitor are identified during the treatment-planning meeting. Typically, the team identifies specific behaviors related to treatment problems and objectives, and administering one, two, or three items suffices for each treatment problem and objective.

To facilitate interrater reliability, scoring guidelines have been developed for each item, as follows:

EXAMPLE

1. Hyper Vigilant

0	1	2	3
Not Present: Behavior was not observed.	**Mild:** Has expressed distrust and need to watch others; tends to scan the environment.	**Moderate:** Intermittent periods of watching others or the environment to the extent that the individual is not attending to immediate tasks. May express belief that others are plotting against him/her.	**Severe:** Watching is pervasive and becomes the primary task to the extent that attention to other tasks is compromised. May associate everyday activities with plots of harm. May not want to interact with others due to these fears.

INSTRUMENT 13.A: BEHAVIORAL RATING SCALE.

Child and Adolescent Inpatient Behavioral Rating Scale

INSTRUCTIONS:

This instrument may be used as either a pretreatment/post-treatment measure or as the basis for repeated (weekly, daily, shift-to-shift, or hourly) observations.

Pretreatment/Post-Treatment Measure

Information to complete this instrument is based on the youngster's behaviors during the first 72 hours after admission (pretreatment) and within 72 hours prior to the youngster's planned discharge (post-treatment). Information to complete the rating scale is based on:

- Direct observation
- Interview and interactions with the youngster
- Chart notes and verbal feedback from other members of the treatment team

The entire form (all items) should be completed. If the behaviors are not observed, use "Not Present" to rate the item. The primary means of comparing pretreatment and post-treatment scores is through the process of "eye-balling" to determine where responses have changed over time. Items can also be graphed and the differences observed through visual comparison.

Daily Behavioral Observation—Clinical Indicators

Behaviors that the treatment team wishes to monitor should be identified at the time of admission and/or during the treatment-planning meeting. Typically, the team will identify those specific behaviors that are related to treatment problems and objectives. Items 65 and 66 provide space to add behaviors which are not included on the checklist, but which the treatment team may chose to monitor using the same scale. Typically, one, two, or three items should suffice for each treatment problem and objective.

Depending on the behavior, the treatment team should determine the frequency of observation; for example, observations could be made hourly or twice a shift. In this way, the behavioral rating scale can be used in conjunction with behavior analysis and the assessment of treatment effects.

The purpose of the rating system is to provide data on which to base continuing assessments of the youngster's response to treatment. The instrument does not replace the need for analysis of the data. For example, if a pattern of behavior is detected, this may suggest that additional information is required, such as a situational analysis to determine factors that may elicit the behaviors. Finally, the utility of the data can also be enhanced by using the data in conjunction with other sources of information, such as anecdotal reports and the results of other assessment measures.

	Anxiety	Not Present	Mild	Moderate	Severe
❑	1. Hyper vigilant	0	1	2	3
❑	2. Difficulty settling at night	0	1	2	3
❑	3. Repetitive behaviors	0	1	2	3
❑	4. Nightmares/flashbacks	0	1	2	3
❑	5. Low startle threshold	0	1	2	3
❑	6. Panic attacks	0	1	2	3
❑	7. Grandiose	0	1	2	3

	Depression	Not Present	Mild	Moderate	Severe
❑	8. Withdrawn	0	1	2	3
❑	9. Sad affect	0	1	2	3
❑	10. Flat affect	0	1	2	3
❑	11. Crying spells	0	1	2	3
❑	12. Tired/loss of energy	0	1	2	3

❑	13. Negative self-statements	0	1	2	3
❑	14. Physical complaints	0	1	2	3
❑	15. Irritable	0	1	2	3
❑	16. Self-harmful statements	0	1	2	3
❑	17. Self-injurious behavior	0	1	2	3

	Communication Problems	Not Present	Mild	Moderate	Severe
❑	18. Loud/shouting	0	1	2	3
❑	19. Under-productive speech	0	1	2	3
❑	20. Incoherent speech	0	1	2	3
❑	21. Pressured speech	0	1	2	3
❑	22. Disorganized speech	0	1	2	3
❑	23. Echolalia	0	1	2	3

	Psycho-Motor Activity	Not Present	Mild	Moderate	Severe
❑	24. Dizziness and/or difficulty standing	0	1	2	3
❑	25. Exaggerated mannerisms	0	1	2	3
❑	26. Stereotypical movements	0	1	2	3
❑	27. Perseveration	0	1	2	3
❑	28. Tremors and tics	0	1	2	3
❑	29. Psychomotor retardation	0	1	2	3
❑	30. Clumsiness	0	1	2	3

	Attention Problems/Hyperactive	Not Present	Mild	Moderate	Severe
❑	31. Difficulty staying on task	0	1	2	3
❑	32. Difficulty following directions	0	1	2	3
❑	33. Distracted by external stimuli	0	1	2	3
❑	34. Distracted by internal stimuli	0	1	2	3
❑	35. Fidgets/restless	0	1	2	3
❑	36. Hyper-kinetic	0	1	2	3

Conduct Problems/ Disruptive Behaviors	Not Present	Mild	Moderate	Severe
❏ 37. Cursing	0	1	2	3
❏ 38. Argumentative	0	1	2	3
❏ 39. Frustration/tantrums	0	1	2	3
❏ 40. Disobedient	0	1	2	3
❏ 41. Does not accept responsibility	0	1	2	3
❏ 42. Rude	0	1	2	3
❏ 43. Manipulates others	0	1	2	3
❏ 44. Lies	0	1	2	3
❏ 45. Verbally threatens	0	1	2	3
❏ 46. Physically intimating	0	1	2	3
❏ 47. Aggressive toward objects	0	1	2	3
❏ 48. Aggressive toward people	0	1	2	3
❏ 49. Demands must be met immediately	0	1	2	3
❏ 50. Passively defiant	0	1	2	3

Social Skills	Not Present	Mild	Moderate	Severe
❏ 51. Touches others when/where they don't want	0	1	2	3
❏ 52. Teases others	0	1	2	3
❏ 53. Does not maintain appropriate social distance	0	1	2	3
❏ 54. Engages in attention seeking behaviors	0	1	2	3
❏ 55. Interrupts or intrudes	0	1	2	3
❏ 56. Difficulty waiting one's turn	0	1	2	3
❏ 57. Difficulty picking up social cues	0	1	2	3
❏ 58. Sexually inappropriate—directed toward self	0	1	2	3
❏ 59. Sexually inappropriate—directed toward others	0	1	2	3

❑	60. Difficulty maintaining personal hygiene	0	1	2	3
❑	61. Incontinence (including bedwetting)	0	1	2	3
❑	62. Bowel management problems	0	1	2	3

Eating Habits

❑ 63.		Ate most of this meal	Skipped most of this meal	Picky about what he/she ate	Overeats or gorges
	Breakfast	1	2	3	4
	Lunch	1	2	3	4
	Dinner	1	2	3	4
	Snack	1	2	3	4

Sleeping Habits

❑ 64.	1	2	3	4
	Sleeps thru the night w/o incident	Difficulty falling asleep	Awakens early	Restless sleeper

Other Behaviors (specify)	Not Present	Mild	Moderate	Severe
❑ 65.	0	1	2	3
❑ 66.	0	1	2	3

Endnote

1. A concern with providing clarification for one respondent but not another is that it may influence the recipient's response and thus raise questions about the validity and reliability of the administration process and the results obtained. If you believe this could be a problem in your study, you might use another typical approach: when a respondent has a question about an item, the interviewer will repeat the item but will not provide additional information, even if asked.

Key Concepts and Terms

cluster sample	informed consent	purposive sample
confidence interval	interval recording	random digit dialing
confidence level	margin of error	random sample
convenience sample	nonprobability sample	sampling
discrete categorization	nonresponse bias	site selection
duration	observer training	stratified sample
frequency measures	probability sample	vignette

CHAPTER FOURTEEN

COMPUTERS AND INSTRUMENT CONSTRUCTION

In this chapter we will

- Examine how computers can assist in designing and organizing an instrument.
- Identify factors to address when administering an instrument through computer technology, including the Internet and e-mail.

Traditionally, artists have painted on a variety of surfaces—canvas, wood, and special papers. In recent years, however, artists have turned to computers to create their works, often with software so sophisticated that they have had to learn entirely different ways of managing the new medium. Similarly, computers are increasingly being used by researchers in the design and administration of questionnaires. During the past decade personal computer (PC) software has made it possible to use PCs in instrument design and development, and the Internet has opened up new approaches for delivering the instrument to the user. In this chapter we will examine how computers can aid you in instrument construction and how e-mail and the Internet can facilitate administration. As with any approach, you should be aware of the pros and cons prior to deciding to use computer-based approaches.

The first computers, or calculators, were designed to analyze the results of survey data, specifically census data. The 1890 census was tallied using a computer that read punch cards (cards carrying numerical codes in the form of holes punched in each card) for data entry. With this equipment, calculation of the census took only six weeks, as compared to the seven and a half years it took to manually tally the 1880 census! Fifty years later, the first electronic computers continued to use punch cards for data entry. These early computers were massive and yet had much less computational power than contemporary hardware (Kroenke, 1984). The early 1980s saw the advent of the personal computer. However, the computer operator had to write, or hire someone to write, his or her own software, which limited the PC's use. The breakthrough came when prewritten software was developed to address specific needs, such as word processing, accounting, and graphic design. In the late 1980s and early 1990s, software designers began to develop applications for survey research. The first applications operated on mainframe computers. Today, however, an individual can purchase software that can operate on a personal computer with the same capabilities to design, administer, and analyze surveys as the software used by large survey research organizations.

We are discussing software here, near the end of this book, for a very important reason. Although survey software can assist you in the design of your instrument and the analysis of your data, it cannot replace your personal knowledge about what constitutes an effective instrument or questionnaire item. At best, it can take a poorly worded question and give it a polished appearance. However, as instrument designer, you are still responsible for the quality of the individual items and the organization and appearance of your questionnaire.

Computer software can do three things to make the process of instrument construction more efficient. First, it can assist in the construction of individual items and particularly in their formatting. Second, it can facilitate questionnaire design, such as the organization of items and the final overall appearance. Third, some (not all) software helps you perform data entry and analysis. Typically, either this last feature is a component of the software or the software allows you to export the data to an application whose primary purpose is statistical analysis. In the next section we will examine how computer software can assist you with item construction and organization of the questionnaire; issues related to administering Web surveys will be addressed in the last section.

Item Construction and Questionnaire Organization

Item Construction

Computer software can assist you in formatting individual items and designing the final appearance they will take. The first step is to articulate the item (following the steps outlined in Part Two of this book). You can then chose an item format, such as Likert scale, numerical scale, rank order, or open-ended sentence, from a menu of styles. With this menu you can also indicate the number of response choices you want, and select such options as making *no opinion* a response choice. Most survey software includes word processing features such as spelling and grammar checkers as well. Once you have selected all your options, the software will add the question to the instrument and prompt you to go on to the next item.

Typically, survey software includes a variety of templates from which you can select the physical appearance of each item. For example, you can select a graphic for recording a response from a menu with various boxes (❏ or ☐) and circles (O or ◯), where boxes are used to mark all-that-apply options and circles are used to make a selection. Although this can be done with word processing software as well, a ready-made template saves time, and once you have established the format you want to use, the software can apply that format to all subsequent items.

Layout and Design of the Questionnaire

Another advantage of using survey software is the ease of constructing an instrument that is appealing in appearance. Templates facilitate arrangements that are easy to read and follow. In the following example, items are easy to read because the stem has been separated from the response set, and response choices are easy to differentiate because they are separated by lines and shading. Although this can be accomplished with word processing software, here again, using preset templates is more efficient. In addition, some survey software will allow you to print item directions in a different color or to apply background shading in colors.

Item	Strongly Agree	Agree	No Opinion	Disagree	Strongly Disagree
Members of Congress should be limited to serving three terms.	❏	❏	❏	❏	❏
Raises to members of Congress should be limited to no more than 2% of their salary each year.	❏	❏	❏	❏	❏
I believe that my Congressman/woman adequately represents my needs.	❏	❏	❏	❏	❏

Special Considerations for Web Instruments

When using a paper-and-pencil document, the user can see the instrument in its entirety at once. However, the amount of information the Web-page user sees is dependent on the display size and resolution the user selects for his or her computer screen. For this reason, what users see may vary from monitor to monitor. If the instrument is no more than a page of written text, you may want to place the entire instrument on one Web page, allowing the respondent to scroll through it. This can be important when the items are related or the respondent needs to refer back to a prior item or response choice. Alternatively, many software programs allow you to break your questionnaire into sections so that the user completes just a few items per page (screen) without having to scroll. Schonlau, Fricker, and Elliott (2001) sum up the issues: "Excessive scrolling can become a burden to respondents and lengthy Web pages can give the impression that the survey is too long to complete, both of which have the potential to negatively impact response rates. . . . Also, there is some evidence that using only a single screen or a few screens for short surveys minimizes respondent 'abandonment' (starting but not completing a survey) whereas using a single screen and forcing the respondent to scroll down in long surveys increases abandonment" (p. 42).

Pretesting will of course assist you in determining how many questions to place on one screen as well as how to organize them. Issues that pretesters may remark on are the size of the font used, the arrangement of the item(s) on the screen, the use of background colors and graphics to highlight information, and also equipment considerations, such as the size of the monitor.

To assist users in moving through multiscreen Web instruments, and to provide feedback about their rate of progress, some software programs allow you to include a counter indicating how many pages or items have been completed and how many more are left to finish. The counter can simply indicate the number of items or can include text such as, "This is item #17, there are eight more items to complete in this section." With long questionnaires a downside of counters can be that the respondent sees there are still many pages to complete and gives up. One way to address this possibility is to use software that allows the user to log off and then log back on at a later time, picking up where he or she left off. This method usually requires assigning each user a unique password that the software can track. Consequently, you may want to look for this feature when purchasing survey software.

Survey software can also create links that support skip items and directions. Rather than manually navigating the instrument, the respondent can click a *yes* or *no*, or *if* or *then*, box and be automatically transferred to the next appropriate question. Another automated process can eliminate missed items; if the respondent does not rate an item, the software will not allow him or her to move on to the next item. The downside to this feature is that respondents may become frustrated and log off without completing the questionnaire: "In our view respondents should not be forced to provide an answer before moving on. Sometimes respondents have legitimate reasons for objecting to providing and answer and may, in fact, be unable to provide the answer to some questions" (Dillman, Tortora, & Bowker, 1998, p. 11).

Schonlau et al. (2001) point out yet another advantage to Web surveys—the designer can easily use color and graphics. Color is helpful for setting off important information. You can use different colors as backgrounds for different sections or highlight text with more than one (but not too many) colors. Graphics can include symbols and pictures, although you should be cautious in using pictures or photos as they can be distracting and increase the time it takes to download a page.

Data Collection and Scoring

Suppose you have constructed a survey that will be sent out to a sample of one hundred respondents and it contains forty items. Depending on your response rate, you could end up with about four thousand pieces of information that you will need to enter into a database for analysis. One of the primary benefits of survey software is that you can perform data collection and scoring very efficiently through scanning or on-line administration. If you have administered a paper-and-pencil instrument, a scanner can transfer the data to a computer. An optical reader, for example, can scan thirty to sixty answer sheets a minute, transferring the data to the database section of the software. A less expensive and more time-consuming method (although still less time consuming than manual entry) is to use a flatbed scanner, which might scan three to four answer sheets a minute. Regardless of the scanner used, if the answer sheets are neatly and completely filled out, this approach should also reduce the number of input errors.

Increasingly, instruments are being designed so that they can be administered over the Internet. The respondent can check boxes or circles with the touch of a computer mouse, and each entry is automatically entered into a database. This increases reliability by avoiding the transfer step of scanning or manual entry and thus reducing data entry errors.

More Pros and Cons of Using Survey Software

One of the primary advantages of using survey software is that you will be purchasing an application dedicated to your task. As we have pointed out, this software combines the features of word processing and desktop publishing for designing and organizing the instrument. In addition, many survey programs include features that facilitate data entry and analysis.

If you are thinking about making an investment in this software, one of your first considerations should be the size of your questionnaire. If it will be more than two pages long and use multiple item formats, then survey software may be beneficial in helping you design and organize your complex document.

A second consideration is whether you will be designing and conducting more than one survey. If you are planning to develop a questionnaire for just one project, then survey software may well be overkill, particularly given the cost of dedicated software. But if you foresee that you will be conducting a number of surveys, the software may be a sound investment.

Also consider the size of your sample and whether you want the software to assist in data entry. Remember that a survey with only twenty-five items going out to a sample of two hundred respondents has the potential to generate up to five thousand responses. That is a lot of information to enter and analyze. If you do decide to buy a program with an analysis function, be sure to check its capacity, as some programs limit the number of respondents and amount of data they can handle.

As with any software purchase, be sure to check that the program you want is compatible with your computer and that you have adequate random access memory (RAM) and hard drive space. If you have to upgrade or purchase a new computer to run the new software, using it may no longer be a cost-effective decision.

Survey software prices vary depending on the features you seek and on whether you need a single copy for an individual's use or a licensing agreement for a large organization's use. Be sure to compare and contrast prices and features before you buy. Many vendors list their products on the Internet (search using the keywords *survey* and *software*). Most vendors display examples of pages that the software can produce, and some offer demos that you can download. At the time we were writing this book, a number of vendors were selling entry-level programs for under $500. Other programs cost as much as $1,200. Because survey software is marketed to a fairly small consumer base, with limited competition between vendors, its price is not usually reduced as quickly as the prices for mass-marketed programs are. Consequently, although survey software features will continue to be enhanced, do not expect to purchase these programs at bargain prices.

A final option is to use an electronic survey service. Rather than purchasing the software, you purchase instrument design and administration services from a vendor's Web site. This is a cost-effective approach when you have just one or two surveys and do not need or want to go to the expense of purchasing the software.

In closing our discussion on survey software, we want to reiterate that this software cannot and will not replace the skill and acumen that you bring to the process of instrument creation. View it as a set of templates and menus that can assist you with design and construction. And remember that the old computer maxim of "garbage in, garbage out" still applies. The quality of your questionnaire will reflect your skills and abilities as an instrument developer; don't blame the software.

Computers and Questionnaire Administration

When combined with telecommunications media, computer technology and systems provide the newest approach for administering an instrument, particularly as ownership of computers and access to the Internet have proliferated. It has been thought that Web surveys might offer such advantages as timeliness in getting the instrument to respondents and in obtaining results, higher response rates, lower costs (from savings on printing or mailing), and ease of inputting data for analysis. However, a review of the literature on Web surveys provides conflicting evidence. Fricker and Schonlau (2002) reviewed fifty-seven published papers that examined the use of Web surveys, and they came to these three conclusions:

> Web surveys are thought to be much faster than conventional survey modes. While there is no question that the delivery time of an Internet-based survey is faster than a survey sent via the mail, there is little to no evidence in the literature to substantiate whether this increase substantially results in a shorter overall fielding period [p. 16].

> [T]here is little evidence in the literature that Internet-based surveys achieve higher response rates, as a general rule, than conventional surveys [p. 2].

> [W]hen only considering postage and printing costs, email and Web surveys almost by definition are cheaper than mail surveys. However, when the total costs of a survey are considered, including labor and other costs, Web surveys may or may not be cheaper depending on whether the additional expenses incurred in that mode, such as programmer costs, are offset by savings, such as postage and data entry costs [p. 15].

These findings suggest that the Internet and other computer-based systems, such as e-mail, are not a panacea for problems associated with questionnaire administration. In making the decision to administer an instrument via computer you should consider your goals, resources, and time constraints and whether there are any designing and formatting advantages. For example, a Web survey may be more efficient for collecting data when you are using a sample of convenience.

There are three challenges you will need to address if you decide to administer an instrument by computer: they concern design, technology, and management of the administration process. We discussed design issues earlier in this chapter. Design is a function of your skills in organizing and formatting the instrument and of the features available in the software you select. For example, some survey software is designed to assist you in structuring and printing the instrument (which can then be sent by mail or e-mail), and other software is designed from the outset to support Internet administration of questionnaires. Therefore the way you plan to administer your instrument should assist you in selecting the appropriate software.

The technology challenge relates to hardware and connections to other computers. The term *electronic survey* has been coined to describe an instrument delivered via computer terminals or dedicated devices such as touch pads connected through a computer network. For a customer satisfaction questionnaire, you might locate the computer or touch pad in a waiting area, where employees can direct clients to complete the instrument. The advantage of this approach is that help is available for the client who has difficulty using the technology. This brings up the essential challenge in using computers, which is that potential respondents must have access to the hardware. Although computers are increasingly ubiquitous, it is possible that your audience of interest has limited or no access to this technology. Dillman et al. (1998) refer to this problem as *coverage error:* "some units in the population may have no chance of selection, some units may have multiple chances, and some units may not even qualify for the survey" (p. 2). In other words, when some members of your target population lack access to a computer, you will likely exclude individuals who should participate. The problem is compounded when you are depending on e-mail to contact individuals and invite them to participate in your survey.

Another technology concern is the speed of the connection. Today a connection speed of 56 megabytes per second, for both uploading and downloading, is the norm and high-speed, broadband, and cable connections are becoming increasingly available (with even higher speed wireless and fiber optic connections replacing DSL and cable in the near future). At slower speeds, respondents may become impatient with document loading times. When you are administering your instrument on a local area network, such as a university campus or business intranet, you can obtain information about access speed and be assured that load times will not be a detriment. However, when users connect via the Internet, you probably will not know their access speed, and slow connections may dissuade some individuals from participating in the process.

Yet another technology issue is monitor resolution (which individual users set using the "display" function on their PC's control panel). If a user's monitor is set for a lower resolution than you used in designing the survey, icons and print will appear larger than they did to you, and it's possible that the respondent will need to scroll down the screen continually or that part of the survey page may not display at all.

Then there is the question of how you let potential respondents know that your survey is available. In some cases an open announcement will do, as when a magazine publisher invites readers to participate in an on-line survey. As we have noted, this can result in a large response rate, but because you are using nonprobability sampling, you cannot generalize beyond the survey respondents to a broader audience. Open invitations are also susceptible to skewing if a few individuals respond more than once. For example, if your on-line survey asks people to vote for a favorite person or product, unless you have some way to control multiple entries, a few respondents can bias the results.

Probability sampling can be done via the Internet when the population of interest is discrete, such as all the employees in an organization or all the undergraduates at a college. For example, in an organization with 800 employees where everyone has access to a computer terminal, you could generate a random sample that is representative of all workers. Due to technical issues, such as access to computers, electronic surveys are not suitable for opinion polls among the general population (Newport, 2004). When probability sampling is used, potential respondents are typically notified of the survey via e-mail, the assumption being that if a person has an e-mail address he or she also has a computer connection. (This is not always the case, however, as there are dedicated e-mail terminals that lack access to the Internet.) Consequently, you need access to potential respondents' e-mail addresses (which may raise confidentiality concerns among these individuals). Typically, each respondent is assigned a password so that he or she and not some other individual completes the instrument. This also allows survey administrators to monitor and control for multiple entries. If you are contacting a limited number of participants—twenty-five or fewer—you can send all the announcement e-mails out at one time. If notifying a larger sample, however, you may want to stagger the invitations so that your Web server is not inundated by replies. Heavy user traffic may prevent other respondents from logging onto the site, and they may become frustrated and decide not to participate (Schonlau et al., 2001). Respondents may also become frustrated if they have to navigate numerous screens to get to your site or if they encounter a complicated log-in process.

Issues related to Web survey confidentiality and anonymity have to be addressed at two levels. Respondents must be assured that adequate safeguards are in place to protect the collected data from hackers. Additionally, respondents who are using company equipment will know that the organization can access information stored on company computers at any time. For example, one study of on-line assessments found that "the on-line method produces a lower response rate to the teaching evaluations than the traditional paper and pencil method. The lower response rate is most likely related to factors such as fear that responses to the on-line survey may not be anonymous and that the on-line method can be inconvenient, time-consuming, and prone to technical problems" (Dommeyer, Baum, & Hanna, 2002, pp. 14–15). Addressing these issues might mean working with computer personnel to ensure that firewalls and other safeguards are in place to prevent external sources from accessing your data or, worse, getting into the survey and skewing the responses. And as we will examine in the next chapter, you should negotiate an agreement with the organization establishing who has ownership of and access to the raw data.

Ultimately, you will have to weigh the advantages against the limitations of using an electronic survey. The use of Web surveys is certainly growing, particularly with samples of convenience. One reason for this growth is that the data can be analyzed immediately. However, there are also limitations that need to be addressed to ensure that the process is efficient and cost effective.

Finally, computer technology can also support the recording of observational data. A number of handheld devices, including compact laptop computers and personal digital assistants (PDAs), can be carried into the field so that an observer can observe and record data simultaneously. Word processing and spreadsheet programs are available for these units. Technological issues to address include battery life and the amount of memory available for storage. Fortunately, both battery life and memory have been increasing in newer units, while the cost of PDAs and accessories has been decreasing. These units can also support the process of administering questionnaires and conducting interviews, as some models allow audio recording and software is available to transcribe audio into written form.

Summary

The medium used in the creation of a painting has not changed much in the past two thousand years. The Egyptians, Greeks, and Romans painted objects using pigments mixed with oil or water, mixtures that remain basic for painting today. However, in just the past twenty years computers have become a totally new medium for creating works of art. The same holds true for survey instruments, which for more than two hundred years have been paper-and-pencil documents. In the last twenty years, computers have created a new platform for creating and administering these instruments.

In this chapter we have examined how computers can support the design and construction of an instrument as well as how they can be used to deliver the instrument to potential respondents. Even as we were writing this text, computer technology was continuing to change significantly, and researchers are just beginning to tap this technology's potential in instrument construction. There may come a time when the paper-and-pencil questionnaire becomes a historical artifact and new media are used to create and administer instruments. However, good instruments will still have to adhere to the principles and guidelines that we have presented.

Instrument 14.A: Example of a Web Survey

Instrument 14.A displays an example of what you might see after you had logged onto a Web site and completed a survey there. This questionnaire takes up the entire computer screen, and you would probably need to scroll down in order to see all the items. The first seven (Likert type) items are answered by selecting a circle (sometimes referred to as a *radio button*) and clicking on it, which changes it to a circle with a dot in the center. The question about the number of children attending the school is answered by selecting a number from a *pull-down* box. Space is also provided for an open-ended response to the last question. The up and down arrows indicate that the respondent can scroll down for additional space if he or she has a lengthy answer. Finally, selecting the exit button enters the responses into a database and logs the respondent out of the survey.

When you are designing a Web questionnaire, survey software will often guide you through the process; it might, for example, suggest appropriate formats for an item, such as buttons or pull-down boxes. If you have more items than will fit on a single screen, it might offer a counter to help the respondent keep track of items completed and items left to finish.

Although it may take additional preparation time to place a questionnaire on the Internet, it is believed that the ease with which these instruments can be completed may enhance response rates. There is also less opportunity for data entry errors, on either the respondent's part when answering or your part when transferring responses to a database.

INSTRUMENT 14.A: WEB QUESTIONNAIRE.

Parent Survey of Stonewall Jackson Middle School (SJMS)

Please click on the button to record your selection. This questionnaire contains 10 items and should take no more than five minutes to complete. Thank you for your participation. Please go to www.stonewalljackson.edu/survey to view the result.

	Strongly Disagree					**Strongly Agree**	
I feel that my child receives a good education at SJMS.	○	○	○	○	⊙	○	○
The faculty of SJMS maintains good classroom discipline.	○	○	○	○	○	⊙	○
The school building is well maintained.	○	○	○	○	⊙	○	○
My child's teacher communicates his or her progress to me regularly.	○	○	⊙	○	○	○	○
Homework assignments appear to be meaningful.	○	○	○	⊙	○	○	○
SJMS faculty do a good job of preparing my child for the state's standardized test.	○	○	○	○	⊙	○	○
Classrooms are decorated attractively (posters, pictures, etc.) to invite learning.	○	○	○	○	○	⊙	○

Number of children attending SJMS: [1 ▾]

I am a member of the SJMS PTO. ○ Yes ⊙ No

My child/children get to school by: ○ walking
⊙ taking the school bus
○ are driven to school by car

Additional Comments:

[   ]

Click here to enter your data and exit this survey:

[Exit]

Key Concepts and Terms

coverage error	e-mail survey	pull-down box
data analysis	instrument design	survey software
data entry	instrument organization	Web survey
database	item construction	

CHAPTER FIFTEEN

MANAGING THE DATA AND REPORTING THE RESULTS

In this chapter we will

- Provide guidance for managing the data produced by an instrument.
- Explore who owns the instrument and the data it produces.
- Describe ways to report survey results to different audiences.

Throughout the United States artists find opportunities to display and sell their work. As we noted earlier, ultimately, an artist must take his or her creation out of the studio and place it before the public, and the time will come when you, the instrument designer, will need to not only administer your instrument but share the results of that endeavor as well.

In this chapter we address managing the data obtained by administering an instrument and also reporting the results. We use the term *data management* broadly here to include such processes as organizing and cleaning the data for analysis as well as securing the rights to the data and the instrument itself. *Reporting* covers how information from an analysis can be presented, to whom, and under what conditions. For example, the results from a psychometric instrument might be used by a clinician or treatment team, in conjunction with the client, to develop a treatment plan. The results from administering a job evaluation might be used to determine who receives a pay raise or gets promoted. The results from an organization survey might be used to improve the service delivery or product quality. Although different situations necessitate different types of instruments, which produce quite different information, if you have followed the advice given in these chapters you will have created a good instrument that provides you and other users with information that can be used with confidence in a variety of decision-making situations.

Data Management

Let's say that you have created a questionnaire containing thirty Likert type rating items that you plan to administer to 150 police officers in the local law enforcement office. Now is the time to consider how you are going to manage the 4,500 pieces of data the survey will produce. Data management is important because it is another step in the instrument construction process that can affect the accuracy and trustworthiness of your results. Considerations include entering the data, organizing data for analysis, coding, handling errors, securing the database, and determining who owns the data. Additionally, qualitative and quantitative data will be managed differently in some respects.

The first phase of data management involves organizing the data for analysis. Fortunately, you can use computer programs dedicated to data management or analysis, such as database, statistical, and spreadsheet software. Database software, such as Microsoft Access and IBM's Lotus Approach, have a user-friendly interface and excel at sorting and tabulation, making them suitable for examining qualitative information generated from open-ended items. Data are entered in a table. The column variables, referred to as *fields*, allow you to organize the data into categories, such as text (names, dates, addresses), and numerical values, such as coded responses. Row variables make up a *record;* a record contains all the data about one person, place, or thing. Certain database software, such as Ethnograph, is intended specifically for analyzing narrative information, including interview or focus group transcripts, field notes, diaries, and meeting minutes. These programs can store, categorize, and sort (based on codes that you develop) words, phrases, sentences, and paragraphs, as well as photographs and audio and video files.

Statistical software is dedicated to handling large data sets and conducting quantitative analysis. Database software supports basic calculations, but statistical software is specifically designed to carry out all manner of quantitative data analysis. There are many statistical software applications on the market, of varying prices and complexity. When you purchase the Statistical Package for the Social Sciences (SPSS), Statistical Analysis Software (SAS), or Minitab, you buy a license to use the software for a limited period, and the price may vary depending on the number of modules you purchase or on whether you can buy a student version at reduced cost. Some free statistical software can be downloaded from the Internet (when this book went to print, links to statistical freeware were available at http://statpages.org).

Spreadsheet software lies somewhere in between database and statistical applications, as it is effective for sorting and tabulating and current versions also support both basic and advanced statistical calculations. Early versions were limited in the amount of data that could be entered. Today one of the more commonly used applications, Microsoft Excel, supplies 256 columns and 65,536 rows, for a total of 16,777,216 cells, in one spreadsheet; this should be more than enough data storage space for most users. Most software applications allow you to transfer data; for example, even if you originally entered your data into a spreadsheet, you may be able to import them into database or statistical software for another level of analysis.

Typically, the choice of software is dependent on the user's knowledge and experience, as learning how to use new software applications adds to the time needed to complete data analysis. For studies where you need to generate frequencies, compute descriptive statistics such as means and standard deviations, and plot graphs, spreadsheet software will be more than adequate. If you are interested in exploring the relationship between variables, such as demographic data and ratings, then statistical software may facilitate that level of analysis. If you have a lot of narrative responses, then database software, particularly applications designed for qualitative analysis, should be considered. Regardless of the type of software you use to organize and analyze your data, there are a number of steps you should take to prepare those data for analysis: (1) develop a coding guide, or structure; (2) enter the data; (3) check and clean the data for accuracy; and (4) create a process to safeguard the data.

Develop a Coding Guide

Coding means using a systematic process for entering data for analysis. Depending on your software you may be able to record text directly; the application may be able to treat terms like *male* and *female* as if they were numerical data, counting the frequency of occurrences as well as using them in quantitative analysis. In many cases the item format will facilitate coding; it may be logical to use 1 and 2 to identify dichotomous variables like gender or *yes* or *no* responses. Back in Chapter Seven we noted that you could label response scale alternatives with numbers such as 1, 2, 3, . . . to represent, for example, *strongly disagree, disagree, undecided,* and so forth. These numbers may also be used to code the responses. Or you may have written responses, such as the name of a political party, that you can code with a number, such as 1 = *Democrat,* 2 = *Republican,* 3 = *Independent.* Although you could use an alphabetical coding scheme (A, B, C, and so on), numerical coding facilitates computer analysis of the data, particularly for multi-item scales that produce a true numeric value.

By convention, the number 9 is used in coding to indicate missing data. If an item has more than nine response choices, or values (as a list of job titles might, for example), then the numbers 99 or 999 can be used for this purpose. The number 9 is used, rather than 0, because a questionnaire may use 0 to represent a null value, such as number of children or number of previous arrests. Similarly, the number 7 is used to code a *don't know* response (Welch & Comer, 2001).

You should record your coding system in a codebook, along with any rules or standards you have created for entering data. Judd, Smith, and Kidder (1991) observe that "all too often, researchers fail to maintain an adequate and detailed codebook. As a result, when they attempt to return to a set of data after some interval, perhaps as short as a few days or weeks, they have a difficult time reconstructing what the numbers in the data matrix really mean. Codebooks should therefore be complete and detailed. Further, multiple copies should be made and they should be stored in safe places" (p. 358). Coding can also help you to maintain confidentiality: if all items are coded, including identifying information such as names, e-mail addresses, and telephone numbers, it may be impossible for someone who does not have access to the codebook to identify a participant from the information in the database.

Enter the Data and Check for Accuracy

As little as fifty years ago databases were paper-and-pencil documents and the data were entered and tabulated by hand. Researchers had to wait until the early 1970s before handheld calculators with basic statistical functions were marketed (and believe it or not these early models sold for $100 to $150). You now have a number of ways to enter data into a computer database, including typing data in manually, using optical character recognition (OCR) software to scan the instrument (or its separate answer sheet), and having respondents enter data directly, as they do in completing an electronic survey on the Internet. All three approaches are open to error as you, the respondent, or the optical scanner might enter data incorrectly. And an error rate of only 2 percent for the instrument producing 4,500 bits of data would result in nearly 90 incorrect database entries.

There are several methods available to improve data coding quality. You can spot-check by selecting items at random and comparing the data entered in the database to the data recorded on the paper-and-pencil instrument. You should always visually inspect the data to identify *blatant* errors, such as a

450-year-old respondent, a rating of 9 on a 5-point Likert scale, or a net income of $19,000 a year. Just as you have someone proofread the instrument for spelling and grammatical errors during the pretesting phase, it is helpful to have someone proofread the database for possible errors. If you have guaranteed confidentiality or anonymity, you must first delete all uncoded data that would give a reviewer sufficient information to identify respondents. Aside from names, you might need to delete birthdates, job titles, and addresses, as well as unique identifiers, such as a driver's license number, that taken singularly or in combination might point to a particular individual.

Some computer programs require you to make each entry twice and will not allow you to save the data if the two entries do not coincide. In some software applications you can (or must) first determine validation rules that govern how data can be entered. For example, you can specify that only text, numbers, dates and times, or monetary values can be entered; i9,000 will be rejected if the field requires a numerical value. You can also specify the number of characters, so that you cannot inadvertently enter two numbers in a field that requires only one.

In an ideal world your pretesting will have been so effective that respondent or raters will not make mistakes as they complete the instrument. In the real world you should anticipate such errors as marking multiple items, scratching out responses, and misaligning responses (Figure 15.1). Multiple marking occurs when the respondent or rater makes a selection, changes his or her mind, and then makes another selection but does not cross out the first choice. Scratch outs appear when a respondent crosses out a first choice and marks another; however, the scanner cannot differentiate between the markings and so may not record the response. Misalignment can occur in two ways. At the item level, the response choices may be grouped together so closely that the respondent inadvertently marks more than one alternative. This is more likely to occur when you ask individuals to circle their choice. Misalignments also occur when the respondent or rater does not align an item and his or her selection for that item, a problem most people have experienced when using a separate answer sheet. Once this happens, all subsequent responses will be misaligned (Macey, 1996). This might be evident on a test, where once an answer is out of position on the answer sheet all the others will be misaligned as well. A teacher seeing a pattern of incorrect answers will probably deduce that it is due to misalignment. However, this would not be as obvious in instruments where individuals are providing subjective responses. To a large extent these problems can be minimized during the design and formatting stage of instrument construction. For example, respondents are less likely to misalign responses when items are separated by lines or shading and when item stems and their corresponding response sets are presented on the same page, rather

FIGURE 15.1: EXAMPLES OF DATA ENTRY ERRORS BY RESPONDENTS.

Marking Multiple Items

About when was this building first built?

☐ 1999 to 2000
☒ 1995 to 1998
☐ 1990 to 1994
☒ 1980 to 1989
☐ 1970 to 1979
☐ Prior to 1970

Rewritten Items/Unsolicited Data

How many rooms do you have in this house?

☐ 1 room   ☐ 5 rooms
☐ 2 rooms   ☐ 6 ~~rooms~~ *closets*
☐ 3 rooms   ☐ 7 rooms
☐ 4 rooms   ☐ 8 or more rooms

Which best describes this building?

☐ A mobile home
☐ A one-family attached house
☐ A one-family detached house
☐ A building with 2 apartments
☐ A building with 3 or 4 apartments
☐ A building with 5 to 9 apartments
☐ A building with 10 or more apartments
× *A building with 1 apartment*

Misalignment

Apartments in my neighborhood are affordable (circle one):

Strongly   Disagree   Agree   Strongly
Disagree   Agree

Scratch-out

Write in today's date and then fill in the corresponding ovals.

Day		Month		Year	
0	3	1	0	0	8
1 ○	○	●	○	○	○
2 ○	○	○	○	○	○
3 ○	●	○	○	○	○
4 ○	●	○	○	○	○
5 ○	○	○	○	○	○
6 ○	○	○	○	○	○
7 ○	○	○	○	○	○
8 ○	○	○	○	○	●
9 ○	○	○	○	○	○
0 ●	○	○	●	●	○

Source: These items, but not the errors shown, are taken from the U.S. Census, 2000.

than having the answers on a separate sheet. You can minimize the circling of more than one response alternative by providing sufficient space between the choices.

A related problem is *unsolicited data*—respondents or raters may cross out your item stem and rewrite it to suit their perceptions, or they may write in a response alternative that you have not provided. We discussed this in relation to Instrument 6.A, where the *yes* or *no* options did not fit some of the checklist items, so raters wrote in *NA, not sure,* or *?* Even unsolicited responses, however, may have value. In the case of Instrument 6.A, unsolicited data pointed out flaws in the checklist design that should be corrected. Or consider an organization survey where unsolicited responses reveal problems that might not have surfaced otherwise given the range of questions. Ignoring these responses would result in the loss of meaningful information. One way to handle this situation is to provide a code for unsolicited data when you design the database. For example, if you were using a 5-point response scale ranging from *unsure* to *definitely,* you could code unsolicited responses as 7 and missing data as 9.

Create a Process to Safeguard the Data

After you have administered your instrument and cleaned, checked, and entered the data, you have a responsibility to safeguard the data. Security measures should ensure that only authorized individuals have access to the data and that backup copies exist in case you lose the original data, in a hard drive crash, for example. Your first step should be to ensure that your computer or the database, or both, are password protected. This will limit unauthorized access to all but the most dedicated of computer hackers. Encryption provides another layer of security; encrypted files are transformed into random codes nearly impossible for hackers to break. In addition to encrypting document files, it is also possible to encrypt computer hardware, including the hard drive, and portable media such as a DVD or memory card. Encryption software can be purchased, and some basic versions of encryption software are available free of charge on the Internet.

You should also plan to back up your database file—on removable media (CD, DVD, or flash drive) if the original file is on your computer hard drive, or on your hard drive if the original file is stored on a network server. The advantage of saving data on a network server is that the files are routinely backed up. However, even with electronic safeguards in place, network servers are often the target of hackers. The bottom line when it comes to security is to have two or more copies of your documentation, including data files, on different platforms: hard drive, removable media, and if possible a server. Additionally, files should be encrypted to reduce the possibility that data will be inadvertently shared or even stolen.

Who Owns and Has Access to the Instrument and the Data?

A painting is an original artwork. As long as the artist maintains possession, it belongs solely to him or her; once it has been sold the artist loses all rights to his or her creation and cannot profit from its resale. If you have been the driving force in creating an instrument—the sole developer, perhaps, or the leader of a team of developers—you are probably assuming that the instrument (and the data it produces), like the artist's painting, belongs to you or your team. However, depending on the circumstances under which it was created, this may not be the case. Issues surrounding ownership of an instrument are complex and dependent on a number of factors. We can provide background information; however, you will still need to consider your unique situation.

If you develop an instrument as part of your job duties as an employee of a federal agency, that instrument belongs to the U.S. government. This is typically true for state and local government agencies as well, but rules do vary from state to state and municipality to municipality and must always be checked. When the government agency owns the instrument, your work may be placed in the public domain and shared openly, and no one is required to get your permission to copy and use it. Agencies may do this to meet various objectives, including supporting research and evaluation in the study area and encouraging other researchers to assess instrument reliability and validity.

Conversely, government agencies may limit access to work you have done for them; in which case people who wish to view the study and its instrument must make a request under the Freedom of Information Act. If you develop an instrument using government funding, such as a grant, ownership rights to the instrument and the data will typically be articulated in the agreement between you and the government agency.

If you develop an instrument for your employer, then under current copyright law it will probably be considered a work product and as such it belongs to the organization. Like government agencies, some nonprofit organizations place instruments in the public domain to support research and information dissemination. They may also be required to place an instrument in the public domain when government funds were used to support its development.

Faculty of colleges and universities are encouraged to engage in research as part of their academic development, and publications generated from these activities are often considered during the process of granting tenure. Therefore, faculty have traditionally assumed that because a survey instrument is a product of their original research, it belongs to them and not to the institution. The American Association of University Professors has taken the following position: "It is the prevailing academic practice to treat the faculty member as the copyright owner of works that are created independently and at the faculty member's own initiative for traditional academic purposes" (Springer, 2004).

In recent years, however, universities have profited by retaining ownership of faculty work products. In particular, inventions and discoveries arising from faculty research, such as medications and vaccines, can become a source of revenue for the university. For that reason faculty should learn their institution's policy regarding ownership prior to engaging in research. The picture can become even more cloudy when the research depends on external funding, such as a government agency or private foundation grant, in which case faculty need to develop an agreement that specifies who owns what. Some faculty have established private corporations to manage outside funding, instead of channeling these funds through the university. In this way they can retain certain rights over their work product that they might otherwise have to relinquish to the university.

The following excerpt from the Copyright Policy of the University of Virginia (2004, pp. 1–2), with which the authors are affiliated, shows how one institution of higher learning views ownership of employee work. However, because standards do vary, it is important to learn and comply with the policies and procedures of your particular institution.

> **Work-for-Hire Rule:** The "work-for-hire" rule, defined by the Copyright Act, provides that when an employee produces copyrightable work within the scope of employment, the copyright to that work belongs to the employer and not the author.
>
> **Employee Ownership:** The employee owns the rights to any work created at his or her own initiative and outside the scope, time, and place of employment.
>
> **University Ownership:** By operation of the copyright law, the University owns all rights, title and interest in copyrightable works created by University employees while acting within the scope of their employment. The University cedes copyright ownership to the author(s) of scholarly and academic works (such as journal articles, books and papers) created by academic and research faculty who use generally available University resources. However, the University asserts its right of copyright ownership if significant resources (including sponsor-provided funds) are used in creation of such works and (a) the work generates royalty payments; or (b) the work is of commercial value that can be realized by University marketing efforts.

The same guidelines apply to University of Virginia students. If a student develops an instrument in conjunction with coursework, the instrument is construed to belong to the student. However, if the student develops an instrument as part of work done for the University—developing a survey of graduates while working in the alumni office, for example—that questionnaire belongs to the university. Our guidance to students is to check institutional policy, as it does vary from institution to institution.

In some cases the owner of an instrument (such as you or your organization) may decide to register the copyright. Constructing a multi-item scale requires a significant investment of resources, including pretesting with a large sample to demonstrate reliability and validity. Consequently, you may want or need to recoup development expenses by charging a fee for use. Registering your copyright makes it much easier to take legal action in the event your instrument is used without permission or payment of the fee. It also helps to clarify ownership when you use the instrument in conjunction with a project for a client. For example, if you are a management consultant and use an instrument you developed for a contracted work project, the organization may require ownership of the data as part of the contract, but it cannot take claim to your instrument. Additionally, instrument developers often obtain a copyright when they use their name in the title, such as the Vineland Scale© or Beck Depression Inventory©. Here the ©symbol clearly indicates that the instrument is under copyright and that permission, and perhaps a fee, is required for use.

The copyright process is managed by the U.S. Copyright Office of the Library of Congress. Its Web site (www.copyright.gov) provides a wealth of information to guide you through the process of protecting your work.

Similar issues relate to the data an instrument produces, and as the designer and user of your instrument, you should be prepared to address these concerns. Consider a teacher who is taking a graduate course in research methods and for her class project wants to conduct a survey of teachers in the school division where she works. She obtains permission from the school administration to carry out the project, using her planning period to develop a questionnaire and administer it to faculty at two high schools and three junior high schools, and she agrees to share the study results with the school administration. The introduction to the instrument states that respondents' identities will not be divulged. After completing her project and sharing the findings with school administrators, she is surprised when they request that she submit all of her data to them for analysis. In particular, she is concerned that data items taken in combination might be used to identify respondents, so that her pledge of confidentiality cannot be fulfilled. What should she do?

This scenario raises questions that should be addressed when you begin your project: What are the parameters of the study? And who has ownership of and access to the data? In this case the teacher approached the study as a class project and so assumed that the data belonged to her and not to the graduate school or the school system. However, school administrators pointed out that she carried out the project during her work hours, therefore the data belonged to the school system and not to the teacher.

Clarifying ownership is important for two reasons. First, a changed interpretation of data ownership can cloud or even abrogate a guarantee of confidentiality. Respondents will have much less trust in you personally, your study, and your findings if they believe confidentiality has been breached. Second, if you cannot guarantee the security of the data, it is possible that others can gain access to it and misuse or manipulate the data for their own purposes. For example, they might obtain identifying data, such as social security numbers, and misuse them in fraudulent activities. Data manipulation might involve modifying data. For example, if the school administrators in the previous example found the study results embarrassing to themselves or to the school system, they could conceivably modify the data to obtain different findings.

Although similar to the issue of who owns the instrument, the question of data ownership and access is more complex. Data may be owned by you, your employer, the project funder, or even stakeholders and participants. Some databases change ownership because they are sold; for example, a database of biological specimens might be sold to another research laboratory (Bagby, 2003; Loshin, 2003).

As with the instrument itself, your relationship to stakeholders helps to define data ownership. You may have developed a questionnaire in conjunction with a work-related quality improvement project. In this case your organization retains ownership of the data because it is a work product. The situation is not always as clear when you enter an organization as an independent consultant. Although you are not directly employed by the organization, it is funding the study, and therefore management may feel it has ownership rights. In this case you will need to negotiate an ownership agreement with your client.

Generally, students retain data ownership when the instrument and data are developed to meet a required academic activity. However, this may not be the case if the data result from a research project with external funding that is channeled through the university. Either the funder or the university, or both, may retain ownership rights. Therefore we again recommend that students check their school's policies and procedures.

If you are a college or university faculty member conducting original research, the institution or an external funder, or both, may own the data. In that case you would be serving as the *principal investigator*, with responsibility for collecting, managing, and retaining the data but without ownership rights.

As with your instrument, you can register the copyright for your database to help ensure that these data cannot be shared or used without your permission. Nonetheless, this is controversial in academic settings because, "in academia, there exists an ideal of maintaining public-domain access to data and a strong belief that society benefits from research findings. Current proposals to tighten the controls over databases, therefore, appear antithetical to longstanding academic values" (Bagby, 2003, p. 1).

Closely related to data ownership is the issue of access to (raw) data, which, as we have discussed, may relate to maintaining confidentiality or even anonymity. For this reason it is important to clarify who will have access to the data. One of the authors conducted an employee quality-of-work-life survey in his place of employment, thus the database was considered a work product. It was agreed, however, that management would receive a summary of the findings but would not have access to the completed questionnaires, which could have been used to trace responses back to the respondents. These conditions were documented in the plan for conducting the survey, creating a formal record of the agreement.

At a minimum you should have a written agreement specifying who will have access to data and how participant identity will be protected. Rules for research involving human subjects, as defined in the Code of Federal Regulations (CFR) (Protection of Human Subjects, 2001) and for protection of health information, as defined by the Privacy Rule of the Health Insurance Portability and Accountability Act (HIPAA) of 1996, provide further guidance for securing and disclosing data. For example, the rules for human research require that research be reviewed and approved by an institutional review board (IRB) prior to implementation, and HIPAA describes the data that must be extracted to ensure that an individual cannot be identified by someone who has access to the database but not to participants' identities. If you are conducting a study funded by an agency of the U.S. Department of Health and Human Services (either directly or through another agency, such as a nonprofit foundation obtaining HHS funding) or if you are doing research to fulfill graduate school requirements, one or both of these sets of regulations will apply.

Reporting Your Results

You have developed an instrument to answer one or more questions or to provide information for decision making. Having administered the instrument and collected and analyzed the data, it is time to formulate your findings and share them with others. Like a painter, you are about to exhibit your hard earned results. And like a painter, you may be somewhat apprehensive about how this outcome will be received. In this final section of this chapter, and this book, we examine three aspects of report writing to help you present your findings—identifying your audience; organizing the material, including graphs and tables; and organizing the final report for your intended audience.

Audience

Audiences and their needs vary across situations and settings. You have designed your study and subsequently your instrument to provide information for a specific audience, and now you need to tailor your report for that audience. For example, each of the following audiences or groups of stakeholders will have specific needs in regard to report content and organization:

- Senior management of a for-profit organization
- Officials of a regulatory agency
- Consumers of a human service program
- Representatives of a local government entity, such as members of a school board
- A thesis or dissertation committee
- Your immediate supervisor
- A peer-reviewed professional journal and the journal's target audience
- The funding authority for a financial grant
- Your colleagues and peers
- A member of Congress

For example, busy executives may want a one-page summary highlighting the important facts. Because they must respond to constituent concerns and questions, school board members may want detailed information. Members of a graduate committee will look at how thoroughly each section of the report has been researched and developed and whether research protocols have been followed. Government officials may expect to see data presented in such handy forms as charts, graphs, and summary tables. Consumers may want to see all documentation related to the services provided to them, including scores on assessment instruments and analytical reports created by providers.

In many cases, you will already know your audience's expectations. For example, peer-reviewed journals typically provide submission guidelines that describe the journal's audience, types of papers accepted, and how papers should be formatted. Government agencies and grant administrators also typically provide materials explaining how they want reports organized and presented. If you negotiate a contract to conduct a study, a section of that contract should detail how the results are to be delivered.

When you are unsure about your audience's expectations, try to find out by contacting a stakeholder or other audience member. This is especially important when you are making an oral presentation. Your audience may, for example, be expecting you to provide the exposition and to limit the written material to handouts of summary data in graphic form. That is, knowledge of audience expectations can help you determine what *not* to include as well as what to include in your report.

A related consideration is to identify all who will be receiving your report and whether any recipients have expectations about how the findings will be disseminated. For example, due to the Freedom of Information Act, many documents developed for or by government agencies are placed in the public domain. This means that anyone can request a copy of the report, and increasingly, federal agencies are making reports accessible by posting them on the Internet. Similarly, both federal and state laws make confidential records available to clients, such as recipients of mental health, social, and educational services.

Finally, you need to determine audience expectations or preferences for writing style. For some audiences a relaxed style, with stories and anecdotes to punctuate important concepts, may be appropriate. Other audiences, such as those made up of fellow researchers, will expect more formal and technical language.

Expectations for Documenting Your Instrument Construction Project

The focal point of student activity in the course we teach is the construction of an instrument, which is often related to the student's graduate thesis or dissertation project. We give the students the following outline of our expectations for the development of the instrument and documentation of the instrument construction process:

- Students will design an instrument of their choice, revise it through pretesting, and pilot-test it to obtain data to support assessment of validity and reliability.
- An initial statement of purpose is due by the second session, which the student will continue to revise and refine.
- A rough draft of the instrument is due by the fifth class session. By meeting in small groups, students will receive feedback and begin the process of revising the instrument and planning for its administration.

- Students will present their instrument to the class along with their initial findings. At that time, a formal, written narrative is due addressing the following elements:
  1. Purpose/operational definition—What is the purpose of this instrument? How did you operationally define your questions?
  2. Why did you choose the item format that was selected? What types of data will this produce, and how will you go about summarizing and analyzing the data?
  3. Describe the activities used to pretest the instrument and to demonstrate validity. Specifically, how did you go about establishing each type of validity for your instrument?
     Face
     Content
     Criterion
     Construct
     Cultural
  4. Describe the activities used to pretest the instrument and to demonstrate reliability. Which type of reliability applies to your instrument, and what approach did you take to make that assessment?
     Internal consistency
     Test-retest
     Interrater
  5. Describe how you have addressed each of the following characteristics of measurement:
     Situation (implementation in a natural versus artificial setting)
     Respondent (mode of administration)
     Object of measurement
     Recording form (if applicable)
  6. Describe issues related to administration, data collection, and data management.

Organization and Presentation of Results

There are a number of meaningful, useful, and simple ways to report data produced by instruments. The usual approach is to report the frequency or the percentage, or both, of responses to each item selection. The advantage of using percentages is that this approach enables comparisons between groups of different sizes. For example, if a college professor teaches two sections of the same course with a different number of students in each section, reporting responses on an instructor evaluation as percentages will allow the professor to make quick comparisons. If some respondents do not complete a particular item, that information should be conveyed as well.

You can use tables and graphs to organize and succinctly display information. The following table is an organized summary of responses to the question of textbook readability. With such a table, you have a method of expressing your results in a manner that is descriptive, is easily understood, and facilitates comparisons.

EXAMPLE

Table 1: Responses to Item 1: "Circle the number that best describes the readability of this textbook."

Item Alternative	Frequency	Percentage
Very difficult to read	23	26%
Difficult to read	29	33%
About average to read	16	18%
Easy to read	7	8%
Very easy to read	9	11%
Not responding	3	4%
Total	87	100%

Frequency data may also be presented with other relevant data, such as the response rate by gender, age, or educational status.

EXAMPLE

Table 1: Responses to Item 1: "Circle the number that best describes the readability of this textbook."

Item Alternative	Frequency	Male	Female
Very difficult to read	23	12	11
Difficult to read	29	14	15
About average to read	16	9	7
Easy to read	7	3	4
Very easy to read	9	3	6
Not responding	3	3	0
Total	87	44	43

Follow these guidelines to make tables readable and easily understood:

- Make sure each table has a title that clearly describes the table content and purpose. If a table is constructed for each item, as in the previous examples, supply the item number and the item stem so the reader can quickly relate each alternative's frequency to the correct stem. Order the tables in logical way. If you are going to present a table of responses for each item, it makes sense to arrange the tables in the same sequence used for the items. However, if the instrument is composed of subscales, it may make more sense to cluster the items and tables of responses in the order in which they appear in the subscale.

- Label columns and rows clearly. Notice in the previous examples that each column has a heading. Notice also that the headings are printed in bold type to set them off from the data contained in the table body.
- Use borders and gridlines as needed to differentiate information. Gridlines are useful for visually separating data and are recommended when the table has a lot of rows and columns or if you need to print the table using a small typeface.
- Present information in a consistent form across all cells in a single category (for example, do not use numerals in some cells and words in others; for example, do not use the number "2" in one cell and the word *two* in another).
- Limit the use of decimal places. For clarity, percentages are often rounded to the nearest whole number. If decimals are used, taking them to one and no more than two places will do. Avoid confusing decimals, such as reporting that "23.67 respondents rated an item 'very difficult to read."
- Order the data in a logical way. In the previous examples, the response alternatives flow from *very difficult* to *very easy* as on the original answer scale. The data thus vary with the alternative. However, when reporting on items making use of rank order, you should list the alternatives by frequency of selection, which may not be the order in which they appeared on the instrument:

EXAMPLE (QUESTION)

2. Rank the following based on the way you typically obtain the news.
————Network television station
————Cable television station
————AM radio
————Internet news site
————Other

EXAMPLE (REPORT)

Table 2: Responses to Item 2: "Rank the following based on the way you typically obtain the news."

Alternative	Ranking	Responses
Internet news site	1	106
Network television station	2	84
Cable television station	3	78
FM radio	4	46
AM radio	5	15
Other	6	3

Care should also be taken in collating and transposing your data, as that is where many errors occur. For example, errors may occur in transposing a score from the instrument to a tally sheet or a computer spreadsheet and again when transposing the aggregate data from your spreadsheet to a table. It is important therefore to double-check your work or have another person proofread the data to reduce data input errors.

Data may also be displayed in the form of graphs. When properly constructed, these visual displays can convey a great deal of information concisely. When making a graph, you should first compile the data in the form of a table. Most computer word processing and spreadsheet software will convert data in the table into any number of graphic formats, such as a pie chart, bar graph, or line graph. Color or shading can differentiate graphical data for quick and easy visual comparisons. As with tables, it is important to label graphs and to provide sufficient information for the viewer to easily read and discriminate information. For example, in the following graph, lines and shading distinguish male and female responses. Every other bar is labeled with the corresponding item alternative. And a legend in the upper-right-hand corner explains which degree of shading refers to which gender.

EXAMPLE

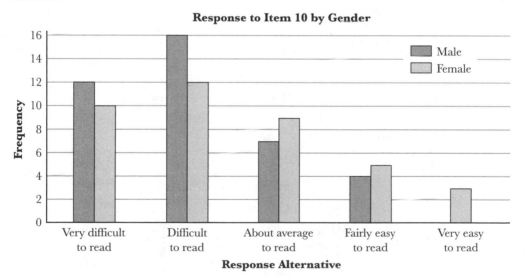

Like the data produced from rating scales, data produced by alternative response sets are suited to frequency tables (reporting data as percentages) and histograms. The following example shows a question and two analyses of the responses.

EXAMPLE (QUESTION)

3. What is your current annual income? Check one of the following income ranges:

- ❑ Less than $15,000
- ❑ $15,001–$20,000
- ❑ $20,001–$25,000
- ❑ $25,001–$30,000
- ❑ $30,001–$35,000
- ❑ $35,001–$40,000
- ❑ $40,001–$45,000
- ❑ More than $45,001

EXAMPLES (RESPONSES)

Table 3: Responses to Item 3: "What is your current annual income?"

Amount	Frequency	Percentage
Less than $15,000	23	12%
$15,001–$20,000	28	15%
$20,001–$25,000	31	17%
$25,001–$30,000	37	20%
$30,001–$35,000	30	16%
$35,001–$40,000	19	10%
$40,001–$45,000	10	6%
More than $45,001	8	4%
Total	186	

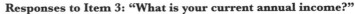

Responses to Item 3: "What is your current annual income?"

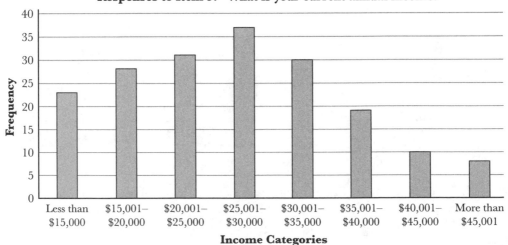

As we have noted throughout this book, a major challenge is ensuring that your instrument is producing valid and reliable results. A number of factors outside your purview as instrument designer can influence the information you obtain. For example, you have no control over the mood of respondents or raters at the time they are completing the instrument, and that mood may influence how they respond to a particular item or the entire instrument. An individual who has had a stressful day at work may be in no mood to complete your marketing survey or respond to your political poll. Conversely, an individual responding to your marketing survey may feel uncomfortable rating products adversely and so may tend to rate most items positively. For this reason, even though you have conducted pretesting to minimize other factors, it is important when analyzing and presenting your data to understand and appreciate the context in which those data were obtained. Any limitations you observe should be shared in your presentation; for example, you might need to discuss factors that might have influenced the data represented in graphs and tables.

Organization of the Final Report

Whether a one-page summary or a two-hundred-page tome, the report, like the instrument, should have a coherent organization. However, the organization of the report may vary slightly based on the target audience and its expectations.

Research Papers and Journal Articles. The purpose of a research paper is to add to the body of knowledge about a specific topic or situation. The paper should demonstrate what is known about the subject, typically through a literature review, and discuss how that existing knowledge helped to focus the study. Returning to our discussion in the first chapter, the social sciences are scientific because their processes are systematic. It should be possible for another researcher to follow your methodology, to determine if the actions or interventions produce similar results under similar conditions. Consequently, a research paper includes a section about methodology, where you would describe the instrument development and administration. The heart of the paper is the presentation of the findings and the discussion of what the findings may mean. By convention, research papers are organized into seven sections (Judd et al., 1991, p. 454):

1. Introduction, which explains the purpose of the research and the problem you are investigating.
2. Methods section, which describes the procedures you used to measure and collect data. This is the section of the paper where you describe how you

constructed your instrument, pretested it, and produced evidence of validity and reliability, and how you addressed administration issues.

3. Results section, which describes your findings. If you summarize findings with tables and graphs, they may be included in this section or placed at the end of the paper as an appendix.

4. Discussion section, which describes your interpretation of the findings and the implications for the problem or topic under investigation.

5. Summary, which brings the study to a conclusion.

6. References, which list all sources used in the study.

7. Appendix, which includes copies of any instruments you used to support the research.

Journal articles tend to follow the same sequence as research papers, although individual journal preferences vary somewhat. Typically, the article begins with an abstract, a brief summary of the article. The introduction provides background information about the topic of study. This is followed by a description of the project, which may include information about methodology. In some journals, the results and discussion sections are combined. This is followed by a conclusion, typically just a few paragraphs in length. The primary difference between journal articles and research papers is depth and length, as most journals limit the number of pages or words they will accept.

Formal Reports. Depending on your audience, a formal report may not need all the elements found in a research paper. For example, if you have conducted a study for an organization whose managers are interested primarily in the findings, you will probably keep the methodology section short. Also, although you will want to include an introduction, explaining why the study was carried out, you probably will not need a literature review.

Because the focus of a formal report is usually on the findings, these documents often rely heavily on tables, charts, and graphs. For example, we recently saw a report describing personnel activities such as turnover, use of annual leave, and grievances in a large state agency. Each section featured a brief, one to two-page summary, which was then followed by ten to twenty pages of graphs and charts.

A formal report may or may not include a section discussing the *implications* of the study. This is similar to the discussion section of a research paper. Its purpose is to describe to stakeholders possible consequences if action is not taken in response to the findings. For example, data on the number of employee grievances filed may imply the need to address issues related to staff morale and workplace conditions.

If the purpose of the report is solely to inform, then it should not include *recommendations* because the assumption is that stakeholders will decide how to use the findings. You determine whether or not to include recommendations through your analysis of audience expectations. These expectations may be described in any directions you receive for preparing the report, in the guidelines attached to a financial grant, for example, or in a study contract. To summarize, a formal report may include the following sections:

1. Introduction, which offers a brief (one- to three-page) explanation of the purpose of the study and report.
2. Findings, which may include charts, graphs, and illustrations. This section may be primarily narrative with supporting graphics or, conversely, primarily graphical with a limited narrative.
3. Implications (optional).
4. Recommendations (optional).
5. Summary (one to three paragraphs).
6. Appendices, which include a copy of the questionnaire(s) used to gather information.

Executive Summaries. Even though you may have gone to considerable time and effort to study a topic, including constructing, administering, and analyzing a survey, your audience may want only a brief summary of your findings. You have painted a masterpiece, and your audience wants a photographic reproduction!

An executive summary is a brief (one- to two-page) document summarizing your findings. The introduction is usually limited to a few lines or a paragraph. The findings are often presented as a numbered or bulleted list of the main points or concepts. Graphics are rarely used, as they may distract from the concise narrative.

An executive summary is usually prepared in addition to a formal report, so that readers have the choice of reviewing the summary for an overview or examining the report itself for detailed information.

Case Studies. The term *case study* describes a methodology as well as a way of organizing and reporting your findings. From a research perspective, a case study is "an empirical inquiry, that investigates a contemporary phenomenon within its real-life context; when the boundaries between the phenomenon and context are not clearly evident; and multiple resources of evidence are used" (Yin, 1989, p. 23). The book *All the President's Men*, by *Washington Post* reporters Bob Woodward and Carl Bernstein, is an example of a case study, one that examines in great depth the Watergate conspiracy and cover-up (Yin, 1989).

Case studies tend to be more expository in structure than research papers or formal reports. In essence, they tell a story—describing the situation, what happened, and what the information may mean in a larger context. Some case studies are organized around comparisons, such as a comparison of what theory suggested should have happened and of what was actually observed. Consequently, the report might be written like a mystery, with the findings being gradually revealed and a case built up to support or refute the hypothesis. Case studies are also organized chronologically, so that the reader can follow an event, such as the Watergate conspiracy, from onset to resolution. When you are interested in obtaining alternative opinions and interpretations of events, the case study is one good way to present opposing viewpoints. Nonetheless, although case studies provide an opportunity for compelling narrative, they must still be based on thoughtful information gathering and analysis.

Client Observations. Many instruments are developed and used to observe an individual, such as a student, patient, or social services consumer. In these situations you may be expected to use a specific formal outline for documenting the results of client observations and measurements. Documentation of a psychological evaluation, for example, typically includes a brief statement describing why the individual was referred for treatment and the presenting problems, results of diagnostic assessment, conclusions, and treatment recommendations. In the section describing diagnostic assessment the clinician should identify any psychometric instruments administered, such as an IQ test, depression inventory, or mental health screening questionnaire, and report the results obtained. If the instruments used are not attached to the report, they should be filed in the client's record, where providers and the client have access to it.

Oral Presentations. In addition to or instead of a written report, your audience may expect an oral presentation of your findings. Your presentation should be organized, and like a written report, it should have an introduction, an explanation of the way you collected your data, and a presentation of your findings. Depending on audience expectations, you might include implications and recommendations as well. For example, if you conduct an evaluation for a school board on the effectiveness of educational materials, board members are likely to expect some recommendations about items to continue or discontinue using.

Compared to the readers of a written report, those listening to an oral presentation have a highly limited amount of time to take in your information. Public speakers use a number of approaches to focus the audience's attention. For example, they incorporate stories, anecdotes, or humor into the presentation. They employ visual aides, such as slides and overheads. Finally, they take advantage of computer technology, using slide show software, animation, and sound effects. If you know that you will be making an oral presentation, you will probably benefit from reading among the many books and articles available on public speaking and using visual aids.

Summary

In this chapter we have presented information to help you effectively manage the data obtained from administering your instrument, and we have provided recommendations for reporting the results of your findings. By now you realize that instrument construction is a thoughtful process that requires a considerable amount of time to develop and implement. Although there may be a few artists who can literally throw paint onto a canvas, most painters engage in a deliberate process that involves planning, testing ideas, and mastering techniques. We suggest emulating them. By following the guidelines we have presented in this book, you should be able to design an effective instrument, which will produce meaningful information for you and other stakeholders.

Key Concepts and Terms

case study	database	research paper
coding guide	executive summary	scratch out
copyright	formal report	spreadsheet software
data access	misalignment	statistical software
data management	public domain	unsolicited data
data ownership	report organization	work for hire

REFERENCES

Achenbach, T. M. (1991). *Manual for the Youth Self-Report and 1991 Profile*. Burlington: University of Vermont.

Aday, L. A., & Cornelius, L. J. (2006). *Designing and conducting health surveys: A comprehensive guide*. San Francisco: Jossey-Bass.

Aiken, L. R., Jr. (1975). Procedures and problems in designing a college course evaluation and questionnaire. *College and University, 50,* 247–253.

Albanese, R. (1981). *Managing toward accountability for performance*. Homewood, IL: Irwin.

Albanese, M., Prucha, C., Barnet, J. H., & Gjerde, C. L. (1997). The effect of right or left placement of the positive response on Likert-type scales used by medical students for rating instruction. *Academy of Medicine, 72*(7), 627–630.

American Statistical Association. (1997). *What is a survey?* Alexandria, VA: Author.

Amin, Z. (2000). Q methodology: A journey into the subjectivity of human mind. *Singapore Medical Journal, 42,* 410–414.

Amoo, T., & Friedman, H. H. (2001, February 26). Do numeric values influence subjects' responses to rating scales? *Journal of International Marketing and Marketing Research.* Retrieved May 10, 2006, from http://academic.brooklyn.cuny.edu/economic/friedman/numeric.htm.

Associated Press. (1999, August 19). Caltech tops best college list. *CNN.com.* Retrieved August 22, 1999, from http://www.cnn.com/US/9908/20/college.rankings.01.

Babbie, E. (1990). *Survey research methods*. Belmont, CA: Wadsworth.

Bagby, J. (2003). Who owns the data? *Research Penn State, 24*(1). Retrieved March 2, 2005, from http://www.rps.psy.edu/0301/data.html.

Baker, F. (2001). *The basics of item response theory*. College Park, MD: ERIC Clearinghouse on Assessment and Evaluation. Retrieved May 4, 2006, from http://edres.org/irt.

Barnette, J. J. (1999, April 23). *Likert response alternative direction: SA to SD or SD to SA: Does it make a difference?* Paper presented at the annual meeting of the American Educational Research Association, Montreal, Quebec.

Barnette, J. J. (2001). Likert survey primacy effect in the absence or presence of negatively-worded items. *Research in the Schools, 8*(1), 77–82.

Bayer, A. E. (1973). Construction of a race item for survey research. *Public Opinion Quarterly, 36*(4), 592–602.

Bellak, L., & Bellak, S. (1993). *Children's Apperception Test (CAT).* Lutz, FL: Psychological Assessment Resources, Inc.

Belson, W. A. (1981). *The design and understanding of survey questions.* Aldershot, Hants, UK: Gower.

Berelson, B. (1954). Content analysis. In G. Lindzey (Ed.), *Handbook of social psychology* (pp. 488–518). Reading, MA: Addison-Wesley.

Biographical Dictionary of Management. (2001). Retrieved September 5, 2001, from http://www.thoemmes.com/dictionaries/bdm_likert.htm.

Bogen, K. (1996). The effect of questionnaire length and response rates: A review of the literature. In *Proceedings of the Section on Survey Research Methods, American Statistical Association.* Retrieved March 30, 2004, from http://www.census.gov/srd/papers/pdf/kb9601.pdf.

Brennan, M. (1997). The effect of question tone on responses to open-ended questions. *Marketing Bulletin, 8,* 66–72.

Brennan, M., & Esslemont, D. (1998). The accuracy of the Juster Scale for predicting purchase rates of branded, fast-moving consumer goods. *Marketing Bulletin, 5,* 47–52.

Brown, S. R. (1991). *A Q methodological tutorial.* Retrieved March 1, 2006, from http://www.facstaff.uww.edu/cottlec/QArchive/primer1.html.

Buckingham, M., & Coffman, C. (1999). *Gallup's discoveries about great managers and great workplaces.* Retrieved April 3, 2001, from www.gallup.com.

Buros Institute of Mental Measurements. (2007). Web site. Retrieved March 21, 2007, from http://www.unl.edu/buros/bimm/html/subburos.html.

Cardillo, J. E., & Choate, R. O. (1994). Illustrations of goal setting. In T. J. Kiresuk, A. Smith, & J. E. Cardillo (Eds.), *Goal attainment scaling: Applications, theory, and measurement* (pp. 39–60). Mahwah, NJ: Erlbaum.

Carroll, J.F.X., & McGinley, J. J. (2000). *Mental Health Screening Form-III.* Tampa, FL: Project Return Foundation.

Centers for Disease Control and Prevention. (2006). *Taking part in research studies: What questions should you ask?* Retrieved December 15, 2006, from http://www.cdc.gov/hiv/pubs/brochure/unc3bro.htm.

Chan, J. (1991). Response-order effects in Likert type scales. *Educational and Psychological Measurement, 51*(3), 531–540.

Chelimsky, E. (2007). Factors influencing the choice of methods in federal evaluation practice. *New Directions for Evaluation, 113*(Spring), 13–33.

Childers, T. L., & Ferrell, O. C. (1979). Response rate and perceived questionnaire length in mail surveys. *Journal of Marketing Research, 16,* 429–431.

Coens, T., & Jenkins, M. (2000). *Abolishing performance appraisals: Why they backfire and what to do instead.* San Francisco: Berrett-Koehler.

Cohen, J. (1960). A coefficient of agreement for nominal scales. *Educational and Psychological Measurement, 20*(1), 37–46.

Colton, D. (2003). *Child and adolescent inpatient behavioral rating scale.* Retrieved November 20, 2005, from http://www.ccca.dmhmrsas.virginia.gov/links.htm.

Colton, D. (2004). *Checklist for assessing your organization's readiness for reducing seclusion and restraint.* Retrieved November 20, 2005, from http://www.ccca.dmhmrsas.virginia.gov/links.htm.

Colton, D. (2005). Instrument for assessing behavioral change. *Residential Group Care Quarterly, 5*(4), 1–4.

Crowne, D. P., & Marlowe, D. (1960). A new scale of social desirability independent of psychopathology. *Journal of Consulting Psychology, 24*(4), 349–354.

Czaja, R. (1998). Questionnaire pretesting comes of age. *Marketing Bulletin, 9,* 52–66.

Dahlberg, L. L., Toal, S. B., & Behrens, C. B. (Eds.). (1998). *Measuring violence-related attitudes, beliefs, and behaviors among youths: A compendium of assessment tools.* Atlanta, GA: Centers for Disease Control and Prevention, National Center for Injury Prevention and Control, Division of Violence Prevention.

DeCoster, J. (1998). *Overview of factor analysis.* Retrieved May 3, 2006, from http://www.stat-help.com/notes.html.

DeMaio, T. J., Rothgeb, J., & Hess, J. (1998). Improving survey quality through pretesting. In *Proceedings of the Survey Research Methods Section, American Statistical Association* (pp. 50–58). Alexandria, VA: American Statistical Association.

Derogatis, L. (1992). *Derogatis Psychiatric Rating Scale.* Minnetonka, MN: NCS Assessments.

DeVellis, R. F. (1991). *Scale development: Theory and applications.* Thousand Oaks, CA: Sage.

Dillman, D. A. (2000). *Mail and Internet surveys.* Thousand Oaks, CA: Sage.

Dillman, D. A., Smyth, J. D., Christian, L. M., & Stern, M. J. (2004). *Multiple answer questions in self-administered surveys: The use of check-all-that-apply and forced-choice question formats.* Retrieved May 23, 2006, from http://www.sesrc.wsu.edu/dillman/papers/Check%20all%20Draft%20_final%20revision_.pdf.

Dillman, D. A., Tortora, R. D., & Bowker, D. (1998). *Principles for constructing Web surveys* (SESRC Technical Report 98–50). Pullman: Washington State University, Social and Economic Sciences Research Center.

Dommeyer, C. J., Baum, P., & Hanna, R. W. (2002). College students' attitudes towards methods of collecting teaching evaluations: In-class versus on-line. *Journal of Education for Business, 78*(1), 11–15.

Donaldson, G. W., Moinpour, C. M., Bush, N. E., Chapko, M., Jocom, J., Siadak, M., et al. (1999). Physician participation in research surveys: A randomized study of inducements to return mailed research questionnaires. *Evaluation and the Health Professions, 22*(4), 427–441.

Emmerson, G. J., & Neely, M. A. (1988). Two adaptable, valid, and reliable data-collection measures: Goal attainment scaling and the semantic differential. *Counseling Psychologist, 16*(2), 261–271.

Employees respond. (1999, March). *Commonwealth Currents, 5,* 2–3.

Evaland, V. B., & Sekely, W. S. (2005). *Effect of response position and number of responses on response selection.* Retrieved July 26, 2005, from http://www.westga.edu/~bquest/2001.response.htm.

Exner, J. E., & Weiner, I. B. (1994). *The Rorschach: A comprehensive system* (2nd ed.). (Vol. 3). Hoboken, NJ: Wiley.

Fink, A. (1995). *How to ask survey questions.* Thousand Oaks, CA: Sage.

Flamm, B. (2004). The Columbia University 'miracle' study: Flawed and fraud. *Skeptical Inquirer, 28*(5). Retrieved June 28, 2005, from http://www.csicop.org/si/2004–09/miracle-study.html.

Foddy, W. (1993). *Constructing questions for interviews and questionnaires* (rpt. ed.). New York: Cambridge University Press.

Fowler, F. J., Jr. (1988). *Survey research methods.* Thousand Oaks, CA: Sage.

Fowler, F. J., Jr. (1995). *Improving survey questions.* Thousand Oaks, CA: Sage.

Fraser, S. (Ed.). (1995). *The bell curve wars: Race, intelligence, and the future of America.* New York: Perseus.

Freedman, W. L., & Turner, M. S. (2003). Cosmology in the new millennium. *Sky and Telescope, 16*(4), 30–41.

Friedman, H. H., & Friedman L. (1994). A comparison of vertical and horizontal rating scales. *Mid-Atlantic Journal of Business, 30,* 107–111.

Fricker, R. D. Jr., & Schonlau, M. (2002). *Advantages and disadvantages of Internet research surveys: Evidence from the literature.* Santa Monica, CA: Rand.

Garland, R. (1990). A comparison of three forms of the semantic differential. *Marketing Bulletin, 1,* 19–24. Available at http://marketing-bulletin.massey.ac.nz/author.asp?aid=30.

Gendall, P. (1994). If the answer was "people who have AIDS get much less sympathy than they deserve," what was the question? *Marketing Bulletin, 5,* 1–12.

Gendall, P. (1998). A framework for questionnaire design: Labaw revisited. *Marketing Bulletin, 9,* 28–39.

Gendall, P., & Hoek, J. (1990). A question of wording. *Marketing Bulletin, 1,* 25–36.

Gendall, P., Menelaou, H., & Brennan, M. (1996). Open-ended questions: Some implications for mail survey research. *Marketing Bulletin, 7,* 1–8.

Gerber, E. R., & Wellens, T. R. (1995). Literacy and the self-administered form in special populations: A primer. In *Proceedings of the Survey Research Methods Section, American Statistical Association* (pp. 1087–1092). Alexandria, VA: American Statistical Association.

Goodlatte, R. (1998). Results of the 1998 congressional questionnaire (Congressional Report). Washington, DC: U.S. House of Representatives.

Goodlatte, R. (2000). *Congressional report.* Washington, DC: U.S. House of Representatives.

Green, R. G., Murphy, K. D., & Snyder, S. M. (2000). Should demographics be placed at the end or the beginning of mailed questionnaires? An empirical answer to a persistent methodological question. *Social Work Research, 24*(4), 237–241.

Grisso, T., & Underwood, L. A. (2004). *Screening and assessing mental health and substance abuse disorders among youth in the juvenile justice system.* Washington, DC: U.S. Department of Justice, National Center for Mental Health and Juvenile Justice.

Gritching, W. (1986). Public opinion versus policy advice. *Australian Psychologist, 34,* 33–39.

Grudens-Schuck, N., & Kramer, B. (2000, March 1–2). *A primer on Q methodology.* Ames, IA: Iowa State University. Retrieved November 15, 2004, from http://ageds.iastate.edu/personne/nancy/qprimer.htm.

Hambleton, R., & Rodgers, J. (1995). Item bias review. *Practical Assessment, Research and Evaluation, 4*(6). Retrieved April 19, 2007, from http://pareonline.net/getvn.asp?v=4&n=6.

Heacock, H., Koehoorn, M., & Tan, J. (1997). Applying epidemiological principles to ergonomics: A checklist for incorporating sound design and interpretation of studies. *Applied Ergonomics, 28*(3), 165–172.

Henerson, M. E., Morris, L. L., & Fitz-Gibbon, C. T. (1987). *How to measure attitudes.* Thousand Oaks, CA: Sage.

Hernstein, R. J., & Murray, C. (1995). *The bell curve: Intelligence and class structure in American life.* New York: Simon & Schuster.

Hinds, P. S., Schum, L., & Srivastava, D. K. (2004). Is clinical relevance sometimes lost in summative scores? *Western Journal of Nursing Research, 24*(4), 345–353.

Hockney, D. (2001). *Secret knowledge: Rediscovering the lost techniques of the old masters*. Corvallis, OR: Studio Books.

Hodges, K. (1996). *CAFAS self-training manual*. Ann Arbor, MI: Child & Adolescent Functional Assessment Scale.

Hossini, J. C., & Armacost, R. L. (1993). Gathering sensitive data in organizations. In P. Rosenfeld, J. E. Edwards, & M. D. Thomas (Eds.), *Improving organizational surveys*, 29–57.

Johnson, T. P., & Fendrich, M. (2002). *A validation of the Crowne-Marlowe Social Desirability Scale*. Retrieved September 15, 2005, from http://www.srl.uic.edu/publist/Conference/crownemarlowe.pdf.

Joinson, A. (1999). Social desirability, anonymity and Internet-based questionnaires. *Behavioral Research Methods, Instruments, and Computers, 31*(3), 433–438.

Judd, C. M., Smith, E. R., & Kidder, L. H. (1991). *Research methods in social relations*. Austin, TX: Holt, Rinehart and Winston.

Kaczmarek, T. L., Hagan, M. P., & Kettler, R. J. (2006). Screening for suicide among juvenile delinquents: Reliability and validity evidence for the Suicide Screening Inventory (SSI). *International Journal of Offender Therapy and Comparative Criminology, 50*(2), 204–217.

Kane, R. L. (1997). *Understanding health care outcomes research*. Gaithersburg, MD: Aspen.

Kanji, G. K., & Asher, M. (1996). *100 methods for total quality management*. Thousand Oaks, CA: Sage.

Kazdin, A. E. (1982). *Single-case research designs*. New York: Oxford University Press.

Kazdin, A. E. (1998). *Research design in clinical psychology* (3rd ed.). Boston: Allyn & Bacon.

Kerlinger, F. N., & Lee, H. B. (1999). *Foundations of behavioral research*. Belmont, CA: Wadsworth.

Kirkhart, K. E. (1995). Seeking multicultural validity: A postcard from the road. *Evaluation Practice, 16*(1), 1–9.

Knäer, B., Schwarz, N., & Fritsch, A. (2006). *The perils of interpreting cohort differences in attitude reports: Question order effects decrease with age*. Retrieved May 28, 2006, from http://www.isr.umich.edu/src/smp/Electronic%20Copies/117.pdf.

Kohn, A. (1999). *The schools our children deserve*. Boston: Houghton Mifflin.

Krathwohl, D. R. (1988). *How to prepare a research proposal* (3rd ed.). Syracuse, NY: Syracuse University Press.

Kroenke, D. M. (1984). *Business computer systems: An introduction*. Santa Cruz, CA: Mitchell.

Krosnick, J. A., Holbrook, A. L., Berent, M. K., Carson, R. T., Hanemann, W. M., Kopp, R. J., et al. (2002). The impact of "no opinion" response options on data quality. *Public Opinion Quarterly, 66*, 371–403.

Lakoff, G. (2004). *Don't think of an elephant: Know your values and frame the debate—The essential guide for progressives*. White River Junction., VT: Chelsea Green.

Likert, R. (1932, June). A technique for the measurement of attitudes. *Archives of Psychology*, pp. 5–55.

Lincoln, Y. S., & Guba, E. G. (1985). *Naturalistic inquiry*. Thousand Oaks, CA: Sage.

Loshin, D. (2003, March). Knowledge integrity: Who owns the data? *DM Review*. Retrieved September 6, 2005, from http://www.dmreview.com/editorial/dmreview/print_action.cfm?articleId=6389.

Lutz, W. J. (2006). *Discover the researcher in you: A guide to understanding and using research*. Columbus: Ohio Department of Mental Health.

Lyons, J. S. (1998). *Acuity of Psychiatric Illness Scale: Child and Adolescent Version*. San Antonio, TX: The Psychological Corporation, Harcourt Brace Jovanovich

Macey, W. H. (1996). Dealing with data collection, processing, and analysis. In A. I. Kraut (Ed.), *Organizational surveys: Tools for assessment and change* (pp. 204–232). San Francisco: Jossey-Bass.

Marsh, H. W. (1986). Negative item bias in rating scales for preadolescent children: A cognitive-developmental phenomenon. *Developmental Psychology, 22*(1), 37–49.

Martin, E., DeMaio, T. J., & Campanelli, P. C. (1990). Context effects for census measures of race and Hispanic origin. *Public Opinion Quarterly, 54*(4), 551–566.

Martin, L. L. (1993). *Total quality management in human service organizations.* Thousand Oaks, CA: Sage.

Matell, M. S., & Jacoby, J. (1971). Is there an optional number of alternatives for Likert scale items? Study 1: Reliability and validity. *Educational and Psychological Measurement, 31,* 657–674.

McCall, W. (2004). *Learn while dreaming.* Retrieved January 21, 2004, from http://abcnews/go.com/sections/Living/WorldNewsTonight/sleep_creativity_040121–3.html.

McLaughlin, C. P., & Kaluzny, A. D. (1994). Defining total quality management/continuous quality improvement. In C. P. McLaughlin & A. D. Kaluzny (Eds.), *Continuous quality improvement in health care: Theory, implementation, and applications* (pp. 3–10). Gaithersburg, MD: Aspen.

McLean Hospital. (1999). *BASIS-32: Behavior and Symptom Identification Scale.* Belmont, MA: Author.

Miller, G. A. (1956). The magical number seven, plus or minus two: Some limits on our capacity for processing information. *Psychological Review, 63,* 81–97.

Mindel, C., & Dangel, R. (1998). *Goal attainment scales.* United Way of Metropolitan Dallas Outcomes Evaluation Web site. Retrieved November 22, 1998, from http://www.the2professors.com/measurement/sld008htm.

Montagu, A. (1984). *Science and creationism.* New York: Oxford University Press.

Mooney, G. M., & Carlson, B. L. (1996). *Reducing mode effects in "mark all that apply" questions.* Retrieved May 23, 2006, from http://www.amstat.org/sections/SRMS/Proceedings/papers/1996_105.pdf.

Mullen, B., Futrell, D., Stairs, D., Tice, D. M., Dawson, K. E., Riordan, C.A. et al. (1986). Newscasters' facial expressions and voting behavior of viewers: Can a smile elect a president? *Journal of Personality and Social Psychology. 51,* 291–295.

Munn, N. L. (1966). *Psychology: The fundamentals of human adjustment.* Boston: Houghton Mifflin Co.

Munshi, J. (1990). *A method for constructing Likert scales.* Retrieved October 3, 2001, from http://munshi.sonoma.edu/working/likert.html.

National Alliance on Mental Illness. (2006). *Protection of research volunteers.* Retrieved March 17, 2007, from http://www.nami.org/Content/NavigationMenu/Inform_Yourself/About_Research/Protection_of_Research_Volunteers.htm.

Newport, F. (2004). *Polling matters: Why leaders must listen to the wisdom of the people.* New York: Warner Books.

O'Muircheartaigh, C., Krosnick, J. A., & Helic, A. (2000). *Middle alternatives, acquiescence, and the quality of questionnaire data.* Retrieved March 28, 2006, from http://www.harrisschool.uchicago.edu/faculty/web-pages/colm-omuircheartaigh.asp.

Odom, J. G. (1979, April 8–12). *Validation of techniques utilized to maximize survey response rates.* Paper presented at the annual meeting of the American Educational Research Association, San Francisco.

Office of the Governor, Commonwealth of Virginia. (1998, August 10). *Virginia State Employee Survey and cover letter*. Richmond, VA: Author.

Osgood, C. E., Suci, G. J., & Tannenbaum, P. (1967). *The measurement of meaning*. Champaign: University of Illinois Press.

Overall, J. E., & Pfefferbaum, B. (1998). *Brief Psychiatric Rating Scale for Children*. Sarasota, FL: Professional Resource Exchange.

Palmer, G. L. (1943). Factors in the variability of response in enumeration studies. *Journal of the American Statistical Association, 38*, 143–152.

Paterson, D., & Tinker, M. (1940). *How to make type readable: A manual for typographers, printers and advertisers*. London: Harper & Brothers.

Patton, M. Q. (1990). *Qualitative evaluation and research methods*. Thousand Oaks, CA: Sage.

Porter, T. M. (1986). *The rise of statistical thinking, 1820–1900*. Princeton, NJ: Princeton University Press.

Presser, S., & Schuman, H. (1978). *The measurement of a middle position in attitude surveys*. Retrieved March 21, 2006, from http://www.amstat.org/sections/SRMS/proceedings/papers/1978_008.pdf.

Protection of Human Subjects, 45 CFR Part 46 (2001).

Redline, C. D. (2005). *Identifying the intended navigational path of an established survey*. Retrieved May, 26, 2006, from http://www.fcsm.gov/05papers/Redline_IXB.pdf.

Redline, C. D., Dillman, D., Carley-Baxter, L., & Creecy, R. (2003). *Factors that influence reading and comprehension in self-administered questionnaires*. Paper presented at the Workshop on Item-Nonresponse and Data Quality, Basel, Switzerland. Retrieved November, 5, 2005, from http://survey.sesrc.wsu.edu/dillman/papers/Basel%20submission%20dillman.pdf.

Reilly, T. (1973). The "T" test: An experimental lecture on traits. In J. W. Pfeiffer & J. E. Jones (Eds.), *A handbook of structured experiences for human relations training* (vol. 4, pp. 41–44). San Diego, CA: University Associates.

Rosenberg, M. (1989). *Society and the adolescent self-image* (rev. ed.). Middletown, CT: Wesleyan University Press.

Sadovsky, R. (2002, May 1). Clinically important changes in pain severity on VAS. *American Family Physician*, p. 1902.

Sarle, W. S. (1995). Measurement theory: Frequently asked questions. In *Disseminations of the International Statistical Applications Institute* (4th ed.). Retrieved May 4, 2006, from http://www.measurementdevices.com/mtheory.html.

Schonlau, M., Fricker, R. D., Jr., & Elliott, M. N. (2001). *Conducting research surveys via e-mail and the Web*. Santa Monica, CA: Rand.

Schuman, H., & Presser, S. (1981). *Questions and answers in attitude surveys: Experiments on question form, wording, and context*. New York: Academic Press.

Schwarz, N., & Norbert. (1999). Self reports: How the questions shape the answers. *American Psychologist, 54*(2), 93–105.

Schwarz, N., & Oyserman, D. (2001). Asking questions about behavior: Cognition, communication, and questionnaire construction. *American Journal of Evaluation, 22*(2), 127–160.

Scriven, M. (2000, June). *The logic and methodology of checklists*. Available at http://www.wmich.edu/evalctr/checklists/papers/index.html.

Sheehan, K. (2001). E-mail survey response rates: A review. *Journal of Computer Mediated Communication, 6*(2). Retrieved November 5, 2005, from http://jcmc.indiana.edu/vol6/issue2/sheehan.html.

Smith, A. (1994). Introduction and overview. In T. J. Kiresuk, A. Smith, & J. E. Cardillo (Eds.), *Goal attainment scaling: Applications, theory, and measurement* (pp. 1–14). Mahwah, NJ: Erlbaum.

Smith, T. (1989). *Thoughts on the nature of context effects.* Retrieved May 29, 2006, from http://webapp.icpsr.umich.edu/GSS/rnd1998/reports/m-reports/meth66.htm.

Sobell, L. (1999). The Brief Situational Confidence Questionnaire (BSCQ). In W. R. Miller (Ed.), *Enhancing motivation for change in substance abuse treatment* (pp. 204–205). Rockville, MD: U.S. Department of Health and Human Services, Center for Substance Abuse Treatment.

Sparrow, S. S., Balla, D. A., & Cicchetti, D. V. (1984). *Vineland Adaptive Behavior Scales: A revision of the Vineland Social Maturity Scale by Edgar A. Doll.* Circle Pines, MN: American Guidance Service.

Spector, P. E. (1992). *Summated rating scale construction: An introduction.* Thousand Oaks, CA: Sage.

Springer, A. (2004). *Intellectual property legal issues for faculty.* Washington, DC: American Association of University Professors. Retrieved March 8, 2005, from http://www.aaup.org/Legal/info%20outlines/legintellprop.htm.

Steers, R. M., & Porter, L. W. (1983). *Motivation and work behavior.* NY: McGraw-Hill.

Stemler, S. (2001). An overview of content analysis. *Practical Assessment, Research & Evaluation, 7*(17), 1–9.

Strauss, S. (1995). *The sizesaurus: Making measures fit for human consumption.* Toronto: Key Porter Books.

Streiner, D. L., & Norman, G. R. (1995). *Health measurement scales: A practical guide to their development and use.* New York: Oxford University Press.

Subar, A. F., Ziegler, R. G., Thompson, F. E., Johnson, C. C., Weissfeld, J. L., Reding, D., et al. (2001). Is shorter always better? Relative importance of questionnaire length and cognitive ease on response rates and data quality for two dietary questionnaires. *American Journal of Epidemiology, 153*(4), 404–409.

Sudman, S., & Bradburn, N. M. (1982). *Asking questions.* San Francisco: Jossey-Bass.

Szasz, T. (Ed.). (1973). *The age of madness.* Garden City, NY: Anchor Books.

Trochim, W. M. (2001). *The research methods knowledge base* (2nd ed.). Cincinnati, OH: Atomic Dog.

Underwood, M. (2000). *Semantic differential.* Retrieved February 23, 2004, from http://www.cultsock.ndirect.co.uk/MUHome/cshtml/introductory/semdif.html.

University of Maryland, Department of Sociology. (2006). *The Rosenberg Self-Esteem Scale.* Retrieved April 10, 2007, from http://www.bsos.umd.edu/socy/grad/socpsy_rosenberg.html.

University of Virginia. (2004). *Copyright policy* (Policy ID: RES-001). Charlottesville, VA: Author.

U.S. Census Bureau. (2006). *Racial and ethnic classifications used in census 2000 and beyond.* Retrieved November 15, 2006, from http://www.census.gov/population/www/socdemo/race/racefactcb.html.

U.S. General Accounting Office. (1986). *Developing and using questionnaires.* Washington, DC: Author.

U.S. Naval Observatory. (1999). *Precise time and the master clock.* Retrieved November 19, 2000, from http://www.tycho.usno.navy.mil/clocks.html.

Ward, J., et al. (1997). *Problem severity ratings: Children's Functional Assessment Rating Scale* (Adapted from the Colorado Client Assessment Record and Functional Assessment Rating Scales).

Tampa: University of South Florida, Florida Mental Health Institute, Department of Child & Family Studies.

Welch, S., & Comer, J. (2001). *Quantitative methods for public administration*. Mason, OH: Thomson/South-Western Press.

Wharton School, Department of Marketing. (2004). *Forecasting principles*. Retrieved November 22, 2004, from http://morris.wharton.upenn.edu/forecast/data/definitions/juster%20scale.html.

Witzig, R. (1996). The medicalization of race: Scientific legitimatization of a flawed social construct. *Annals of Medicine, 125*(8), 675–679.

Worthen, B. R., Borg, W. R., & White, K. R. (1993). *Measurement and evaluation in the schools*. White Plains, NY: Longman.

Worthen, B. R., & Sanders, J. R. (1987). *Educational evaluation: Alternative approaches and practical guidelines*. White Plains, NY: Longman.

Yin, R. K. (1989). *Case study research: Design and methods*. Thousand Oaks, CA: Sage.

Zimmerman, S. M., & Icenogle, M. L. (1999). *Statistical quality control using Excel*. Milwaukee, WI: ASQ Quality Press.

INDEX

J